T0314632

the **HITCHCOCK** complete

**Paul Condon
and Jim Sangster**

Virgin

The authors dedicate this book to:

Mark & Audrey Condon
Jim & Marge Sangster

First published in 1999 by
Virgin Publishing Ltd
Thames Wharf Studios
Rainville Road
London
W6 9HT

Reprinted 2000, 2001

ISBN 0 7535 0362 X

Typeset by TW Typesetting, Plymouth, Devon

MIX
Paper | Supporting
responsible forestry
FSC® C018179

Printed and bound in Great Britain by Clays Ltd, St Ives PLC

Contents

Acknowledgements

The authors would like to thank the following for use of their scissors, knives, ropes and other useful implements:

John Ainsworth (who knows far more about *Falcon Crest* than anyone really should), the gang at Amazon Books, David Bailey, Jane Barclay, Ian Beck, Marc Bellevret, Liam Brison, Mike Burnhill, Peter Cooke, Paul Cornell, Andrew Cornes, Paul and Trish Evans, Lynn Fox, Ian Garrard, Gary Gillatt, Carolyn Hall, Clayton Hickman, Ian Hodge, Rob Jones, Julian Knott, Rod Molinaire, Richie Moosbally, Stephen Mouette, Alyssa Padia, Gareth Roberts, Eddie Robson, Gary Russell, Jim Smith, Bob Stanley, Kaff Trainer, David Waddell, Gary Wah, Lisa Wardle, Simon Winstone, Birgit Zich.

Special thanks to Miss Riley, Miss Jones, Mr Cullen, Mr Entwistle, Miss Burns and Mr Spencer for childhood inspiration, and to Jackie Miller and Tom Paulin for the letters after our names.

Extra special thanks to Peter Darvill-Evans for his trust, patience and encouragement, and to Joanne Brooks for suffering paper-cuts beyond the call of duty in arranging our picture sections.

Good Evening …

Our story tonight concerns a small boy who committed an act that his father thought deserved punishment. Rather that beating him or shouting at him, the father chose an altogether more psychologically damaging castigation. He handed his son a note and told him to take it to the local police station. The boy then passed the note to the duty officer, who led the boy through the station and locked him in a cell. He was there for only a few minutes but to the confused and terrified boy it felt like an eternity.

'That's what we do to naughty boys,' the officer later told him. The boy was released and allowed to return home.

The above story is more than likely apocryphal. However, it's one that Alfred Hitchcock often told to interviewers and friends by way of explanation for his lifelong mistrust of the police and for the theme of an innocent man accused that featured in so many of his films. Coming from a Catholic household and receiving a Jesuit education, the young Hitchcock would be all too aware of the preachings of 'Original Sin' and of a God who sees and judges all. This is an attitude that Hitchcock both represented and rebelled against throughout his career. His films often show how even the smallest of crimes or wrongdoings must be accounted for, and how every man can be 'tested', like the biblical figure Job, until such time as they can be said to have 'atoned' for their sins. But he also bucked against authority, reacting against the repression left over from the Victorian age, ridiculing the inefficiencies of the police, and challenging the social and cinematic mores on more than one occasion.

Many writers have tried, with varying degrees of success, to discover just who Alfred Hitchcock was, through the scant historical evidence available and through interviews with the people who claimed to have known him best. They have examined his work and decided that he was a misogynist, or that he just loved women too much; he was an *auteur*, or just a self-indulgent man making the same film again and again; he was a genius, or just good at what he did.

But these biographical details are not what this book is about. To suppose that we might be in a position to expose his inner psyche or lay claim to hidden knowledge would be both conceited and misguided, and it would distract due attention from the films themselves. If you're looking for a biography, then this book probably isn't for you.

We're unapologetic in admitting that we're 'Generation X-ers', those annoying 'twenty/thirty-somethings' who are culturally aware and seem to absorb a constant stream of useless trivia to regurgitate and bore each other with at parties. For our generation, Steven Spielberg represents everything that we call 'cinema'; his new releases are almost always 'event movies' and he's just about the only film director *everybody* knows. In 1975, Spielberg released his first made-for-cinema feature film, the shark thriller *Jaws*. Of note was one small sequence, where a character seemed to move closer to the camera while the background stayed the same distance away. This technique, achieved by pulling back the camera and zooming in at the same time, had been pioneered on Alfred Hitchcock's 1959 picture *Vertigo*; but from this year on it would cease to be known as 'the Hitchcock shot' – now it was well and truly Spielberg's.

The following year saw the release of Alfred Hitchcock's final film, *Family Plot*.

We mention all this because we feel it's important to note that we approach Hitchcock's legacy the only way we can: through TV reruns and videotapes. We watch through the eyes of a modern audience spoilt by the technological advances of the end of the twentieth century, for whom Norman Bates has been superseded by Freddie Krueger, Grace Kelly by Gwyneth Paltrow, tight plot and strong characters by outlandish special effects and spiralling budgets. Like, we imagine, most of the readers of this book, we never had the luxury of watching a Hitchcock 'event' on its first night in the cinema. We had *Star Wars*, *Pulp Fiction* and *Titanic* instead, and it's only fair to acknowledge that these have probably been a greater direct influence on our generation than Hitch. But, as this book attempts to show, just as Hitchcock himself was inspired by the works of FW Murnau, Eisenstein and Fritz Lang, so too would his work shape the future of contemporary cinema. Whether they admit it themselves or not, such film-makers as Quentin Tarantino, James Cameron and Oliver Stone owe their careers to the man we celebrate here.

The aim of this book is to provide a comprehensive guide through the fifty-odd films directed by Alfred Hitchcock. That's all. No mission statement, no axe to grind, just an appreciation of and enthusiasm for a man who understood that the primary function of the cinema is to entertain.

The guide is divided into three uneven sections, separating Hitchcock's silent movies from the 'talkies', and his feature films from the episodes of his television series. Donald Spoto, a respected biographer of Hitchcock, describes the early silent films as 'interesting works by a gifted novice rather than cinematic masterpieces'. Certainly, owing to the nature of film-making at the time, even the best of these come across as crude and overly theatrical with little of the spark that would ignite his later works. Additionally, access to these films is severely limited, with, at the time of writing, only one of them available for home viewing in the UK. For both these reasons, we present these first titles in a briefer form than the later entries. We've highlighted *The Lodger* (Hitch's third film, but the first one to be released) to represent the silent era, as it contains many of the visual and thematic motifs that would populate his greatest achievements – an innocent man accused, a glamorous blonde female lead, and a long, imposing staircase. The bulk of this book, therefore, focuses on the films from 1929 onward.

Each film is taken in turn with basic information such as year of release, alternative or working titles where appropriate, plus production and cast lists and a summary of the plot. The rest of the entry is made up of a number of different categories, which pop up as and when we feel they're appropriate. Among them are:

ROOTS/LEGACY: Hitchcock's interests in film history, as well as art, literature and music, is evident in a number of his films, an influence that was passed on as he inspired others along the way. We examine the trails of inspiration in both directions in these two sections.

WHO'S WHO?: To hopefully save you from asking yourself, 'Where have we seen him/her before?', we've tried to help you out here with a guide to the major players. We also keep track of 'repeat offenders' in a section entitled **THE USUAL SUSPECTS**.

ANIMAL CRUELTY: Blowing up a dog in *Sabotage*, shooting a horse in *Marnie*, it's a wonder Hitch wasn't attacked by the RSPCA – but then he'd have used this for some superb publicity.

THERE HE IS!: Be the smuggest 'Hitchphile' at every party as we help you play that most popular of cinema games, 'Spot the Director'.

THE MACGUFFIN: Hitchcock used this word to describe an item or objective upon which the plot hangs that is immaterial to the actual story. To illustrate the concept, he often told a story of two men on a train. One of them has a huge trunk in the luggage rack and the other man asks him what its contents are. The first man explains that it's a 'MacGuffin'. 'What's a MacGuffin?' he asks. 'It's a device for trapping lions in the Scottish Highlands,' he explains. 'But there aren't any lions in the Highlands,' says the second man. The final reply is either, 'Well that's no MacGuffin' or 'See, it works!'

The MacGuffin may be the secret plans that cause our hero to go on the run, or the wedding ring that proves a man has just murdered his wife, or any number of other things. What it actually *is* is unimportant, as it's merely the catalyst that sets the drama in motion.

TABOOS: For all his acclaim as the Master of Suspense, Hitchcock also had an appreciation of schoolboy humour and an interest in the lewd and the outrageous. He regularly included elements simply to get up the noses of the ever-restrictive censors. We note how he tried to shock, whether through suggestive behaviour, nudity or just being the first film director to show a toilet being flushed.

MUSIC: Many of Bernard Herrmann's scores have passed into popular culture, notably the one for *Psycho*. Music plays an integral part in many of Hitchcock's films, a contribution we acknowledge here.

MARKETING (POSTERS, TRAILERS, ETC.): Hitchcock's controlling influence extended way past the limits of the screen, through the posters, trailers and marketing campaigns, which often featured Hitch himself as an extension of his TV persona, and contribute greatly to the films they were trying to sell.

THE ICE MAIDEN: We chart the rise of what would come to be known as 'the typicial Hitchcock blonde' from June Tripp in *The Lodger* to Tippi Hedren in *Marnie* and beyond.

WHAT THE PAPERS SAID: Reviews from critics at the time or on rerelease. Some show how Hitchcock's talents were recognised early on in his career; others just show how even the beloved men of the press can often completely miss the point.

COSTUME: Film critics often refer to the *mise-en-scene* in a shot – meaning that everything in the frame contributes to the meaning the director wishes to convey. One of the most important aspects of this can be seen in the tight control Hitchcock held over the appearance of his female stars. Here we note some of the more interesting of Hitch's experiments with colour, hairstyles and fashion.

FINAL ANALYSIS: Lastly, we offer a brief, subjective review of each film, where we either debunk accepted wisdom or just toe the line. Some of the films just don't work for a modern audience – a few of them never really worked at all. When Hitch is at his best, however, we'll shout it from the rooftops. Just to be really controversial we give a mark out of ten, based on each of the individual categories themselves combined with our feelings towards the film as a whole. It's worth pointing out here that, even at his worst, Hitch was more innovative than most of his peers, striving to do something new every time (with a few exceptions that we'll come to in turn).

Throughout this book we've tried to remember the words of the great man himself: 'It's only a movie'.

Of course, as we all know, it was always so much more than that.

the complete

HITCHCOCK

the silent films

The British film industry had a very slow start. Cinema was not appreciated as an art form for many years and films tended to come from America and mainland Europe. Identifying a gap in the market, Famous Players-Lasky, the parent company who controlled the Paramount Corporation in the States, opened a studio in Islington, London, where a twenty-year-old called Alfred Hitchcock was eventually hired as a designer, creating titles for a number of their features. His enthusiasm was limitless and he soon found himself making his first foray into direction with *Always Tell Your Wife* after the original director, Hugh Croise, fell out with the producer, Seymour Hicks. Such was the success of the project, Hicks offered Hitchcock his own film, called alternately *Number 13* or *Mrs Peabody*. But the studio was winding down production owing to financial difficulties and despite investment from Clare Greet, one of the cast, the film was never completed.

At around the same time, the independent producer Michael Balcon and his associate, Victor Saville, formed Victory Films, a small distribution company based in Birmingham. Invited to London by CM Woolf to represent W and F Distribution, Balcon soon found himself heading the production of a number of theatrical adaptations for the cinema under the banner of Gainsborough Pictures. He hired Alfred Hitchcock, initially as assistant to the director Graham Cutts, but as different personnel dropped out along the way Hitchcock found himself filling in a number of roles, from set designer to scriptwriter.

Hitchcock later asserted that he had never intended becoming a film director, but that he fell into it as a result of a political problem at the studio. Graham Cutts took a dislike to him and refused to have him as his assistant. When Cutts took his grievances to Balcon, the producer decided to give Hitchcock a chance to helm his first feature. However, Balcon was all too aware of the resistance distributors had to change and that they preferred familiar names to newcomers. He decided to test the fledgling director out in Germany, so that if he was a success he could return to Britain as a 'new talent'.

On 5 June 1925, and accompanied by his fiancée, the respected editor Alma Reville, Hitchcock arrived at the Emelka Studios in Munich to commence the shooting of his first film, *The Pleasure Garden* ...

Hitchcock worked on a number of films in different capacities over the years. Very few of these pictures have survived; many of them had been destroyed within ten years of their release. Though many of Hitchcock's silent features have survived, very few of them are available for public viewing. In this section, we look at these early works, leading up to his first sound feature, *Blackmail*, in 1929.

Title Designer for: *Dangerous Lies, The Princess of New York, The Mystery Road, Appearances, The Great Day, The Call of Youth, The Bonnie Brier Bush* (all 1921), *The Spanish Jade, Love's Boomerang,*

Three Live Ghosts (uncredited), *The Man from Home*, *Tell Your Children* (all 1922).

Note: All listed films are directed by Alfred Hitchcock unless otherwise specified in the production credits.

Always Tell Your Wife (1922)

Produced by Seymour Hicks/Wardour & F. Distribution
Directed by Hugh Croise & (uncredited) Alfred Hitchcock
Written by Seymour Hicks, based on his play

CAST: Seymour Hicks (*The Husband*), Gertrude McCoy (*The Wife*).

Number 13 (1922 – unfinished)
(aka *Mrs Peabody*)

Produced by Seymour Hicks/Wardour & F. Distribution

CAST: Clare Greet, Ernest Thesiger.

USUAL SUSPECTS: Clare Greet would later work with Hitchcock on *The Manxman*, *Murder!*, *Sabotage* and *Jamaica Inn*.

Woman to Woman (1923)

Produced by Michael Balcon
Directed by Graham Cutts
Written by Graham Cutts & Alfred Hitchcock, based on the play by Michael Morton
Photography: Claude L McDonnell
Film Editor/Continuity: Alma Reville
Art Direction/Assistant Director: Alfred Hitchcock

CAST: Betty Compson (*Louise Boucher/Deloryse*), Clive Brook (*David Compos/Davis Anson-Pond*).

The White Shadow (1924)

Produced by Michael Balcon & Victor Saville

Directed by Graham Cutts

Written by Alfred Hitchcock, based on the novel *Children of Chance* by Michael Morton

Photography: Claude L McDonnell
Film Editing/Art Direction/Assistant Director: Alfred Hitchcock

CAST: Betty Compson (*Nancy Brent/Georgina Brent*), Clive Brook (*Robin Field*), Henry Victor (*Louis Chadwick*), AB Imeson (*Mr Brent*), Olaf Hytten (*Herbert Barnes*), Daisy Campbell (*Elizabeth Brent*).

The Passionate Adventure (1924)
(German title: *Ehe in Gefahr*)

Produced by Michael Balcon/Gainsborough Pictures

Directed by Graham Cutts

Written by Alfred Hitchcock & Michael Morton, based on a novel by Frank Stayton

Photography: Claude L McDonnell
Art Direction/Assistant Director: Alfred Hitchcock

CAST: Clive Brook, Mary Brough, Marjorie Daw, Lillian Hall-Davis, John F Hamilton, Alice Joyce, Victor McLaglen, JR Tozer.

The Prude's Fall (1925)
(German title: *Seine Zweite Frau*)

Produced by Michael Balcon/Gainsborough Pictures

Directed by Graham Cutts

Written by Alfred Hitchcock, based on the novel by Rudolf Besier & May Edginton

Art Direction/Assistant Director: Alfred Hitchcock

CAST: Betty Compson.

The Blackguard (1925)
(German title: *Die Prinzessin und der Geiger*)

Produced by Michael Balcon/Ufa/Gainsborough Pictures
Associate Producer: Erich Pommer

Directed by Graham Cutts
Assistant Director/Art Director: Alfred Hitchcock

Written by Alfred Hitchcock, based on a novel by Raymond Paton

CAST: Fritz Alberti, Dora Bergner, Bernhard Goetzke, Jane Novak, Walter Rilla (*The Blackguard*), Frank Stanmore, Rosa Valetti.

The Pleasure Garden
(produced 1925/released 1927)
(German title: *Irrgarten der Leidenschaft*)

Produced by Michael Balcon & Erich Pommer/Gainsborough Pictures/Emelka

Written by Eliot Stannard, based on the novel by Oliver Sandys

Photography: Baron Ventimiglia
Assistant Director/Continuity: Alma Reville
Art Directors: Ludwig Reiber & CW Arnold

CAST: Virginia Valli (*Patsy Brand*), Carmelita Geraghty (*Jill Cheyne*), Miles Mander (*Levett*), John Stuart (*Hugh Fielding*), Nita Naldi (*Native*), Florence Helminger, Frederick Martini, George Snell, C Falkenburg.

SUMMARY: Jill Cheyne, a naive girl from the country, arrives at the Pleasure Garden Music Hall looking for work. She carries with her a letter of recommendation, but, when her purse is stolen, she is helped out by one of the dancers, Patsy Brand, who succeeds in getting her a place in the chorus line. Patsy introduces Jill to Hugh, a friend of her fiancé, Levett. Patsy and Levett marry before he and Hugh set off to work in the Middle East. While Patsy misses her husband terribly, Jill has all but forgotten Hugh, and as her career rises she rejects Patsy's friendship, her eyes locked on the Big Time.

Patsy learns that her husband is ill and travels across the globe to be with him. She is horrified to discover that not only has he taken to drink, but he is consorting with a native woman and in a drunken state he accidentally kills a young girl. Haunted by guilt, Levett turns on Patsy and tries to kill her. Hugh arrives and shoots Levett in the chest. Hugh and Patsy decide to stay together.

THE USUAL SUSPECTS: Miles Mander also pops up in *Murder!*, Nita Naldi (*the native*) played Beatrice in *The Mountain Eagle*, and John Stuart appeared as the detective in *Number Seventeen*.

ROOTS: The scene where Patsy is rescued by Hugh from her sword-wielding husband is inspired by the scene in *Birth of a Nation* (DW Griffith, 1915), where the Ku Klux Klan shoot a black rapist just in the nick of time.

THEMES AND MOTIFS: As Patsy dances, as part of the chorus, an oily man watches her through binoculars (*Rear Window*).

TRIVIA: Although shot a year before, the film was held back after Graham Cutts, senior director at Gainsborough, convinced the producers that Hitchcock had a flop on his hands. It was eventually released after *The Lodger* became a massive hit and confirmed to the producer Michael Balcon that Hitchcock had been worth the risk.

The Mountain Eagle
(produced 1925/released 1927)
(German title: *Der Bergadler*/US title: *Fear O'God*)

(B&W – 68 mins)

Produced by Michael Balcon/Gainsborough Pictures

Written by Eliot Stannard & Charles Lapworth

Photography: Baron Ventimiglia
Assistant Director: Alma Reville
Art Direction: Willy & Ludwig Reiber

CAST: Bernhard Goetzke (*Pettigrew*), John F Hamilton (*Edward Pettigrew*), Malcolm Keen (*Fear O' God*), Nita Naldi (*Beatrice*).

SUMMARY: A store owner lecherously pursues Beatrice, a young schoolteacher. Desperate to avoid his advances, Beatrice flees into the mountains, where she is saved by a hermit, known as Fear O' God. The couple fall instantly in love and are soon married.

THE USUAL SUSPECTS: Nita Naldi also appeared in *The Pleasure Garden* (1925), while Malcolm Keen can be seen in *The Lodger* and *The Manxman*.

TRIVIA: Like *The Pleasure Garden*, *The Mountain Eagle* was caught up in the internal wrangles at Gainsborough and was held back until after the success of *The Lodger*. No prints of this film are known to have survived, which Hitchcock himself claimed was no bad thing, considering it to be 'a very bad movie'.

The Lodger: A Story of the London Fog
(produced 1926/released 1927)
(US title: *The Case of Jonathan Drew*)

(B&W – 83 mins)

Produced by Michael Balcon & Carlyle Blackwell Sr/Gainsborough Pictures

Written by Eliot Stannard & Alfred Hitchcock, based on the novel by Marie Belloc-Lowndes

Photography: Baron Ventimiglia
Art Directors: C Wilfrid Arnold & Bertram Evans
Title Designers: E McKnight Kauffer, Ivor Montagu
Assistant Director: Alma Reville

CAST: Ivor Novello (*Lodger*), June Tripp (*Daisy Bunting, a Mannequin*), Malcolm Keen (*Joe Betts, a Police Detective*), Marie Ault (*Landlady, Mrs Bunting*), Arthur Chesney (*Her Husband, Mr Bunting*), Helena Pick (*Anne Rowley*).

SUMMARY: London is terrorised by a spate of murders attributed to 'the Avenger'; the victims are always blondes and the attacks always occur on a Tuesday night. At a fashion house, Daisy Bunting and her fellow models complete another show and prepare to make their way home. Mindful of the Avenger's peculiarities, Daisy hides her blonde hair under a hat and attaches brown curls to complete the effect.

She returns to her home, a boarding house run by her parents. Her fiancé, Joe, is a detective and she finds him waiting for her; he's obviously keen to get her on her own. The lights go out and, as they try to find a coin for the meter, a stranger comes to the door asking to rent a room. He seems withdrawn and mysterious but Mrs Bunting allows him to stay and shows him his room. He immediately requests that she remove all of the paintings from his room – pictures of blonde women.

One Tuesday night, while her husband is out working as a waiter at a dinner function, Mrs Bunting hears the lodger sneak out of the house. His behaviour worries her and she decides to look around his room, but, before she can find anything, the lodger returns. Mrs Bunting rushes back to her bed and spends the rest of the night awake.

The next morning, Joe arrives at the house in a state of excitement – he's been put on the Avenger case and vows that once he's arrested the murderer he'll ask Daisy to marry him. Just then he and Daisy's parents hear a scream from the lodger's room – it's Daisy! The policeman and the Buntings race up the stairs to find Daisy and the lodger laughing. She explains she had been startled by a mouse and is surprised when she realises Joe is jealous of their house guest. He drags her downstairs and kisses her, but she is distracted by the sound of the lodger, pacing up and down in his room. Meanwhile Mrs Bunting tells her husband that she believes their lodger is the Avenger. At first he laughs off her suspicions but soon the pair of them become worried for their daughter.

The lodger and Daisy begin to spend a lot of time together. He visits her at the fashion house and buys her an expensive dress from the collection she models. Both her father and Joe admonish Daisy for associating with him, but Daisy tires of their interference and breaks off her engagement to Joe. As Daisy leaves to go on a date with the lodger, Joe suddenly jumps to the same conclusions as Mrs Bunting. He also works out that the murders have been following a trail that leads directly to the Buntings' boarding house.

Joe arrives at the house accompanied by his fellow officers with a warrant for the lodger's arrest. They search his room and find a gun, a map with the precise location of each murder marked on it and a photograph of the first victim. The lodger breaks down in tears and tells them the first victim was his sister. Unconvinced, Joe arrests the man, who manages to whisper to Daisy to meet him where they met for their date. He then struggles free from the police and escapes into the night.

Daisy finds him and he tells her about the night of his sister's coming-out ball. During the evening, the lights had been switched off and when they came back on he was horrified to find that his sister was dead, strangled by an unseen maniac. His mother never recovered from the shock, and before she died she made him promise to avenge his sister's death.

Daisy takes him to a pub to get some 'medicinal' brandy, and, as his hands are still bound by handcuffs, she tells him to keep his hands covered while she brings the drink to him, arousing the suspicions of the other customers. They leave and, soon after, Joe comes to the same pub to use the phone. The patrons overhear Joe tell his station that they are looking for an escaped criminal who is handcuffed. The customers realise that the mysterious man must be the killer and a mob runs out of the pub in pursuit. But then Joe learns that the Avenger has already been caught red-handed and realises that he's sent the mob after an innocent man. Trying to climb over an iron fence, the lodger gets his handcuffs caught on the railings. The mob catch up with him and try to pull him off the railings until Joe manages to intercede and pull the lodger to safety.

The lodger is taken to hospital and, after making a full recovery, he invites Daisy to his family home where they are married with her parents' blessing.

TITLES: Though the titles are run on simple caption cards, the logo, a triangle containing the silhouette of a man, is quite innovative. As the credits sequence ends, the sides of the triangle close in on the silhouette, suggesting both the way the police are slowly closing in on the killer, and the love triangle of Daisy, Joe and the lodger.

ROOTS: In the original novel by Marie Belloc-Lowndes, the lodger is the murderer, but, as Novello was a matinée idol, it was felt best to make him innocent for the film. Obviously the novel was inspired by the Whitechapel murders of the 1880s, and indeed Hitch often referred to the lodger as 'Jack The Ripper' in interviews. The screaming of the blonde girl in the opening scene and some subsequent shots is a clear nod to Edvard Munch's notorious painting *The Scream*.

LEGACY: In July 1940, Hitchcock adapted his screenplay for radio, starring Herbert Marshal (*Murder!*), Lurene Tuttle (*Psycho*) and Edmund Gwenn in the role played by his brother Arthur Chesney in Hitch's film version (see the section on Hitch's television work at the back of this book for more information). Two more film versions followed, *The Lodger* (John Brahm, 1944) and *Man in the Attic* (Hugo Fregonese, 1954), and it was spoofed in the Oscar-winning animated film *The Wrong Trousers* (Nick Park, 1993). See also **Themes** below.

WHO'S WHO?: Ivor Novello (*the Lodger*) was a Welsh-born matinée idol, Britain's Rudolph Valentino. He also starred in Hitch's *Downhill*, having written the play the movie was based on, and was the lyricist for *Elstree Calling*. Though his career began in films, Novello's cinematic career stalled with the arrival of sound and he became more famous for his stage work (indeed his obituary in *The Times* omitted his film career entirely). His name is now given to an annual award for songwriting. Past recipients include Elton John, George Michael and Gary Barlow.

Arthur Chesney (Mr Bunting) was the brother of Edmund Gwenn, a regular collaborator with Hitchcock.

THE USUAL SUSPECTS: Malcolm Keen (*Joe Betts*) appeared in *The Mountain Eagle* and *The Manxman*.

KILLER LINES: On hearing of a seventh murdered blonde, one of the women from Golden Curls remarks: 'No more peroxide for yours truly.'

After telling the family about his appointment to the Avenger's case,

Joe boasts: 'When I've put a rope around the Avenger's neck, I'll put a ring around Daisy's finger.'

In what is supposed to be a tense scene, Mrs Bunting's cry to her husband is rather comical: 'I let her go out with the lodger – and it's Tuesday night!'

THERE HE IS!: Hitch makes his first cameo with his back to the camera, sitting at a desk in the newsroom early in the film. He can also be seen in the crowd baying for the lodger's blood towards the end of the film (he's wearing a grey flat cap). Though at the time this was to cut costs on extras, it would soon become a regular occurrence.

THEMES AND MOTIFS: *The Lodger* establishes a number of images and themes that become familiar Hitchcock elements over the years. As Joe comes down the back stairs of the house (No. 13, both a reference to 'unlucky for some' and Hitchcock's aborted first feature) we see a black cat run past his legs. The staircase at the Buntings' boarding house bears a frightening resemblance to those seen in the Newtons' house in *Shadow of a Doubt* and the Bateses' house in *Psycho*. We have the first of the Hitchcock blonde heroines (although *The Pleasure Garden*'s Jill is a blonde, she's not the heroine, acting as a contrast with the brunette Patsy) and the first innocent man on the run.

WHAT THE PAPERS SAID: The critic for *The Bioscope* (16 September 1926) wrote: 'It is possible that this film is the finest British production ever made . . . Mr Hitchcock's sense of dramatic values is magnificent; and individually and collectively the scenes show thought, care and skill. The tempo of the whole film has seldom been equalled, and there is hardly a scene which is a foot too long or a foot too short. Mr. Hitchcock builds up his evidence against the lodger relentlessly and logically. It is a directorial triumph.'

TRIVIA: Having succeeded in preventing the release of Hitchcock's first features, Graham Cutts went to town on this one, convincing CM Woolf, the head of W & F, that he had a disaster on his hands. The producer Michael Balcon had spent over £12,000 in the making of the film, and he saw Hitchcock himself as an investment that was about to be squandered. He delayed the trade preview till the following September, then contacted Ivor Montagu, a renowned film critic and respected editor. He asked him to help shape the film into a more commercial release and so Montagu, assisted by E McKnight Kauffer, reduced the number of title cards from three hundred to eighty while Hitchcock went about performing minor reshoots. Though Hitchcock never referred to Montagu's contribution to the film, it undoubtedly saved his career.

FINAL ANALYSIS: As noted in **Themes and Motifs** above, *The Lodger* displays many of the elements that would become staple ingredients in future Hitchcock successes. Surprisingly, the greatest achievement of the film is the way Hitchcock appears to overcome the limitations of silent film. The opening sequence shows us the murder of a blonde woman whose screaming mouth appears to all but fill the screen, another recurring Hitchcock image. Later, when the lodger paces in his room, Hitchcock uses a trick shot involving Ivor Novello walking across a glass floor, which he filmed from beneath and then superimposed on to a shot of a rocking chandelier to convey the 'sound' of his footsteps. Throughout the film, little touches of genius such as this help to make it one of the noisiest silent movies ever made.

Obviously, *The Lodger* cannot hope to compete with the later, 'talkie' classics in Hitchcock's canon. With a performance as camp as Ivor Novello's it's difficult to take the film quite as seriously as we suspect we should; but in a way it's easy to see why Graham Cutts was so obstructive, trying to prevent Hitchcock's rise in the company. He could obviously see that Hitchcock possessed a style of film-making that would show up the rest of the British Film Industry's output as the mannered and insubstantial stuff it was. **7/10**

Downhill (1927)
(US title: *When Boys Leave Home*)

(B&W – 74 mins)

Produced by Michael Balcon/Gainsborough Pictures

Written by Eliot Stannard (as David Lestrange), based on the play by Ivor Novello & Constance Collier

Photography: Claude L McDonnell
Film Editing: Ivor Montagu

CAST: Lilian Braithwaite (*Lady Berwick*), Ian Hunter (*Archie*), Robin Irvine (*Tim Wakely*), Isabel Jeans (*Julia*), Hannah Jones, Ivor Novello (*Roddy Berwick*), Sybil Rhoda (*Sybil Wakely*), Jerrold Robertshaw, Ben Webster (*Dr Dowson*), Annette Benson, Violet Farebrother, Alfred Goddard, Barbara Gott, Norman McKinnell.

SUMMARY: At a private school, a schoolboy is accused by a waitress of fathering an illegitimate child. As the actual father is his best friend, Roddy Berwick decides to take the blame and is summarily expelled to protect the school's good name. Roddy is shunned by his former friends and his family are humiliated and so he decides to leave for Paris. He soon squanders what money he has and is forced to take a job as a dancer. He slowly descends into alcoholism and finds himself being sent back home to his now forgiving family.

Alma Hitchcock (née Alma Reville) (1900–1982)

When Alfred Hitchcock received the American Film Institute's Lifetime Achievement Award in 1979, he dedicated it to four people: a film editor, a script writer, the mother of his daughter and a talented cook; 'And their names,' he announced '. . . are Alma Reville.' His constant companion for fifty-four years, he regarded his wife as both his most loyal collaborator and his harshest critic.

She came to his attention in the early 1920s, when she was earning her reputation as a film editor and he was filling in jobs at Gainsborough. They got engaged during production of *The Prude's Fall* in 1925 and married the following year. In 1928, Alma gave birth to their only child, Patricia, who would follow her parents into the entertainment industry as an actress, and appeared in a number of her father's films. When Hitchcock finally earned the chance to direct his first feature, the producer Michael Balcon dispatched Reville to work as his assistant director, confident that he would learn from her greater experience in the film industry. This was the beginning of a partnership that would endure for the rest of their lives, with Alma providing adaptations, scenarios, screenplays and continuity on many of his features.

Alma Reville outlived her husband by just two years, and died in 1982 after suffering a series of strokes.

THE USUAL SUSPECTS: Hannah Jones would later appear in *Blackmail, Murder!* and *Rich and Strange*. Ivor Novello (*Roddy*) starred in *The Lodger* and was the lyricist for *Elstree Calling*. Ian Hunter (*Archie*) appears in *The Ring* and *Easy Virtue*. Isabel Jeans (*Julia*) was in *Easy Virtue* and *Suspicion*. Robin Irvine (*Tim Wakely*) was in *Easy Virtue*. Violet Farebrother was in both *Easy Virtue* and *Murder!*. Finally, Ben Webster pops up in *Suspicion*.

Easy Virtue (1927)

(B&W – 74 mins)

Produced by CM Woolf & Michael Balcon/Gainsborough Pictures

Scenario by Eliot Stannard, based on the play by Noël Coward

Photography: Claude L McDonnell
Art Director: Clifford Pember
Assistant Director: Frank Mills
Film Editing: Ivor Montagu

CAST: Isabel Jeans (*Larita Filton*), Franklin Dyall (*Her husband, Mr Filton*), Robin Irvine (*John Whittaker*), Frank Elliott (*His father*),

Dacia Deane (*His elder sister*), Dorothy Boyd (*His younger sister*), Violet Farebrother (*His mother*), Ian Hunter (*The Plaintiff's Counsel*), Eric Bransby Williams (*The Co-respondent*), Enid Stamp-Taylor (*The Switchboard Operator*).

SUMMARY: Larita Filton is named as co-respondent by her husband in a scandalous divorce case. When her lover kills himself, she escapes to France, changing her identity and starting a new life for herself. She thinks she is finally free of the past when she meets a man called John Whittaker. He asks her to marry him and introduces his new bride to his family. They refuse to take to her, believing her to be a woman of easy virtue. Eventually, John's mother discovers her secret and tells her son everything. Disgusted by her new family's intolerance, Larita sneaks away into the night.

THE USUAL SUSPECTS: Many of the cast can also be found in *Downhill* with appearances from Robin Irvine, Ian Hunter (who was also in *The Ring*), Isabel Jeans (who also appears in *Suspicion*) and Violet Farebrother (also seen in *Murder!*). Enid Stamp-Taylor can be seen in *The Farmer's Wife* (1928).

THERE HE IS!: During a scene in a tennis court, we see him leaving through a side gate, carrying a walking stick.

The Ring (1927)

(B&W – 72 mins)
Produced by John Maxwell/British International Pictures
Written by Alfred Hitchcock and Alma Reville (uncredited)
Photography: John J Cox
Assistant Director: Frank Mills
Art Director: CW Arnold

CAST: Carl Brisson (*'One Round' Jack Sander*), Lillian Hall-Davies (*Nelly*), Gordon Harker (*Jack's Trainer*), Ian Hunter (*Bob Corby*), Forrester Harvey (*Harry, the Promoter*), Harry Terry (*Showman*), Billy Wells, Tom Helmore (*uncredited*).

SUMMARY: Nelly, a ticket girl at a circus, finds herself the object of desire for both her fiancé, the celebrated boxer Jack 'One Round' Sander, and an Australian stranger named Bob Corby. Bob challenges Jack to a fight and, for the first time in his career, Jack is defeated. Bob steals Nelly away from him, but, after a revenge match at the Albert Hall, Jack defeats the Australian and wins back the heart of his girlfriend.

THE USUAL SUSPECTS: Carl Brisson and Harry Terry also appeared in *The Manxman*. Lillian Hall-Davies can also be seen in *The Farmer's Wife*, as can Gordon Harker, who worked on *Champagne* (1928) and *Elstree Calling*. An uncredited Tom Helmore is in *Secret Agent* and, more significantly, as Gavin Elster, the man who ruins James Stewart's early retirement in *Vertigo*. Ian Hunter pops up in *Downhill* and *Easy Virtue*, and Forrester Harvey was in *Rebecca*.

The Farmer's Wife (1928)

(B&W – 67 mins)

Produced by John Maxwell/British International Pictures Ltd

Adapted by Eliot Stannard, based on the play by Eden Philpotts

Photography: John J Cox
Art Director: C Wilfred Arnold
Assistant Director: Frank Mills
Film Editing: Alfred Booth

CAST: Jameson Thomas (*Farmer Samuel Sweetland*), Lillian Hall-Davies (*Araminta Dench, the Housekeeper*), Gordon Harker (*Churdles Ash, the Handyman*), Gibb McLaughlin (*Henry Coaker*), Maud Gill (*Thirza Tapper*), Louise Pounds (*Widow Windeatt*), Olga Slade (*Mary Hearn, the Postmistress*), Ruth Maitland (*Mercy Bassett*), Antonia Brough (*Susan*), Haward Watts (*Dick Coaker*), Mollie Ellis (*Sibley Sweetland*).

SUMMARY: A farmer decides to find himself a wife and tries to decide between three women from the area. As the three women fight among themselves, the farmer finds himself falling in love with his maid and chooses her instead.

THE USUAL SUSPECTS: Lillian Hall-Davies was the star of *The Ring*, which also starred Gordon Harker. Harker also appeared in *Champagne*, and *Elstree Calling*.

Champagne (1928)

(B&W – 88 mins)

Produced by John Maxwell/British International Pictures (BIP)

Written by Alfred Hitchcock & Eliot Stannard, based on the novel by Walter C Mycroft

Photography: Jack Cox

CAST: Betty Balfour (*Betty*), Jean Bradin (*Boy*), Vivian Gibson, Gordon Harker (*Father*), Clifford Heatherley (*Manager*), Claude Hulbert (*Guest*), Phyllis Konstam, Jack Trevor Story (*Officer – credited as Jack Trevor*), Marcel Vibert, Ferdinand von Alten, Theo von Alten.

SUMMARY: After her millionaire father forbids his daughter, Betty, to marry a penniless boy, she runs away to France, where she decides to live off her father's profits. Her father decides to put a stop to her decadent lifestyle and informs her that he is bankrupt, forcing her to work in a nightclub serving the champagne that once made her father's fortune.

THE USUAL SUSPECTS: Gordon Harker appeared in *The Ring*, *The Farmer's Wife* and *Elstree Calling* (1930). Phyllis Konstam has roles in *Blackmail*, *Murder!* and *The Skin Game* (1931). Jack Trevor Story wrote the novel *The Trouble with Harry*, filmed by Hitchcock in 1955.

TRIVIA: A future film director, Michael Powell was employed by Hitch to take still photographs for both this and Hitch's next production, *The Manxman*.

The Manxman (1929)

(B&W – 80 mins)

Produced by John Maxwell/British International Pictures Ltd

Scenario by Eliot Stannard, based on the story by Sir Hall Caine

Assistant Director: Frank Mills
Photography: Jack Cox
Art Director: C Wilfred Arnold
Film Editing: Emile de Ruelle
Still Photographer: Michael Powell

CAST: Carl Brisson (*Pete Quilliam*), Malcolm Keen (*Philip Christian*), Anny Ondra (*Kate Cregeen*), Randle Ayrton (*Caesar Cregeen*), Clare Greet (*Mother*), Kim Peacock.

SUMMARY: Kate, the daughter of a wealthy landlord, falls in love with Pete, a poor fisherman. Kate's father disapproves, believing Pete will be unable to support his daughter, so the fisherman decides to leave the island to earn his fortune. He asks his best friend Philip to look after Kate, unaware that Philip also has feelings for the girl. When news reaches Philip that Pete has been lost at sea after a shipwreck he proposes to Kate and the couple plan their wedding. But then Pete returns . . .

ROOTS: Remake of *The Manxman* (George Loane Tucker, 1916).

THE USUAL SUSPECTS: Clare Greet had worked in Hitch's very first (unfinished) film *Number 13*, as well as *Murder!*, *Sabotage*, and *Jamaica Inn*; Malcolm Keen (*Philip Christian*) worked on *The Mountain Eagle* and *The Lodger*; Carl Brisson appeared in *The Ring*; Anny Ondra also appeared in Hitch's next film, *Blackmail*.

the complete HITCHCOCK

films 1929–39

Blackmail (1929)

(B & W – 78 mins)

Producer: John Maxwell/British International Pictures/Gainsborough Pictures

Adapted by Alfred Hitchcock, dialogue by Benn W Levy & Michael Powell (uncredited), based on the play by Charles Bennett

Music: Campbell & Connely, compiled and arranged by Hubert Bath and Henry Stafford, played by the British Symphony Orchestra, conducted by John Reynders
Photography: Jack Cox
Art Director: WC Arnold
Assistant Director: Frank Mills
Film Editing: Emile de Ruelle

CAST: Anny Ondra (*Alice White*), Sara Allgood (*Mrs White*), Charles Paton (*Mr White*), John Longden (*Detective Frank Webber*), Donald Calthrop (*Tracy*), Cyril Ritchard (*Mr Crewe, the Artist*), Hannah Jones (*Landlady*), Harvey Braban (*Chief Inspector*), Ex-Det. Sgt Bishop (*Detective Sergeant*).

UNCREDITED CAST: Joan Barry (*voice of Alice White*), Johnny Butt (*Sergeant*), Phyllis Monkman (*Gossip*), Percy Parsons (*Crook*) and Phyllis Konstam.

SUMMARY: After a busy day's work, Detective Frank Webber is met at the police station by his girlfriend Alice. She complains about his keeping her waiting, as they had planned to go to the cinema. The couple go to a busy café where, unbeknown to Frank, Alice has arranged to meet another admirer, and, when he turns up, Alice abruptly cancels her date with Frank, waits for him to leave and then walks off with her new man, Mr Crewe.

Crewe is an artist and invites Alice up to his studio. As they enter the front door, a man calls out to Crewe from the shadows. The two talk for a short while, and when Crewe returns he tells Alice the stranger is just a scrounger trying to get money from him. After scaling the long flight of stairs to Crewe's attic studio, Alice admires the artist's work and asks if he'd consider using her as a model for one of his paintings. The couple flirt and Crewe steals a kiss. Alice decides she must leave but Crewe grabs her by the hands and drags her over to his bed. As she struggles, Alice's hand brushes against a knife lying on a bedside table. Instinctively, she grasps the knife and stabs him. She dresses and sneaks out of the apartment in a daze. Unseen by Alice, the stranger from earlier watches her leave.

Racked with guilt, Alice walks through the West End of London until dawn, reaching her bed only seconds before her mother comes to wake her. The family home adjoins her father's shop and, as Alice sits down to breakfast, she overhears a customer gossiping. The news of Crewe's murder is spreading and Alice can barely conceal her guilt.

Frank is assigned to the murder case, and as he searches the dead man's room he finds a glove that he recognises as belonging to Alice. Frank goes to see her on the pretence of needing to use their telephone, but once he gets Alice alone he returns her missing glove to her, thereby revealing that he knows she is somehow involved. Before he can talk further though, a man enters the shop: it's the man who was lurking outside Crewe's flat the previous night. His name is Tracy and he reveals that he managed to obtain Alice's other glove from the scene of the crime. He hints that she might be open to blackmail, then invites himself to breakfast, confident he can exploit the situation to his advantage. However, at the local police station, Crewe's landlady makes a statement claiming she'd seen Tracy hanging around recently. On this evidence, the order is given for Tracy to be arrested for Crewe's murder.

Back at the shop, Frank learns of this new development. Though he is confident he can lay the blame on Tracy, Alice is terrified and begs her boyfriend to let her confess. Tracy tries to talk Frank round and pleads with Alice to persuade him not to take the matter any further. The police arrive and Tracy escapes through a back window. A chase ensues and eventually Tracy is cornered at the British Museum, where, trying to escape via the roof, he falls to his death. Meanwhile, Alice goes to the police station to turn herself in, but, before she can make her confession, Frank returns to tell her that Tracy is dead. He persuades her to let the blackmailer take the blame and the couple leave the station together.

ROOTS: Obviously, *The Jazz Singer* (Alan Crossland, 1927) with Al Jolson's proclamation 'You ain't heard nothin' yet!' must be seen as a major influence on every sound picture, but we'll mention it just the once here.

WHO'S WHO?: Born in Poland in 1903, Anny Ondra (Alice) worked on over 30 silent movies before *Blackmail* – including Hitchcock's *The Manxman*. But, after the development of sound features, Ondra moved to Germany to continue her career. The Irish actress Sara Allgood, seen here as Alice's mother, was the star of Hitchcock's *Juno and the Paycock*, and made a brief appearance in *Sabotage*. She also played the mother in the remake of *The Lodger* (John Brahm, 1944). John Longden also appeared in *Juno and the Paycock*, as well as *The Skin Game* and *Young and Innocent*. Listen out for him as the Narrator in *A Matter of Life and Death* (1947).

THE USUAL SUSPECTS: Donald Calthrop can be seen in *Murder!*, *Juno and the Paycock*, *Number Seventeen* and in Hitchcock's contribution to the sketch-based *Elstree Calling* (1930). Hannah Jones (the Landlady) had already worked with Hitch in *Downhill*, and would return for *Murder!* and *Rich and Strange*, while Phyllis Konstam appeared in *Champagne*, *Murder!*, and *The Skin Game*.

KILLER LINES: Obviously foreshadowing later events, Alice says to Crewe: 'I always think a girl knows instinctively if she can trust a man.'

The gossip in the shop is hilarious, rabbiting on about the murder and setting Alice's nerves on edge: 'A good, clean honest whack over the 'ead with a brick is one thing. There's something British about that. But *knives*? No, knives is not right.'

THERE HE IS!: After Alice and Frank leave the police station near the beginning, they board a London Underground tube train. We see Hitch sitting behind them in the train carriage being pestered by a small boy.

MISOGYNY: At the close of the film, a policeman jokes with Frank, saying: 'I suppose we should have lady detectives up at the yard, eh?' and laughing heartily. I'm sure Stella Rimmington, head of MI5, might find it equally amusing!

THEMES AND MOTIFS: Some of the images that were becoming Hitch standards are used here, notably a long, spiralling staircase first seen as early as *The Lodger* right through to *Frenzy*. And, as with *The Lodger*, the murder itself takes place on a Tuesday night. Note also the blonde heroine, a kitchen knife as a murder weapon (*Murder!*, *Sabotage*, *Psycho*, *Torn Curtain*), and a police officer taking the law into his own hands out of self-interest (Frank willingly allows his fellow officers to chase Tracy to his death).

TABOOS: Anny Ondra is shown to reveal a surprising amount of flesh for the times, but more shocking is the apparent suggestion that after her flirty and coquettish behaviour Alice gets what is coming to her.

POSTER: With stills from the movie, the poster invites patrons to 'See and Hear Blackmail. Britain's all-talkie challenge to the World . . .' 'The first full length all talkie film made in Great Britain. SEE & HEAR it – our mother tongue as it should be – spoken! 100% talkie, 100% entertainment. Hold everything till you've heard this one!'

THE ICE MAIDEN: Because of Anny Ondra's East European accent, her voice was dubbed 'live' by Joan Barry, standing in the wings reading the lines into a microphone as each scene was shot. Unfortunately, Barry's accent was more Royal Family than East End shop girl, giving Alice a voice that sounds like nails down a blackboard. As a consequence, Ondra fails to appear natural in any of her scenes containing dialogue. She's trying to throw off the shackles of the silent screen, and many of her mannerisms come across as severely overplayed. However, her jerky movements immediately following the murder are quite chilling, where she emerges from the bed still holding the knife and looking off into the distance blankly.

WHAT THE PAPERS SAID: Reaction was universally positive, largely due to this new nine-day wonder called 'sound'. Hugh Castle, editor of *Close Up*, wrote that *Blackmail* was 'perhaps the most intelligent mixture of sound and silence we have yet seen', while on 24 June the reviewer in the *Daily Mail* jingoistically declared the picture to be 'the best talking film yet – and British'. The London reviewer for *Variety* summed up its historical importance in its 1 July edition, where he noted how 'silent, it would be an unusually good film; as it is, it comes near to being a landmark'.

TRIVIA: It was originally filmed as a silent movie, running 75 minutes; Hitchcock later added newly shot scenes and had other existing footage dubbed to create the talkie version, running 86 minutes. A German-language version was produced at the same time, also directed by Hitchcock.

An early version of the script had Alice arrested for the crime. We were to have seen her charged and processed just like the criminal Frank arrests at the beginning of the film, but it was felt the film needed a more commercial happy ending.

In an interview, led by the director François Truffaut, Hitchcock boasted that in *Blackmail* he had created 'something amusing, a kind of a parting greeting to the silent movie. In silent movies the rogue mostly has a beard. My painter does not have a beard; but an iron lattice, which is in his studio, throws a shadow on his face, which looks like a beard, but even more genuinely and more threateningly.'

During filming, the Duchess of York – now the Queen Mother – visited the studio and was given a tour by Hitchcock. Hitch apparently committed a faux pas by removing the Duchess's hat to enable her to wear a pair of headphones – since Victorian times it had been accepted etiquette that royalty were always seen with their heads covered by a hat.

Having worked as an uncredited still photographer on *Champagne* and *The Manxman*, Michael Powell claimed to have made contributions to the script for *Blackmail*. Powell would later write, direct and, along with his long-time collaborator Emeric Pressburger, produce such great British classics as *The Life and Death of Colonel Blimp* (1943), *A Matter of Life and Death* (1947) and *The Red Shoes* (1948). His widow, Thelma Schoonmaker, is the award-winning film editor on such films as *Raging Bull* (Martin Scorsese, 1980) and *Goodfellas* (Scorsese again, 1990).

The climax to the film, set in the British Museum, was achieved using the complicated 'Schufftan process', where mirrors are combined with miniatures to rear-project an image.

FINAL ANALYSIS: While there are many moments in *Blackmail*, such as the lengthy opening sequence, that are obviously reconstructed silent sections, the film displays many innovative touches in Hitchcock's use of the newly developed sound technology. As Alice strolls through the streets her daze is disrupted by the sight of a tramp reaching out to her like the man she's just murdered. She is startled and her scream merges with that of the landlady discovering the body – cinema's first example of a 'shock cut'. As Alice returns to her bed, Hitch intercuts shots of a birdcage in her room with the bird's song disturbing the silence. But it's in the notorious 'knife' sequence that Hitch really shows off, giving us an insight into Alice's state of mind as she half listens to a gossip discussing news of the murder. Her voice falls to a low murmur, only the word 'knife' audible. The word gets louder and louder until it's almost screamed, making Alice jump and sending the bread knife she's holding darting across the table.

Technically, *Blackmail* is a fascinating exercise in a still-young form of entertainment. However, the plot is, at times, painfully slow, the acting stilted and awkward, and it is interesting more as a historical artefact than as an entertaining film. 5/10

Elstree Calling (1930)

Produced by British International Pictures

A collaborative work directed by André Charlot, Alfred Hitchcock, Jack Hulbert, Paul Murray

Written by Val Valentine

Music: Reg Casson, Vivian Ellis & Chic Endor
Lyrics: Ivor Novello & Jack Strachey Parsons
Photography: Claude Friese-Greene
Supervising Director: Adrian Brunel
Sound Engineer: Alex Murray

CAST: Donald Calthrop, Gordon Harker, Tommy Handley, Nathan Shacknovsky, John Stuart, Jameson Thomas, Anna May Wong.

SUMMARY: *Elstree Calling* was a series of vaudeville sketches presented in the form of a live broadcast hosted by the top comedian Tommy Handley. Hitchcock's segment stars Donald Calthrop as a would-be Shakespearean actor who finally gets his big chance to appear in a scene from *The Taming of the Shrew*. Unfortunately, the Chinese woman playing Katherine (Anna May Wong) is prone to throwing custard pies and Calthrop ends up making his entrance on a runaway bicycle at great speed.

THE USUAL SUSPECTS: Donald Calthrop can be seen in *Murder!*, *Juno and the Paycock*, and *Number Seventeen*, while the lyricist Ivor Novello starred in Hitchcock's *The Lodger* and *Downhill*.

FINAL ANALYSIS: Played for the crudest of farce, it's not a major part of Hitch's canon, and, in the famous interviews with François Truffaut, Hitch's sole comment was that the sketches were 'of no interest whatsoever'.

Juno and the Paycock (1930)
(aka *The Shame of Mary Boyle*)

(B & W – 85 mins)

Produced by John Maxwell/British International Pictures

Adapted by Alfred Hitchcock, scenario by Alma Reville, based on the play by Sean O'Casey

Photography: JJ Cox
Art Director: J Marchant
Assistant Director: Frank Mills
Sound Recordist: C Thornton
Film Editing: Emile de Ruelle

CAST: Barry Fitzgerald (*Orator*), Maire O'Neill (*Mrs Madigan*), Edward Chapman (*Captain Boyle*), Sidney Morgan (*Joxer Daly*), Sara Allgood (*Mrs Boyle – Juno*), John Laurie (*Johnny Boyle*), Dave Morris (*Jerry Devine*), Kathleen O'Regan (*Mary Boyle*), John Longden (*Charles Bentham*), Dennis Wyndham (*Mobiliser*), Fred Schwartz (*Mr Kelly*), Donald Calthrop (*Needle Nugent*).

SUMMARY: In a time of civil war in Ireland, an orator speaks to the people of Dublin with cries for a united country. His speech is disrupted by gunfire and the crowd flees into a nearby pub. Here, Jack Boyle, known as 'the Captain', discusses the Troubles with his friend, Joxer Daly. The two manage to scrounge a drink from a neighbour, Mrs Madigan, before deciding to retire to Boyle's house and take advantage of the fact that Boyle's wife Juno will not be there to nag them. But Boyle is surprised when his wife comes home early and admonishes him for having spent the afternoon wasting her hard-earned money in the pub.

Jerry Devine, a young man with an eye to Boyle's daughter Mary, comes to tell him of a vacancy at the local mine. This instantly brings on agonising twinges in Boyle's legs, much to the amusement of his unconvinced wife. Jerry tells Juno that he saw Mary leave a local dance with another man. The man in question turns out to be Charles

Bentham, a local solicitor who brings news of the death of Boyle's cousin William. It appears that William has left Boyle a legacy that could amount to as much as two thousand pounds. The news sends Juno and, particularly, Jack into a premature spending spree, investing in new furniture, curtains, a gramophone and a well-stocked drinks cabinet. Juno invites Mr Bentham to dinner, though they are soon joined by Joxer and Mrs Madigan, who are drawn by the possibility of free drinks.

Boyle's son, Johnny, is unimpressed by his father's news. Unable to work after losing an arm in the recent conflicts, Johnny has given up on life and treats his entire family with resentment. He is evidently troubled by something else, though, and his family put it down to the death of Robbie Tancred, his old friend and fellow Republican who was recently shot, accused of being an informer. Johnny's absence at recent Republican staff meetings is beginning to cause concern and suspicion with the battalion members, and a man known as 'the Mobiliser' comes to visit Johnny, warning him to attend the next meeting or face the consequences. Johnny insists he's done enough for his country – he lost an arm and took a bullet in the hip fighting for freedom – but the Mobiliser insists that 'No man can do enough for Ireland'.

Inevitably, Boyle's jubilation about his new wealth comes to nothing, and, as his creditors begin to realise they have little chance of ever being paid, all of the Boyles' new acquisitions are repossessed. Worse, having found out that a legal loophole will leave the Boyles penniless, Bentham absconds, unaware that Mary is pregnant. Juno tells the family of Mary's plight, but both Jack and Johnny are scornful of her, realising the shame she will bring on the house. Determined to protect her daughter, Juno vows to leave Jack and Johnny to fend for themselves and start a new life at her sister's to help raise Mary's child. But, as Juno makes arrangements to leave, she learns that her son has been shot dead by the Republicans for betraying Robbie Tancred. This last news is too much to take, and the strong Juno finally crumbles with grief.

ROOTS: *Juno and the Paycock* is set against the political and social background of Ireland in the 1920s. After centuries of unrest, the Irish Free State was created by the 1921 Anglo-Irish agreement. Sinn Fein, the dominant political party in Ireland, eventually proclaimed independence from British rule and formed its own government, an act that eventually led to civil war. The character Johnny Boyle is a quartermaster in a Republican association which, though not stated explicitly here, is the organisation that would evolve into the Irish Republican Army (the IRA).

LEGACY: Like Hitchcock's, Sean O'Casey's work would enjoy an upsurge of interest in the 1960s, with many of his plays being revived and re-examined. The character of Joxer Daly has become a mythological figure, lending his name both to a bar in New York (on

43rd Avenue, Woodside) and to a character played by Ted Raimi in the fantasy television series *Xena: Warrior Princess*.

WHO'S WHO?: Sean O'Casey is one of the most influential names in twentieth-century Irish drama, with many of his plays focusing on the Civil War and ensuing unrest in Ireland. His plays *The Shadow of a Gunman* (1923) and *Juno and the Paycock* (1924) were huge successes, both domestically and on mainland Britain. However, the opening of *The Plough and the Stars* in 1926 led to a riot due to Nationalist anger over his treatment of the Easter Rebellion of 1916. O'Casey fled to England, where he remained until his death in 1964.

A young John Laurie appears as the guilt-ridden Johnny Boyle. He also appeared in Hitch's *The 39 Steps* (1935), but is much better known as Private Fraser in the WW2-based comedy series *Dad's Army*.

THE USUAL SUSPECTS: Sara Allgood (*Juno*) appeared in *Blackmail* (1929), and made a cameo appearance in *Sabotage* (1936). John Longden (*Charles Bentham*) also appeared in *Blackmail* (1929), *The Skin Game* (1931), and *Young and Innocent* (1937). Donald Calthrop (*Needle Nugent*) can be seen in *Blackmail* (1929), *Murder!* (1930), *Number Seventeen* (1932) and in Hitchcock's contribution to *Elstree Calling* (1930). Edward Chapman, almost unrecognisable here as Captain Boyle, also appeared in *Murder!* (1930) and *The Skin Game* (1931).

KILLER LINES: Mrs Madigan pawned her blankets to lend money to Boyle, but when she hears that the legacy has fallen through she orders him to repay the debt: 'I've decided, if I'll be too hot in the next world aself, I'm not goin' to be too cold in this one!'

At the film's climax, Juno tells her daughter that 'These things have nothing to do with the will of God – what can God do against the stupidity of man?' She then echoes the words of the mourning Mrs Tancred when she cries: 'What are the pains I suffered, Johnny, bringin' you into the world and carryin' your cradle, to the pains I'll suffer now? Bringin' you out o' the world to carry you to your grave?'

THEMES AND MOTIFS: At the beginning, the familiar image of a black cat is seen, as it runs up the length of a street light to escape the panicked crowd. Hitch's fear of the police is transferred to the Irish's distrust and outright hatred of them here.

TABOOS: The political problems faced by the Irish are almost washed over here. Some delicate editing of dialogue from the original play (such as suggesting the Republicans are right to attack the Royal Irish Constabulary) have been removed, and, despite the fact that we all know what the 'shame' of Mary Boyle refers to, there's a lot of euphemism and hinting at work here. An illegitimate birth could ruin an entire family, something that might seem odd today with both unmarried single parents and abortion on demand a common occurrence.

WHAT THE PAPERS SAID: James Agate summed up a generally enthusiastic reaction in his review for *The Tatler* when he wrote that '*Juno and The Paycock* appears to me to be very nearly a masterpiece. Bravo, Mr. Hitchcock! Bravo the Irish Players and Bravo Edward Chapman! This is a magnificent British picture.' However, Hitch himself claimed to have felt uneasy at such praise, mainly because, as with most of Hitchcock's early literary adaptations, the film's success was due more to O'Casey's original play than anything Hitch himself brought to it.

FINAL ANALYSIS: 'When we have thought together and fought together we have always won!' This adaptation of O'Casey's examination of the struggles of the Irish does not transfer easily to cinema. The lengthy party sequence in the middle of the film appears to be merely a showcase for the talents of the Irish Players, with each of them in turn performing a song. Edward Chapman, however, is superb as 'the Captain', a deluded and lazy waster who believes the world owes him a living. Completely unlike the other roles he'd perform in a couple of Hitch's later films, the totally repulsive Dubliner is utterly convincing as played by Chapman. Equally strong is Sara Allgood, as the titular Juno. Although she's almost a pantomime dame in the early scenes, her grief over her son's execution in the final act is heartbreaking, especially as, allegorically, she cries not only for the collapse of her family but the tragedy of the entire Irish nation. *Juno and the Paycock* illustrates perfectly how sometimes a successful play cannot be adapted effectively to the screen, a problem Hitch wouldn't really solve until *Dial 'M' For Murder* in 1954. **4/10**

Murder! (1930)

(B & W – 92 mins)

Produced by John Maxwell/British International Pictures

Adapted by Alfred Hitchcock & Walter Mycroft, scenario by Alma Reville, based on the novel *Enter Sir John* by Clemence Dane and Helen Simpson

Musical Director: John Reynders
Photography: JJ Cox
Film Editing: Rene Marrison, under the supervision of Emile de Ruelle
Art Director: JF Mead
Assistant Director: Frank Mills
Sound Recordist: Cecil V Thornton

CAST: Herbert Marshall (*Sir John Menier*), Norah Baring (*Diana Baring*), Phyllis Konstam (*Dulcie Markham*), Edward Chapman (*Ted Markham*), Miles Mander (*Gordon Druce*), Esme Percy (*Handel Fane*), Donald Calthrop (*Ian Stewart*), Esme V Chaplin (*Prosecuting Counsel*), Amy Brandon Thomas (*Defending Counsel*), Joynson Powell (*Judge*), SJ Warmington (*Bennett*), Marie Wright (*Miss Mitcham*), Hannah Jones (*Mrs Didsome*), Una O'Connor (*Mrs Grogram*), RE Jeffrey (*Foreman of the Jury*), Alan Stainer, Kenneth Kove, Guy Pelham, Matthew Boulton, Violet Farebrother, Clare Greet, Drusilla Wills, Robert Easton, William Fazan, George Smythson, Ross Jefferson, Picton Roxborough (*Members of the Jury*).

SUMMARY: Late one night, a repertory actress, Diana Baring, is discovered in a daze holding an iron poker. Beside her is the dead body of a fellow actress, Edna Bruce. Circumstantial evidence points towards Diana's being responsible for Edna's murder, although she claims to be unable to remember a thing. With such a weak defence, Diana is found guilty of murder and imprisoned to await her execution, despite the efforts of one of the jury members, the noted theatrical producer Sir John Menier. Sir John is not convinced by the evidence of the prosecution and resolves to discover the truth.

He engages some of Diana's fellow actors to help him in his investigations and learns that Diana is trying to protect a dark secret involving another member of the cast. Sir John suggests that Diana must be protecting the real killer because she's in love with him, though Diana tells him this is impossible. Eventually she confesses that the killer is of mixed race. Sir John then shows her some new evidence, a cigarette case that Diana identifies as belonging to Handel Fane, the female impersonator. Sir John deduces that Fane killed Edna Bruce to prevent her from exposing him as a 'half-caste'.

Sir John traces Fane to a circus and invites him to audition for a part in a script he has written based on the murder case. Fane realises that the script is simply a ruse created in the hope that it might make him reveal his part in the real murder, and declines the role. However, terrified of being caught, Fane commits suicide, dramatically hanging himself during a circus trapeze act. He leaves behind a note for Sir John that explains everything.

Sir John invites Diana to play herself in his theatrical adaptation of the case, and it is clear that he has, by now, fallen madly in love with her.

ROOTS: The biographer Donald Spoto notes how the two scenes where the Markhams struggle into their clothes were inspired by Hitchcock's remembering his mother dressing in a state of panic during an air raid in World War One. The scene where Sir John shows Fane the script loaded with hidden meaning is a steal from Shakespeare's *Hamlet*, where the depressed Prince stages a play that he calls *The Mousetrap* in the hope of unveiling his stepfather's guilt.

LEGACY: What Hitchcock dispenses with in just over ten minutes took Sidney Lumet an hour and a half with his tense jury drama *12 Angry Men* (1957). See also **Themes and Motifs** below.

WHO'S WHO?: Herbert Marshall, who plays his first 'talkie' role here, also appeared in Hitchcock's *Foreign Correspondent* as well as the original version of *The Fly* (Kurt Neumann, 1958). Marshall lost his leg during World War One and wore a wooden prosthetic, a fact that was kept from the public for most of his career. Miles Mander, who had worked with Hitch on *The Pleasure Garden*, also played Mr Lockwood in *Wuthering Heights* (William Wyler, 1939), opposite Laurence Olivier as Heathcliffe.

THE USUAL SUSPECTS: Donald Calthrop had appeared in *Blackmail*, *Juno and the Paycock*, *Number Seventeen* and *Elstree Calling*. Hannah Jones can also be seen in *Downhill*, *Blackmail* and *Rich and Strange*. Clare Greet (one of the jury members) had worked in Hitch's very first (unfinished) film *Number 13*, as well as *The Manxman*, *Murder!*, *Lord Camber's Ladies*, *Sabotage*, and *Jamaica Inn*. Other familiar faces include Violet Farebrother (*Easy Virtue*), Phyllis Konstam (*Champagne*, *Blackmail*, *The Skin Game*), and Edward Chapman (*Juno and the Paycock*, *The Skin Game*). Matthew Boulton and SJ Warmington both played policemen in *Sabotage*.

KILLER LINES: Mrs Ward, a juror with a rather basic understanding of criminal psychology, advises the jury on the meaning of the defence's argument: '[the murder] was due to the independent activity of the suppressed experience, in other words, disassociation, which in this particular form is called a fugue. So that a person displaying the strangest behaviour for a considerable period of time would be quite unaware of this when he or she regained normality.' Despite such a clear grasp of the case, Mrs Ward seems surprised by the notion that such a person might be a danger to society.

A young male juror also provides us with an interesting ethical debate: 'Twenty years cut out of life – the best years – and to spend them in hell! It takes a civilised community to think out a punishment like that!' Strangely, having agonised over the weight of his vote, the juror then casually dismisses the accused as 'guilty, I suppose'.

THERE HE IS!: Hitch walks past the scene of the crime, accompanied by a woman, in the scene where Sir John leaves the boarding house with Dulcie and Ted Markham.

THEMES AND MOTIFS: Hitch's familiar theme of an innocent accused of a crime they didn't commit is complicated here by the willingness of the accused to accept her fate. What makes it interesting though is the way Hitch creates the trial and its aftermath in the style of a play within a play (film). The jury (acting as both the audience and the critics) enter the courtroom. The accused and her counsel deliver a barely adequate defence, the prosecution and the judge all play their parts, then the jury retires to 'review the evidence'. Before they deliver their verdict, the jury take the form of a Greek chorus chiding Sir John to make a decision as to whether Baring is innocent or guilty.

Later, at the theatre, we see the audience take their seats as the safety curtain rises. We cut to a shot of a cell door with the observation hatch, matching the curtain, rising to reveal Diana. We hear someone giving her a curtain call, and then the audience are heard to applaud. We cut to backstage at the theatre as the performance continues. When Sir John asks Fane to audition, the scene mirrors the earlier events in the courtroom. The accused (Fane) is presumed guilty before he begins his performance, and as with Diana, he does little to dissuade his judge of that opinion.

The Lodger, *Number Seventeen*, *Sabotage*, *Stagefright*, *The Man Who Knew Too Much* (1956 version), *Vertigo* and *North by Northwest* also feature people playing dual roles to conceal guilt or purpose. The traditional murder weapon, a kitchen knife, plays a part in *Blackmail*, *Sabotage*, *Psycho* and *Torn Curtain*, and, thirty years before *Psycho*, *Murder!* provides us with a discussion about the possibilities of a dual personality being responsible for turning someone into a murderer.

TABOOS: When Diana lets slip Fane's secret, Sir John exclaims: 'A half-caste . . . black blood!' summing up the cultural backdrop to this movie. In 1930, it might, conceivably, have been legitimate for a killer's motivation to be that he's a transvestite homosexual desperate to conceal the fact that he's of mixed race (and possibly, by implication, illegitimate). In the allegedly politically correct society of today, however, this view sits uncomfortably. Viewed retrospectively, this scene is so outrageous it actually provides one of the less intentionally comic highlights of the film.

MUSIC: The title music is an arrangement of Beethoven's 5th Symphony, and the scene where Sir John thinks out loud in front of a mirror features an excerpt from Wagner's *Tristan und Isolde*. Interestingly, the shaving scene features an innovative 'interior monologue' for Sir John using a prerecorded soliloquy played through a speaker on set. The music for the scene, ostensibly coming from a radio, was actually performed by an orchestra hidden behind the set as it was not possible to dub the scene in post-production. The rest of the production features very little music of note, however.

TRIVIA: Hitchcock filmed a German version called *Mary* at the same time, but using German actors on the same sets. He came into conflict with Alfred Abel, the actor playing Herbert Marshall's role, who refused to perform the farcical bed scene in the boarding house as he felt it was degrading.

FINAL ANALYSIS: *Murder!* is unusual for a number of reasons. First, it's a whodunnit, a genre Hitch generally avoided. Secondly, owing to time constraints, many of the scenes had to be improvised, leading to the odd fluffed line or strange sentence construction. However, most unusual is that, despite the obvious trappings of a thriller, *Murder!* is quite clearly mounted as a comedy. Our first clue (if the wonderfully melodramatic title doesn't give it away) comes during the scenes where the jury deliberate over the case. Here, the pompous Mrs Ward (see **Killer Lines** above) spouts some ludicrous cod psychology, prompting us to recall the comedian Harry Enfield's spoof information films instructing: 'Women – know your place'. The jury also includes Mr Daniels, whose only reason for voting not guilty is because he fancies the accused, and Mr Matthews, whose stupidity serves the purpose of showing the shortcomings of living in a democracy.

Another scene, reminiscent of the Catholic household from *Monty Python's Meaning of Life*, has Sir John staying at a boarding house. As the landlady wakes him with breakfast in bed, a horde of young children run riot in the room, shaking the bedposts and crawling all over him. It's almost understandable that Alfred Abel felt it was undignified when his turn came to film the scene for the German version.

But there are some subtler moments, such as when Sir John visits Diana in prison and she invites him to sit down. They take their place either end of an enormously long table, meaning they have to almost shout across to each other. In any other setting there would almost certainly be a laughter track. As it is, the scene ends with Diana alone in her cell, with the morning light casting the shadow of the gallows across her cell wall in a sobering reminder of the possible fate that awaits her. Everything after this comes as an anticlimax as Sir John gets on with piecing together the evidence to expose Handel Fane as the weak, murderous 'sexual deviant' we suspected he was from the start. **6/10**

The Skin Game (1931)

(B & W – 85 mins)

Produced by John Maxwell/British International Pictures

Adapted by Alfred Hitchcock, scenario by Alma Reville, based on the play by John Galsworthy

Photography: JJ Cox
Assistant Director: Frank Mills
Sound Recordist: Alec Murray
Art Director: JB Maxwell
Film Editing: A Gobett & R Marrison

CAST: CV France (*Mr Hillcrist*), Helen Haye (*Mrs Hillcrist*), Jill Esmond (*Jill Hillcrist*), Edmund Gwenn (*Mr Hornblower*), John Longden (*Charles Hornblower*), Phyllis Konstam (*Chloe Hornblower*), Frank Lawton (*Rolf Hornblower*), Herbert Ross (*Mr Jackman*), Dora Gregory (*Mrs Jackman*), Edward Chapman (*Dawker*), RE Jeffrey (*First Stranger*), George Bancroft (*Second Stranger*), Ronald Frankau (*Auctioneer*).

SUMMARY: Hornblower, a leading industrialist, issues eviction orders to some of his tenants to enable him to build new homes for his own employees. However, when Hornblower bought the land from the Hillcrist family he did so on the understanding that the existing tenants would be left alone and his decision to go back on his word soon reaches the enraged Hillcrists.

Visiting them at their home, Hornblower tries to explain his plans to Mr Hillcrist, who remains unimpressed; even less impressed when Hornblower goes on to reveal that he also plans to buy the Century, a plot of land that backs directly on to the Hillcrists' estate. It is here that he plans to build a new factory. Recriminations and threats begin to fly, with Mrs Hillcrist and their daughter Jill throwing their weight behind their family's commitment to their land. During a lengthy conversation, Mr Hillcrist reassures Jill that he won't let the land go without a fight.

At the auction for the Century, the Hillcrists and the Hornblowers turn out in force. Hornblower's daughter-in-law Chloe tries in vain to make peace between the two families, claiming that she has pleaded with her husband and father-in-law to abandon their plans. Despite her peacemaking efforts, she is publicly snubbed by Mrs Hillcrist, causing her much shame and embarrassment. Hearing about this incident, Hornblower vows not to be beaten in the auction – no matter what the cost. Chloe seems deeply upset and seeks comfort from her husband.

The bidding moves forward quite quickly, with Dawker (one of Mrs Hillcrist's staff) acting as Mr Hillcrist's agent. Hornblower, however, bids himself, and is on the verge of winning when Mr Hillcrist enters the bidding personally. The price goes up and up to sums that neither party can really afford. At the last moment, a mystery agent enters the bidding race and outbids them all. Believing this third party to be acting on behalf of the local duke, Hillcrist is shocked to discover that the mystery agent was in fact also working for Hornblower.

Dawker informs Mrs Hillcrist that he has uncovered a shocking secret about Chloe Hornblower. Mrs Hillcrist writes to Hornblower, telling him that she has some information about Chloe that he urgently needs to hear. Hornblower receives the letter and asks Chloe outright what Mrs Hillcrist could mean. Though she is visibly concerned, Chloe claims she has no idea what the letter could be referring to. However, later that night, Chloe meets with Dawker, who explains that he knows her dark secret and is prepared to use the information to the Hillcrists' advantage. Dawker leaves just as a curious Charlie turns up. He is worried about

Chloe's odd behaviour until she reveals that she's pregnant. He is thrilled by this unexpected news.

Hornblower storms up to the Hillcrists' house to demand an explanation for the letter. Mrs Hillcrist explains to Hornblower that they have discovered Chloe's former profession – she was regularly hired to be the 'third party' in divorce cases, with the implication being that Chloe was often required to act the part on a 'professional' basis. Hornblower realises he must act quickly to protect his family's reputation, and, reluctantly, he agrees to sell the Century back to the Hillcrists in exchange for their silence over his daughter-in-law's past.

In desperation, Chloe visits the Hillcrists, unaware that Charlie has followed her. When he bursts into the Hillcrists' home demanding an explanation, Chloe hides behind a set of curtains. The Hillcrists try to protect Chloe's reputation, but Charlie has already learnt the truth from Dawker and declares he will abandon the pregnant girl rather than suffer the shame. Jill Hillcrist calls to the hiding Chloe, but she has fled, so Charlie, Mr Hillcrist and Jill search the gardens for her.

At that moment, Mr Hornblower arrives. The gossip about Chloe is by now common knowledge. Believing the Hillcrists have betrayed him, he demands his land be returned to him. Just then, a devastated Charlie returns with Chloe's body. Unable to bear the scandal, she has drowned herself. With his son's life ruined, his daughter-in-law and unborn grandchild dead, and his name for ever tarnished, Hornblower decides to leave the village, cursing Hillcrist and his family. Thoroughly humbled by his part in a young woman's death, Hillcrist can only apologise and contemplate the terrible cost both families have had to pay.

ROOTS: The General Strike and the Depression of the late 1920s led to a near-resurrection of the industrial novel, with writers such as Galsworthy and Arnold Bennett drawing from the works of Victorian authors like Thomas Hardy and George Eliot.

LEGACY: The never-ending British obsession with class and trying to better themselves was parodied in the satirical 1980s comedy series *Brass*, with Timothy West portraying a character not too dissimilar to Hornblower.

WHO'S WHO?: Jill Esmond (*Jill Hillcrist*) was at this time married to Laurence Olivier, who later starred in Hitchcock's *Rebecca* (1940).

THE USUAL SUSPECTS: John Longden appears in *Blackmail, Juno and the Paycock* and *Young and Innocent*. Helen Haye pops up in *The 39 Steps*; Phyllis Konstam is in *Champagne, Blackmail* and *Murder!*; Edward Chapman also appeared in both *Murder!* and *Juno and the Paycock*; and Edmund Gwenn offered support in *Waltzes from Vienna, Foreign Correspondent* and *The Trouble With Harry*.

KILLER LINES: Hornblower, to Jill Hillcrist: 'I'll answer to God for my actions, not to you, young lady.' 'Poor God . . .' she replies.

Chloe Hornblower, realising fatalistically that her past would eventually catch up with her: 'I know it was in the wind. What gets in the wind never gets out. Ever. It blows.' We imagine Hitchcock found this line less profound than just plain amusing.

MISOGYNY: Compare the shame that Chloe suffers, used by men eager for a quickie divorce, with the similar circumstances of Cary Grant in *Suspicion*, who, believed to have been named as a co-respondent in a divorce case, almost receives a commendation.

THEMES AND MOTIFS: 'Scenes from the Class Struggle in the English Countryside' no less! It's interesting to note that the working classes are very poorly represented in *The Skin Game*. Chloe is, we are supposed to believe, little more than a whore who has gained her new social position through deceit; Dawker is a duplicitous coward who is quite happy to threaten women, but who caves in to physical threats himself; and the Jackmans are pathetic losers who go running for help from the upper classes to stop themselves losing their homes. It's clear where Hitchcock's sympathies lay.

TABOOS: It's very heavily implied that Chloe used to work as a professional co-respondent, being hired to sleep with men in order to get them a divorce or to give their wives a reason for escaping from their marriages. This was so shocking, so scandalous, that Hornblower is prepared to lose thousands of pounds to protect his family from its revelation. Even worse, it causes Chloe herself to commit suicide, rather than face the shame.

THE ICE MAIDEN: There are no classical Hitch blondes in *The Skin Game*, just a smattering of rather dull brunettes. Although Phyllis Konstam's performance as Chloe is endearingly over-the-top and melodramatic, Jill Esmond has a voice like cut glass falling from a great height on to a pebble beach. To add insult to injury, Jill's behaviour and attitude make her a prime candidate for the most annoying character ever to be seen in a Hitchcock movie.

FINAL ANALYSIS: *The Skin Game* falls into the traditional mould of many early Hitchcock pictures, with the first half of the film verging on the unwatchable, and the second half being rather tense. It's possible to sympathise with the situation of each of the families (although the Jackmans are such clichéd 'honest working folk' that one might feel they deserve to be kicked out of their home!), but impossible to actually *like* any of them. The Hillcrists incorporate all of the baseless arrogance that's so easy to despise about the 'upper classes', using their status and position to keep the other classes in their place, and it could be argued that their dislike of Hillcrist is as much to do with his refusal to compromise as his unwillingness to bow and scrape before them. While the Hillcrists fight to maintain the status quo, Hornblower strives to elevate his family through the accumulation of land and money, and, though the Hillcrists regret the final outcome of the dispute, it's clear – to them at least – that Hornblower brought about his own downfall. As with Julius Caesar, it was his own unrestrained ambition that would ultimately destroy him.

The movie now seems little more than a curio, despite the themes of class warfare and land rights still being as relevant as ever. It just seems very clear that Hitchcock was terminally bored while making this film, and it's a great shame that his audience ends up equally bored for most of the time, too. Thank heavens it's less than an hour and a half long. 3/10

Number Seventeen (1932)

(B & W – 63 mins)

Produced by Leon M Lion & John Maxwell/British International Pictures

Written by Alfred Hitchcock, scenario by Alfred Hitchcock, Alma Reville & Rodney Ackland, based on the play by J Jefferson Farjeon

Photography: John J Cox & Byran Langley
Assistant Director: Frank Mills
Art Director: Wilfred Arnold
Sound Recording: AD Valentine
Film & Sound Editing: AC Hammond
Musical Score: A Hallis

CAST: Leon M Lion (*Ben*), Anne Grey (*Girl, Nora*), John Stuart (*Detective*), Donald Calthrop (*Brant*), Barry Jones (*Henry Doyle*), Ann Casson (*Rose Ackroyd*), Henry Caine (*Mr Ackroyd*), Garry Marsh (*Sheldrake*), Herbert Langley (*Guard*).

SUMMARY: Snooping around an old derelict house, a man discovers both a nervous tramp called Ben and the dead body of a man. Claiming all innocence of the crime, Ben tries to escape, but the man, Thordyke, restrains him and enlists his help in searching the house. Ben inspects the body and is surprised to find a pair of handcuffs and a gun.

As the men continue their investigation a young woman falls through the roof and lands dazed at their feet. When she comes round she introduces herself as Rose Ackroyd. She lives next door at No. 15 and is looking for her father, who disappeared from their home just before a telegram arrived for him. She shows Thordyke the telegram, which states that the sender, 'Barton,' has traced the whereabouts of a necklace to a person called Sheldrake, who will somehow try to make his escape via this house sometime after midnight.

At 12.30 a.m., the trio hear the doorbell. Thordyke goes to investigate. Meanwhile, Ben discovers that the 'dead' body is missing. At the front door, Thordyke watches as someone outside pushes what looks like a ticket through the letterbox. Thordyke opens the door to two men and a woman, who appears to be mute. One of the men tells him he's a house hunter and begins to look around. Ben panics and pulls the gun on them. He's quickly restrained and locked in one of the spare rooms, unaware that this is the hiding place of another man. He attacks Ben, who quickly falls to the ground and pretends to have passed out, having pickpocketed a necklace from the stranger.

Rose's father, Mr Ackroyd, turns up and helps Thordyke and Rose bundle the newcomers into another room, locking the door behind them. But when they try to free Ben they are surprised by his attacker. He knocks Ackroyd to the ground and wrestles Ben's gun from his trembling hands. The attacker frees the house hunters and identifies himself as Sheldrake, the man they were looking for. He has arranged to meet the trio to help them escape the country with a stolen necklace. He chains Thordyke and Rose to a rickety balustrade before escorting his entourage down to the house's cellar.

Rose and Thordyke try to escape but the balustrade suddenly breaks, leaving them dangling dangerously over a massive drop to the ground. The mute woman returns and not only saves them, but reveals she can speak, introducing herself as 'Nora'. She returns to the escapees and tries to slow them down but they drag her along after them. Using a secret staircase they head towards a nearby railway, the reason the house was chosen as a meeting point. They find the train they need and stow away in some storage wagons.

Ben and Thordyke chase after the departing train. Ben climbs aboard, leaving Thordyke to call the police. Meanwhile, having commandeered the train, Sheldrake finally notices that the diamonds are missing from his pocket and suspects that one of his accomplices is an undercover policeman. One of the men announces that he is in fact Barton of Scotland Yard and orders him to hand over the diamonds. A fight breaks out, during which the train driver is shot, sending the train speeding out of control. Despite the efforts of the criminals, the train careers off the end of a pier, sending the carriages crashing into the sea. Thordyke manages to save both Nora and Ben and gets them both to dry land. In a confusing switch, the man posing as Barton is revealed to be a criminal called Doyle, and Thordyke finally unveils himself to be the real Inspector Barton. Watching the police lead the villains away, Barton invites Nora to breakfast just as Ben opens up his gabardine to reveal the necklace safe around his neck.

THE USUAL SUSPECTS: Donald Calthrop (*Brant*) appeared in *Blackmail, Murder!, Juno and the Paycock* and *Elstree Calling*. John Stuart (*the Detective*) from *The Pleasure Garden* is also in *The Hound of the Baskervilles* (Gareth Gundrey, 1931) as Sir Henry Baskerville and was last seen as one of the Kryptonian Elders in *Superman: The Movie* (Richard Donner, 1978).

THEMES AND MOTIFS: A black cat is seen running up the staircase of the deserted house (see, among others, *The Lodger* and *To Catch A Thief*). Originally a whole alleyful of moggies was meant to dart up the stairs at the sound of a gunshot, but the untrainable creatures refused to respond to Hitch's direction and the idea was abandoned.

MUSIC: It's no wonder this is Hallis's sole contribution to cinema. An inappropriately loud and unnecessarily melodramatic score succeeds only in ruining any real tension. Maybe it's all done in the spirit of pastiche that Hitch had intended but, like the rest of the film, it fails on every count. Definitely just cause for a speedy return to silent pictures.

THE ICE MAIDEN: Ann Casson is charming as the dizzy Rose Ackroyd. Hanging from the broken balustrade she notes with glee that she's just fainted, looks down to the ground far below and faints again. Anne Grey as the mysterious mute woman is more in the vein of the traditional Hitchcock *femme fatale*, pretending to be mute to avoid attracting attention to herself, then betraying her companions in the hope that Thordyke can rescue her in time. Two of the few redeeming features of the picture.

FINAL ANALYSIS: 'Messin' about, that's all you're doing! Messin' about!' In some ways, a film such as this provides a greater insight into the mind of Hitchcock than some of his more notorious work, like *Vertigo* and *Marnie*. If his producers allocated him to a project he didn't want, or if he lost interest in the project along the way (see *Waltzes from Vienna*), his destructive urges would often take hold of him and he'd send the whole thing up. Such was the case with *Number Seventeen*, which he intended to be a pastiche of gritty espionage thrillers. Unfortunately, whereas in other films Hitch has calculated the degree of humour and counterpoints it with suspense (and vice versa), here the 'satire' is misjudged at almost every level.

What we are left with is a setup where the detective and the tramp spend far too much time lurking about on the same landing for no good reason, a neighbour who comes looking for her father in the abandoned house next door for no good reason and a secret (though not very well-hidden) trapdoor that leads down to a railway siding for no good reason. Surely the previous owners would have no need to have easy access to the railway, and if the spies created it surely someone would have heard them. This collection of plot holes, loose ends and mistaken/concealed identities might well be a clever and biting satire, but where the strokes should be broader they're almost invisible, and where the humour should be subtle it's way too crude. The worst example of this is Leon M Lion's eye-scratchingly awful performance as Ben the tramp, playing every line with the most embarrassing slapstick approach possible and an incredibly thick 'cockernee' accent to boot.

Through all this we've felt completely uninvolved, so it came as a great surprise to find ourselves on the edge of our seats during the climactic chase sequence where, thanks to the wonders of miniatures, Thordyke commandeers a bus to race after the runaway train. As the two vehicles tear across the (model) countryside the whole sequence feels like a hypertense episode of *Thomas the Tank Engine*, but it's by far the only satisfying segment of the picture. Definitely Hitchcock's weakest film. **2/10**

Rich and Strange (1932)
(US title: *East of Shanghai*)

(B & W – 83 mins)

Produced by John Maxwell/British International Pictures

Adapted by Alfred Hitchcock, scenario by Alma Reville & Val Valentine, based on the novel by Dale Collins

Music by Hal Dolphe
Photography: JJ Cox (credited as John Cox) & Charles Martin
Assistant Direction: Frank Mills
Sound Recording: Alec Murray
Art Director: C Wilfred Arnold
Musical Direction: John Reynders
Film Editing: Winifred Cooper & Rene Marrison

CAST: Henry Kendall (*Fred Hill*), Joan Barry (*Emily Hill*), Percy Marmont (*Commander Gordon*), Betty Amann (*The Princess*), Elsie Randolph (*Old Maid*).

UNCREDITED CAST: Aubrey Dexter (*Colonel*), Hannah Jones (*Mrs Porter, their housekeeper*).

SUMMARY: Fred and Emily Hill are a happily married, if rather dull, middle-class couple. Bored with the daily trauma of commuting to work in London, Fred longs for excitement and adventure in his life. Unexpectedly, Fred receives a letter from his uncle:

'I've thought a lot about our conversation of the other day. You say you want to enjoy LIFE as a change from your existence – well, see my solicitors and they will fix you up with the money to experience all the life you want by travelling everywhere. You might as well have the money now instead of waiting until I die.'

Following Fred's uncle's advice, they decide to spend the money on a grand tour around the world. The tour kicks off with a visit to Paris, where the couple are pleasantly scandalised by the scantily clad performers at the Folies-Bergère. Emily gets her bottom pinched by a Toulouse Lautrec lookalike, then the couple get quite drunk and end up staggering back to their hotel room.

They then begin a 'round-the-world' cruise on a luxury ship, joining it at Marseilles. Unfortunately, Fred soon discovers that he suffers from extreme seasickness, and ends up spending the vast majority of the trip unable to leave his bed. Meanwhile, Emily begins to socialise with her fellow passengers, notably a dizzy 'old maid' who seems oblivious to her own lack of social skills, and a certain Commander Gordon. Gordon is a charming gentleman who flatters and enthrals Emily, and, deprived of her husband's company, she begins to fall in love with the dashing commander.

Fred is introduced to a beautiful, dark-haired woman who claims to be a princess; he is instantly smitten by her beauty. They travel on through the Mediterranean to Port Said and the Suez Canal. Fred becomes increasingly jealous of Gordon, and turns for comfort to the princess. Inevitably, Fred and Emily's relationship starts to break down as they bicker about the journey and their respective new friends. By the time they reach Colombo, it is clear that they are both spending far more time with their partners than with each other. Eventually, something has to give. On the last night of the voyage, both of them decide that they will run away with their new partners when they hit land in Singapore. As Gordon and Emily leave for his plantation in Kuala Lumpur, Gordon criticises Fred for failing to see what a wonderful woman Emily is. Furthermore, Gordon knows that the princess is misleading Fred – she is in fact nothing more than a common German actress willing to do anything to separate a fool from his money.

Horrified, Emily abandons Gordon, rushing back to save Fred from making an even bigger mistake. She returns to the Singapore hotel and confronts Fred with the news. He refuses to believe her until he discovers that the princess has abandoned him and caught a train to Rangoon. It doesn't take them long to realise that the 'princess' has actually stolen the majority of the money that they had left. Unhappy with their decisions and fed up with travelling, they decide to book a ticket straight back to Britain. Unfortunately, they have only enough money left to buy passage on one of Brown's Steamers' rickety cargo ships – and for one twin room.

Partway through the voyage, just off the coast of China, the boat they are on starts to sink. Trapped in their cabin and with water starting to flood in under the door, Fred and Emily hold each other and fall asleep on their bed. When they wake up, they are shocked to discover that they are still alive. The boat has only partially submerged, but the entire crew has fled in the lifeboats or drowned. Climbing out of their porthole and on to the deck, Fred and Emily wander round the abandoned ship, the true scale of their predicament hitting them. They are relieved when a passing Chinese junk stops to salvage the wrecked ship, and, just as they climb on board the junk, their ship finally sinks.

On board the junk, they witness what life at sea can really be like: cramped, squalid conditions and a young Chinese woman forced to give birth using only sea water. Their journey to civilisation is arduous, but it brings them together again. Finally back home in Britain, Fred and Emily decide to try for a baby, but have a friendly squabble about whether or not they will need to move to a bigger house.

CASTING: Hitchcock was really not at all keen about using Joan Barry for *Rich and Strange*, probably due to the experience he had previously had working with her on *Blackmail*. He interviewed several other actresses signed to BIP, including Anna Lee, but reluctantly plumped for Barry.

ROOTS: The title comes from Shakespeare's *The Tempest* ('But doth suffer a sea-change/Into something rich and strange' – as stated on screen on one of the caption cards). The sequence on the sinking ship is very reminiscent of the *Titanic* tragedy, which is curious considering that a filmed version of the disaster was planned to be Hitch's first project on moving to America. However, more than anything else, *Rich and Strange* is inspired by Mr and Mrs Hitchcock's autobiographical anecdotes of their own round-the-world trip. Whether or not the Hitchcocks suffered as much marital strain as Fred and Emily is unknown, but Alfred's bouts of severe seasickness and the couple's visit to a burlesque show in France pop up.

LEGACY: The sinking of the ship foreshadows by 66 years (and some $200 million) James Cameron's version of *Titanic* (1998), notably the scene where, as the ship sinks, a married couple cling to each other in terror as the water seeps into their cabin underneath the door.

THE USUAL SUSPECTS: Elsie Randolph had been one of the London stage's most popular comedy stars and Hitch had admired her for many years. She appears here as the 'old maid' on board the cruise ship. Elsie's performance and presence in the film particularly impressed Hitch – so much so that he invited her back to appear in another movie. Sadly for Elsie's long-term film career, her much-anticipated return to the Hitchcock fold didn't occur until *Frenzy* in 1972. That's patience for you.

Hannah Jones had earlier appeared in *Downhill*, *Blackmail* and

Murder!. Percy Marmont would meet an icy fate in *Secret Agent* and appear in *Young and Innocent* as the heroine's father. Joan Barry *didn't* actually appear in *Blackmail* – but she did provide the voice for Alice, played by Anny Ondra.

ANIMAL CRUELTY: Black cats don't seem to have much luck in *Rich and Strange*. It's clear that Fred isn't exactly fond of his own – spitefully throwing a book at it, for example. The cat that they rescue from the sinking steamer meets an even more unpleasant fate: it ends up in the stew that Fred and Emily tuck into with gusto. The final insult to feline admirers comes when the Chinese chef nails up the cat's skin on the wall of the boat to dry.

KILLER LINES: Emily: 'Love is a very difficult business, Mr Gordon – you'd be surprised. It makes everything difficult and dangerous. You know, I don't think love makes people brave, like they say it does in books. I think it makes them timid. I think it makes them frightened when they're happy and sadder when they're sad. You see – everything's multiplied by two. Sickness. Death. The future. It all means so much more.'

THEMES AND MOTIFS: This film is largely an analysis of how oddly matched couples can often end up staying together. Fred is so disenchanted with what he sees as a boring life that he willingly abandons the relationship he already has with the only woman who will put up with his strange little ways. Of course, Fred throws his stable marriage away for an infatuation with an actress. He comes to his senses only when faced with the brutal truth that the actress doesn't really want him, and returns to his loyal and dependable – if a little odd – wife. This theme is repeated time and again in Hitchcock's work, most notably in *Vertigo*. However, in *Vertigo*, there is of course no happy ending.

Also of note is the opening sequence, which features a long tracking shot through the office where Fred works. The office workers leaving the building raise their umbrellas in unison, almost like a Busby Berkeley chorus line. Compare this to the waves of umbrellas in both *Foreign Correspondent* and *Stage Fright*.

TABOOS: After realising they are all alone on an abandoned, half-sunk ship in the middle of the ocean, Emily comes out with this pearl of 1930s discretion: 'Fred, hadn't we ought to find some clothes or something? Someone might come!' Fred: 'Yes, that's *very* likely . . .'

Fred's xenophobic comments following the birth of the baby on board the junk are just priceless with a modern sensibility: 'Why, these damn Chinese breed like rabbits . . .'

And perhaps the defining moment for this pair of vacuous fools: 'I like being shipwrecked. It's not half as bad as people make out!'

THE ICE MAIDEN: Only the most generous of reviewers could describe Joan Barry as a typical Hitchcock Ice Maiden. Quite simply, she just doesn't seem quite right for the part – a fact that Hitch himself realised from almost the beginning. Although she's blonde and has the typical Hitchcockian cheekbones, Joan Barry is simply the Wrong Woman.

FINAL ANALYSIS: *Rich and Strange* is not one of Hitch's greatest, by any stretch of the imagination. It's a curious little film, with three distinct sections – a lively, humorous and fast-paced beginning, a deadly dull central section, and a pseudo-*Titanic* conclusion. If you can avoid falling asleep during the middle half-hour, you will find that it's almost an entertaining movie. It is very clear to a modern viewer that *Rich and Strange* is an interim film between the world of the silent movie and the talkie – the caption cards that litter the film reinforce this view perfectly. In fact, there is so little dialogue that it sometimes feels as if *Rich and Strange* needs a piano accompaniment.

There are several nice touches and set pieces that make the film less of a burden to watch. The cruise ship is greeted with clear skies, romance and glamour on its initial stretch of the journey. On the way back, however (when both of our heroes have 'cheated' on each other), the audience is treated to fog, budget accommodation and a cut-price reconstruction of the sinking of the *Titanic*. Fred and Emily are no Leo and Kate, however. A total lack of empathy with them as heroes means that the audience is almost hoping that they drown in the sinking ship. Nevertheless, the sinking sequence is quite atmospheric and scary, as the noises on the decks above them slowly die down and the water starts seeping into their cabin.

The film must also surely boast one of the very earliest instances of an old horror-film cliché. Fred and Emily are alone on the deserted ship, when a door slowly creaks open behind them. What could it possibly be? It must have been innovative back in 1932 for the culprit to be the ship's cat – today it's a pleasant nod to the past. For another giggle, it's worth keeping an eye out for a totally incomprehensible sequence where the Chinese sailors are leaving the sinking ship. One of the crew starts to slide head first down a rope and drowns, for no adequately explicable reason – madness! 4/10

Lord Camber's Ladies (1932)

Produced by Alfred Hitchcock/British International Pictures

Directed and written by Benn W Levy

Based on the play *The Case of Lady Camber* by Horace Annesley Vachell

Photography: James Wilson

CAST: Nigel Bruce (*Lord Camber*), A Bromley Davenport (*Sir Bedford Slufter*), Hal Gordon (*Stage Manager*), Clare Greet (*Peach*), Benita Hume (*Janet King*), Molly Lamont (*Actress*), Gertrude Lawrence (*Lady Camber*), Betty Norton (*Hetty*), Hugh E Wright (*Old Man*), Gerald du Maurier (*Dr Napier*).

THE USUAL SUSPECTS: Nigel Bruce would later appear in *Rebecca* and *Suspicion*. Clare Greet (*Peach*) worked on *Number 13*, *The Manxman*, *Murder!*, and *Jamaica Inn*.

FINAL ANALYSIS: Originally slated to direct and produce this adaptation of *The Case of Lady Camber*, Hitchcock instead handed over the lens duties to Benn Levy, who had provided the dialogue for *Blackmail* and was a close friend of Hitch's. With Gertrude Lawrence and Gerald Du Maurier hired, two of the most popular actors at the time, things looked set to work out favourably. However, Hitch and Levy fell out during the production, never to speak again. With Hitch at an all-time low and becoming increasingly disillusioned, this would be his last picture for the company.

Waltzes from Vienna (1933)
(aka *Strauss' Great Waltz*)

(B & W – 80 mins)

Produced by Tom Arnold/Gaumont-British Picture Corporation Ltd

Adapted by Guy Bolton, scenario by Guy Bolton & Alma Reville, based on *Walzerkrieg* by Heinz Reichhart, Dr AM Wilmer & Ernest Marischka

Musical Director: Lois Levy
Musical Accompaniment: Julius Bittern & EW Kongold
Featuring the music of Johann Strauss Sr and Johann Strauss
Production Manager: Henry Sherek
Photography: Glen MacWilliams
Art Director: Oscar Werndorff
Editor: Charles Frend
Recordist: Alfred Birch

CAST: Marcus Barron (*Drexter*), Fay Compton (*Countess*), Frank Vosper (*Prince*), Hindle Edgar (*Leopold*), Sybil Grove (*Mme Fouchett*), Edmund Gwenn (*Strauss the Elder*), Robert Hale (*Ebezeder*), Charles Heslop (*Valet*), Betty Huntley-Wright (*Lady's Maid*), Esmond Knight (*Strauss the Younger*), Jessie Matthews (*Rasi*), Billy Shine Jr, Cyril Smith, Bertram Dench, BM Lewis.

SUMMARY: By chance, Johann Strauss, son of the famous composer, finds himself in conversation with the countess. As they chat, Johann tells her he also writes music, but complains that his father offers him little support or encouragement. He plays one of his compositions for her, and she is immediately impressed. She confesses to being something of a lyricist and suggests that they might collaborate; he could compose some music to fit her lyric, then she could present the piece to his father under her name and ask him to conduct it. She enlists the support of her husband, who has never been an admirer of Strauss Sr and when the prince hears Strauss's work he immediately offers to sponsor him, if only to spite the boy's famous father.

Johann visits his fiancée, Rasi, at her father's restaurant and plays her his latest piece. As ever, she is encouraging, though she suggests he might consider using another piece of music, one he wrote for her some time ago. It fits the lyric perfectly and the lovers dance joyfully. However, Rasi's father is unconvinced that Johann has what it takes to be a great composer, and insists that if he wants to marry his daughter Johann must work in the family bakery. Johann reluctantly accepts the job, but he soon finds himself distracted. Inspired by the daily sounds of the bakery, Johann manages to arrange his latest composition in his head and rushes home to write it up. When he plays the finished piece to a proud Rasi she insists he dedicate it to her, even though he has secretly dedicated another copy of the manuscript to the countess.

The countess arranges a meeting with Anton Drexter, manager and friend of Strauss Sr, and shows him young Strauss's manuscript. At the same time, and ignorant of the second manuscript, Rasi takes her copy to Strauss Sr, who refuses to even look at it. As Rasi storms from Strauss's rehearsal room, she hears her fiancé's music coming from one of the other rooms. She investigates and finds Drexter performing it for the countess. The girl is puzzled as to how the countess could have obtained a manuscript she'd believed to be unique – until she spies the different dedication on the countess's copy. Rasi runs from the room in some distress. The countess realises that Strauss will probably be held back by his love for the girl, and asks Drexter to play it through so she might hear it once and then burn it. However, Drexter is so impressed he persuades her to let him orchestrate the piece.

Still working at the bakery, Strauss is visibly unhappy. He receives a message from the countess inviting him to a forthcoming festival, much to Rasi's anger. Jealous of his relationship with the countess, Rasi threatens to leave him if he even considers attending the festival, but then she learns that, as her father has been asked to do the catering, Strauss will have to be there anyway.

The countess and Drexter indulge in a little subterfuge. Knowing that Strauss Sr is the star guest at the festival, they arrange for him to be delayed. Drexter has already trained Strauss's orchestra to play the son's composition and when the father fails to appear for the main performance, Drexter pushes Johann forward. The confused man takes his father's place and conducts the first performance of 'The Blue Danube'. The delayed Strauss Sr arrives to see his son receiving a rapturous ovation. Once his son escapes the crowds he accuses him of plotting with Drexter to humiliate and ridicule him. Worse, Rasi is now of the belief that her boyfriend and the countess are lovers.

Strauss returns home, convinced his career is irreconcilable with his love for Rasi. The countess learns of this and tries to convince him otherwise. Back at the festival, both the prince and Rasi learn that their partners have left together and both race off separately to find Strauss. The prince arrives first, baying for Strauss's blood and looking for his wife, who by now is hiding in a back room, mindful of the fact that her presence in the young man's room could send her husband into a jealous rage. With the help of Rasi, she manages to escape via a window and then runs to the front door as if she had only just arrived. She praises her husband for wanting to congratulate the young composer and the prince is forced to accept that his behaviour was a little rash. Rasi realises that Strauss will never be happy without his music and decides to support him in his chosen career.

Alone in the festival park, Strauss Sr contemplates his future. A young girl approaches him and begs for his autograph. Realising that he is still respected despite his son's success, he scrawls his name, 'Johann Strauss', in the child's book, adding as an afterthought the word 'senior' in recognition that his son will no doubt be a success.

ROOTS: Johann Strauss the Younger (1825–99) was the most famous of Viennese waltz composers. By the age of nineteen he was running his own orchestra. At 25 he was appointed the 'Imperial-Royal Director of Music for Balls' by the Emperor Franz-Joseph I.

The original stage version of *Waltzes from Vienna*, *Walzerkrieg*, had enjoyed a hugely successful run at the Alhambra Theatre in London's West End from 1931–2, where Esmond Knight had played the role re-created here.

THE USUAL SUSPECTS: Frank Vosper (*the Prince*) also appears in Hitch's next film, *The Man Who Knew Too Much*. Edmund Gwenn (*Strauss the Elder*), appears in *The Skin Game* and *Foreign Correspondent*.

KILLER LINES: The countess explains Strauss Sr's resentment for his son's talent: 'Like all great men, he has a peculiar dislike for hearing you knocking at the door.'

Reading the countess's lyric, the prince is less than impressed by some of her imagery: 'My dear, the Danube's never looked *blue* in its life. Couldn't you make it silver?'

THEMES AND MOTIFS: Even in something as un-Hitchcock as this, there's at least one moment where his guiding hand is evident, where the camera pans across the park where the festival is held and passes nonchalantly past a young couple kissing passionately behind a tree. Even in a historical setting like this, he can't resist a spot of voyeurism.

TABOOS: Though there are a number of scenes featuring women running around in their undergarments, they're unfortunately Victorian undergarments – bloomers, corsets and stockings (so there's not an inch of bare flesh to be seen). A taboo in Strauss's time, but not in Hitch's, and certainly not now, where it all seems very innocent.

When her father remarks that her mother wouldn't let him kiss her until six months after they were married, Rasi remarks saucily: 'Now I know why you were over fifty when I was born!'

ICE MAIDENS: At the time, Jessie Matthews was one of Britain's biggest stars – but then we all know Hitchcock's feeling about highly paid stars. In her autobiography, Matthews claims that Hitch often disrupted rehearsals with his customary practical jokes and tried to undermine her by cutting back her role and overwhelming her with a constant stream of corrections. This might account for Matthews's quite unlikable performance as Rasi. Quite why anyone should fall in love with such a spoilt and demanding character is unfathomable. Much more appealing is Fay Compton as the countess, a captivating blonde whose warm and commanding performance provides much-needed restraint among so much silliness.

MUSIC: We hear brief snatches of 'The Blue Danube' (or 'On the Beautiful Blue Danube' to give its full title) before the climactic 'First Performance', and Hitch sends it up by suggesting Johann's arrangement of the now legendary tune was inspired by hearing the clanking of a dough-mixing machine and the sound of croissants dropping into a tray. Witty, if not altogether historically accurate.

COSTUME: Some splendid numbers, but none of them really contribute to the themes beyond making Fay Compton look really glamorous.

FINAL ANALYSIS: A curious undertaking for Hitchcock. A musical with very little music, this sits uncomfortably among the many more successful experiments in Hitch's early films. Though the idea of directing a romantic period piece must have appealed to Hitch at some point, it's evident that he soon tired of both the minuscule budget and the uninvolving storyline. His only reaction was to send the whole thing up, turning the story of one of Vienna's most celebrated composers into an uneven farce. An early scene featuring firefighters rushing to a blaze, which might have been a dramatic opener, is instead played solely for laughs: the fire wagon is delayed by a brass band marching through the streets; the fire is at a restaurant, where everybody seems completely unconcerned by the apparent risk to their lives, watching as a cake is removed for safety and placed in front of a greedy boy, then quickly whisked away by the owner of the restaurant – who promptly drops the cake before being accidentally drenched by a firehose. It's no wonder *Waltzes from Vienna* remains an almost forgotten film, being by turn an immature slapstick comedy, a rather thin love story and a biopic that seems completely unimpressed by its subject.

That said, it's an interesting experiment for Hitch, even if only for the fact that it confirmed for him what he had probably always suspected, that his talents were best reserved for comic or suspenseful thrillers, or, as he himself put it: 'I hate this sort of stuff. Melodrama's the only thing I can do.' Had it been made by a director with an appreciation for the subject matter, *Waltzes from Vienna* might have been an interesting film, as the actual story, when it gets going, is a familiar and not unappealing one. Hitch's resentment at being lumbered with a subject he neither cared for nor knew anything about is blatant, as is the fact that he was simply biding his time until he could make a start on his next picture, one that was infinitely more suited to his own personal tastes. 5/10

The Man Who Knew Too Much (1934)

(B & W – 76 mins)

Produced by Michael Balcon/Gaumont-British Picture Corporation Ltd
Associate Producer: Ivor Montagu

Written by Charles Bennett & DB Wyndham-Lewis, scenario by Edwin Greenwood & AR Rawlinson, additional dialogue by Emlyn Williams

Photography: Curt Courant
Art Direction: Alfred Junge & Peter Proud (uncredited)
Editor: Hugh Stewart (as HStC Stewart)
Recordist: F McNally
Unit Production Manager: Richard Beville
Music: Arthur Benjamin
Musical Director: Louis Levy

CAST: Leslie Banks (*Bob Lawrence*), Edna Best (*Jill Lawrence*), Peter Lorre (*Abbott*), Frank Vosper (*Ramon*), Hugh Wakefield (*Clive*), Nova Pilbeam (*Betty Lawrence*), Pierre Fresnay (*Louis Bernard*), Cicely Oates (*Nurse Agnes*), DA Clarke-Smith (*Binstead*), George Curzon (*Gibson*).

SUMMARY: Bob and Jill Lawrence, accompanied by their daughter, Betty, are enjoying a skiing holiday in St Moritz, where they meet Louis

Bernard, a French skier. They instantly become friends and Betty begins to treat the man as an honorary uncle. Jill is an expert markswoman and enters a clay-pigeon tournament where she's narrowly defeated by a man called Ramon, thanks to the chiming of a watch owned by a Mr Abbott.

As he is due to leave the next day, Bernard invites the Lawrences to dinner. Jill drags him up to dance and Bob plays a prank on them by unravelling Jill's knitting and tying the thread to the back of Bernard's jacket, so that as they dance they end up ensnaring the entire dance floor in a web of wool. In the chaos, there's a loud smash. A small bullet hole is spotted in a windowpane and it is with a mixture of confusion and shock that Bernard discovers he has been shot. He pulls Jill to him and urgently tells her to send Bob to his room – there's a brush containing a message that must be given to the British Consul. He gives her his room key, then dies in her arms. Jill explains Bernard's instructions to Bob and gives him the key. He dashes up to Bernard's room and soon finds the message. It contains two names: G Barbour, who, it says, can be found in Wapping, and A Hall. As he leaves the room he's accosted by Ramon, who reveals he is aware of both the message and its importance, but luckily the hotel manager arrives to inform Bob that the police wish to speak with him about the murder. Bob is led away, and Ramon sneaks off.

While the police question Jill, Bob tries to find someone who can contact the British Consul for him. A note is delivered to him warning him not to tell the police anything or else they will never see their daughter again: Betty has been kidnapped.

Returning to London, the couple are questioned by the police on the disappearance of their daughter. Bob tells them she is staying with a relative in Paris, but the police tell him that they know she's been kidnapped. Gibson of the Foreign Office informs Bob that Louis Bernard had been an agent for the 'Deuxieme Bureau' and had been in the process of preventing the assassination of a world leader. He begs Bob to tell him if Bernard said anything before he died. At that moment the telephone rings and Bob receives another threat from the kidnappers, who then allow him and Jill to speak to Betty. Jill asks her if she knows where she is, but the phone goes dead. The police manage to trace the call to a public phone box in Wapping and dash off in pursuit. Aware that a heavy police presence in the area may endanger his daughter, Bob enlists the help of his friend Clive and the pair rush off to Wapping to find 'G Barbour'.

The men find Barbour; he's a dentist. Bob pretends to have toothache to gain entry to the dentist's surgery, and as he sits in the chair he sees a man leaving from a side door – he recognises him as Abbott, whom he had met while in St Moritz. Barbour makes idle chat but soon realises that Bob is spying and tries to put him to sleep with gas. Bob manages to wrestle the gas nozzle from his hand and clamps it across the dentist's face until he stops struggling. By the time Abbott returns, Bob is posing as the dentist and manages to overhear a conversation between Abbott and another man, whom Bob recognises as Ramon, the marksman. The two men soon leave and head for the Tabernacle of the Sun, followed by Bob and Clive.

Inside the Tabernacle, a mass is in process. The priestess identifies the two men as strangers and calls Clive up to the stage where she proceeds to hypnotise him. She then dismisses all but those who are 'members of the fourth Circle', leaving Bob cornered by Abbott, Ramon and their hired thugs. A fight ensues, during which Bob catches sight of tickets in Ramon's pocket for a performance at the Albert Hall and realises that this must be what Bernard's message regarding 'A Hall' must have meant. He manages to bring Clive round and helps him escape with instructions to call Jill and tell her to meet them at the Albert Hall. As he himself tries to escape, Bob is knocked unconscious.

Clive phones Jill, telling her Bob's message. He then alerts the police and leads them to the Tabernacle, but there Abbott is able to twist events to his advantage and gets Clive arrested for disorderly conduct in a place of worship. In their hideout, Abbott allows Bob to see Betty. He then plays Ramon an excerpt from the piece being performed that night at the Albert Hall, pointing to a section that features a loud clash of cymbals that will, he says, provide the perfect cover for a shot at the foreign statesman.

Jill reaches the Albert Hall and as she searches for Bob she spies Ramon, who reminds her that only her silence can ensure her daughter's safety. He climbs the stairs to take his place in his reserved box on the opposite side of the auditorium to the statesman. The performance begins and as the orchestra reach the specified section Ramon takes aim. Unable to bear the tension, Jill screams, putting him off his shot so that he barely wounds the statesman. Ramon flees the hall in an awaiting cab, but it's too late. Thanks to Jill the police are able to follow him to the spies' hideout.

Having been listening to a radio broadcast of the performance, Abbott and the gang are unaware of Ramon's failure until later on in the evening. By the time Ramon returns, the police have tracked them down. A shoot-out begins and in the confusion Bob manages to free Betty and help her on to the roof, but as he himself tries to escape Ramon shoots him. The assassin pursues Betty across the roof, watched in horror by Jill and the police on the ground below. Unused to rifles, the officers are unwilling to use them for fear of hitting the girl by mistake. Jill snatches a rifle and dispatches Ramon with one shot. The police finally storm the stronghold and the rest of the gang are found to be already dead. They search for the missing Abbott, whose chiming watch ultimately gives him away. The police fire at a doorway, and as the door swings open Abbott collapses to the floor. Outside on a landing, a wounded Bob Lawrence is finally reunited with his wife and daughter.

TITLES: After a hand leafs through some holiday brochures, the camera settles on one for St Moritz. Cut to a shot of some snowy mountains with the titles overlaid.

ROOTS: The title comes from the collection of short stories of the same name, written by GK Chesterton. Hitchcock had negotiated for the rights to a number of Chesterton books, having been impressed by the better-known Father Brown series. Despite this, the film has very little to do with Chesterton's story, which is more akin to a latter-day vigilante novel.

Though Hitch is careful not to identify the nationality of the kidnappers, the fact that the final shoot-out is inspired by real historical events, the infamous 'Sidney Street Siege', is a bit of a giveaway. After a failed revolt in Latvia in 1905, many refugees settled in London's East End, where they continued revolutionary activity for a number of years. In December 1911, a gang of Latvian thieves attempted to rob a jeweller's by tunnelling through the wall of an adjoining property. The noise of their work alerted the police and when, unarmed, they went to investigate they were gunned down and the gang went into hiding. Over the space of a few weeks, many of the gangsters were found and arrested, and on New Year's Eve the police traced two of the fugitives to an address in Sidney Street. By 3 January, the police had cordoned off the area and a shoot-out ensued. Overpowered by the fugitives' massive arsenal of ammunition, the police requested assistance and Winston Churchill, then Home Secretary, granted his permission for them to use whatever force necessary to put an end to the siege. Churchill attended the scene and after a fire broke out on an upper floor of the building he refused access to the fire brigade in the belief that the fire would flush the gunmen out. In the event, it killed them. Aware of the close similarity between the real events and Hitchcock's fictional interpretation of them, a line was inserted into the script to reassure the public that the police were not used to handling firearms, stressing that they were forced to acquire the rifles from a local gunsmith.

Listen out for Abbott's paraphrase of Hamlet's famous soliloquy when he says that Bob and Betty will be going to the place 'from which no traveller returns' (see also *Topaz*).

LEGACY: This film really kick-started Hitchcock's interest in the nonspecific foreign espionage thriller, so we can trace back to here every spy movie from *The 39 Steps* to *Topaz*. See also *Marathon Man* (John Schlesinger, 1976), which takes dentistry torture that little bit further. See also Hitchcock's own remake in 1956.

WHO'S WHO?: Edna Best would no doubt have got to know Hitchcock through her then husband, Herbert Marshall (*Murder!*, *Foreign Correspondent*).

THE USUAL SUSPECTS: Peter Lorre was the General in *Secret Agent*. Lorre (born László Löwenstein) appears here in his first English-speaking role after achieving notoriety as the child killer in Fritz Lang's *M* (1931). He would later make the inevitable trip to Hollywood, where he would play a series of shady Europeans in films such as *The Maltese Falcon* (John Huston, 1941) and *Casablanca* (Michael Curtiz, 1942), as well as starring in a number of features as Mr Moto, the Oriental detective. He provided the inspiration for Surface Agent X-20 in Gerry Anderson's puppet adventure series, *Stingray*.

George Curzon (*Gibson*) appears in *Young and Innocent* and *Jamaica Inn* as well as starring in Sexton Blake movies. Leslie Banks also stars in *Jamaica Inn* and Nova Pilbeam took the female lead in *Young and Innocent*. Frank Vosper (*Ramon*) played the Prince in *Waltzes from Vienna*.

KILLER LINES: The shooting contest at the beginning is loaded with ironic dialogue. Jill jokes with Ramon after Betty distracts her during the contest: 'Let that be a lesson to you – never have any children', and teases Bob over Betty, saying: 'You *would* have this child!' Though it's obviously good-natured banter, Jill soon regrets her flippancy. Also, when she offers to have another 'battle' with Ramon, he says: 'I shall live for that moment' – at the end of the film, Jill shoots him from the rooftops in one shot.

THERE *SHE* IS!: Getting in on her boss's act, Joan Harrison, Hitchcock's assistant, appears as a secretary.

AWARDS: Listed by the *New York Times* as one of the top ten movies of 1935.

TRIVIA: Peter Lorre married Cecelie Lvovsky during the making of the film; Hitchcock had him working that morning, he was married at noon and was back on the set within an hour – and according to Hitchcock Lorre had spent the whole time with the horrific scar make-up that his part required!

Patricia Hitchcock has recently allowed a cinema re-release of this original version of *The Man Who Knew Too Much*.

POSTER: The British release was accompanied by a shot of Jill and Bob Lawrence, clinging to each other accompanied by insets of Nova Pilbeam and Peter Lorre. The American artwork was much simpler, depicting a sneering Peter Lorre, with the strapline 'Public Enemy No. 1 of all the world . . .'

FINAL ANALYSIS: Peter Lorre visibly relishes his role as the most despicable man in the world. In comparison with the oily Ramon, Lorre's Abbott is charming and sophisticated, offering Bob Lawrence a 'last' cigarette and a drink and generally upholding his impeccable manners till the end. Here Lorre sets the standard for later Hitchcock villains, men with unpleasant jobs to do and the correct psychological profile to recognise that just because they're killers doesn't mean they can't also be polite about it. His obvious sense of loss at the death of his 'nurse' hints at his profound sense of compassion and love for her that he has kept hidden for most of the film, and when he is ultimately betrayed by his watch, a symbol of his vanity as well as time finally running out for him, we almost pity him.

Perceived wisdom holds this as infinitely superior to its 1956 counterpart. We disagree, but only just. Wittier and more concise, this English version has probably as many strengths and weaknesses as the remake and it's purely a matter of taste which one you'll prefer. The Lawrence family appear much more secure than the McKennas, with Jill openly flirting with Louis Bernard as an accepted joke between the couple that there's absolutely no possibility that any of the parties would let it go too far. As is shown above, Jill pokes fun at her daughter, knowing full well that it is just light-hearted teasing.

Even when their daughter has been kidnapped, and 'Uncle' Clive joins in, the events seem more like an exciting romp than a desperate attempt to save the lives of both Betty and the diplomat. However, this serves to make the climax all the more chilling, with the horrific image of a policeman having been shot in the head, blood trickling away from the back of his skull, other policemen gunned down without a second's thought and an overall atmosphere contributing to one of the most tense and dramatic scenes in Hitchcock's British films. **7/10**

The 39 Steps (1935)

(B & W – 81 mins)

Produced by Michael Balcon & Ivor Montagu/Gaumont-British Picture Corporation Ltd

Adapted by Charles Bennett, with dialogue by Ian Hay, based on the novel *The Thirty Nine Steps* by John Buchan

Continuity: Alma Reville
Photography: Bernard Knowles
Art Director: O Werndorff
Editor: DN Twist
Recordist: A Birch
Wardrobe: Marianne
Dress Design: J Strassner
Musical Director: Louis Levy
Music: Hubert Bath (uncredited)

CAST: Robert Donat (*Richard Hannay*), Madeleine Carroll (*Pamela*), Lucie Mannheim (*Miss Annabella Smith*), Godfrey Tearle (*Professor Jordan*), Peggy Ashcroft (*Margaret, the Crofter's Wife*), John Laurie

(*John, the Crofter*), Helen Haye (*Mrs Jordan*), Frank Cellier (*Sheriff*), Wylie Watson (*Memory*), Gus MacNaughton, Jerry Verno (*Commercial Travellers*), Peggy Simpson (*Maid*).

SUMMARY: Richard Hannay, a Canadian staying in Britain, visits a music hall one evening. During a fracas, gunshots are fired and a stampede occurs. Hannay bumps into a beautiful and mysterious-acting woman who calls herself 'Miss Smith', and takes her back to his rented apartment. Unfortunately, she has been followed by two shadowy figures and Miss Smith believes that both her life and her mission are in jeopardy. She reveals to Hannay that she is a mercenary, hired to stop foreign agents from stealing state secrets. She asks Hannay if he has ever heard of 'the 39 Steps', which he hasn't, and claims she must go to Scotland the next day to stop some vital secrets falling into enemy hands.

In the middle of the night, Miss Smith staggers into Hannay's room with a knife in her back, a map of Scotland clutched in her hand. Before she dies, she warns Hannay of a man with a part of a finger missing. Hannay travels to Scotland, to the place marked on the map with a circle – Alt-Na-Shellach. En route by train to Scotland, Hannay becomes alerted by a newspaper headline to the fact that Miss Smith's body has been discovered and that he is the prime suspect for her murder. Attempting to avoid the police, Hannay throws himself at a blonde woman in a carriage and kisses her before making a daring escape from the train on to the Forth Bridge.

Travelling on foot further north towards Alt-Na-Shellach, Hannay encounters a bible-bashing crofter and his wife. Hannay briefly shelters with the couple until the police arrive. Margaret, the crofter's wife, suspects that Hannay may be the murder suspect she has read about in the newspapers, but still lends him an overcoat and helps him to escape the police. A wild hunt across the moors then follows, with Hannay only just managing to avoid his pursuers. Arriving in Alt-Na-Shellach, Hannay heads for the largest house in the area in the hope he might find help there. He meets the owner of the house, Professor Jordan, a local bigwig, who is entertaining guests. After they leave, Hannay tells Professor Jordan about Miss Smith's murder and her concerns about possible spies leaking secrets abroad. Unfortunately for Hannay, he then notices that Professor Jordan has part of his little finger missing, and is therefore one of the spies. Jordan pulls out a gun and shoots Hannay in the chest.

Hannay's life is saved by a thick bible in the breast pocket of the crofter's overcoat. He wakes up, steals the professor's car, and goes to see the local sheriff, protesting both his innocence and the professor's guilt. The sheriff doesn't believe a word and has Hannay handcuffed to be taken back to London to stand trial for Miss Smith's murder. Hannay escapes once again by diving through a window before his second wrist can be handcuffed. Now being pursued by both Professor Jordan's henchmen *and* the police, Hannay darts into the local assembly hall.

Inside he is mistaken for the overdue guest speaker, and forced on stage to address a political rally.

Once again, Hannay's luck fails him, and the blonde he kissed on the train is in the audience. Spotting him, she goes to fetch the police. Hannay tries to avoid capture by rousing the crowd up into a frenzy, but at that moment the real guest speaker arrives and Hannay is arrested. He is led away to rapturous applause from the audience. The blonde – Pamela – refuses to help Hannay and gladly accompanies the police to give evidence against him. However, Hannay quickly realises that he and Pamela have in fact been taken away by secret agents, not the police, and that they are being taken to meet the professor. In order to clear a flock of sheep from the road, the agents handcuff Hannay and Pamela together. Seizing his chance, Hannay makes a break for freedom into the foggy night, dragging a very reluctant Pamela with him.

Hannay and Pamela check into a local pub for the night, where to her horror the only room left is a double. While Hannay is asleep, Pamela manages to get the handcuff off her wrist, and is about to call for the police when she overhears the two secret agents on the telephone to the professor's wife. She realises that Hannay has in fact been telling the truth all along and that the professor is going to warn the 39 Steps and meet at the London Palladium.

Pamela goes to Scotland Yard with her story. They don't believe her, but arrange for her to be followed to the Palladium – just as Hannay hoped. At the theatre, Hannay hears the melody that he's been whistling for the past few days. It's the theme tune to Mr Memory, the cabaret act he saw back at the theatre where he met Miss Smith. Hannay realises that Memory and the professor obviously know each other. As the police start to close in on him once more, Hannay poses Memory a question, shouting it from the audience: 'What are the 39 Steps?' Memory, shocked and horrified, starts to automatically recite the answer – that the 39 Steps is an organisation of spies collecting information on behalf of a foreign government – before being shot down by the professor.

The professor tries to make his escape by jumping from his box down on to the stage, where he is arrested by the police. Memory makes a dying statement confirming that he'd been paid by the 39 Steps to memorise a formula to make silent aircraft engines. As Memory breathes his last, Hannay and Pamela hold hands – this time with no handcuff, to hold them together.

ROOTS: *The Thirty Nine Steps* was originally published in 1915 by William Blackwood and Sons. According to Hitchcock's biographer Donald Spoto, the character of Mr Memory is based on a Vaudeville act that Hitch saw as a child, Mr Datas. And it could be argued that the dénouement is, perhaps, a little too similar to the Albert Hall sequence in Hitch's previous film.

LEGACY: It was remade with Kenneth More as Hannay in 1956 (by Ralph Charles) and in 1978 (by Don Sharp) with Robert Powell, and spoofed in both *High Anxiety* (Mel Brooks, 1977) and *Foul Play* (Colin Higgins, 1978). *The Defiant Ones* (Stanley Kramer, 1958) had Sidney Poitier and Tony Curtis handcuffed and on the run. See also **Themes and Motifs** below.

WHO'S WHO?: Robert Donat starred in the original *Goodbye, Mr. Chips* (Sam Wood, 1939) and *The Magic Box* (John Boulting, 1951), which told the story of the birth of cinema. His last film, *The Inn of the Sixth Happiness* (Mark Robson), in which he starred opposite Ingrid Bergman, was released in 1958. He died the same year of chronic asthma.

Hitch's wife Alma spotted Madeleine Carroll's potential as a leading lady after meeting her in 1928. After a twenty-year career, in which she appeared in Hitch's *Secret Agent*, as well as *The Prisoner of Zenda* (John Cromwell, 1937) and *The Fan* (Otto Preminger, 1949), Carroll retired from acting and emigrated to Canada. She died in 1987, having lived for a number of years in Spain.

The 39 Steps was Peggy Ashcroft's second feature film, but she would emerge as one of the most respected British actresses of her generation. She was made a Dame of the British Empire in 1956 and in 1984 she starred in David Lean's film adaptation of EM Forster's *A Passage To India* for which she won an Oscar. The same year she appeared in the Granada Television drama *The Jewel in the Crown*.

THE USUAL SUSPECTS: John Laurie (*the Crofter*) also appeared in *Juno and the Paycock* (1930), but is much better known as the lugubrious Fraser in the comedy series *Dad's Army*. Wylie Watson (*Mr Memory*) plays a smuggler in *Jamaica Inn*.

KILLER LINES: Richard Hannay: 'I know what it is to feel lonely and helpless and to have the whole world against me, and those are things that no men or women ought to feel.'

Richard Hannay: 'There are twenty million women in this island and I get to be chained to you!'

THERE HE IS!: About seven minutes in, tossing some litter as Richard and Miss Smith run from the music hall.

THE MACGUFFIN: There's a double MacGuffin at play here – the unknown nature of the 39 Steps is raised at the very beginning and forgotten about until practically the very end of the film. At least with this movie Hitch actually tells us what the 39 Steps actually are – although not until the final reel, where it's revealed by Mr Memory in his dying words. Additionally, the factor that drives forward the actions of the characters in the film is to prevent the formula for a new aeroplane engine being smuggled out of the country.

MISOGYNY: In some ways, *The 39 Steps* acts as a none-too-subtle critique on the institution of marriage. In a scene reminiscent of a *Carry On . . .* film, Hannay asks a milkman if he's married. The milkman replies: 'Don't rub it in!' Then there's the crofter, who looks and acts more like an abusive father than a husband, as we realise that he has assaulted his wife (off camera, thankfully) for helping Hannay to escape. In addition, there's the scene where Hannay grabs Pamela by the throat to stop her from squealing to the innkeeper's wife. Hitchcock's obsession with sexualising the act of strangulation makes for uncomfortable viewing. Having spent a good portion of the film handcuffed to Pamela, it's almost as if he's being prepared for being 'shackled' to her for the rest of his life.

THEMES AND MOTIFS: One of the earliest examples of the 'innocent man on the run', this is actually one of the very best. Copied mercilessly in *Young and Innocent*, *Sabotage* and *North by Northwest*, it's easy to see why Hitch felt the format was strong enough to use again and again. *The 39 Steps* also falls into a series of spy thrillers and espionage films that preoccupied Hitch during the mid-30s, and then again and again throughout his career (*Saboteur*, *North by Northwest*, *Torn Curtain*, *Topaz*, etc.)

TABOOS: Much fun is made of Hannay and Pamela pretending to be a married couple so that they can share a double room. The innkeeper and his wife seem to believe that they have either eloped together or – even more scandalous – that they may not even be married! Gosh! The smutty conversation that the underwear salesman engages Hannay in on the train must have raised an eyebrow or two as well.

POSTER: The lobby posters rather erroneously boasted that this is 'John Buchan's famous novel!' Very nearly, Hitch. Very nearly.

THE ICE MAIDEN: Madeleine Carroll is excellent throughout *The 39 Steps*, pouting and bitching away at Robert Donat's Hannay for all her worth. She is a feisty character, totally confident in her own opinions and superiority to Hannay, and therefore totally untouchable – at least until she discovers the truth. Definitely the strongest contender to the Ice Maiden throne so far.

TRIVIA: The train escape sequence was filmed at the Forth Bridge in Scotland. The first scene of the film to be shot was the handcuff escape sequence where Hannay and Pamela run into the foggy night through a flock of sheep. It was actually filmed in the studio, and Hitch allegedly arranged for the keys to the handcuffs to be 'mislaid' for the entire first day, leaving his stars literally shackled to each other. Whether this was an attempt by him to help his actors understand the plight of the characters they were playing, or he was merely enjoying another bondage fantasy being lived out by real people, is entirely open to your personal interpretation.

FINAL ANALYSIS: *The 39 Steps* is regularly ranked as one of Hitch's very best films, and it's easy even for a modern audience to see why. It's very tightly plotted and remains genuinely thrilling even today. We sympathise with Hannay's plight and share in his frustration at his escalating chain of bad luck. The plot twists are nicely timed, and the whole movie rattles along at a cracking pace. Best of all, though, are the performances, from Donat and Carroll's sparkling sexual chemistry to Peggy Ashcroft's sympathetic crofter's wife. Hitch's love for satire is on display in the scene where Hannay spouts utter rubbish at a political meeting yet still manages to gain the support of the audience simply because his meaningless rally cries are delivered with such charm! Definitely a good place to start if you're hoping to get a taste of the British movies. **8/10**

Secret Agent (1936)

(B & W – 86 mins)

Produced by Michael Balcon & Ivor Montagu/Gaumont-British Picture Corporation Ltd/The Rank Organisation

Screenplay by Charles Bennett, with dialogue by Ian Hay and additional dialogue by Jesse Lasky Jr, based on the 'Ashenden' stories of W Somerset Maugham and the play by Campbell Dixon

Continuity: Alma Reville
Photography: Bernard Knowles
Art Director: Oscar Friedrich Werndorff (credited as O Werndorff)
Editor: Charles Frend
Recordist: Phillip Dorté
Dresses: Joe Strassner (credited as J Strassner)
Musical Director: Louis Levy

CAST: John Gielgud (*Edgar Brodie/Richard Ashenden*), Peter Lorre (*General*), Madeleine Carroll (*Elsa Carrington*), Robert Young (*Robert Marvin*), Percy Marmont (*Caypor*), Florence Kahn (*Mrs Caypor*), Charles Carson ('*R*'), Lilli Palmer (*Lilli*).

UNCREDITED CAST: Tom Helmore (*Colonel Anderson*), Andreas Malandrinos (*Manager*), Michael Redgrave (*Army Captain*), Michel Saint-Denis (*Coachman*).

OPENING TITLES: A series of silhouettes depict soldiers in the trenches, setting the scene but not really the tone for this World War One escapade.

SUMMARY: 10 May 1916. A small crowd has assembled for the pre-funeral lying-in-state of a gentleman called Brodie, who has apparently died while on leave from the conflict in World War One. When the crowd leaves, Brodie's one-armed servant lights up a cigarette and struggles to move the coffin, which promptly falls to the ground, empty.

On the other side of town, during an air raid, Captain Edgar Brodie is ushered into the office of a mysterious figure, 'R'. Brodie is shocked and angry that he has been reported as having died, and demands an explanation from 'R'. It is clear that, since Brodie is a well-respected soldier and a bachelor, the government could stage his death with minimal impact on family. Brodie will assume the name of Richard Ashenden. 'R' supplies him with British and American passports, and tells him he is to go to Switzerland. There he will locate and terminate a German agent who is heading for Arabia via Constantinople, in order to set up an alliance between Germany and the Arab states. Unfortunately, Ashenden's predecessor in the role died before he could send a description of the German agent back to London.

Ashenden is introduced to his assistant, a short greasy-looking man nicknamed 'the General'. Chasing one of the secretaries upstairs during the middle of a bombing raid, Ashenden notes that the General seems to be a bit of a lady-killer. 'Not just ladies,' quips 'R'.

Arriving in Switzerland, Ashenden checks into the Hotel Excelsior. He is somewhat surprised to discover that he has a wife, and that she has already arrived at the hotel. He goes up to his room, where he finds a young American man, Robert Marvin, chatting and flirting with his 'wife'. Marvin beats a hasty retreat. Mr and Mrs Ashenden check each other's official credentials – it transpires that 'Mrs Ashenden' (real name Elsa Carrington) has also been sent by 'R', to help Ashenden with his cover story. The General arrives at the hotel too, and is disgusted to discover that Ashenden has been 'given' a beautiful woman by 'R' when he hasn't. Ashenden and Elsa have their first row as a 'married' couple.

A mysterious, bearded pipe-smoker purchases a bar of chocolate. Throwing the bar of chocolate away, he reads a message written in German inside the wrapper: 'Novelist Brodie reported dead arrived today Hotel Excelsior on espionage work. Take steps.'

Ashenden and the General go to the small village of Langenthal to meet a double agent, who may possibly have information on the German they're looking for. The double agent – the organist at the local church – is already dead, strangled and slumped over the keyboard of his organ. In the palm of his hand is a coat button, presumably belonging to the killer.

Meanwhile, Elsa is being entertained by Marvin at the Casino. Ashenden and the General arrive and show Elsa the button they have discovered. The button is dropped by accident on to the roulette table and it wins. By luck, Ashenden realises that the man who claims the button is an elderly gentleman whom he met at the Hotel Excelsior. They befriend the man and his German wife and discover that his name is Mr Caypor. Ashenden and the General, suspecting that Caypor is the agent they're after, hatch a plot to kill him by persuading him to act as their guide on a mountain walk up the Langham Alp.

The General pushes Caypor off a cliff while Ashenden watches from a distance through a telescope. However, on returning to the hotel, they are horrified to discover that they have in fact killed the wrong man – Caypor was completely innocent. Elsa in particular takes this turn of events very hard and turns for emotional support to Marvin, finding the company of Ashenden difficult to stomach – despite the fact that she acknowledges that she has fallen in love with him.

Ashenden and the General follow another lead to a chocolate factory in Geneva. Narrowly avoiding the security forces, they discover that the real spy is in fact Robert Marvin. They dash back to the hotel only to realise that Elsa and Marvin have already left, on a train bound for Constantinople. They manage to catch up with Marvin on board the train just as it passes the border into enemy territory. Elsa finds it difficult to believe that Marvin could be the spy, and turns her gun on Ashenden and the General to prevent them from committing what she believes would be murder. At that moment, Allied aeroplanes bomb the train, derailing it. The terminally injured Marvin shoots and kills the General before dying himself. Elsa and Ashenden are reconciled in the wreckage, and they manage to make their way home.

Newspaper headlines show that the Allies have won a major victory in Palestine, most likely as a direct result of their efforts. The couple read the news as newly-weds.

ROOTS: *Secret Agent* is based on W Somerset Maugham's 'Ashenden' stories, specifically 'The Traitor' and 'The Hairless Mexican'.

LEGACY: For modern audiences, the most obvious legacy from *Secret Agent* is James Bond. The secret base in Whitehall for a shadowy agency, the glamorous woman attached to our hero as an assistant, the 'colourful' mercenary who proves to be both a help and a hindrance – all of these elements were clear influences on Ian Fleming and Cubby Broccoli. And as for calling the hero's boss by a single initial . . . well, admittedly 'M' and 'Q' have appeared regularly in Bond films for around four decades, so the arrival of John Cleese as 'R' in the forthcoming movie *The World Is Not Enough* (Michael Apted, 1999) is about time! Even the initial concept of the agent's death being faked to divert the attentions of foreign agents was copied almost identically in *You Only*

Live Twice (written by Fleming in 1964, filmed by Lewis Gilbert in 1967).

WHO'S WHO?: John Gielgud was appearing in a stage production of *Romeo and Juliet* at the same time as filming *Secret Agent*. He would later gain a knighthood and become one of the most respected actors of his generation – though this didn't stop him playing a rather crude butler in *Arthur* (Steve Gordon, 1981). Hitchcock cast Florence Kahn after seeing her in a performance of Ibsen's *Peer Gynt* at the Old Vic. Not only was this her first film, but she'd never even entered a film studio before. Robert Young would find fame later on in life as star of the 1970s TV series *Marcus Welby, MD*.

THE USUAL SUSPECTS: Tom Helmore (*Colonel Anderson*) appeared in *The Ring* (1927) and would later play Gavin Elster in *Vertigo* (1958). Peter Lorre returns to the Hitchcock fold after his appearance in *The Man Who Knew Too Much*. Of course, Madeleine Carroll had appeared in *The 39 Steps*, and Percy Marmont, who plays the unluckiest button-wearer in the world, Caypor, had earlier portrayed Emily's love interest, Commander Gordon, in *Rich and Strange* and would also appear in *Young and Innocent*.

ANIMAL CRUELTY: Caypor's dog, somehow aware that its master is about to be killed, lets out the most agonising howl as the General pushes Caypor off the top of the mountain.

KILLER LINES: When 'R' asks Ashenden if he loves his country, he replies grimly: 'Well, I just died for it.'
    Ashenden (to Elsa): 'We aren't hunting a fox, we're hunting a man. It's an oldish man with a wife. Oh, I know it's war and it's our job to do it, but it doesn't prevent it being murder, does it? Simple murder. And all you can see in it is fun.'

MISOGYNY: Marvin (to Ashenden, in jest): 'Thank heavens you've come to take your wife off my hands. I'm tired of talking in words of one syllable.'

THEMES AND MOTIFS: The scene where the factory workers escape after the fire alarm is raised evokes similar scenes in *Saboteur*, and, to a lesser extent, in *Rich and Strange*, where the office workers finish for the day and walk towards the camera. The use of miniatures to create the illusion of the train crash, a plot element first seen in *Number Seventeen*, is here executed much more successfully.

TABOOS: Eager to get toilet humour in at every opportunity, Ashenden tears toilet paper during his discussion with Elsa about the virtues of marriage.

MUSIC: Very much in the style of a newsreel, in keeping with the pseudo-documentary style of the top-and-tail sequences of the film, but not particularly memorable apart from that.

ICE MAIDEN: Madeleine Carroll is in fine form in *Secret Agent*. Slightly reserved and haughty, Elsa flirts with both Marvin and Ashenden with great aplomb. She's possibly a bit too warm to be a typical Hitchcock Ice Maiden, but as a leading lady she's superb. Elsa moves rapidly from being a bored socialite eager for excitement and adventure to being a confused and frightened young woman caught up in a violent chain of circumstances. The moment when she turns her gun on Ashenden and the General, in order to prevent them from cold-bloodedly killing Marvin, is a gem and completely understandable in the circumstances – even if the audience feels like giving her a jolly good slapping at this point. A possible indicator of why Madeleine Carroll never again appeared in a Hitchcock film may be found in a comment he made when being quizzed about his potential film about the *Titanic*: 'Oh yes, I've had experience with icebergs. Don't forget, I directed Madeleine Carroll . . .'

COSTUME: Pretty pedestrian and utilitarian, with the exception of Elsa's ball gown at the casino which wouldn't look out of place in an episode of *Dynasty*.

TRIVIA: The bizarre character of the Swiss coachman was specifically created during filming to find a role in the movie for John Gielgud's friend, the French actor Michel Saint-Denis. This was an almost unprecedented move for Hitchcock, who normally had every word of dialogue and camera angle prepared before entering the studio. Some people have speculated that Hitch was so bored with making *Secret Agent* that this act of spontaneity was the only way he could find of maintaining his interest in the film. This is a great shame, as the scene adds little to the movie as a whole.

It has also been alleged that, by the time of filming *Secret Agent*, Peter Lorre had become a hopeless morphine addict, regularly needing to get a fix between filming scenes. This might explain the outrageous, unrestrained performance that he delivers.

Oh, and despite what some other books or videotape covers might tell you, the title of this film is *Secret Agent*, not THE *Secret Agent* – there are many different agents in this movie, and the title just wouldn't make sense otherwise!

FINAL ANALYSIS: *Secret Agent* is, along with *The 39 Steps*, one of the most entertaining of all of Hitch's early movies, and an educational one at that – how many modern viewers would be aware that there had been air raids on London during World War One? We certainly didn't!

Though it responds to the very real concerns of the British public in the late 30s about the growing strength of Germany, *Secret Agent* is still an old-fashioned *Boy's Own* adventure story, populated by dashing heroes and dastardly villains. Peter Lorre is marvellous as the pseudo-Mexican General, although it's fairly obvious his origins are closer to Central Europe than Central America.

However, it is difficult to watch John Gielgud in this movie without finding his cut-glass accent and old-fashioned attitudes fairly reminiscent of his *Spitting Image* puppet. Despite his reputation as one of the greatest actors of his generation, his performance here is more than a little stiff, particularly when compared with the naturalistic performances of Madeleine Carroll and Robert Young, and with the wildly over-the-top Lorre. Sadly for Hitch, although *Secret Agent* was well received by the critics, it wasn't as big a success at the box office as either *The Man Who Knew Too Much* or *The 39 Steps*. Today it remains very much a 'forgotten' Hitchcock movie, with few television screenings and very limited availability on home video. As it is a far more enjoyable film than some of his better-known offerings, this seems a massive oversight. **7/10**

Sabotage (1936)

(Working titles: *I Married a Murderer/The Hidden Power*/US title: *The Woman Alone*)

(B & W – 76 mins)

Produced by Michael Balcon & Ivor Montagu/Gaumont-British Picture Corporation Ltd/Shepherd

Screenplay: Charles Bennett, with dialogue by Ian Hay & Helen Simpson
Additional dialogue: EVH Emmett, based on the novel *The Secret Agent* by Joseph Conrad

Continuity: Alma Reville
Photography: Bernard Knowles
Editor: Charles Frend
Art Director: Oscar Friedrich Werndorff (credited as O Werndorff)
Dresses: Joe Strassner (credited as J Strassner)
Recordist: A Cameron
Wardrobe: Marianne
Musical Director: Louis Levy

CAST: Sylvia Sydney (*Mrs Verloc*), Oscar Homolka (*Carl Verloc*), Desmond Tester (*Mrs Verloc's Young Brother, Stevie*), John Loder

(*Police Sergeant Ted Spencer*), Joyce Barbour (*Renee*), Matthew Boulton (*Superintendent Talbot*), SJ Warmington (*Hollingshead*), William Dewhurst (*Professor*).

UNCREDITED CAST: Peter Bull (*Michaelis*), Martita Hunt (*Professor's Daughter*), Torin Thatcher (*Yunct*), Austin Trevor (*Vladimir*), Charles Hawtrey (*Youth*), Aubrey Mather (*Contact*), Clare Greet, Sam Wilkinson, Sara Allgood, Pamela Bevan, Frank Atkinson, DA Clarke-Smith, Hal Gordon, Frederick Piper.

SUMMARY: The West End of London is plunged into darkness after a power generator is sabotaged. But, rather than spreading panic, the event is treated by the public as an amusing distraction. The only people angered by the disruption appear to be the patrons of the Bijou Theatre, a cinema run by Mr and Mrs Verloc. Distracted by the crowd, Mrs Verloc fails to see her husband using the cover of darkness to sneak into the house through a back door. When she finds him later, he pretends to be unaware of the power cut and claims he's been asleep the whole time. To keep his regular customers happy, Mr Verloc agrees to let them have their money back. Mrs Verloc returns to the ticket booth to find the crowd being pacified by Ted Spencer, a shop hand at the greengrocer's next door. Fortunately, the power soon comes back on and the customers retake their places for the remainder of the film.

Ted finishes for the day and leaves the greengrocer's – heading straight for Scotland Yard. He is a detective sergeant working undercover and is keeping an eye on Verloc, who is prime suspect for the recent spate of sabotages. The police believe that a foreign power is employing someone to do its dirty work and by capturing this person they hope to trace the organisation responsible.

The next day, Verloc heads for the London Zoo Aquarium, trailed by Ted's colleague Hollingshead. Inside the aquarium, Verloc is met by an agent of his employers. It seems the act of sabotage the previous day did not have the desired effect and the agent shows Verloc the newspaper headlines declaring: LONDON LAUGHS AT BLACKOUT. The agent tells Verloc he will not be paid unless he causes a major disruption – he must plant a bomb to coincide with the Lord Mayor's parade the coming Saturday. Verloc is distressed by this, not wishing to be responsible for loss of life, but the agent insists that even if he doesn't plant the bomb himself it is his responsibility to ensure it goes off at the desired time. He leaves Verloc with directions to a contact who will supply him with a bomb.

Ted, meanwhile, has been following Mrs Verloc and her brother Stevie. He approaches them, as if meeting them by coincidence, and invites them both to dinner at an expensive restaurant. While they wait for their food, Ted asks Mrs Verloc about her husband's business interests, and is relieved that she appears completely ignorant about how he is able to afford to run a loss-making theatre. As conversation turns to lighter matters, a waiter approaches Ted and greets him, and it's obvious to Mrs Verloc that this 'greengrocer' is in fact a regular patron.

Verloc follows the directions he's been given, which lead him to a bird shop in Islington. The proprietor, Professor Chatman, arranges to deliver two birds to Mr Verloc for Saturday morning with an incendiary device hidden in the bottom of the cage. Verloc must place the device in the cloakroom of Piccadilly Circus Underground Station. The bomb is set to go off at exactly 1.45 p.m.

At home, Verloc is visited by three men – contacts whom he hopes to persuade to plant the bomb on his behalf. Ted sneaks into the cinema and manages to listen in on most of the saboteur's conversation, but when one of the men spies Ted's hand poking through the window he drags him into the room. Ted pretends he was just playing about with Stevie and leaves, but not before one of the men recognises him. When they are alone again, the man tells Verloc that Ted is Detective Sergeant Spencer of Scotland Yard. Afraid of being entrapped by Verloc's plans, the men leave. Later, while his wife speculates how Ted can afford to eat in fancy restaurants on a greengrocer's assistant's wages, Verloc tells her what he has discovered. Mrs Verloc is obviously upset that he has used her and her brother to get at her husband, and offers to speak to him, but Verloc tells her he will deal with it. However, when he goes to the greengrocer's, Verloc learns that Ted no longer works there.

Saturday morning and the birds arrive. Verloc tells his wife that they are a gift for Stevie and, as she goes to find her brother to give him the good news, Verloc removes the explosive device from beneath the birdcage. Inside the birdcage's tray, he also finds a note reminding him that 'the birds will sing at 1.45 p.m.' Ted comes to explain his actions, telling Mrs Verloc that he was just doing his job and that he needs to speak with her husband. Mr Verloc meanwhile is preparing to leave with the bomb when he sees his wife talking to Ted, blocking the main exit. He is about to leave by the back door when he sees the head of a policeman visible on the other side of the back fence. He is trapped. Reluctantly he asks Stevie to run him an errand, returning some film canisters to a nearby cinema, and entrusts him with an additional 'package', telling him he must get it to Piccadilly Circus by 1.30 at the latest. With Stevie on his way, Verloc consents to making a statement to Ted, explaining his actions during the last week and declaring his innocence of any illegal actions.

Unaware of the importance of the package, Stevie meanders through London's West End. On the way he is delayed, first by a street hawker who ropes him into helping him with his presentation, then by the procession of the Lord Mayor's parade. When the streets finally clear, it is already 1.30, so Stevie catches a bus to Piccadilly. However, the bus is still too slow and it turns into Piccadilly Circus just on 1.45p.m. The bomb explodes, wrecking the bus and killing everyone on board.

The news reaches Ted, who has just concluded his interview with Verloc. When Ted tells the couple about the explosion, Verloc appears relieved as he has a perfect alibi. But when Ted goes to investigate the wreckage he finds the film canisters that Stevie left with.

By the end of the day, Mrs Verloc is worried that Stevie has not returned in time for tea. She buys an evening newspaper, which states that film canisters were found in the wreckage. She suddenly realises that her brother must have been killed and passes out. Racked with guilt, her husband explains all, telling her that he never meant any harm to come to the boy. She begins to prepare dinner, carving the joint, but her husband's insensitivity drives her over the edge and in a daze she stabs him. She panics and is about to run to the police when Ted arrives to arrest Mr Verloc. Seeing the dead body, Ted makes a snap decision – he tells Mrs Verloc he's in love with her and offers to help her run away. As the couple walk through the streets, Mrs Verloc is haunted by the face of the dead brother and becomes hysterical. Meanwhile, Professor Chatman has come to collect the birdcage in fear that it might incriminate him in the bombing. He discovers Verloc's body just as the police arrive. They evacuate the cinema and then make to arrest the professor. Determined to avoid capture, he detonates a bomb that rips the cinema apart, conveniently destroying the evidence that would have incriminated Mrs Verloc. The police begin to organise a clear-up and Ted walks off with Mrs Verloc in his arms.

TITLES: The titles run over a dictionary definition, helpfully informing us that sabotage is the 'wilful destruction of buildings or machinery with the object of alarming a group or persons or inspiring public uneasiness'.

CASTING: Hitch once again tried to get Robert Donat for the role of Ted Spencer, but when he wasn't available he accepted John Loder.

ROOTS: As a reworking of Conrad's *The Secret Agent*, *Sabotage* is surprisingly faithful in terms of structure, but in the updating Verloc changes from peddler of pornography to cinema owner and Stevie shifts from retarded adult to clumsy child. The role of Ted is a composite of two characters from the novel, the inspector who hounds Verloc and the anarchist Ossipon. Ossipon befriends Mrs Verloc after she kills her husband and helps her escape to the Continent, but ultimately abandons her after stealing her money and Mrs Verloc commits suicide. Thankfully, *Sabotage* has a marginally happier ending. One downside is that while *Sabotage*'s professor is hugely entertaining we lose the chilling monomaniac of the original, walking calmly through the streets of London with a bomb strapped to his chest.

The animated sequence shown after Mrs Verloc kills her husband is an excerpt from *Who Killed Cock Robin?* (David Hand, 1935), with bird characters clearly inspired by the blonde bombshell Mae West and the crooner Bing Crosby.

LEGACY: The source novel was filmed as *Joseph Conrad's The Secret Agent* (Christopher Hampton, 1996), starring Bob Hoskins as Verloc, Patricia Arquette as his wife and Christian Bale as Stevie.

See also **Animal Cruelty** below to see how the mistake Hitch made in blowing up a dog perhaps influenced the producers of *Independence Day* (Roland Emmerich, 1996) into letting their dog *live*!

WHO'S WHO?: A native New Yorker, Sylvia Sidney was a major Hollywood star when Hitch managed to cast her in *Sabotage*. Though they planned to work together again, nothing came of this. Though her career stalled in the 1960s, it picked up again in the 70s with appearances in a few TV movies. She can be seen in *Damien: Omen II* (Don Taylor, 1978) as Damien's Aunt Marion, and as Grandma Norris in Tim Burton's sci-fi spoof *Mars Attacks!* (1996). She and Oskar Homolka both appeared in a film called *The Tamarind Seed* (Blake Edwards, 1974).

THE USUAL SUSPECTS: Among the extras are Sara Allgood (*Blackmail* and *Juno and the Paycock*) and Clare Greet (*Number 13*, *The Manxman*, *Murder!*, *Lord Camber's Ladies* and *Jamaica Inn*). Matthew Boulton and SJ Warmington played jury members in *Murder!*.

ANIMAL CRUELTY: As if the death of young Stevie wasn't emotionally manipulative enough, the boy was sitting next to an old lady holding an adorable puppy just before the bomb went off.

KILLER LINES: When Ted claims the power cut is an act of God, a heckler asks him to explain what he means: 'I'd call your face [an Act of God] and you won't be getting your money back on that.'
  In a scene reminiscent of Monty Python's parrot sketch, a customer complains to Professor Chatman that the canary she bought won't sing. He claims it sang all day before she bought it but the customer doesn't believe him: 'I've tried all ways: whistling to it, clapping my hands, frying bacon – no use, it just sits there and makes me look silly!' When the professor suggests she must continue to whistle to it, she replies: 'P'raps you'd like me to sit in the cage and him to do the housework!'

THEMES AND MOTIFS: The Verlocs keep a black cat. A kitchen knife is used for the murder (*Blackmail*, *Murder!*, *Psycho*, *Torn Curtain*) and a policeman takes it upon himself to help a murderess to evade admitting her guilt (*Blackmail*). Note also the transference of guilt (*Murder!*, *Stage Fright*, *Strangers on a Train*) as Verloc gets young Stevie to plant the bomb for him, but the innocent boy dies through no fault of his own. As with the young heroine in *Rebecca*, Mrs Verloc is identified only in relation to her husband (though the character is named Winnie in the original novel). Birds play a pivotal role, first as the front for the professor's other exploits and as the housing for the bomb, and then in the cinema when the audience laugh at the sequence from *Who Killed Cock Robin?* while Mrs Verloc sobs for the loss of her brother (see also

Psycho and, of course, *The Birds*). The setting is very reminiscent of *Frenzy*, specifically the West End of London and a greengrocer with a secret identity.

TABOOS: During the scene in the London Aquarium, a courting couple walk by. The man (played by a very young Charles Hawtrey, camp member of the *Carry On . . .* team) walks by discussing the sex life of the oyster. He informs his date that after laying a million eggs the female oyster changes sex. 'I don't blame her!' exclaims the girl.

POSTER: '. . . A Bomb Plot . . . A Killing . . . Justice'. The American release, entitled *The Woman Alone*, featured a passable likeness of Sylvia Sidney being terrorised by a shadowy Oskar Homolka.

THE ICE MAIDEN: The glamorous Sylvia Sidney is perhaps a little too sophisticated for the role of Mrs Verloc, but her star status probably helped raise the character from the vapid, humble child who appears in the original novel. The little sailor suit she wears in the first scene is so sweet.

TRIVIA: In mentioning *Sabotage* in an article for *Film Weekly* prior to the film's release, Hitchcock asserted that 'this title will be changed'. He'd adopted it to avoid confusion with his previous film, and had also announced the film under the title *The Hidden Power* (a pun on the blackout at the beginning of the film as well as the unnamed organisation who employ Verloc), though it seems the only working title actually used (briefly) was a rather lurid *I Married A Murderer*.

The restaurant to which Ted takes Stevie and Mrs Verloc is the famous Simpsons in London, one of Hitchcock's personal favourites.

In the on-screen credits (as shown above), both Sylvia Sidney's and Oskar Homolka's names are misspelt.

FINAL ANALYSIS: Hitchcock always regretted the way the bomb sequence ended, feeling that he had cheated the audience by building up the suspense intolerably and then not releasing it in a way that would let them breathe easily. We feel he was being way too hard on himself, especially as the sequence is expertly edited, with its constant reminders that 'the birds will sing at 1.45 p.m.' When the bomb finally explodes, killing the innocent Stevie, the old woman and her dog, we can almost picture Hitch rubbing his hands with glee at the thought of delivering cinema's sickest joke, only to be later convinced by adverse reviews that he'd gone too far. Not a bit of it, Hitch. 7/10

Young and Innocent (1937)

(US title: *The Girl Was Young* – 1938)

(B & W – 82 mins)

Produced by Edward Black/Gaumont-British Picture Corporation Ltd

Screenplay: Charles Bennett, Edwin Greenwood & Anthony Armstrong, with dialogue by Gerald Savory, based on the novel *A Shilling For Candles* by Josephine Tey

Continuity: Alma Reville
Photography: Bernard Knowles
Recording: A O'Donoghue
Film Editor: Charles Frend
Art Director: Alfred Junge
Musical Director: Louis Levy
Wardrobe: Marianne
Songs: Al Goodhart, Samuel Lerner and Al Hoffman

CAST: Nova Pilbeam (*Erica Burgoyne*), Derrick De Marney (*Robert Tisdall*), Percy Marmont (*Col. Burgoyne*), Edward Rigby (*Old Will*), Mary Clare (*Erica's Aunt*), John Longden (*Det. Insp. Kent*), George Curzon (*Guy*), Basil Radford (*Erica's Uncle*), Pamela Carme (*Christine*), George Merritt (*Detective Sergeant Miller*), JH Roberts (*Solicitor*), Jerry Verno (*Lorry Driver*), HF Maltby (*Police Sergeant*), John Miller (*Police Constable*).

UNCREDITED CAST: Torin Thatcher (*Dosshouse Caretaker*), Gerry Fitzgerald (*Singer*), Frank Atkinson, Clive Baxter, Pamela Bevan, Albert Chevalier, Syd Crossley, William Fazan, Richard George, Anna Konstam, Fred O'Donovan, Frederick Piper, Bill Shine, Peggy Simpson, Beatrice Varley, Jack Vyvian, Humberston Wright.

SUMMARY: A man and a woman are arguing furiously. He accuses her of hanging around with 'boys' and she tells him that the marriage is over. He storms on to the balcony of the room they are in, which overlooks a tumultuous sea. The man stares back into the room at his wife, his eyes twitching rapidly.

The next morning, Robert Tisdall, a screenwriter, is walking along the beach when he spots the body of his friend Christine Clay washed up on the shore. Robert dashes off to get help, but is observed by two young women who assume that he is the killer. On this rather flimsy evidence, Robert is arrested. Things then go from bad to worse for Robert. Under questioning, he confirms that he knew Christine Clay. Christine had been an international film star, and Robert had written some scripts for her in the past. It transpires that Christine had been strangled by the belt from an overcoat. The fact that Robert's overcoat had been stolen from his car some time previously doesn't help matters. The final nail in his coffin is the motive – Christine had left him £1,200 in her will. This news takes Robert completely by surprise, and he collapses from shock. He is revived by Erica Burgoyne, daughter of Colonel Burgoyne, the local police chief, who having heard some of his tale is not quite as quick to judge him as is his lawyer, a short-sighted, money-grabbing buffoon who seems utterly convinced of his client's guilt. Stealing the lawyer's glasses, Robert improvises a disguise and manages to escape from the courthouse.

A manhunt is quickly organised, and everyone is drafted in to help, including Erica. Unfortunately, Erica runs out of petrol in the middle of the countryside, and she is both shocked and pleasantly surprised when Robert appears, and helps her push the car to the nearest garage. His persuasive manner begins to convince her of his innocence. He asks her to drive him to Tom's Hat, the transport café where his overcoat was stolen. Erica begins to get nervous and decides to drop him off outside an abandoned mill, where he is able to hide. Erica goes home, where conversation and news around the dinner table leads her to sympathise with Robert and suspect his innocence even more.

Erica returns to the mill and helps Robert escape from the police, who are closing in on him. They then travel on to the transport café, where Erica asks the clientele if any of them know anything about a stolen overcoat. One of them tells her that Old Will the China-Mender, a local vagrant, recently came into possession of a brand-new overcoat. He thinks that Old Will is currently staying at a dosshouse about thirty miles away.

Concerned to cover her tracks with her father about being away from home, Erica decides to pop into her aunt's house to give herself an alibi. She has forgotten, though, that it is her cousin Felicity's birthday, and gets involved in organising party games for the children. Her aunt soon becomes suspicious of Erica's relationship with Robert, and after they leave she phones Colonel Burgoyne to alert him that something is afoot. Unsurprisingly, Erica is soon flagged down by a police officer who instantly recognises Robert from his description. In a moment of panic, Erica drives off with Robert. Realising she's now an accessory, she is forced to accept that they can't go back to her father unless they find the overcoat. Hiding out, Robert and Erica share their fears. She realises just how tired and scared she is, but refuses to give up, having come so far.

Robert goes to Nobby's Lodging House where he eventually tracks down Old Will. Robert recovers his overcoat, but unfortunately the belt is missing, turning his potential alibi into even more incriminating evidence. Will tells Robert that the coat didn't have a belt on it when he received it – the man who gave it to him was a man with rapidly blinking eyes. Trying to avoid the police, who are closing in, Erica drives the car into a disused mine, which collapses underneath them from the weight of the car. Robert, Erica and Will narrowly avoid death, but Erica is arrested. Her father tries to get her to reveal Robert's whereabouts, but Erica continues to protest his innocence. Erica faces a real dilemma when her father threatens to resign his position as Chief Constable if she refuses to cooperate, but she decides not to betray her new love.

Later that evening, Robert boldly climbs into Erica's bedroom. The situation looks grim for him, as the police now have his coat as evidence. However, there is a book of matches in the pocket of the coat from the Grand Hotel, and, as neither Robert nor Will has ever been there, that must mean that the killer has either been there or is still there. The next day, Will, Robert and Erica search the Grand Hotel in the hope of spotting the man who gave the coat to the old vagrant. They stop for tea and listen to a minstrel band. The drummer spots Will sitting in the audience and tries to hide his blinking eyes. Once he has finished playing, he runs outside and spots the police closing in (who are actually there to arrest Robert). The drummer collapses from stress and guilt, and when Erica goes to help him she notices his blinking eyes. In the presence of the police, the drummer confesses that he murdered Christine. Free at last, Robert and Erica embrace and receive her father's blessing.

ROOTS: Based on the novel by Josephine Tay, the plot was entirely reworked by Hitchcock. The young romantic heroes were originally supporting characters playing second fiddle to the detective. Note instead how the police roles are played out like sequences from the Keystone Kops films.

THE USUAL SUSPECTS: Mary Clare, Erica's aunt, would reappear in *The Lady Vanishes* as the sinister baroness. John Longden had already appeared in *Blackmail*, *Juno and the Paycock* and *The Skin Game*. Percy Marmont was following up his appearances in *Rich and Strange* and *Secret Agent*. Finally, George Curzon had played Gibson in *The Man Who Knew Too Much* and would later appear in *Jamaica Inn*.

Nova Pilbeam played Betty, the kidnapped daughter in *The Man Who Knew Too Much*. This would be the last time that Hitch worked with her, although he had actively considered using her in a project that never materialised.

THERE HE IS!: Outside the courthouse holding a camera (typical director!) during Robert's escape.

THE MACGUFFIN: The overcoat belt is the sole driving force behind the movie's plot, but it's the romance between Erica and Robert that's the most interesting aspect for Hitchcock.

THEMES: Sight and seeing are the key themes explored here. References abound throughout – the twitching eyes of the killer, the shortsighted lawyer, the children's game of blind man's buff, among many others. This corresponds with the regular use of disguise and concealment, not least with the villain's use of black make-up and with Will's transparently obvious attempt at playing a dandy during his time in the Grand Hotel.

Hitch gives another prominent role to a tramp, as he did in *Number Seventeen* and would do again in *Rebecca*. See also Dick Blaney's visit to a dosshouse in *Frenzy*. Compare also the similarities between the sequence where Robert rescues Erica from her car during the mineshaft collapse, and the final moments of *North by Northwest*, where Roger rescues Eve. Even their names aren't dissimilar – the framing of the shots is almost identical.

TABOOS: For anyone brought up after the 70s, the concept of the Black-and-White Minstrel band must seem archaic and more than a little offensive. At the time, however, the concept of a married woman dallying with a series of boys probably caused a great deal more indignation from the audience. Of course, Christine pays for her infidelity (from a loveless marriage) with her life.

FINAL ANALYSIS: *Young and Innocent* is a really sweet movie. In short, it's a remake of *The 39 Steps*, but without the sinister overtones that make the earlier film a much more 'serious' work. There are no spies to fight, no web of deceit and intrigue, just a series of mistakes and people jumping to the wrong conclusions. The police are so ineffectual in their attempts to catch Robert that it's not surprising that the young Erica is often able to run rings about them. It's a pleasant respite from the dark subject matter of the previous three espionage thrillers. Nonetheless, it's one of the most easily accessible and charming of the British movies. **7/10**

The Lady Vanishes (1938)

(B & W – 97 mins)

Produced by Edward Black/Gainsborough Pictures

Written by Sidney Gilliat & Frank Launder, based on the novel *The Wheel Spins* by Ethel Lina White

Continuity: Alma Reville
Photography: Jack Cox
Editing: RE Dearing
Cutting: Alfred Roome
Recording: Sydney Wiles (credited as S Wiles)
Settings: Alex Vetchinsky (as Vetchinsky)
Musical Director: Louis Levy
Original music: Louis Levy & Cecil Milner (uncredited)

CAST: Margaret Lockwood (*Iris Henderson*), Michael Redgrave (*Gilbert Redman*), Paul Lukas (*Dr Hartz*), Dame May Whitty (*Miss Froy*), Cecil Parker (*Eric Todhunter*), Linden Travers (*'Mrs' Margaret Todhunter*), Naunton Wayne (*Caldicott*), Basil Radford (*Charters*), Mary Clare (*Baroness*), Emile Boreo (*Hotel Manager*), Googie Withers (*Blanche*), Sally Stewart (*Julie*), Phillip Leaver (*Signor Doppo*), Zelma Vas Dias (*Signora Doppo*), Catherine Lacey (*Nun*), Josephine Wilson (*Madame Kummer*), Charles Oliver (*Officer*), Kathleen Tremaine (*Anna*).

SUMMARY: A small Tyrolean town pays host to a variety of travellers after an avalanche blocks the railways. As a mad scramble for rooms ensues, Iris Henderson discusses her impending marriage with her friends. Though her friends are against the idea, Iris is set on being married, largely, it seems, because she feels she's done everything else. In the room above, a music scholar by the name of Gilbert Redman is writing a traditional folk song, singing as he does so, much to Iris's annoyance. When she bribes the concierge to throw him out, he moves his luggage into her room and threatens to make her share her bed. She quickly makes a call to the concierge and allows him to return to his old room. Meanwhile, another singer disturbs the peace of Miss Froy, a middle-aged governess and music teacher. She is relieved when the singing stops, unaware that the man has actually been murdered.

By the next morning the tracks have been cleared, so the travellers board the train to continue their journey. At the station, a window box is pushed from a window – its target is Miss Froy. Instead it hits Iris, and Miss Froy helps the dazed girl aboard the train. She takes her to the dining car and tries to introduce herself, but Iris can't understand her, owing to the noise of the train, so Miss Froy writes her name on the steamed-up carriage window. They return to their carriage and Iris promptly falls asleep, and when she awakes some time later Miss Froy has disappeared. When she asks the other passengers of her whereabouts, they tell her that no such person exists. Iris walks the length of the train but is told by all that they never saw such a woman.

She eventually bumps into Gilbert, who appears willing to forgive their initial meeting and offers to help her look for the old woman. At the next stop they see two passengers get on, a fully bandaged patient accompanied by a nun. They encounter a doctor, called Hartz, who tells Iris she's delusional and still suffering from concussion thanks to the bump on the head she suffered. Iris begins to suspect she imagined the whole thing, especially when she's shown another passenger dressed identically to Miss Froy only much younger.

The couple go to the dining car. As Iris gives up all hope of finding any evidence that the old woman ever existed she spies the name written on the glass, but before she can show Gilbert the train enters a tunnel and when they emerge the letters have been covered by grime from the smoke outside. Now certain she's not imagining things, she pulls the emergency cord and promptly passes out.

When she comes round the train is moving again and she realises she's now managed to alienate all the other passengers – except Gilbert, who luckily believes her story. They search the luggage compartment and after finding what looks like Miss Froy's glasses they are attacked by an Italian man, a magician by the name of Doppo. Together they manage to knock him out and lock him in a case – only to discover the case has a false bottom and he has escaped. As they try to work out what happened to Miss Froy, Iris suddenly realises that the nun who came on board can't be a real nun – she was wearing high heels. They realise that Miss Froy must have been swapped with Miss Kummer, the bandaged patient. They go to the doctor to ask for his help, unaware that he is behind the entire conspiracy. He boasts that he has drugged the drinks that they had earlier and that any minute now they'll fall asleep. In fact, they did not receive these drinks. The doctor leaves them apparently unconscious but once alone they stop faking. Gilbert climbs along the carriage and frees Miss Froy, exchanging her with Miss Kummer again.

At the next stop, Dr Hartz leaves with the patient, only to discover it's Miss Kummer. He instructs some railworkers to reroute the train to keep it within the borders of his country. The train eventually comes to a halt and an 'official' steps on board to apologise for the delay, offering a free lift to the passengers back to the town. Gilbert realises it's a trap and knocks the man out, stealing his gun. Miss Froy explains that she is in fact a spy working for the British Embassy. She has memorised a piece of music that contains a coded peace treaty that must reach London. She sings the tune to Gilbert, telling him where to take it if he reaches home safely, then she escapes from the train. After a shoot-out, Gilbert manages to get the train moving again and soon they are all home.

As Gilbert and Iris say goodbye at Victoria Station, Iris spies her husband-to-be and realises she doesn't love him as much as she feels for Gilbert. The couple hide in a carriage and go to the embassy together. By this time Gilbert is embarrassed to discover he has forgotten the tune he was given, but fortunately Miss Froy managed to reach London safely. The travellers are reunited at last.

ROOTS: The lighting of some scenes reveals Hitch's interest in German expressionistic cinema of the 20s and 30s. Compare the murder of the singing messenger – the shadow of outstretched hands slinking across the wall just as the strangler attacks him – to similar scenes in *Nosferatu* (FW Murnau, 1922). In a similar vein, the montage shots used to convey the compression of time, such as those mixing the wheels of the train with shots of the track, are a cinematic device all but lost after the advent of the talkie.

As the couple try to decipher the evidence, Gilbert plays at being both Sherlock Holmes (with Iris acting as his Watson) and Will Hay, the long-suffering comedy actor from such farces as *Oh, Mr Porter!* (Marcel Varnel, 1937).

LEGACY: Remade in 1979 by Anthony Page, starring Elliott Gould, Cybill Shepherd and Angela Lansbury.

WHO'S WHO?: Michael Redgrave had popped up in Hitch's *Secret Agent* as an uncredited soldier, but here he won the starring role. Acting was a family affair for Redgrave – he was the son of the Australian silent-movie star Roy Redgrave, father of Lynn, Vanessa and Corin Redgrave and grandfather of Natasha, Joely and Jemma Redgrave. He was knighted in 1959, and his filmography includes the roles of Ernest Worthing in Oscar Wilde's *The Importance of Being Earnest* (Anthony Asquith, 1952), Dr Barnes Wallis in *The Dambusters* (Michael Anderson, 1954) and the uncle in *The Innocents* (Jack Clayton, 1961), the film adaptation of Henry James's gothic novel, *The Turn of the Screw*. Redgrave died in 1985 after a long struggle with Parkinson's disease.

Margaret Lockwood would become best known for playing the villainess, thanks in no small measure to her starring role in *The Wicked Lady* (Leslie Arliss, 1945). Her last film, *The Slipper and the Rose* (Bryan Forbes, 1976), saw her play the wicked stepmother of Cinderella.

Cecil Parker was forever the haughty military gentleman, as seen in *The Ladykillers*, (Alexander MacKendrick, 1955) and Hitchcock's *Under Capricorn*. He also appeared as a lawyer in the *Alfred Hitchcock Presents* episode, 'I Spy'. Paul Lukas also found himself typecast for much of his career, playing mainly professors, doctors and slightly shifty Europeans, in films like *20,000 Leagues Under the Sea* (Richard Fleischer, 1954) and *Watch on the Rhine* (Herman Shumlin, 1943), for which he won a Best Actor Oscar.

One of Iris's friends is played by a young Googie Withers, who later played the governor of a British prison in the ITV drama *Within These Walls* (1974–7).

KILLER LINES: Iris explains to her friends why she's decided to wed: 'I've no regrets. I've been everywhere and done everything. I've eaten caviar at Cannes, sausage rolls at the dogs. I've played baccarat at Biarritz and darts with the rural dean. What is there left for me but marriage?'

Gilbert gets more than his fair share of one-liners. When Iris gets him thrown out of his room, he moves into her bathroom, citing 'An eye for an eye, a tooth for a toothbrush' as justification. Later, he tells her with regard to their fellow passengers that he's 'about as popular as a dose of strychnine'. He also points out the ethos of British diplomacy: 'Never climb the fence if you can sit on it – it's an old Foreign Office proverb.' When the official boards the train, he claims he had lived in England, where he attended Oxford University. After Gilbert knocks him out, he says by way of an explanation: 'I was at Cambridge.'

THERE HE IS!: Near the end of the movie at Victoria Station wearing a black coat and smoking a cigar.

AWARDS: Won the New York Film Critics' Circle Award for Best Director, and was listed by the *New York Times* as one of the top ten movies of 1938.

THEMES AND MOTIFS: The high-thrills chase across a train is a familiar technique, popping up in *Number Seventeen*, *The 39 Steps* and *Secret Agent*. Due largely to the climate in Europe at the time, the exact nature of the enemy spies remains unspecified – which is probably no bad thing as it allows everybody on the train to be considered part of the conspiracy. Note also how, in the inn when Gilbert plays his folk music, we see Iris's chandelier swaying, similar to the scene in *The Lodger*.

TABOOS: The scene where Caldicott and Charters are forced to share a bed is made even more risqué when it's revealed they've also shared a pair of pyjamas, with Caldicott getting the bottom half and Charters the top. If it works for Morecambe and Wise, and Bert and Ernie, we shouldn't be too shocked really.

MUSIC: It is entirely relevant that the agents have chosen a piece of music in which to hide their coded message. As the message is an extract from a peace treaty, the play on the word 'harmony' is clear in both a musical and universal sense.

FINAL ANALYSIS: The film that helped clinch the deal between Hitchcock and the American producer David Selznick, *The Lady Vanishes* is a fine example of both the best and worst of Hitch's British period. Certainly the model shots that are used for the train exterior, grand as they are, fail to convince, having none of the realism of the train sequences for *The 39 Steps* and *Secret Agent*. However, such a minor quibble cannot detract from a fine ensemble piece with a perfect mix of espionage, romance, comedy and suspense. Michael Redgrave breezes through the piece, clearly enjoying every minute of the adventure, while Margaret Lockwood makes for a feisty travelling companion and attractive female lead. The two English cricket fans, Caldicott and Charters, while evidently present for light relief, do have an important role to play – to ridicule their homeland: note how they are desperate to 'get out of Europe', and yet immediately ask for help from a German. In the political climate of the time, this kind of satire was amazingly daring on Hitch's part. Even today, *The Lady Vanishes* is still an engaging piece, though possibly not nearly as thrilling as its reputation might suggest. 7/10

Jamaica Inn (1939)

(B & W – 108 mins)

Produced by Erich Pommer/Mayflower Pictures

Screenplay: Sidney Gilliat & Joan Harrison, dialogue by Sidney Gilliat, additional dialogue by JB Priestley, based on the novel by Daphne du Maurier

Continuity: Alma Reville
Original Music: Eric Fenby
Photography: Harry Stradling in collaboration with Bernard Knowles
Settings: Thomas Morahan
Costumes: Molly McArthur
Film Editing: Robert Hamer
Musical Director: Frederick Lewis
Special Effects: Harry Watts
Sound Recordist: Jack Rogerson
Make-up Artist: Ern Westmore
Production Manager: Hugh Perceval

CAST: Charles Laughton (*Sir Humphrey Pengallan*), Horace Hodges (*Chadwick, the Butler*), Hay Petrie (*Groom*), Leslie Banks (*Joss Merlyn*), Emlyn Williams (*Harr*), Robert Newton (*Jim Trehearne*), Marie Ney (*Patience*), Wylie Watson (*Salvation*), Maureen O'Hara (*Mary Yelland*), Frederick Piper (*Broker*), Herbert Lomas, Clare Greet, William Devlin (*Pengallan's Tenants*), Jeanne De Casalis, Mabel Terry-Lewis, A Bromley Davenport, George Curzon, Basil Radford (*Pengallan's Guests*), Morland Graham (*Sea Lawyer Sydney*), Edwin Greenwood (*Dandy*), Mervyn Johns (*Thomas*), Stephen Haggard (*Boy*).

SUMMARY: A large sailing ship is being buffeted in the middle of a huge storm, and is heading unawares towards the jagged rocks of the Cornish coast. A gang of pirates are waiting on the shore. One of them deliberately covers the warning lantern on the cliff top, and the ship runs aground. The pirates swarm forward and brutally murder the few survivors of the wreck. Within a few minutes, the ship is stripped of everything of value.

A young Irish woman, Mary Yelland, arrives by coach, intending to visit Jamaica Inn, but the coach driver refuses to stop, telling her that the inn is far too dangerous a place. He drives some way past the inn before stopping to let her off. Mary walks to the nearest large house to ask for directions, where she is introduced to the rotund and eccentric local squire, Sir Humphrey Pengallan. Sir Humphrey seems quite infatuated with the young Irish woman, and he escorts her personally to the front door of Jamaica Inn before heading off.

Mary discovers that Jamaica Inn is managed by her Aunt Patience's loutish husband, Joss Merlyn. Patience is upset to learn that her sister, Mary's mother, died some three weeks before. With no other family to turn to, Mary has travelled to Cornwall in the hope that her relatives will look after her. Patience takes Mary upstairs to a spare bedroom, and en route she is observed by the inn's many intimidating patrons, most of whom seem to be as transfixed by her beauty as Sir Humphrey had been.

It transpires that Joss is the real leader of the gang, and that they use Jamaica Inn as their base. He tries to pacify the gang, angry that the last wreck didn't contain as much bounty as they had been led to believe. They argue about the possibility that some of the booty could have been stolen by one of their number, and suspicion begins to fall on their newest member Jim Trehearne. Their discussion is interrupted by Patience, who has just discovered from Mary that she had been brought to the inn by Sir Humphrey, and is worried because Sir Humphrey is not only the local squire, but also the local magistrate. Has he discovered that Jamaica Inn is the source of the wrecking attacks? A furious Joss storms out of the downstairs room and upstairs into another room, where he apologises to *his* boss about the poor quality of the bounty. His boss is Sir Humphrey, who is happily living a double life as the real leader of the brigands. Sir Humphrey entertains the rich and wealthy at his mansion, and then informs Joss which ships should be worth pillaging. Sir Humphrey tells Joss that he's hungry for more money – and for Mary.

Downstairs, the gang decide to lynch Trehearne. From her upstairs bedroom, Mary has an eagle-eye view of the lynching. As Trehearne starts to lose consciousness, the pirates lose interest and brawl among themselves. Mary reaches through a gap in the floor to cut through the lynching rope, and Trehearne falls to the floor, still alive. Mary helps Trehearne to escape from the inn, but her uncle soon realises what she has done and vows to kill her. Patience manages to get Mary out of the inn before the pirates can get to her. She bumps into Trehearne and together they head off down to the coastline to hide, pursued by the gang.

Mary wakes up the next morning in a cave with Trehearne. They are shortly cornered by the gang, and are able to escape only by swimming out to sea themselves. They make a dash for Sir Humphrey's house, where they explain to him what a den of thieves Jamaica Inn really is. Trehearne reveals to Sir Humphrey that he is actually an undercover officer of the law. Although he knows that Merlyn is the leader of the gang, Trehearne is waiting to discover who the mastermind behind the enterprise really is before reporting back to his superiors. Sir Humphrey offers to take Trehearne to Jamaica Inn to discover the true identity of the ringleader. However, Mary overhears Trehearne telling Sir Humphrey that he already has enough evidence to hang Merlyn and his conspirators. Torn between doing what's right and saving her only remaining family members, Mary steals Sir Humphrey's coach and gets to Jamaica Inn first.

Patience refuses to leave without Joss, much to Mary's annoyance. 'He's a wrecker, a murderer!' she exclaims. 'But he's my husband,' Patience replies. Joss answers a knock at the front door and is immediately arrested by Sir Humphrey and Trehearne. Sir Humphrey gestures to him to keep quiet and play along with him for Trehearne's benefit. When Trehearne leaves the room to prepare for the arrival of Joss's partner, Sir Humphrey tells Joss about another ship that his gang should try to wreck that night. He needs the money from the wreck to go away 'on a holiday'. Trehearne, instead of capturing Joss's mastermind, is captured by the pirate gang. Joss, playing along with the act for the moment, tells the gang that he has captured Sir Humphrey. The gang want to kill Sir Humphrey, but Joss diverts them with the news of the next wreck, which is due at 9 p.m. Joss ties up Trehearne and Sir Humphrey, and leaves Patience guarding them with his gun. The gang leave for the coast.

Now that they are alone, Trehearne is horrified when Sir Humphrey shakes off his ropes, stands up and admits that he is the mastermind behind the pirates. He tells Patience that if Trehearne escapes her husband's life will be in great danger. Sir Humphrey leaves to go home and pack for his 'holiday' abroad. Somehow Trehearne manages to appeal to Patience's better side, and she releases him. He hijacks a coach and goes for help from the authorities in Truro.

On the shore, the gang are waiting for the wreck. Mary slips away from them and, during an attempt to put the beacon back on the cliff top, starts an even bigger fire, which alerts the ship, preventing another disaster. The gang are ready to kill her then and there, but Joss manages to get her away from them and they make their escape back to Jamaica Inn – but not before Joss takes a bullet wound from one of his pirates. Patience tends Joss's wounds, which are clearly very serious indeed. Patience is just about to tell Mary that Sir Humphrey has been behind all of the plotting when a gunshot rings out and Patience collapses dead on her already deceased husband. Sir Humphrey fired the shot, in order to protect his secret. He binds and gags Mary and drags her out of Jamaica Inn seconds before the gang arrive. The gang discover the bodies of Joss and Patience, and are about to leave themselves when Trehearne and the militia arrive and clap them all in irons.

Sir Humphrey and Mary arrive at the overnight packet steamer to St Malo and start to relax and settle in to their cabin. The boat is just leaving the dock when the militia arrive and stop it. Sir Humphrey makes a final bid for freedom by holding Mary at gunpoint and ordering them to leave. Sir Humphrey ends up climbing the rigging, clearly insane, with Mary begging her rescuers not to hurt her former captor, because 'he can't help himself'. Sir Humphrey throws himself from the top of the mast to his death on the deck below. Mary is led off to be comforted by Trehearne.

ROOTS: It's based quite loosely upon the Daphne du Maurier novel of 1936, but du Maurier herself was less than impressed with the adaptation. As a result of this, she insisted that the script for her next novel, *Rebecca*, be far more faithful to its source material. The stories of the pirates and shipwrecking gangs are, unsurprisingly, very close to the historical evidence of the events in Cornwall in the seventeenth and eighteenth centuries.

LEGACY: Remade for TV in 1985 by Lawrence Gordon Clark, starring Trevor Eve, Jane Seymour and Patrick McGoohan.

WHO'S WHO?: Charles Laughton was one of the biggest British movie stars of the 40s. He moved to Hollywood to develop his career and became an American citizen in 1950. Not content simply to act, he formed his own film company, Mayflower Pictures Corp., with the infamous producer Erich Pommer in 1937. Laughton was married to Elsa Lanchester (aka *The Bride of Frankenstein*). Some of Laughton's most famous films include *Mutiny on the Bounty* (Frank Lloyd, 1935) as Captain William Bligh; *Hobson's Choice* (David Lean, 1954); *Spartacus* (Stanley Kubrick, 1960); and Hitchcock's *The Paradine Case*.

Robert Newton played Bill Sykes in the David Lean adaptation of *Oliver Twist* (1948), and Long John Silver in both the film *Treasure Island* (Byron Haskin, 1950) and the TV series *The Adventures of Long John Silver* (1955).

Maureen O'Hara was born Maureen Fitzsimmons near Dublin, Ireland, on 17 August 1920. She made her stage debut with the Abbey Players of Dublin (*Juno and the Paycock*). After appearing in *Jamaica Inn* in 1939, Maureen followed Hitchcock's and Laughton's examples and moved to Hollywood to try her luck there. Her first film in the US was *The Hunchback of Notre Dame* (William Dieterle, 1939), again with Laughton. Maureen's best-remembered films are probably the Christmas perennial *Miracle On 34th Street* (George Seaton, 1947) and *The Quiet Man* (John Ford, 1952) opposite John Wayne.

THE USUAL SUSPECTS: Leslie Banks also stars in the 1934 version of *The Man Who Knew Too Much*, Clare Greet (*Number 13*, *The Manxman*, *Murder!*, *Lord Camber's Ladies* and *Sabotage*) once again has a small role. Wylie Watson played Mr Memory in *The 39 Steps*.

KILLER LINES: One of the pirates issues a terrifying warning: 'If you want a public hanging . . . you won't have to wait long. And you'll get a fine view of it from the best position – inside the rope!'

Sir Humphrey's vainglorious final words to his people: 'What are you all waiting for? A spectacle? You shall have it! Tell your children how the Great Age ended – make way for Pengallan!'

THERE HE IS!: Although there is no cameo appearance by Hitchcock in *Jamaica Inn* as such, it's extremely tempting to interpret Charles Laughton's Sir Humphrey as a substitute.

MISOGYNY: It's quite uncomfortable viewing for a modern audience to see Sir Humphrey binding and gagging Mary before dragging her off to be his concubine. The fact that Sir Humphrey is clearly insane, protesting his undying love for the woman, makes it all the more unsettling.

THEMES AND MOTIFS: The focal point of *Jamaica Inn* is clearly Charles Laughton's Sir Humphrey, and the dual nature of his character. On the surface, he is the benevolent local squire concerned with the prosperity and safety of his tenants. Underneath, however, he is a self-serving egomaniac who believes he is above the law he is meant to represent. This Jekyll-and-Hyde aspect to character is later examined in *Shadow of a Doubt*, *Strangers on a Train*, *Psycho* and *Frenzy*.

TABOOS: Maureen O'Hara strips down to her underclothes for her impromptu swim with Trehearne. Admittedly, there's very little flesh on show, but this is still the 1930s!

MUSIC: Eric Fenby's score recalls the 1930s Saturday-morning adventure serials such as *Buck Rogers* and *Flash Gordon*, full of bombastic overtures and melodramatic crescendos. For such an over-the-top picture, it's actually very appropriate indeed.

WHAT THE PAPERS SAID: As *Jamaica Inn* followed the smash successes of *The Man Who Knew Too Much* and *The Lady Vanishes*, critical response was less than kind. The *New York Herald Tribune* described the film as 'singularly dull and uninspired. *Jamaica Inn* is a mannered and highly lackadaisical melodrama.' *Film Weekly* was no more enthusiastic. 'The makers of this film seem less at pains to make our hair stand on end than to prove to us that they can fake a shipwreck as well as Hollywood.'

COSTUME: As one of Hitchcock's three period costume dramas (alongside *Waltzes from Vienna* and *Under Capricorn*), *Jamaica Inn* boasts some spectacular costumes for almost all of its characters. The scavenging criminals look like the rancid, unwashed scum they ought to have been, while Sir Humphrey's opulent outfits are as camp and melodramatic as the man who wore them. Revealing one of Hitchcock's personal preferences, Sir Humphrey promises to dress his captive love-slave Mary in dresses made of the finest 'pale-green' silk.

FINAL ANALYSIS: 'Oh, Lord, we pray thee – not that wrecks should happen, but that if they do happen, thou wilt guide them to the coast of Cornwall, for the benefit of the poor inhabitants.' Considering just how much *Jamaica Inn* is loathed by critics and fans alike, it comes as a great surprise to discover just how much fun it is. The shipwreck sequences are so convincing that it's easy to believe that they were filmed on a Cornish beach, instead of a studio in London. The plot is a fast-paced, breathless affair, with twist after twist to hold most viewers' attention.

However, it's hard to see much of Hitchcock in this movie. Produced by Erich Pommer and made by his (and Laughton's) Mayflower company, it seems clear that Hitch was simply biding his time before heading off to America to work for David O Selznick on *Rebecca*. The few sequences where Hitch's character clearly shines through – such as the brutal treatment of Mary by Sir Humphrey – are probably best glossed over. It's a real shame that Hitchcock seemed to be happy to forget about this movie, as he very rarely spoke about it in hindsight. Its undeserved reputation must largely come from its lack of exposure and its swashbuckling storyline, a genre that traditionally has never received much critical interest in Britain. *Jamaica Inn* is easily the most spectacular of Hitchcock's British movies, and a film that deserves urgent re-evaluation. **7/10**

the complete
HITCHCOCK

films 1940–49

Rebecca (1940)

(B & W – 130 mins)

Produced by David O Selznick/Selznick International Pictures

Screenplay: Robert E Sherwood & Joan Harrison, adaptation by Philip MacDonald & Michael Hogan, based on the novel by Daphne du Maurier

Photography: George Barnes
Music: Franz Waxman
Associate: Lou Forbes
Art Director: Lyle Wheeler
Interior Art Director: Joseph B Platt
Special Effects: Jack Cosgrove
Interior Decoration: Howard Bristol
Supervising Film Editor: Hal C Kern
Associate Film Editor: James E Newcom
Scenario Assistant: Barbara Keon
Recorder: Jack Noyes
Assistant Director: Edmond F Bernoudy

CAST: Laurence Olivier (*Maxim de Winter*), Joan Fontaine (*the Second Mrs de Winter*), George Sanders (*Jack Flavell*), Judith Anderson (*Mrs Danvers*), Gladys Cooper (*Beatrice Lacy*), Nigel Bruce (*Major Giles Lacy*), Reginald Denny (*Frank Crawley*), C Aubrey Smith (*Colonel Julyan*), Melville Cooper (*Coroner*), Florence Bates (*Mrs Van Hopper*), Leonard Carey (*Ben*), Leo G Carroll (*Dr Baker*), Edward Fielding (*Frith*), Lumsden Hare (*Tabbs*), Forrester Harvey (*Chalcroft*), Philip Winter (*Robert*).

UNCREDITED CAST: Billy Bevan (*Policeman*), Leyland Hodgson (*Chauffeur*), Edith Sharpe.

SUMMARY: On holiday in Monte Carlo with her wealthy employer, Mrs Van Hopper, a young woman chances across an elegant older man. He appears distracted and suicidal but when she approaches him the man runs away. Some time later, her employer introduces the man as Maxim de Winter. Mrs Van Hopper explains to the girl that Maxim is a widower who apparently adored his wife, Rebecca, and is now in mourning after she was killed in a tragic boating accident. After Mrs Van Hopper falls ill, the girl finds herself spending a great deal of time with the mysterious de Winter. He asks her to marry him and whisks her away on a whirlwind honeymoon, leaving Mrs Van Hopper to return home alone.

They finally return to Maxim's ancestral home, Manderley. The new Mrs de Winter is presented to the staff by his rather austere housekeeper,

Mrs Danvers. Danvers guides her new mistress to a freshly decorated room in the house's east wing and tells the girl that before her mistress's death the de Winters had lived in the west wing, which overlooks the sea. She then begins to show the girl her daily business and it soom becomes clear that Mrs Danvers has instructed the entire household to continue with the routine established when Rebecca was alive. Even the girl herself finds it hard to accept her new identity, refusing a telephone call for 'Mrs de Winter' because she identifies that name with her husband's dead wife.

Maxim and his new wife go for a walk along the cliff top. When Maxim's dog scampers down to the beach, the girl runs after it despite Maxim's orders. Down on the beach she finds an old cottage, where a tramp has been dossing. He recognises the dog as having belonged to Rebecca and asks the girl not to tell anyone that he's been there. She takes a quick look around the cottage and it clearly has Rebecca's influence all over it. When Maxim catches up with her he is furious and orders her never to go to the cottage again. Almost as if she weren't there, he mutters that he regrets bringing her to Manderley.

For a brief while, everything appears to be as it should, but one evening, as Maxim and his wife watch a home movie of their honeymoon together, a butler disturbs them, saying that Mrs Danvers has accused one of the staff of breaking an expensive china ornament. As Maxim moves to intervene, his wife confesses that it was she who was responsible for the breakage, but she was so scared of what Mrs Danvers might have said that she simply hid the pieces. Realising how overwhelming this new life is for her, he suddenly feels very selfish for marrying her.

Maxim is called away to London, leaving his wife distraught with worry. From her room she sees movement in the west wing. Going to investigate, she overhears a man talking to Mrs Danvers. She enters the room and the man introduces himself as 'Flavell', Rebecca's favourite cousin. He asks her not to tell Maxim that he was there, then leaves. A little curious, the girl decides to inspect the rest of the wing. Mrs Danvers intervenes and begins to show the girl around, parading Rebecca's clothes proudly as if they were her own. Danvers is evidently obsessed with her dead mistress, gloating that the woman had known everyone who mattered and that everyone had loved her.

Idly looking through Rebecca's effects, the girl discovers a letter that suggests the first Mrs de Winter and Flavell had been lovers. The girl decides to take control of her own house and instructs Danvers to get rid of all of Rebecca's things. To lighten the atmosphere, she suggests to Maxim that they throw a fancy-dress party. Mrs Danvers recommends that the girl might find a suitable inspiration for a costume in the family portraits and points her to one that, she claims, is Mr de Winter's favourite.

The night of the party arrives and the girl has managed until now to keep her costume a surprise. Almost bursting with pride and excitement, she walks proudly down the long flight of stairs to the ballroom; but far from being impressed Maxim is enraged and orders her to take the dress off. The girl realises that Danvers has set her up. She confronts the housekeeper, who procedes to taunt the girl, goading her that she will never be able to take Rebecca's place. She carefully guides her to an open window and encourages her to kill herself. Just then, a flare goes up over the sea – a sunken boat has been found with a body aboard. From the window, the girl sees Maxim leave the house and dashes off to be with him.

She finds him in the beach cottage, where the visibly shaken man tells his wife that he knows who the body in the wrecked boat is – it's Rebecca. He's certain of this because, he claims, he put her there. His wife confesses that she knows he will always compare her with Rebecca and that he must have loved her very much. Much to her surprise he reveals he hated her. All their married life she had been unfaithful to him, having married him only for his money; he'd stayed with her only to protect the honour of his family. One night he followed her to the cottage and saw Flavell there. He waited until Flavell left before confronting Rebecca and it was then that she told him she was expecting Flavell's child, spelling out for him that another man's son would inherit his family's entire estate. As she taunted him she tripped on some ship's tackle, banged her head and died. Maxim panicked and, having placed her body inside her yacht, went out into the ocean, bashed a hole in the deck and escaped to the shore, where he watched the yacht sink. When another body conveniently washed up on the shore some weeks later, he had identified it as that of his late wife.

The girl takes control of the situation, offering him a believable alibi: that the fake identification was down to his distress over the death of his wife. The girl then returns to the house and gives instructions that all newspapers must be kept away from her husband.

At the inquest, a boat builder is able to confirm that Mrs de Winter was an expert sailor and claims that the holes in the boat were made from the inside, thereby suggesting that the woman had committed suicide. When Maxim is interviewed, they ask him if 'relations' with his wife were happy. Maxim becomes agitated, so the second Mrs de Winter faints, causing a distraction in the courtroom. The case is adjourned until the following morning. Maxim escorts his wife to their car where he's met by Flavell. He accuses Maxim of murder and proceeds to blackmail him with a letter he was sent by Rebecca that he claims will prove she was not suicidal at the time of her death. He has also asked Mrs Danvers to give evidence against Maxim. The housekeeper knows that Rebecca had been seeing a doctor in London but refuses to tell either Maxim or Flavell who it was. But when Flavell tells her of his suspicion that Maxim killed her beloved Rebecca she blurts out the name 'Dr Baker'.

Flavell and Maxim take the local chief of police, Colonel Julyan, with them to visit Rebecca's doctor. There they learn that Rebecca had discovered she had cancer. Maxim realises that she must have been certain she had very little time left and that, unable to bear the agony of a drawn-out death, she had tried to goad him into killing her, only to die accidentally. Surprised at this outcome, Flavell phones Danvers to tell her that Rebecca had kept the truth from both of them.

Maxim returns to Manderley to see it in flames. His wife tells Maxim that Mrs Danvers has gone mad – she'd rather destroy the home than see the two of them live there. Free at last from the past, Mr and Mrs de Winter watch as Manderley burns to the ground with Danvers trapped inside.

CASTING: When the producer David Selznick began discussions to film *Rebecca*, he had considered both William Powell and Leslie Howard for the role of Maxim de Winter before offering it to Ronald Coleman. Coleman, however, was worried about the fact that the character was a murderer and that the film would focus too much on the female characters, so the part went to Laurence Olivier.

For the female lead, Selznick was determined to create a media frenzy as big as that for the quest for Scarlet O'Hara for his previous production, *Gone With the Wind* (Victor Fleming, 1939). Eventually more than twenty actresses would be screentested, including Margaret Sullavan, Olivia de Havilland, Vivien Leigh (Olivier's then fiancée) and Anne Baxter (who, unsuccessful here, would be remembered by Hitchcock for *I Confess*). The choice of Fontaine was not a popular one, summed up by Olivier, who at one point said to Hitchcock: 'Fontaine's horrible, ol' boy!'

ROOTS: The original novel was clearly infuenced by the traditions of gothic literature, drawing most notably from Charlotte Brontë's *Jane Eyre* (young bride marries a wealthy man burdened with a dark secret concerning his ex-wife and a mad woman burns down the house).

LEGACY: Remade for television no fewer than three times: in 1962, starring James Mason as de Winter and Anna Massey as Mrs Danvers; in 1978, with Jeremy Brett and Anna Massey (again); and in 1997, with Charles Dance and Dame Diana Rigg.

WHO'S WHO?: Laurence Olivier came to prominence as the star of such films as *Wuthering Heights* (William Wyler, 1939), *Spartacus* (Stanley Kramer, 1960) and *Marathon Man* (1976). He was highly regarded as a Shakespearean actor on both stage and screen, directing cinematic adaptations of *Henry V* (1944), *Hamlet* (1948) and *Richard III* (1956) as well as the more lightweight *The Prince and the Showgirl* (1957) opposite Marilyn Monroe. He married Vivien Leigh in 1940, though they divorced in 1960. In 1970 he was made a life peer. He died in 1989, survived by his third wife, the actress Joan Plowright.

Joan Fontaine, was the younger sister of the actress Olivia de Havilland, and for many years it was rumoured that the two were bitter rivals. Fontaine was Oscar-nominated three times for Best Actress, an award she won in 1942 for her role in Hitchcock's *Suspicion*.

George Sanders tended to play oily playboys and charming villains, most notably in an Oscar-winning performance as the theatre critic Addison De Witt in *All About Eve* (Joseph L Mankiewicz, 1950), and as Shere Khan the Tiger in Disney's *The Jungle Book* (Wolfgang Reitherman, 1967). Sanders also pops up as the slightly more sympathetic ffolliott in *Foreign Correspondent*.

Having delivered such an unsettling performance as Mrs Danvers, we can't help but note what a shame it is that Judith Anderson would be remembered by many sci-fi fans for playing a high priestess in *Star Trek III: The Search For Spock* (Leonard Nimoy, 1984).

Gladys Cooper carved a niche for herself playing bitter old battle-axes, most memorably as the oppressive mother of Bette Davis in *Now Voyager* (Irving Rapper, 1942).

THE USUAL SUSPECTS: Nigel Bruce appeared in Hitch's production of *Lord Camber's Ladies*, and played a role not too dissimilar to Major Giles as Cary Grant's best friend in *Suspicion*. It's as the bumbling Dr Watson that he is best remembered, having starred alongside Basil Rathbone in fourteen Sherlock Holmes pictures. Leo G Carroll (*Dr Baker*) can be seen in *Suspicion*, *Spellbound*, *The Paradine Case* and *North by Northwest*, while Forrester Harvey also appeared in *The Ring* (1927).

KILLER LINES: One of the most famous opening lines in movie history: 'Last night I dreamt I went to Manderley again.'

When Maxim asks if Mrs Van Hopper is a relation, the girl explains that she's her 'paid companion'. 'I didn't know companionship could be bought,' he notes dryly.

The key scene in the film comes after the discovery of the body in the sea. The second Mrs de Winter tells her husband how difficult she's found living up to his first wife: 'Whenever you touched me I knew you were comparing me with Rebecca. Whenever you looked at me or spoke to me or walked with me in the garden I knew you were thinking "This I did with Rebecca, and this, and this". Oh, it's true, isn't it?' 'You thought I loved Rebecca?' he asks, genuinely surprised, only to reveal the shocking truth – 'I *hated* her!'

THERE HE IS!: As George Sanders phones Mrs Danvers from a telephone booth towards the end of the film, Hitchcock waits patiently to use the phone.

AWARDS: Won Oscars for Best Picture and Best Photography (for George Barnes), and was nominated for a further eight – Best Actor

(Laurence Olivier), Best Actress (Joan Fontaine), Best Art Direction, Best Special Effects, Best Film Editing, Best Original Music Score, Best Supporting Actress, Best Screenplay and, of course, Best Director. Listed by the *New York Times* as one of the top ten movies of 1940.

TRAILER: The film was sold very much as a follow-up to *Gone With The Wind*, with carefully highlighted passages from the book to point out how faithful the adaptation to the cinema is. A trailer for the film's rerelease reminded audiences not only that *Rebecca* had won the Academy Award for Best Film, but that a national poll had proclaimed it to be 'the most exciting love story of our time'. An enthusiastic voice-over asks the loaded questions: 'What is the mystery of Rebecca? What dread secret is hidden within the silent walls of Manderley? . . . There is mystery, love and laughter in *Rebecca*. The motion picture still unsurpassed for suspenseful romance.'

COSTUME: The costumes of the female leads were selected to act as cyphers for the emotions of each woman: the plain cardigans and skirts of the second Mrs de Winter offer a contrast to both the perceived glamour of her predecessor and the mourning dresses of Mrs Danvers, who glides along the corridors of Manderley like Queen Victoria. Hitchcock instructed Fontaine to carry her handbag as she enters Manderley, saying that she should think of it as if she were staying at a hotel rather than her own home, to convey her awkwardness and lack of stability in her new home.

TRIVIA: Just as in the novel, Mrs de Winter has no name of her own, and is referred to only in relation to Maxim (taking the name de Winter) and Rebecca (who was the *first* Mrs de Winter). In an early draft of the screenplay, Hitch had tried to give the girl the name 'Daphne' after Daphne du Maurier – much to Selznick's disgust!

FINAL ANALYSIS: It was the only one of Hitchcock's pictures to win an Oscar for Best Film, and it's significant that the award went to the film's producer, David Selznick. The whole production has Selznick all over it: the tortured romance, the huge, oppressive sets and, most telling of all, a respect for the original novel that Hitchcock would never have had – it was Selznick's experience with *Gone With the Wind* that, after all, convinced him that *Rebecca* would be a suitable property for his studio, and, having made that commitment, he wasn't about to allow Hitch to perform his customary rewrites of the original source.

There are, however, a number of Hitchcockian touches. The character of Danvers is a skilful creation: one character describes her as being 'no oil painting' but that is exactly what she is – every time we see her she's simply standing there, her arms folded under her bosom, her face as still as the paintings she so admires on the grand staircase. In contrast, though the second Mrs de Winter is very animated in a nervous kind of way, she is so irritatingly meek and withdrawn that it's almost frustrating to watch her squirm and shrink away from everyone she meets. Despite this, it's difficult to imagine why she would fall for someone as cold and unloving as Maxim; one can only assume that she feels flattered that anyone would pay her such attention, or that Maxim is considerably warmer to her when they're alone.

Whether the credit should go to Hitchcock or Selznick, *Rebecca* is a splendid production, managing to tell a romantic ghost story with neither a ghost nor that much romance and still make it compelling. 8/10

Foreign Correspondent (1940)
(Working title: *Personal History*)

(B & W – 120 mins)

Produced by Walter Wanger/United Artists

Written by Charles Bennett & Joan Harrison, with additional dialogue by James Hilton & Robert Benchley and uncredited additions by Richard Maibaum, John Lee Mahin & Ben Hecht, inspired by the novel *Personal History* by Vincent Sheean

Music composed by Alfred Newman
Photography: Rudolph Maté
Production Design: Alexander Golitzen
Film Editing: Dorothy Spencer
Assistant Director: Edmond F Bernoudy
Process Photography: Ray Binger
European Photography: Osmond Borradaile
Construction: Oscar Brodin
Camera Assistant: Frank Bucholtz
Operator, Second Unit: Ellis W Carter
Production Manager: James Dent
Hair Stylist: Carmen Dirigo
Assistant Camera: Tom Dowling
Special Effects/Photographer, Second Unit: Paul Eagler
Camera Assistant: Norman Freed
Art Director: Alexander Golitzen
Camera Operator: Burnett Guffey
Set Decorator: Julia Heron
Associate Art Director: Richard Irving
Assistant Camera: James King
Special Effects Cutter: Louis R Loeffler
Editorial Supervisor: Otho Lovering
Sound: Frank Maher
Pilot: Paul Mantz
Special Production Effects: William Cameron Menzies

Second Assistant Director: Marty Moss
Sound Effects: James T Moulton
Additional Photographer: Roy F Overbaugh
Make-up Artist: Norman Pringle
Sound Film Cutter: Walter Reynolds
Still Photographer: William Walling
Special Effects Assistant: Paul Wtuliska
Special Effects: Lee Zavitz

CAST: Joel McCrea (*Johnny Jones*), Laraine Day (*Carol Fisher*), Herbert Marshall (*Stephen Fisher*), Albert Bassermann (*Van Meer*), Edmund Gwenn (*Rowley*), George Sanders (*Scott ffolliott*), Edward Ciannelli, (*Mr Krug* – credited as Eduardo Ciannelli), Charles Halton (*Bradley*), Ian Wolfe (*Stiles*), Barry Bernard (*Steward*), Robert Benchley (*Stebbins*), Harry Davenport (*Mr Powers*), Martin Kosleck (*Tramp*), Barbara Pepper (*Dorine*), Emory Parnell (*Captain of the* Mohican), Frances Carson (*Mrs Sprague*), Charles Wagenheim (*Assassin*), Edward Conrad (*Latvian Diplomat*), John Burton (*English Announcer*), Roy Gordon (*Mr Brood*), Marten Lamont (*Plane Captain*), Holmes Herbert (*Asst. Commissioner ffolliott*), Leonard Mudie (*Inspector McKenna*), Gertrude Hoffman (*Mrs Benson*).

UNCREDITED CAST: Samuel Adams (*Impersonator*), Jack Rice (*Donald*), Meeka Aldrich (*Donald's Wife*), Betty Bradley (*Cousin Mary*), EE Clive (*Mr Naismith*), Alexander Granach (*Valet*), Crauford Kent (*Toastmaster*), Joan Leslie (*Jones's Sister*), Ted Mapes (*Double for Joel McCrea*), Mary Young (*Auntie Maude*), Eily Malyon (*Hotel Cashier*), Dorothy Vaughan (*Jones's Mother*), Ferris Taylor (*Jones's Father*), Harry Depp (*Uncle Buren*), Jane Novak (*Miss Benson*), Hilda Plowright (*Miss Pimm*).

SUMMARY: Johnny Jones, a reporter for the *New York Morning Globe*, is expecting dismissal after a brawl with a policeman. He is summoned to the office of the paper's proprietor, Mr Powers. It appears that Jones is completely ignorant of the current political state in Europe, but, as Powers wants to hear a fresh approach to the situation, he tells Jones he is to be dispatched to London to work as the *Globe*'s new foreign correspondent, and that he must try to speak to a diplomat called Van Meer, one of the linchpins in the European peace movement. None of the foreign correspondents have been able to get anything out of him, and Powers believes if he can find out the content of a treaty Van Meer's been working on he'll be able to gauge the possibility of war breaking out in Europe. Powers also thinks Jones's name won't command the right amount of respect and suggests he change it to Huntley Haverstock. He then introduces him to Stephen Fisher, head of the Universal Peace Party and a close friend of Van Meer.

After saying a tearful goodbye to his family, Johnny departs for

London, where he meets Stebbins, the current London correspondent. He's been in London for 25 years and sees it as an easy ride. Johnny hardly has any time to get his bearings before he is instructed to cover an important conference in Amsterdam. En route to the conference, Johnny coincidentally sees Van Meer getting a cab outside his hotel. The old man offers to give Johnny a lift but, despite Johnny's attempts to veer the conversation towards politics, Van Meer seems willing only to make idle conversation. When they reach their destination, Van Meer reveals that he has guessed Johnny is a reporter. However, he is impressed by Johnny's frankness, and tells him that the current political situation is making him feel both old and helpless. He wanders off into the crowd.

Jones meets a girl called Carol who tells him she's working at the conference, and Jones mistakenly thinks she works in publicity. He tactlessly asks her if she believes this assembly of 'well-meaning amateurs' can stand up to the professional soldiers of Europe, and then invites her to sit with him on the press table, claiming no one there ever listens to the speeches, so they won't be troubled. Angered by his complete lack of understanding, she storms off. When the speeches begin, Stephen Fisher makes an announcement that Mr Van Meer has telegrammed him to say he is unable to attend, much to the surprise of Jones. In his place, Fisher announces the first speaker, his daughter, who Jones is embarrassed to discover is Carol.

Having heard that the political situation is worsening, Fisher tells Jones that he has been called back to London. Outside the peace conference, Jones goes up to Mr Van Meer to reacquaint himself, but the old man seems not to recognise him. Just then, a man posing as a photographer shoots Van Meer, who falls backward down a flight of steps dead. Jones gives chase and asks the driver of a passing car for help. He's surprised to find the car's passenger is Carol, being driven by a fellow correspondent, Scott ffolliott. They follow the getaway car as far as a field of windmills, but then the car disappears. Johnny notices that one of the windmills is blowing in the wrong direction and sends ffolliott and Carol to fetch the police while he investigates. He works out that the sails of the windmill are being used to signal aeroplanes to land. He enters the mill and hears voices. Keeping himself out of sight from a gang of shady-looking men, Johnny snoops around until he stumbles across Van Meer, recovering from a sedative. It seems the gang used a *doppelgänger* to make the world think Van Meer had been assassinated. Struggling against the drugs, Van Meer tries to say something to Johnny but blacks out without making much sense. Hearing the gang members climbing the steps to Van Meer's room, Johnny escapes and manages to fetch the police, though unsurprisingly all trace of the gang's presence has disappeared.

Jones wires home to say he's on the trail of a huge story. Two policemen come to his hotel room to say their chief wants to question him back at the station. Jones says he needs to make a quick phone call, but his suspicions are aroused when he sees that his phone wire has been cut. He tells the men he needs to take a quick bath and locks himself in the bathroom. Through the keyhole he watches one of the men remove a gun from his pocket and is convinced they are not policemen. He climbs out through the bathroom window and across the rooftops into Carol's room. Carol is, not surprisingly, furious. He explains to her that he believes his life is in danger and persuades her to help him. With the assistance of the hotel valet, he manages to rescue some clothes from his room and he and Carol escape.

They board a ship bound for London, but they're unable to get a cabin and spend the journey sleeping under some blankets on deck. It becomes obvious to the pair that they have fallen inexplicably in love with each other. They manage to reach London safely and rush to see Carol's father to tell him their news. However, when they arrive he has a man with him whom Jones recognises as one of the kidnappers, despite Fisher introducing him as Mr Krug, a member of his own staff. As Krug steps out of the room, Jones tells Fisher that he has seen Van Meer alive, that he is almost definitely in London and that Krug must have brought him there. Fisher reassures him, saying he'll sort it out. However, Fisher is part of the conspiracy and he and Krug discuss ways of ridding themselves of Jones's interference. Krug suggests that, as Jones has such valuable information, they should get Jones a 'bodyguard' who'll sort him out. Fisher then manages to persuade Jones not to act on his news for a few hours, with promises that he's sure the story will be even bigger if they wait.

Jones is introduced to his new bodyguard, an unimposing man called Rowley. Claiming they're being followed, Rowley takes Jones to Westminster cathedral and takes him up to the Cathedral tower to 'put them off the scent'. As soon as the observation platform is clear of tourists, Rowley lunges at him but instead falls to his death.

Rowley's attack on him has made Jones suspicious of Fisher. He visits Stebbins for advice, and is surprised when Scott ffolliott turns up to inform him he's been tracking Fisher for almost a year. He then tells him why Van Meer was kidnapped: he is the only person who knows the contents of a secret passage to a treaty that could be used to avert – or *start* – a war in Europe. ffolliott has an unusual plan – he suggests they kidnap Carol. When Jones refuses he explains that they would merely pretend to kidnap her; Jones would keep her out of the way while ffolliott uses her disappearance to force Fisher's hand. At that moment Carol arrives and begs Johnny to go into hiding. She takes him away while ffolliott smiles smugly to himself, having suggested the idea to Carol half an hour earlier.

When ffolliott is unable to contact Fisher, he calls Jones and tells him he must keep Carol busy a little longer. He arranges for Carol to have a separate room, much to her distress.

Fisher finally arrives home to get ready to return to America and ffolliott tells him that Carol has been kidnapped and that he arranged it. He tells him he knows he's got Van Meer and that Carol is being used to keep Van Meer safe. Then Krug calls and tells him Van Meer is ready to talk. But Carol arrives home safely so ffolliott is forced to leave. Fisher tells his daughter that they are leaving for America, then departs to conclude some final business. Just as he leaves, Carol answers the telephone and hears Krugs's voice – she is suddenly concerned.

Fisher goes to meet Krug and his agents, and is shown to the room where they are keeping the disorientated Van Meer. He tries to get the old man to talk, but is disturbed by ffolliott, who has been found snooping and is brought in at gunpoint. ffolliott warns Van Meer not to speak. Van Meer suddenly realises with dismay that Fisher has been a traitor all along and refuses to tell him anything. The spies begin to torture him and finally he starts to talk. ffolliott struggles to prevent the spies from escaping just as Jones arrives. Though the two men are able to save Van Meer, Fisher escapes.

ffolliott pulls some strings to get himself and Jones on to the same plane as Fisher and his daughter. Fisher intercepts a message for ffolliot that states that Fisher will be met by American agents and arrested on his arrival in the States. He decides to confess all to his daughter, who tells him she had suspected as much. Though Fisher managed to disguise his true identity by adopting an English accent, he has been acting in the interests of his own country all along.

Jones approaches Carol and tries to explain to her that he does not want to incriminate her father: he merely wants to tell the story he's been sent to write. As the couple talk, their plane comes under attack and after sustaining irreparable damage it crashes into the sea. The survivors, including Johnny and Carol, cling to the floating wreckage, but Fisher allows himself to be swept away by the sea rather than be captured. They're rescued by an American ship, but the captain refuses to let them cable their editor. Johnny tells ffolliott that he won't betray Fisher, but Carol overhears and tells him it's his duty. Jones phones Powers and leaves the line open so that the editor can listen in as he tells the full story to the captain – a story that is reprinted in the *New York Morning Globe* that night. Soon Johnny and Carol return to London, from where Johnny reports war events to America during an air raid.

TITLES: A spinning globe, which pans out to reveal it's the roof-mounted standard of the *New York Morning Globe* newspaper.

SCROLLED INTRODUCTION: *To those intrepid ones who went across the seas to be the eyes and ears of America . . . To those forthright ones who early saw the clouds of war while many of us at home were seeing rainbows . . . To those clear-headed ones who now stand like recording angels among the dead and dying . . . To the foreign correspondents . . . this motion picture is dedicated.*

CASTING: When he first mounted the project, the producer Walter Wanger envisaged it as a vehicle for Charles Boyer and Claudette Colbert. By the time Hitchcock was on board, Wanger was pursuing Joan Fontaine and her husband Brian Ahearne, but they had already been released by Selznick to do a play (which fell in with his plans for promoting *Rebecca*). Hitchcock had approached Gary Cooper with the script, but, as thrillers were regarded as 'second-rate' pictures, Cooper turned it down. He later told Hitchcock it was a decision he had regretted. Instead Hitch got what he considered to be second best, Joel McCrea.

ROOTS: In addition to the source book, *Personal History*, Hitchcock returned to one of his favourite books, John Buchan's *The Thirty Nine Steps*, where he appropriated the idea of a mill being a hideout for spies and made it a windmill to suit the Dutch setting.

Van Meer's assassination owes much to Eisenstein's *Battleship Potempkin*, and the introduction to the film notes that foreign correspondents were warning of 'the clouds of war' while in America many were merely 'seeing rainbows', which might be seen as a subtle dig at Hitchcock's producer, David Selznick, who also produced *The Wizard of Oz* (Victor Flemyng, 1939).

LEGACY: The scene with a sea of umbrellas outside the Savoy is copied in Brian De Palma's *Bonfire of the Vanities* (1990). See also the garden party scene in *Stage Fright*.

WHO'S WHO?: Laraine Day (*Carol*) was well known through her role as Sister Mary Lamont in *Dr Kildare*. She later appeared in the *Alfred Hitchcock Presents* episode 'Death and the Joyful Woman'. Robert Benchley (*Stebbins*) was a member of the notorious Algonquin Round Table, a social circle of New York's wittiest minds that included Dorothy Parker and Harpo Marx. His son, Peter, was the author of the novel *Jaws*.

THE USUAL SUSPECTS: Herbert Marshall (*Stephen Fisher*) played Sir John Menier in *Murder!*. Edmund Gwenn (*Rowley, the bodyguard*) appears in *The Skin Game*, *Waltzes from Vienna* and *The Trouble With Harry*, as well as Hitchcock's radio dramatisation of *The Lodger*; George Sanders played Flavell in *Rebecca*; Ian Wolfe appeared in *Saboteur*; Charles Halton also appeared in *Mr. and Mrs. Smith*.

KILLER LINES: When the captain of the *Mohican* asks Johnny why he didn't tell him he was a reporter, Johnny says: 'My dear Captain, when you've been shot down in a British plane by a German destroyer, three hundred miles off the coast of England (latitude forty-five), and have been hanging on to a half-submerged wing for hours, waiting to drown with half a dozen other stricken human beings, you're liable to forget you're a newspaperman for a moment or two!'

As Carol Fisher begins her speech, a journalist comments. 'The female of the speeches is deadlier than the male.'

After discovering that he and Carol want to marry each other, Johnny notes flippantly: 'That cuts down our love scene quite a bit, doesn't it?'

Johnny's closing words in a broadcast to America: 'Hello, America, hang on to your lights: they're the only lights left in the world!'

THERE HE IS!: Eleven minutes in, Hitch strolls past Johnny Jones's hotel reading a newspaper.

THE MACGUFFIN: The reason Van Meer is kidnapped is for Clause 27 from a peace treaty that was never written down, merely memorised by the old man. He is the only person who knows the clause and the (unidentified) enemy want it.

GOOFS: Despite the explicit dialogue and written appearances of the name that make it clear that the character Scott ffolliott has no capital F, the name still appears as 'Ffolliott' in the end-credit cast list.

AWARDS: Oscar-nominated for Art Direction, Photography, Special Effects, Best Supporting Actor (Albert Bassermann), Best Picture, Original Screenplay.

POSTER: Announcing 'The thrill spectacle of the year', the poster declared, like a tabloid headline: 'He wanted his story, she wanted love!'

TRIVIA: With a final budget of $1,500,000, *Foreign Correspondent* was Hitchcock's most expensive picture so far, though thanks to the war in Europe most of the money went on building full-sized re-creations of Amsterdam locales, the largest of which being a ten-acre reconstruction of the Amsterdam public square complete with a sewer system to handle the artificial rain.

The scene where the plane crashes into the sea and water streams in without a cut was achieved by releasing a tank of water that tore the rear projection screen open, flooding the cabin. Hitchcock boasted to François Truffaut that this was achieved in one shot.

FINAL ANALYSIS: Despite the lack of a 'wrong man' theme, *Foreign Correspondent* smacks just a little of Hitchcock simply recreating his British 'chase' movies like *Secret Agent* and *The 39 Steps* for an American audience. Though this is no bad thing it does seem a little like a step backward compared with the sophistication of *Rebecca*. Joel McCrea makes for an appealing but lightweight hero, but Laraine Day is forced to make the best of a bad job with Carol, who rapidly descends from being a strong-willed and intelligent woman to a mere accessory.

It's also painfully obvious that the love story, which kicks in rather too suddenly, is just a means to an end, tagged on to the more important story of the awakening of Johnny (representing his country in more ways than one) from an ignorant hack writer to a politically aware reporter playing his part in asking the citizens of the States to support the Allies in their difficult times.

The allusion to America's isolationism during the first few years of the war is obvious, and, while it cannot lay claim to persuading the American people to enter into World War Two (the events at Pearl Harbor hold that dubious honour), *Foreign Correspondent*'s well-meaning intentions go much further than any other studio-led picture of the time in alerting its audience to the real problems in Europe. It's little more than an enjoyable lightweight crowd-pleaser, but at least its heart, if not its mind, is in the right place. **6/10**

Suspicion (1941)

(B & W – 99 mins)

Produced by Alfred Hitchcock/RKO Radio Pictures, Inc.

Written by Samson Raphaelson & Joan Harrison & Alma Reville, based on the novel *Before the Fact* by Francis Iles (pseudonym for Anthony Berkeley Cox)

Original music: Franz Waxman
Photography: Harry Stradling Sr
Costume Design: Edward Stevenson
Film Editing: William Hamilton
Assistant Art Director: Carroll Clark
Art Director: Van Nest Polglase
Set Decorator: Darrell Silvera
Assistant Director: Dewey Starkey
Sound: John E Tribby
Special Effects: Vernon L Walker

CAST: Cary Grant (*Johnnie Aysgarth*), Joan Fontaine (*Lina McLaidlaw Aysgarth*), Sir Cedric Hardwicke (*Mr McLaidlaw*), Nigel Bruce (*Beaky*), Dame May Whitty (*Mrs McLaidlaw*), Isabel Jeans (*Mrs Newsham*), Heather Angel (*Ethel*), Auriol Lee (*Isobel Sedbusk*), Reginald Sheffield (*Reggie Wetherby*), Leo G Carroll (*Captain Melbeck*), Billy Bevan (*Ticket Taker*), Ben Webster (*Registrar*), Lumsden Hare (*Inspector Hodgson*), Gertrude Hoffman (*Mrs Wetherby*), Hilda Plowright (*Postmistress*).

UNCREDITED CAST: Faith Brook (*Alice Barham*), Leonard Carey (*Butler*), Clyde Cook (*Photographer*), Alec Craig (*Receptionist at the Hogarth Club*), Carol Curtis-Brown (*Jessie Barham*), Vernon Downing

(*Benson*), Rex Evans (*Mr Bailey*), Edward Fielding (*Antique Shop Proprietor*), Gavin Gordan (*Bertram Sedbusk*), Kenneth Hunter (*Sir Gerald*), Doris Lloyd (*Miss Wetherby*), Aubrey Mather (*Mr Webster*), Nondas Metcalf (*Phyllis Swinghurst*), Clara Reid (*Mrs Craddock*), Maureen Roden-Ryan (*the Maid, Winnie*), Pax Walker (*the Maid, Phoebe*), Elsie Weller (*Miss Wetherby*), Constance Worth (*Mrs Fitzpatrick*).

SUMMARY: A tall, handsome man shares a train carriage with a rather studious, bookish young woman. An inspector comes to check their tickets and, finding that the man possesses only a third-class ticket for a first-class carriage, he orders him to pay the surplus. The man has virtually no money and scrounges a postage stamp from his fellow traveller to cover the deficit. The woman tries to avoid eye contact with the cad, until she comes across a picture of him in the society pages of a magazine.

Some time later, Johnnie attends a local hunt, accompanied by an entourage of female friends, where he sees the woman from the train. She looks completely different in her riding suit, and he is obviously taken with her. He discovers her name is Lina McLaidlaw and decides to visit her at her home and invites her to go for a walk. He playfully teases her all afternoon and as he walks her home he hurriedly arranges to meet her later that day. Lina is at first reluctant, but after hearing her parents air their fears she'll end up a spinster she rushes back to him and kisses him passionately.

Excited, she tells her parents about her new suitor, and when he hears her suitor's name her father is immediately wary, aware that the man has a bad reputation. Lina defends him but, soon after, she receives a call from Johnnie cancelling the date. For a week, Lina tries to contact him to no avail and by the time of the hunt ball she is distraught and lovesick. When at last she receives a telegram from him arranging to meet her at the ball she is overjoyed.

When Johnnie arrives at the ball, it appears he has not been invited. As he tries to clear up what he believes is an oversight, Lina rushes over to him and drags him on to the dance floor. Noticing the attention they appear to be receiving, he suggests they duck out of the ball and go for a drive. Overcome with the excitement, Lina lets slip that she has fallen in love with him. Johnnie tells her that he loves her too, but that he is afraid, which is why he stayed away from her for an entire week. The couple decide to elope.

On their return, Lina is met at the station by her mother, who, seeing how happy her daughter is, offers to smooth things over with Lina's father. The newly-weds move into their new home, which Johnnie has arranged while they were away. Lina's father phones and tells her that he is overjoyed for her and that he has sent round a wedding gift as a token of his love. The gift arrives – a pair of antique chairs, much to the disappointment of Johnnie. Lina asks Johnnie how he intends to pay for their beautiful house and it is then that she discovers that her husband is penniless. She orders him to find a job, so he reluctantly accepts an offer from his cousin to be his estate manager.

Soon after, Beaky, an old friend of Johnnie's, pops round to introduce himself to Lina. He tells her he decided to visit after seeing Johnnie at the races a few days earlier. Lina tells him that this isn't possible, now that Johnnie is working, but then she notices that her father's chairs are missing and Beaky tactlessly speculates that Johnnie has sold them and that if she were to ask him about them he'd probably construct an elaborate lie. When Johnnie finally returns home, he explains the disappearance of the chairs by telling his wife that an American had offered him £100 apiece for them, and that he mistakenly thought she'd sooner have the money. However, some time later she spies the chairs in a local antique shop and rushes home upset. Beaky comforts her and asks her not to rebuke Johnnie for his actions. Just then, Johnnie arrives home laden with presents, claiming he's just won £2,000 on a horse. He apologises for lying to her, and, in addition to the gifts he's bought, tells her he's retrieved the chairs too.

Concerned by Johnnie's behaviour, Lina decides to visit his cousin and employer to ask if he might shed some light on the matter, only to be told that Johnnie was sacked six weeks previously after an audit revealed a deficit of £2,000. She decides she's had enough and packs her bags. Before she can leave, however, Johnnie returns home with a telegram – her father has just died of a heart attack.

Some time later, Lina tackles the subject of Johnnie's dismissal, but he claims it was simply a clash of personalities. He has an eye to the bigger picture, he tells her, and takes her to a place by the sea that he intends to develop and sell on – with investment from Beaky so they can form a corporation together. The plan seems unwise to Lina, and when she says this to Johnnie he seems furious. Nevertheless, he eventually tells a disappointed Beaky that the corporation cannot go ahead, and promises to show him early the next morning how unsuitable the site would have been for development.

Waking after the men have left, Lina is suddenly hit with a wave of panic, believing that Johnnie might hurt Beaky to get money from him. She drives up to the cliffs but there is no sign of her husband or his friend. Returning home she's relieved to find the two men playing like children with a record player. Beaky tells her that Johnnie actually saved his life – as he was moving the car he knocked it into reverse and it was Johnnie's quick actions that stopped him plummeting to his death. He tells her that he is taking Johnnie to London to celebrate dissolving their brief partnership, after which time he intends to go to Paris to finish off the paperwork.

While Johnnie is away, Lina is visited by two police officers, who inform her that Beaky is dead: he suffered a massive heart attack in Paris after drinking a huge brandy for a bet. They tell her they wish to question her husband as another Englishman was with him shortly before he died. She tries to contact Johnnie at his club, only to be told he left there the previous morning. Johnnie arrives home some time later, visibly distraught, and when he telephones the police he tells them he was at his club until that afternoon, making Lina even more suspicious.

Lina visits her friend Isobel, a crime writer. As they discuss her murder stories, Lina innocently asks if it's possible to poison someone without their knowing. Isobel tells her of a murder case which she says had circumstances not unlike those of Beaky, in which a man killed someone by drowning the poison in a large brandy. She thinks she has a book on the subject, then remembers that Johnnie borrowed it a few weeks earlier. Lina finds the book on Johnnie's table, and inside she finds an unposted letter from Johnnie to his cousin promising he'll get the money he stole back to him. She then receives a phone call from an insurance company telling her that a claim that Johnnie has made has been delayed. The next morning, Johnnie receives two letters from other insurance companies. Lina manages to steal a look at one of the letters – it informs him that he can make a claim on the insurance policies only in the event of her death.

Isobel invites the couple to dinner, during which Johnnie lightly mocks the complicated murder in her latest novel. He guides the subject towards a discussion of poisons and learns of the existence of an untraceable poison. When they return home, Lina is so suspicious of him she refuses to sleep with him and he storms off to sleep in his study. Overcome with worry, she faints.

She wakes to find Isobel and Johnnie sitting by her bed. Apparently she's slept an entire day. As Isobel talks, Lina learns that Johnnie has quizzed her even further regarding the poison and Lina is now convinced he is trying to kill her. She decides to pack her bags and escape to her mother's. When Johnnie realises what is happening he insists on driving her there. Speeding along the coast, Lina is terrified for her life and when the car door swings open she screams. Johnnie brakes and Lina runs from the car. Johnnie grabs her and demands an explanation. He then confesses he has been contemplating suicide after being unable to repay his mounting debts. Lina suddenly realises that she has been foolish in suspecting Johnnie of being anything other than financially inept and begs him to come back home with her so they can work things out.

CASTING: The RKO studio had been keen to produce a version of *Before the Fact* since 1935, with Louis Hayward as the smooth philanderer. A few years later the project was resurrected for Robert Montgomery. By the time Hitch had been assigned the film, Maureen O'Hara (fresh from her performance in Hitch's *Jamaica Inn*) was up for the part of the delusional wife, with Laurence Olivier as frontrunner for the male lead. It was at this point, while Olivier was still under consideration, that script amendments were made to make Johnnie's murderous acts the result of his wife's paranoia. This contradicts Hitchcock's version of events, claiming that he insisted on the rewrites to appease Cary Grant's fans.

ROOTS: The original story had Lina's suspicions confirmed when she discovers that Johnnie is both a con artist and a murderer. When she becomes pregnant, she decides she doesn't want her husband to bring another monster into the world, so she commits suicide by drinking a glass of milk that she knows has been poisoned – but not before she sends a letter to her mother explaining her husband's entire plan.

The house that Johnnie acquired as the marital home might seem familiar to fans of *Gone With the Wind*, who'll remember Tara – the front of David Selznick's studio was used for both properties.

LEGACY: *Suspicion* was remade for television in 1987, starring Anthony Andrews, spoofed in *High Anxiety* (Mel Brooks, 1977) and edited into Steve Martin's noir spoof *Dead Men Don't Wear Plaid* (Carl Reiner, 1982).

WHO'S WHO?: The screenwriter Samson Raphaelson was the author of the play *The Jazz Singer*, which was the inspiration for the landmark talkie film of the same name.

THE USUAL SUSPECTS: Joan Fontaine had previously played the female lead in *Rebecca*, while Sir Cedric Hardwicke, who plays her father, appears in *Rope* and Dame May Whitty (her mother) was the eponymous lady in *The Lady Vanishes*. Isabel Jeans (*Mrs Newsham*) previously worked with Hitch on *Easy Virtue*, and in *Downhill*, alongside Ben Webster (*the Registrar*); Hilda Plowright played an uncredited role in *Foreign Correspondent*; Heather Angel (*Ethel*) worked on *Lifeboat*; and finally Leo G Carroll (*Captain Melbeck*) can be seen in *Rebecca*, *Spellbound*, *The Paradine Case* and *North by Northwest*.

KILLER LINES: Johnnie tries to rearrange Lina's hairstyle, joking that 'for a moment I became a passionate hairdresser', then tells her that she looks 'like a monkey with a bit of a mirror. What do your friends call you?' he asks, ' "Monkey Face"?' A name he continues to call her throughout the film. He later berates Isobel for the convoluted murders in her novels, telling her: 'If you're going to kill someone, do it simply.'

THERE HE IS!: About 45 minutes in, posting a letter at the village post office.

AWARDS: Joan Fontaine won both an Oscar and a New York Film Critics' Circle Award for Best Actress, while *Suspicion* also won Oscar nominations for Best Dramatic Score and, once again, Best Picture.

THEMES AND MOTIFS: A traditional Selznick device, use of shadows, is seen here when Lina learns of Beaky's death and stands alone in the hallway of her house. The skylight above her casts a shadow like a huge spider's web, and later the window frame's shadows resemble the bars of a cage. In the infamous 'glass of milk' scene, we see Johnnie's shadow briefly surrounded by a triangle of light, which is also strongly reminiscent of the titles from *The Lodger*.

Look out for the climactic car chase across the cliffs – mirrored in Hitch's three other films with Cary Grant: *Notorious*, *To Catch a Thief* and *North by Northwest*.

POSTER: 'Each time they kissed, there was the thrill of love . . . the threat of murder!'/'Thrill to them together in the greatest emotional hit ever directed by that master of suspenseful drama – Alfred Hitchcock!'/'In his arms she felt safety . . . in his absence, haunting dread!'/'Cary Grant in his most powerful role as a wastrel husband intent on riches at any cost. Joan Fontaine in her first since Rebecca, as the bride whose love turned to terror! Completely compelling mystery romance!'/'Alfred Hitchcock, who gave you Foreign Correspondent and Rebecca, creates his most romantic mystery hit!'/' She won your heart in "Rebecca". He drew your cheers in "Philadelphia Story". Thrill to them together in a suspense-romance from the man who did "Rebecca", Alfred Hitchcock.'

TRAILER: Joan Fontaine performs a specially recorded, almost confessional sequence, intercut with clips from the movie. 'There was something strange about John Aysgarth,' she tells us; ' . . . something you couldn't put your finger on, and yet you were always conscious of it. Conscious of something vague, restless, frightening.' She goes on to explain how, though she loved Johnnie, she was terrified of him, spending sleepless nights waiting for 'it' to happen. 'These are the facts,' she concludes, 'the evidence before the crime. I wanted you to know in case I met a violent end . . .'

WHAT THE PAPERS SAID: While audiences loved the film, critics were divided. Howard Barnes of the *Herald Tribune* thought it a 'far finer film than *Rebecca*', but the ever-critical Bosley Crowther believed it was not up to Hitch's usual style, though he noted begrudgingly that it was nevertheless 'a psychological thriller which is packed with lively suspense'.

TRIVIA: After the title *Before the Fact* received a less-than-enthusiastic reception, alternative suggestions included *Fright*, *Suspicious Lady*, *Search For Tomorrow*, *Last Lover*, *Love In Irons* and the delightful *Men Make Poor Husbands*. Just before the film's release, the studio finally accepted one of Hitchcock's suggestions, *Suspicion*.

Cary Grant (1904–1986)

It's often suggested that Hitchcock cast James Stewart as an extension of himself but cast Cary Grant as the ideal of how he'd like to be. Tall, slim and sophisticated, Grant was the embodiment of the best of Hollywood's old-style charm – a construction as artificial as the characters he played. He started out in show business as a trapeze artist under his real name, Archie Leach, and his move to Hollywood led to the creation of Cary Grant, a debonair man whose smooth voice was a casual mix of gentrified English and Bostonian dignity.

Grant was not what could be called a passionate performer; his acting was subtle, stylish and easygoing, which accounts for the success of his early screwball and romantic comedies. In films such as *Bringing Up Baby* (Howard Hawks, 1938) and *The Philadelphia Story* (George Cukor, 1940), Grant showed he was open to the idea of self-mockery, building himself up as the height of cool, only to suffer a pratfall or engage in slapstick – yet always with great dignity.

By the time he came to work with Hitchcock, Cary Grant had become accustomed to playing a specific type that he could exploit and play off. In *Suspicion* his charm hides his con-artistry; in *Notorious* it's the perfect cover for an agent compromised by his love for a woman he's forced to use. By the time of *To Catch a Thief*, Grant's self-parody had come full circle, when he played an ex-criminal who is compelled to return to his old ways to prove how he's changed. More than any other of these collaborations, *North by Northwest* sums up the screen image of Cary Grant: a man who is forced to play a role, yet manages to seize it as his own; who adopts a fake identity and makes it real; who is faced with the dawning realisation that he's far too old to keep up his playboy lifestyle.

In 1966, he eventually retired from public life, conscious that his age was making his glamorous persona somewhat unbelievable. Perhaps this was the ultimate indication of a man who knew his limits and more than anything did not want to disappoint. As Pauline Kael noted: 'We didn't want depth from him; we asked only that he be handsome and silky and make us laugh.'

Equally troublesome was the search for an ending to the picture, with suggestions that Johnnie should join the air force and die in combat justly stamped on. In an attempt to get round the controversial ending of the original story, scenes were shot that suggested Lina had enjoyed an extramarital affair, thereby making her suicide her penance for her infidelity, but, after test audiences mocked this, Hitch was forced to shoot the ending again.

In the film's key scene, where Johnnie brings a glass of milk up to Lina, Hitchcock had a light hidden in the glass to make it appear more sinister, making it glow through the darkness.

FINAL ANALYSIS: Though at the time *Suspicion* was greeted enthusiastically by the public, this can be seen more as good luck than skilful artistry. Cary Grant was arguably at his peak, both in looks and success, and as a rising star Joan Fontaine would go on to win an Oscar for her performance, yet both play incredibly annoying people here. Johnnie is a selfish and irresponsible man whose character would have improved immensely if the producers hadn't been such cowards and instead made him the out-and-out villain he originally was. Fontaine's Lina, meanwhile, is frustratingly blind to her husband's faults, having been unable to accept him as a philanderer, yet in only a matter of seconds she stumbles upon the conclusion that her husband is a murderer. While Nigel Bruce goes through the motions with his lovable but annoyingly stupid Beaky, only Isobel, the crime writer, really shines out in the supporting cast.

Having established the early part of the film as a light-hearted romantic comedy, Hitchcock's sudden lurch towards psychological thriller happens too quickly for us to really believe in any of Lina's convictions. Maybe Hitchcock was right: we simply can't accept Cary Grant as a killer after all. 5/10

Mr. and Mrs. Smith (1941)

(Working titles: *No for an Answer/Here We Go Again!/And So To Wed/Slightly Married/ Temporarily Yours* . . . and many, many more)

(B & W – 94 mins)

Produced by RKO Radio Pictures, Inc.

Executive Producer: Harry E Edington

Written by Norman Krasna

Original music: Edward Ward
Photography: Harry Stradling Sr
Costume Design: Irene
Film Editing: William Hamilton
Art Director: Van Nest Polglase
Set Decorator: Darrell Silvera
Assistant Director: Dewey Starkey
Recording Director: John E Tribby
Special Effects: Vernon L Walker
Musical Director: Roy Webb
Associate Art Director: Lawrence P Williams

CAST: Carole Lombard (*Ann Krausheimer Smith*), Robert Montgomery (*David Smith*), Gene Raymond (*Jeff Custer*), Jack Carson (*Chuck Benson*), Philip Merivale (*Mr Custer*), Lucile Watson (*Mrs Custer*), William Tracy (*Sammy*), Charles Halton (*Mr Deever*), Esther Dale

(*Mrs Krausheimer*), Emma Dunn (*Martha*), Betty Compson (*Gertie*), Patricia Farr (*Gloria*), William Edmunds (*Proprietor*), Adele Pearce (*Lily*).

UNCREDITED CAST: Ernie Alexander (*Bellhop*), Murray Alper (*Harold, driver*), Pamela Blake (*Lily*), Ralph Brooks (*Waiter Captain*), Georgia Carroll (*Girl*), Francis Compton (*Mr Flugle*), Alec Craig (*the Clerk, Thomas*), Ralph Dunn (*Cop*), James Flavin (*Escort*), Jack Gardner (*Elevator Boy*), Beatrice Maude (*Jeff's Secretary*), Frank Mills (*Taxi Driver*), Emory Parnell (*Conway*), James Pierce (*Doorman*), Ronald R Rondell (*Waiter*), Ralph Sanford (*Store Checker*), Stanley Taylor (*Clerk*), Allen Wood (*Bellhop*), Barbara Woodell (*David's Secretary*), Sam Harris.

SUMMARY: A New York couple, Ann and David Smith, are in the middle of one of their legendary rows. So far, it's lasted for three days, five days short of their record. They make up, reaffirming their premarriage vow that neither party will ever leave the bedroom before they settle their arguments – no matter how long they last.

Over breakfast, Ann asks David if he would marry her if he were given the chance to make that decision all over again. To Ann's shock, he says no – although he loves her and doesn't want to leave her, he probably wouldn't have married her if he'd known what it entailed.

David leaves for work, where he is a partner in a law firm. His partner Jeff Custer is very understanding about David and Ann's relationship, as he is very fond of Ann too. A Mr Deever has been waiting to speak to David. Deever tells David that due to a minor legal technicality anyone who got married with an Idaho marriage licence in Nevada wasn't legally married – and as such Mr and Mrs Smith aren't actually Mr and Mrs. Mr Deever tells David that, just to be on the safe side, they had better get married again. David is quite amused by the concept, and books a meal for them that night at a restaurant they used to go to before they got married.

Mr Deever drops in on Ann, mainly because he remembered her from his old home town, Beecham. He tells her the truth, and she is appalled. Ann's mother, who is also there, is horrified and determined that David will make an honest woman of her. Ann tries to fit into the dress she wore on her wedding night, but it doesn't fit her any more. 'I can't understand anything hanging in a closet shrinking so much . . .'

When David fails to mention the marriage difficulty over dinner, Ann is furious. 'You beast! You know we're not married! You were never gonna tell me! You were gonna wait until . . . and then throw me aside like a squeezed lemon!' She is convinced that her marriage is over and throws him out. He goes to his gentlemen's club, the Beefeater, where he gets a room for the night. There he meets up with his old friend Chuck, who advises him to ignore the argument. Before he knows it, Chuck says, she'll be begging for him back.

Next day, he goes home only to find that the staff refuse to let him in, and that Ann is now calling herself Miss Krausheimer. David gets increasingly exasperated with Ann's behaviour – she even gets a job in a department store to try to support herself as a single woman. David's partner Jeff tries his best to reconcile the two of them. He has asked Ann to invite him over for dinner, and wants David to drop by unannounced at 9 p.m. When David drops by, he is shocked to discover that Jeff has agreed to be Ann's lawyer in their impending settlement case.

Jeff invites Ann to dinner the next night. David says that if she goes their relationship is over. When she agrees a time, David storms out, horrified.

Chuck then tries to set David up on a date with one of his friends of dubious morals. At the date, David is initially horrified by the woman he's being set up with, then realises that Ann and Jeff are dining there too. Ann is clearly jealous of David's behaviour, and decides to make a point by spending the rest of the night with Jeff.

They go to the funfair, where they get stuck on the parachute ride, suspended in midair as the rain pours down. When they get down from the ride, Ann takes Jeff home and gives him some brandy to ward off a potential cold. The alcohol goes to Jeff's head, and Ann misinterprets Jeff's drunken incapacity for good manners. Increasingly charmed by him, Ann goes home.

The next day, Ann goes to see Jeff at the office. Jeff's parents are visiting on their way to a vacation in the ski resort of Lake Placid. When David realises that Mr and Mrs Custer think that Jeff and Ann are a couple, he takes great pleasure in embarrassing her in front of them.

Despite their reservations, Mr and Mrs Custer invite Ann and Jeff to visit them in Lake Placid the next weekend. On their arrival, they are surprised to discover that David has been waiting all week in Lake Placid for Ann, clearly spending most of the week drunk. They put the insensible David to bed, but unbeknown to them David is neither ill nor drunk – just acting. Jeff comes to the conclusion that Ann won't be happy unless she's with David – despite the fact that he thinks she would be better off with him. Ann rushes back to David's room to care for him, but spots David through the window clearly conscious and smoking. She storms in and they have another row, David admitting that he is still in love with her.

She goes back to Jeff and asks him to marry her. He accepts. After dinner, Ann is clearly still having doubts and worries about David. She decides to make him hate her by play-acting that she and Jeff are getting carried away in a romantic clinch. Hearing this through the thin walls, David rushes next door, jealous. He grabs Ann in a headlock 'You have just seen her in one of her quieter moments . . .' adds David when Jeff's parents return at an inopportune moment. Still bickering, Ann tries to make a point and head back to the hotel on skis. She falls over and is completely unable to move. She rants and rages, impotent with fury.

Their gaze meets, and they hold each other, finally making up after their longest row yet.

CASTING: With Carole Lombard already committed to the film, the task of finding her sparring partner was considerably more difficult. They initially approached Cary Grant, who was unable to take the role owing to prior commitments, and then considered practically every leading man in Hollywood before finally settling on Robert Montgomery. Montgomery received a considerably higher salary for starring in the film than Hitchcock did for directing it.

ROOTS: The genesis of *Mr. and Mrs. Smith* came from a discussion. Carole Lombard, the well-known film actress, had become close friends with Alma and Alfred Hitchcock; indeed she was often invited for dinner at the Hitchcocks', along with her husband Clark Gable. She begged to work with her friend, and expressed a desire to appear in one of the 'screwball comedies' that were so popular at the time. The original story and screenplay, written by Norman Krasna, was submitted to RKO without a title, but both Hitchcock and Lombard were apparently desperate to work on it. It was only in hindsight that Hitchcock claimed to have never wanted to direct the film.

LEGACY: A cliché even in its day, the relationship between Mr and Mrs Smith has been slavishly copied by every sitcom couple since, from Desi Arnaz and Lucille Ball to Fred and Wilma Flintstone.

WHO'S WHO?: Robert Montgomery was the father of Elizabeth Montgomery, who would gain international fame from her role in the TV comedy series *Bewitched*.

THE USUAL SUSPECTS: Charles Halton also appeared in *Foreign Correspondent*.

KILLER LINES: David is impressed by the verbal dexterity and cultured manners of his dinner date, who tucks into her pheasant: 'Do you know what this peasant [sic] is? Chicken. And *tough* chicken at that!'
  When Jeff makes a sudden play for Ann's affections, she tells David that her new beau believes her husband is 'lucky it's not the South and I'm not his sister'. In retaliation, David resorts to a most profound legal insult, calling her a 'hillbilly ambulance chaser!'

THERE HE IS!: About halfway through the movie passing David Smith in front of his building.

MISOGYNY: It's amusing to a modern audience to discover that Ann is thrown out of her job at the department store because it's not 'company policy to employ married women'. For the particularly politically correct, many of the scenes could be considered to be objectionable. However, as Ann gets her own back on David on many, many occasions, the battle of the sexes is finely balanced here.

TABOOS: The Smiths have no concept at all of how privileged they are. They go to dine at a restaurant they used to frequent, and are appalled that a group of poor children are content to stand and watch them eat.

Ann's mother is utterly, utterly horrified that her daughter might be 'living in sin', albeit through no fault of her own. She pushes Ann to ensure that David puts things right as quickly as possible, and is firmly of the opinion that they should not spend any time together until the problem is sorted.

Finally, there is a very entertaining scene where Jeff tries to speak to his parents in the bathroom of his office. The constant banging and rattling of the pipes makes it almost impossible for them to hear each other. When Hitch originally planned the scene, it wasn't just the sound of banging pipes – it was the sound of flushing toilets that interrupted the dialogue. The studio executives believed this to be just too risqué and dubbed less obvious noises over the scene.

THE ICE MAIDEN: Carole Lombard excels in a role that marked her out as a typical Ice Maiden. Ann Smith is haughty, cold and totally convinced of her own infallibility. Despite this, she comes across as a sympathetic and almost likable character. Ann is so hurt by David's careless remark about not wanting to marry her again that she not only jumps to the wrong conclusions but she also appears to actively want to hurt her husband. It's more of a relief that the two of them end up back together at the end of the film, because surely nobody else would have either of them.

While Hitchcock was filming *Saboteur*, he learnt that Lombard – in whose house Hitch and his wife were living at the time – had been killed in a plane crash, at the tragically early age of 33.

WHAT THE PAPERS SAID: The American *Look* magazine was ecstatic in its praise for the film and for Hitchcock in particular: 'The striking thing about this film is that Hitchcock has employed the same strategy that marks his blood-chilling melodramas . . . The net effect is the same, too – another Alfred Hitchcock hit.'

FINAL ANALYSIS: Your appreciation of this film will depend less on your knowledge of Hitchcock, and more on whether or not you enjoy the 'screwball comedy' genre. If you dislike such films, you'll find *Mr. and Mrs. Smith* annoying and frustrating. If, however, you don't object to such movies, you may well find yourself appreciating the witty and sarcastic script and the ever more farcical situations that Ann and David find themselves in.

It's hard to actually like or admire either of the two main characters, though. David is a thoughtless buffoon and Ann a spoilt little madam. For a while, our sympathies switch to the generous and thoughtful Jeff. However, when we discover he's a teetotal puritan, we realise that once again Hitchcock has strung us along. All in all, an average film that has only just about stood the test of time. 5/10

Saboteur (1942)

(B & W – 108 mins)
Produced by Frank Lloyd & Jack H Skirball/Universal Pictures
Written by Alfred Hitchcock (story), Peter Viertel & Joan Harrison & Dorothy Parker

Original music: Frank Skinner
Photography: Joseph A Valentine
Film Editing: Otto Ludwig
Art Director: Robert F Boyle
Sound: Bernard B Brown
Set Continuity: Adele Cannon
Assistant Director: Fred Frank
Set Decorator: Russell A Gausman
Technician: William Hedgcock
Art Director: Jack Otterson
Musical Director: Charles Previn

CAST: Priscilla Lane (*Patricia Martin*), Robert Cummings (*Barry Kane*), Otto Kruger (*Charles Tobin*), Alan Baxter (*Mr Freeman*), Clem Bevans (*Neilson*), Norman Lloyd (*Fry*), Alma Kruger (*Mrs Van Sutton*), Vaughan Glaser (*Phillip Martin*), Dorothy Peterson (*Mrs Mason*), Ian Wolfe (*Robert the Butler*), Frances Carson (*Society Woman*), Murray Alper (*Truck Driver*), Kathryn Adams (*Young Mother*), Pedro de Córdoba (*Bones*), Billy Curtis (*Midget*), Marie LeDeaux (*Fat Woman*), Anita Sharp-Bolster (*Lorelei*), Jeanne Roher, Lynn Roher (*Siamese Twin*).

UNCREDITED CAST: Al Bridge (*Marine Sergeant*), Ralph Dunn (*Detective*), Pat Flaherty (*George*), Charles Halton (*Sheriff*), Selmer Jackson (*FBI Chief*), Milton Kibbee (*Man Killed in Movie Theatre*), Frank Marlowe (*Man in Newsreel Truck*), Emory Parnell (*Actor on Movie Screen*), Lee Phelps (*Plant Security*), Matt Willis (*Sheriff*).

SUMMARY: Barry Kane is a young man working in an aeroplane factory in California. He bumps into an unfamiliar colleague, Fry, who drops an envelope containing several $100 bills. Barry and his best friend

Ken return the money to Fry, who acts in a very suspicious manner. Before they can do anything about it, a fire breaks out in the factory. Barry rushes to help fight the fire, and is about to take a fire extinguisher from Fry when Ken snatches it off him, shouting 'Don't I get to play, too?' As Ken starts to tackle the blaze, the flames overwhelm him and Barry watches in horror as his friend burns to death.

Some hours later, Barry is explaining to the police exactly what happened. He tells them that Fry handed him the fire extinguisher, but no one else apparently saw anyone with Barry and Ken. Barry goes to visit Ken's mother to tell her how brave her son was. While Barry is with a neighbour looking for brandy, the police arrive. They don't believe Barry's story at all, as there is no record whatsoever of a worker called Fry. There was also evidence of sabotage at the factory, and the final straw is the fact that the extinguisher Barry gave to Ken was filled with gasoline. Barry returns just as the police have left, and is horrified to hear their accusations. Realising that he needs to find the mysterious Fry in order to clear his name, Barry heads to the only place he can – the address on the outside of the envelope that Fry dropped.

Barry catches a lift from a truck driver to Deep Springs Ranch in Springville. He discovers that the ranch is owned by the charming Mr Charles Tobin. Tobin denies knowing anything about Fry, but Barry accidentally discovers a telegram from Fry stating: 'All finished here. Joining Neilson in Soda City.' When confronted with this fact, Tobin admits his involvement in the plot to sabotage the factory, and that the police are on their way to arrest the dangerous saboteur Barry Kane. 'I'm a prominent citizen, widely respected . . . now which of us do you think the police will believe?' Barry tries to make a daring escape, but is eventually handcuffed and arrested.

On his way back to the police station, Barry causes a diversion and escapes from the police car. He then leaps from a high bridge into the river far below, making his escape. Later that day, Barry stumbles across a log cabin in the woods. He meets the owner, a nice old man called Phillip Martin. Barry tries to hide his handcuffs until he realises that the old man is in fact blind. Phillip's niece Patricia arrives home, and spots Barry's handcuffs. Phillip had heard them rattling as soon as Barry arrived, but had decided to trust the young man. Pat is horrified that her uncle could harbour a saboteur, but Phillip believes in Barry's innocence. Phillip tells Pat to take Barry to his friend, the local blacksmith, in order to get the handcuffs removed. Pat drives Barry, but tries to take him to the police instead. Barry manages to grab the wheel and steers the car out into the middle of the desert. Barry manages to sever through the chain of the handcuffs on the car engine's cooling fan. This of course causes the car to overheat shortly afterwards, leaving Pat and Barry stranded in the middle of the desert.

Barry and Pat stumble across a travelling circus, where they are hidden from the police by some of the performers, including a bearded lady, a pair of Siamese twins and a malevolent dwarf who acts and dresses a bit like Hitler. By the end of the night, Pat has become almost convinced of Barry's innocence. The circus drops them off the next morning in Soda City, a derelict old 'western'-type town. While searching a ramshackle deserted building, they hear a telephone ring in its locked back room. Breaking into the room, they discover a tripod and telescope which when aligned properly looks over at a nearby dam. A car pulls up outside the building, and Pat hides in an adjacent room. Barry waits to meet the occupants of the car, admits his identity and pretends to be part of the sabotage conspiracy. Barry tells the men (Neilson and Freeman) that he has been sent to meet them by Mr Tobin, and that they must help and protect him. Barry agrees to travel with them to New York, while Pat slips away and informs the police that the saboteurs are planning to blow up the dam.

Back in New York, the conspirators are getting worried. Their main office has been closed down, as the police have been closing in. Barry learns that they are planning 'a job' in Brooklyn the next day. Freeman takes Barry to Mrs Sutton's house. A wealthy socialite, Mrs Sutton provides sanctuary for the saboteurs. She is deeply worried that the huge ball she is holding that night will be disrupted by the arrival of new people such as Barry. Barry is astonished to discover that Pat is being held there too – when she heard the saboteurs planning to blow up the dam, she ran off to tell the local sheriff. Unfortunately for her, the sheriff was part of the conspiracy too. She assumes that Barry is indeed part of the conspiracy and gives him a piece of her mind. However, when Tobin arrives in the room, Barry is revealed to be the patriot he really is, and the spies decide to kill him. Barry and Pat create a diversion and escape downstairs into the middle of the society ball, determined to stop the act of terrorism planned for the next day – the bombing of a ship during its launch ceremony at the naval yards.

Both Pat and Barry try to convince the guests that they are actually in the middle of a nest of spies, but of course nobody believes them. They dance as the spies subtly close in on them, but get separated. With Pat nowhere to be seen, Barry grabs a microphone and is ready to denounce Mrs Sutton publicly. However, he soon notices that Pat is being held by the conspirators, and with her life in the balance gives himself up.

The next morning, Pat is being held in a high tower block in midtown Manhattan. While her guards are busy, she scribbles a 'help' note on a napkin using her lipstick and throws it out of the window, where a group of cab drivers find it. Barry is shut in the basement storeroom of Mrs Sutton's elegant mansion. He makes his escape by setting the sprinklers off, and makes his way to the Brooklyn Navy Yard.

He searches desperately for a sign of anything suspicious, when he suddenly notices Fry sitting in the back of a newsreel van. Barry dives for Fry, and they fight. A radio commentary runs in the background, counting down the seconds to the launch. Fry reaches for the button that will detonate the bomb on the launch ramp, and presses it. He is just too late, and the ship escapes major damage, foundering on to its side nonetheless. The van driver locks the rear doors, trapping Barry and Fry inside, and drives the newsreel van into the basement of the Rockefeller Center.

The police have rescued Pat from her captors and are lying in wait for Fry. When he returns with Barry and the van driver, there is an exchange of gunfire, and Fry runs for it. He makes his escape through the Radio City Music Hall Cinema, where once again shots are exchanged and one of the patrons is shot. A stampede takes place, and in the confusion Fry escapes once again. Barry is detained by the police yet again, so it is down to Pat to follow Fry. At a safe distance, she watches him as he heads for the Statue of Liberty. She phones the FBI and alerts them to the spy's whereabouts. The FBI tell her to keep him busy until they arrive. Fry notices Pat looking at him, and, mistaking it for a come-on, starts chatting to her. Eager to prevent him getting away again, Pat flirts back, making a terrible mistake when she lets slip that she already knows his name. Fry tries to escape, but the police and FBI have arrived, along with Barry. He climbs further upward, into the torch of the statue. Barry pursues Fry, and after a brief altercation Fry loses his footing and falls over the safety rail. Barry climbs over the rail himself in an attempt to save the only man who can confirm his innocence, but Fry plummets to his death. Despite this, Pat and Barry embrace as the police help them back to safety.

CASTING: Hitchcock originally wanted Gary Cooper and Barbara Stanwyck for the leading roles, with Harry Carey Sr as the chief villain. Cooper and Stanwyck both turned Hitchcock down, despite Hitch's previous attempts to cast Cooper in *Foreign Correspondent*. Gene Kelly, Henry Fonda and Gene Tierney were also linked with the parts.

ROOTS: There's a nod to Mary Shelley's *Frankenstein* in the sequence where Barry stumbles across the wise, blind old man in the countryside. As in the classic horror story, it's the blind man who can 'see' the truth about the stranger who has stumbled into his cottage and chastises his niece Pat for not being able to look past the handcuffs that Barry is wearing.

Another famous film had ten years previously seen the blonde heroine get dragged across New York by the charming villain, only to see the bad guy plummet to his death from the top of a famous landmark. We are not, of course, suggesting that *King Kong* (Merian C Cooper, Ernest B Schoedsack, 1933) had any impact on *Saboteur*!

WHO'S WHO?: The screenwriter Dorothy Parker was a member of the notorious Algonquin Round Table, a social circle of New York wit that included Robert Benchley (who appeared in and contributed to the script of *Foreign Correspondent*) and Harpo Marx. Parker suffered from suicidal tendencies, a problem she wrote about in her famous poem 'You Might As Well Live'.

Priscilla Lane also appeared in the black comedy *Arsenic and Old Lace* (Frank Capra, 1944), where she played the fiancée of the Cary Grant character.

Norman Lloyd, the eponymous saboteur, was later the associate producer and occasional director for *Alfred Hitchcock Presents*. He is perhaps best known these days for his long-running role in the TV series *St. Elsewhere*.

THE USUAL SUSPECTS: Ian Wolfe appeared in *Foreign Correspondent,* as did the uncredited Charles Halton. Norman Lloyd is also in *Spellbound*, while Robert Cummings returned to kiss Grace Kelly in *Dial M for Murder*.

THERE HE IS!: About an hour in, standing in front of Cut Rate Drugs in New York as the saboteurs' car stops.

POSTER: Against a backdrop of exploding planes and a huge, threatening shadow cast by the fleeing Cummings and Lane, the strapline states theatrically: '3000 miles of terror!' . . . which doesn't really tell us anything.

TRAILER: Captions proudly announce: 'The screen's Master of the unexpected brings you a significant story of today'. Then Robert Cummings, in character, tells us he is 'Barry Kane, *American*', before filling in the details that he's a fugitive accused of sabotage, but that he is searching for the real culprits. Another caption challenges that 'you'd like to say it can't happen here . . . but every jolting scene is true!'

THE ICE MAIDEN: Priscilla Lane is another classic Hitchcock blonde, cast very much from the Madeleine Carroll mould. Although she stands up to Robert Cummings's Barry with gutsy aplomb, she does tend to be a little too sweet for her own good once she realises that Barry is a good guy after all. Her final confrontation with Fry, using her feminine wiles to charm the villain into the police trap, is particularly well realised.

WHAT THE PAPERS SAID: The reviewer in *The Times* notes how Hitchcock fails to attempt anything startlingly original with *Saboteur*: 'He is content to take the old counters in the game of sabotage, flight and pursuit, and his interest, and that of the audience, lies in the cinematic pattern he makes of them.'

TRIVIA: The shot of the ship on its side towards the end (when Fry looks out of the cab window on his way to the Statue of Liberty) was an actual shot of the sinking of the USS *Normandie*, which had been sunk at its pier in what turned out to be an actual act of sabotage. (But it was the Mafia, not Nazi spies, who did it – they were hoping to persuade the government to pay them to provide protection against Nazi sabotage.) The US Navy wanted Hitchcock to delete it from the film, but he refused.

The world premiere of *Saboteur* took place in the Radio City Music Hall Cinema, which itself features in a prominent sequence in the picture.

There is no on-screen credit for the actor who portrays Barry's ill-fated best friend Ken, despite the fact that he gets several lines and acts as the catalyst for the rest of the plot.

FINAL ANALYSIS: In many respects, *Saboteur* is an amalgamation of two of Hitchcock's British films – *The 39 Steps* and *Sabotage*. Despite its many thematic and plot similarities, *Saboteur* stands up as a good movie in its own right. It's the second of three attempts (along with *Foreign Correspondent* and *North by Northwest*) to remake *The 39 Steps* for an American audience, taking in a number of familiar landmarks on the way. It could be rightly argued that it is little more that a series of set pieces (extremely well done set pieces, though) linked by a fragile plot that stands up to little in-depth scrutiny. Nevertheless, it's a very entertaining picture, with a clear message that Hitchcock felt needed to be told to an American audience – that their allies in Europe were suffering and needed their support. Having tried to get this message across subtly in *Foreign Correspondent*, here Hitch resorts to using his lead actor to ram the point home.

Robert Cummings is a strong and sympathetic lead, and it's intriguing why Hitch decided not to use him again for another ten years. His chemistry with Priscilla Lane, although not quite as electric as that between Robert Donat and Madeleine Carroll, still makes the film worth watching at moments when the plot seems to drag a little. **7/10**

Shadow of a Doubt (1943)
(Working title: *Uncle Charlie*)

(B & W – 106 mins)

Produced by Jack H Skirball/Universal Pictures

Written by Gordon McDonell (story), Thornton Wilder & Sally Benson & Alma Reville

Original music: Dmitri Tiomkin
Photography: Joseph A Valentine
Costume Design: Adrian, Vera West
Film Editing: Milton Carruth

Sound: Bernard B Brown
Set Continuity: Adele Cannon
Set Decorator: Russell A Gausman
Art Directors: John B Goodman & Robert F Boyle
Musical Director: Charles Previn
Sound Technician: Robert Pritchard
Set Decorator: Edward R Robinson
Assistant Directors: Ralph Slosser & William Tummel

CAST: Teresa Wright (*Young Charlie Newton*), Joseph Cotton (*Charlie Oakley*), MacDonald Carey (*Jack Graham*), Henry Travers (*Joseph Newton*), Patricia Collinge (*Emma Newton*), Hume Cronyn (*Herbie Hawkins*), Wallace Ford (*Fred Saunders*), Edna Mae Wonacott (*Ann Newton*), Charles Bates (*Roger Newton*), Irving Bacon (*Station Master*), Clarence Muse (*Railroad Porter*), Janet Shaw (*Louise*), Estelle Jewell (*Girlfriend*).

UNCREDITED CAST: Virginia Brissac (*Mrs Phillips*), Frances Carson (*Mrs Potter*), Earle S Dewey (*Mr Norton*), Edward Fielding (*Doctor on Train*), Sarah Edwards (*Doctor's Wife on Train*), Vaughan Glaser (*Dr Phillips*), Ruth Lee (*Mrs MacCurdy*), Eily Malyon (*Librarian*), John McGuire (*Detective*), Shirley Mills (*Young Girl*), Constance Purdy (*Mrs Martin*), Isabel Randolph (*Mrs Green*), Grandon Rhodes (*Reverend MacCurdy*), Byron Shores (*Detective*), Edwin Stanley (*Mr Green*), Minerva Urecal (*Mrs Henderson*).

SUMMARY: In a Philadelphia boarding house, Charlie Oakley hides out in his room, hundreds of loose dollar bills strewn across the floor. He's tired of life, bitter and cynical. His housekeeper tells him two men have been asking after him – the same two men who are watching his window from across the street. Charlie decides to visit his sister and favourite niece in Santa Rosa. Giving the two men the slip, he manages to wire his sister to warn her of his visit before boarding a train.

In Santa Rosa, his niece, also named Charlie, is similarly bored. She resents her family, who she feels are in a rut, and prays for a miracle. She decides to telegram her Uncle Charlie and on receiving his telegram for her mother, Emma, is surprised to discover he's already on his way.

Charlie finally arrives in Santa Rosa laden with gifts, including an emerald ring for his favourite niece. Young Charlie notices that the ring carries an inscription: 'TS from BM'. Her uncle offers to have it removed but she says she doesn't mind it; the thought that the previous owner was happy with the ring appeals to her.

Soon after, Uncle Charlie reads something in the newspapers that causes him some concern. He engages young Charlie's little brother Roger in a game that involves tearing up the newspaper. He successfully removes the page with the offending article, and hides it in his pocket. Later, young Charlie spies the page in her uncle's pocket and teases him, saying she knows he's hiding something. Uncle Charlie snaps at her, telling her he'd read something about someone he'd once known. He grabs her by the arm and snatches the page from her, telling her to mind her own business.

Emma brings Charlie breakfast in bed and tells him she has exciting news – the local paper want to interview him, and the Women's Guild, of which Emma is a member, want him to give a talk. She also tells him that while he was sleeping two men came to visit, asking if they could interview the household for a national survey. It seems they have been identified as a representative American family and the two men have asked to photograph them. Charlie rebukes her, believing she's foolish for agreeing to let strangers into her house, and tells her that he's never been photographed. Emma corrects him and sends young Charlie to fetch a photograph of him as a child. Emma remembers that the picture was taken the day her brother suffered a terrible accident. He had been riding on the bicycle their father had bought him for Christmas and as he'd rounded an icy corner he'd skidded out under a street car. He'd escaped with his life but, as Emma recalls, the event changed him: after that date he regularly found himself in 'mischief'.

The next morning, young Charlie escorts her uncle to the bank where her father works. Her uncle opens an account with a deposit of $40,000, making both Mr Newton and his boss very happy. As he's about to leave, Charlie is introduced to a Mrs Potter, a particularly merry widow, gleefully spending her late husband's money.

Returning to the Newtons' home, Uncle Charlie watches as two men approach the house. His niece realises they must be the survey-takers, but Uncle Charlie refuses to see them and slips round the back way. Young Charlie goes to find her mother in a state of great excitement trying to bake one of her favourite recipes to impress the men, but they seem more interested in Uncle Charlie and ask young Charlie to show them his room. She warns them that her uncle is unwilling to take part in the survey, but at that point one of the men sees him enter through the back stairs and photographs him. Uncle Charlie rips the film from the man's camera. The other man, Jack Graham, asks Emma if she might allow her daughter to act as his guide around town, and young Charlie accepts.

As they walk around the town, Jack continues to question Charlie about her uncle and she soon realises the survey was a cover for something else. Jack confesses to her that he's a police officer, sent to look for one of two suspects who match the description of a man who has murdered a number of widows out east. Charlie defends him and Jack promises that if her uncle turns out to be the man they're looking for they'll escort him out of town before arresting him, to spare her mother's feelings.

This news gets Charlie thinking. She visits the library late that night and finds an edition of the newspaper her uncle damaged and reads an article about the so-called 'Merry Widow Murderer'. Then she sees that the most recent victim had the same initials as those on the ring her uncle gave her.

When the family are next assembled for dinner, young Charlie has noticeably cooled towards her loving uncle. She refuses to sit next to him and after he gets particularly morbid and brooding at the dinner table she runs from the house. Her uncle runs after her and drags her into a bar. There he confronts her, asking her what she thinks she knows. She returns the ring he gave her and tells him to leave her and her family alone.

A few days later, Charlie overhears her father talking to a friend about the Merry Widow Murderer and learns that the police had tried to apprehend a man but that he ran away to an airport where he died tragically after running into a propeller. Uncle Charlie also hears the news and appears relieved – until he realises that his niece is not going to let him off the hook.

Jack Graham tells Charlie that they've called the search off and confesses that he's fallen in love with her. He lets her think about it and returns home. As he drives away, Charlie realises this leaves her to face her uncle alone. The next day, leaving by the back stairs, Charlie loses her footing and falls. Later on, she inspects the staircase to find one of the struts in the banister has obviously been sawn away. Uncle Charlie disturbs her and she asks him when he intends to leave. He tells her he's decided to settle down, to never leave. He points out to her that she can never air her suspicions without endangering her father's job at the bank and running the risk of breaking her mother's heart. And, as she no longer has the ring, she has no evidence against him.

The family prepare for Uncle Charlie's speech to the women's club. He manipulates things so that his niece is to travel to the club with him in the car with the rest of the family going by taxi. But when young Charlie goes to inspect the car she finds it has been left running and the garage is filled with fumes. As she struggles to turn the car off, the door to the garage slams shut, locking her in. Her father's friend Herbie happens to be passing and hears her cries. He runs into the house and raises the alarm and manages to save her. She recovers and insists on staying behind to prepare for their guests after the speech. Once the family have left, she tries to phone Jack at all the numbers he left her but to no avail. Then she sneaks into her uncle's room and manages to find the ring just as her family and their guests return. The speech was a great success and Charlie is basking in the glory until he spies the ring back on his niece's hand. He announces that he has decided to leave town the next day, much to his sister's distress.

The family see Charlie off at the station. He invites the children on board to see his cabin and takes Charlie aside to tell her that he accepts that she was right to tell him to leave. But just as the children step off the train he seizes Charlie, waiting for the train to speed up so he can throw her on to the tracks. In the struggle, he slips, falling into the path of another train.

Santa Rosa arranges a huge funeral procession, lamenting the loss of one of their own. Only young Charlie and her boyfriend Jack know of the truth.

TITLES: Couples waltz across the screen in full ballroom suits and gowns to *The Merry Widow*, seemingly an inappropriate image until its relevance is revealed by the revelation of Charlie Oakley's crimes. This image also appears at a number of key scenes in the movie.

ROOTS: It's often said that Orson Welles's *The Magnificent Ambersons* had a major influence on Hitch for this movie, notably the nostalgic tone. Another possible inspiration is the real-life murder case of Earle Nelson, who killed a succession of mainly middle-aged women in the US and Canada and who was hanged at Winnipeg in 1928.

LEGACY: *Shadow of a Doubt* was remade as *Step Down to Terror* in 1958 by Harry Keller, and as a TV movie in 1991 starring Mark (*St. Elsewhere*) Harmon. The 1974 movie, *Impulse* (William Grefe) acts almost like a prequel to the film, with William Shatner (yes, William Shatner!) scamming widows out of their savings before killing them.

WHO'S WHO?: Teresa Wright made her debut in William Wyler's *Little Foxes* (1942) alongside Herbert Marshall, Bette Davies and Patricia Collinge (who here plays her mother Emma). Wyler cast her again in *Mrs Miniver* (1943), for which she won an Oscar. Most recently she appeared in Francis Ford Coppola's *The Rainmaker* (1997).

Henry Travers (*Joseph Newton*) is fondly remembered as Clarence, James Stewart's guardian angel in Frank Capra's *It's a Wonderful Life* (1946).

THE USUAL SUSPECTS: Joseph Cotton got his big break thanks to his friendship with Orson Welles, who cast him in *Citizen Kane* (1941) and *The Magnificent Ambersons* (1942) as well as co-starring with him in *The Third Man* (Carol Reed, 1949). He also appears in Hitch's *Under Capricorn* as well as the *Alfred Hitchcock Presents* episodes 'State of the Union', 'Breakdown', 'Together' and 'Dead Weight'.

Hume Cronyn also appeared in *Lifeboat* and the *Alfred Hitchcock Presents* episodes 'Kill with Kindness' and 'The Impromptu Murder', as well as providing the adaptations for *Rope* and *Under Capricorn*. He starred opposite his wife, Jessica Tandy (*The Birds*), in both *Cocoon* (Ron Howard, 1985) and **batteries not included* (Matthew Robbins, 1987).

MacDonald Carey (*Jack Graham*) appeared in the *Alfred Hitchcock Presents* episode 'Coyote Moon'. Wallace Ford pops up in *Spellbound*.

KILLER LINES: The ever-precocious Ann observes: 'The ones that say they don't want anything always get more in the end,' and later boasts: 'I never make up anything. I get everything from my books. They're all true.' Brat.

Uncle Charlie shares at least one philosophy with the authors of this book: 'I can't face the world in the morning. I must have coffee before I can speak.'

Uncle Charlie lets slip his view of city women in a chilling speech at the dinner table: 'The cities are full of women, middle-aged widows, husbands dead, husbands who've spent their lives making fortunes, working and working. And then they die and leave their money to their wives, their silly wives. And what do the wives do, these useless women? You see them in the hotels, the best hotels, every day by the thousands, drinking the money, eating the money, losing the money at bridge, playing all day and all night, smelling of money, proud of their jewellery but of nothing else, horrible, faded, fat, greedy women . . . Are they human or are they fat, wheezing animals, hmm? And what happens to animals when they get too fat and too old?'

When young Charlie confronts him he is scornful of her: 'What do you know really? You're just an ordinary little girl living in an ordinary little town. You wake up every morning of your life and you know perfectly well that there's nothing in the world to trouble you. You go through your ordinary little day and at night you sleep your untroubled, ordinary little sleep filled with peaceful, stupid dreams. And I brought you nightmares.'

THERE HE IS!: On the train to Santa Rosa, Hitchcock sits with his back to us, playing cards. He has the entire suit of spades in his hand.

AWARDS: Selected for preservation by the National Film Registry of the Library of Congress.

THEMES AND MOTIFS: Early on in the film, young Charlie claims that she and her uncle are like twins, and Hitchcock plays upon the idea of doubles, just as he would later in *Strangers on a Train*: when we first see Uncle Charlie, he is stretched along his bed, facing left, bored with his life; when we first see his niece, Charlie Newton, she too is lying on her bed, facing right and bemoaning how dull her life is; there are two sets of detectives (a pair outside Charlie Oakley's apartment, another outside the Newtons') and two suspects for the killings; a bar called Till Two where Uncle Charlie orders two double brandies; and of course the recurring image of the waltzing couples dancing to 'The Merry Widow'. This also adds to the idea of the transference of guilt – Charlie acts like the conscience that is missing from her uncle, and when the police come looking for him it is she who feels trapped, knowing that Uncle Charlie's arrest could destroy her mother.

There's also a common thread of superstition: Charlie Oakley is first seen living at an address with the house number 13 (unlucky for some), and when Charlie Newton puts her hat on her bed her father removes it, saying that he doesn't want to invite trouble; the ring that Uncle Charlie gives his niece is an emerald, traditionally a gem linked with bad luck; Young Ann chants a skipping rhyme as she hops from paving stone to paving stone: 'Step on a crack and break your mother's back', and gleefully tells Jack Graham that she's broken her mother's back three times already that day.

TRAILER: Over a series of clips comes the powerful strapline: 'Terror warning her to kill . . . or be killed'.

WHAT THE PAPERS SAID: In a review headed MR. HITCHCOCK RETURNS TO FORM the critic for *The Times* declares the films of Hitchcock to be 'one of the greatest treats the cinema has to offer'. Enthused by the performance of Joseph Cotton, the reviewer nevertheless accounts the film's success squarely at Hitch, saying: 'The end is neat and ironical, but not too artificially so, and *Shadow of a Doubt* will long stay in the mind as a film of tense and cumulative interest.'

FINAL ANALYSIS: 'He said people like us had no idea what the world was really like.' *Shadow of a Doubt* is possibly Hitchcock's most nostalgic and sentimental film, and it's one he frequently cited as being a particular favourite of his. Certainly it's his most personal. Completed so soon after the death of his mother, *Shadow of a Doubt* contains a mother figure so lovingly realised as to bear open Hitchcock's loss: he names Charlie's mother Emma, after his own, and slips in a few small biographical details, such as the mother's lack of comprehension over the technology behind the telephone: 'Mama, you don't have to shout,' her daughter says, before observing to her father how she appears to be trying to 'cover the distance by sheer lung power', a habit of his late mother's. Charlie's younger sister is, like Hitchcock, an avid reader of adventure novels such as *Ivanhoe*, and Hitchcock even seems to identify with the murderous Uncle Charlie, who compliments the bank manager on his attention to detail.

A side plot, that of Joseph Newton and his pal Herbie, sees the two men discussing murder novels with great enthusiasm. As he had done before, in *Suspicion*, and would do again in *Strangers on a Train*, Hitchcock has the two characters discussing various possible methods of dispatching an intended victim. Herbie seems to misunderstand the motive behind the need to murder, being more concerned with the planting of carefully thought-out clues than actually getting away with the crime. Herbie's a sweet comic character who clearly hides a dark side, just like the charming Uncle Charlie, with the suggestion that he harbours desires to rid himself of his infirm mother. This again hints at the conflict that Hitchcock may have been feeling at the time, trapped thousands of miles away from his dying mother, wishing her suffering would end, yet feeling guilt-ridden when she eventually died.

Shadow of a Doubt has dated slightly over the years, largely thanks to the lack of subtlety behind most modern cinematic psychopaths. Nothing major seems to happen for most of the film, with Hitchcock preferring to take his time building up the evidence against Uncle Charlie, and as a result it may be a little dull for some viewers. Yet it's a film of amazing depth and a gamut of conflicting emotions that's almost as hard to pin down as some of his later classics like *Vertigo* and *Marnie*. 7/10

World War Two Short Films (1944)

(B & W)

Produced by the Ministry of Information

Written by Angus MacPhail & JOC Orton

Photography: Günther Krampf
Filmed at Welwyn Studios, with 'the co-operation of French writers, artists and technicians serving in Britain'

Bon Voyage

CAST: John Blythe (*Dougal*)

SUMMARY: A young RAF pilot, Sergeant Dougal, is being debriefed in London by French officials about his escape from occupied territory that was 'too good to be true'. Dougal recounts the tale of how he and his colleague Godowski were hiding in Reims, awaiting instructions from the Resistance on how to escape. Godowski goes to a café to meet their next contact, but instead is followed by 'a bounty-hunting Vichy bastard', whom he ends up having to kill in a wine cellar. Worried that the Vichy government will react extremely badly to the death of one of their operatives, they go back to the cellar in order to hide the corpse, but it has already been moved by their Resistance contacts. The contacts give them directions to their next destination, a hotel operated by another sympathiser. The following morning in the hotel, two policemen question Dougal, who claims to be an Irish factory worker.

Dougal and Godowski leave, and are contacted on a train by a female

Resistance fighter. The train stops in a tunnel and they make their escape. Dougal explains to the French officer that the woman took them to her father's farm, where he and Godowski were forced to roll dice in order to decide who got the one space on the escape plane bound for England. Talking to Jeanne, the Resistance worker, Dougal raises some doubts in her mind about Godowski. He tells her that he found Godowski smoking an English cigarette, and that he had been followed by the Vichy spy from the wrong café.

The French officer tells Dougal that his friend Godowski was in fact a Gestapo agent, following the escape route in order to identify key Resistance workers. Learning that Jeanne was murdered by Godowski, Dougal is contrite and realises that in war it is important to know exactly whom you are putting your trust in.

Aventure Malgache
(aka *Madagascar Landing*)

SUMMARY: *'The exploits of the Resistance in France are acclaimed the world over. The story we are about to tell you is true. It may not help you to share these heroic times with the French people, but it shows how the same spirit animated even the furthest colonies.'*

The Molière players are in their dressing room, getting ready to go on set. One actor mentions to another that his face reminds him of an opportunist turncoat he knew when he was in the Resistance. He then relates the adventure that he had in the Resistance, running an illegal radio station and dodging the Nazis. Although on many occasions he ran the risk of execution, he made a stand against the Madagascan official who sided with the Vichy regime and encouraged his people not to support the Allies.

FINAL ANALYSIS: These two short movies are, if truth be told, little more than an interesting diversion. Of the two, it's *Bon Voyage* that is clearly the more accomplished, with a plot that holds the interest of the viewer, some decent characterisation and a genuinely shocking moment (the murder of Jeanne). Even though it's presented in French, Bon Voyage is an entertaining film and well worth a look. The same, unfortunately, cannot be said of *Aventure Malgache*, which has to be the most tedious 35 minutes in the entire Hitchcock canon. There is no suspense, no involvement in the activities of the characters, and a plot so limp that it's barely noticeable.

Although it was conceived as part of the war effort, it's hardly surprising that *Aventure Malgache* was never screened, as it would be unlikely to inspire acts of heroism from anybody. However, it's a great

shame that *Bon Voyage* was never used to promote its 'careless talk costs lives' message, as it gets its point across economically and effectively.
Bon Voyage – 7/10; *Aventure Malgache* – 2/10

Lifeboat (1944)

(B & W – 96 mins)

Produced by Kenneth MacGowan/20th Century Fox

Written by John Steinbeck, screenplay by Jo Swerling

Music: Hugo Friedhofer
Photography: Glen MacWilliams
Costume Design: René Hubert
Film Editing: Dorothy Spencer
Art Director: James Basevi
Technical Adviser: Thomas Fitzsimmons
Recording Directors: Bernard Freericks & Roger Heman
Set Decorators: Frank E Hughes & Thomas Little
Musical Director: Emil Newman
Make-up Artist: Guy Pearce
Art Director: Maurice Ransford
Special Effects: Fred Sersen

CAST: Tallulah Bankhead (*Constance Porter*), William Bendix (*Gus Smith*), Walter Slezak (*Willi, the German Submarine Commander*), Mary Anderson (*Alice MacKenzie*), John Hodiak (*John Kovac*), Henry Hull (*Charles D 'Ritt' Rittenhouse*), Heather Angel (*Mrs Higgins*), Hume Cronyn (*Stanley Garrett*), Canada Lee (*George 'Joe' Spencer*), William Yetter Jr (*German Sailor*).

SUMMARY: A freighter is torpedoed in the Atlantic Ocean during World War Two. Already inside the one remaining lifeboat, a journalist, Connie Porter, is waiting to see if anyone else has survived the attack. Connie has managed to salvage many of her prize possessions from the wreck – a fur coat, her Cartier diamond bracelet, a typewriter and a miniature film camera. Her first companion turns out to be John Kovac, one of the crewmen from the ship, whom she takes an instant dislike to when he accidentally knocks Connie's camera overboard as he helps some more survivors clamber into the lifeboat, a radio operator called Stan Garrett, Nurse Alice MacKenzie and a millionaire, Charles 'Ritt' Rittenhouse. Alice is trying to care for a seaman, Gus Smith, who has a badly injured leg. Also joining the lifeboat's complement are the steward Joe Spencer – nicknamed 'Charcoal' in a politically incorrect fashion by Connie – and an English woman, Mrs Higgins, who is carrying the corpse of her recently deceased baby. The final passenger is a German from the U-boat that torpedoed their freighter – apparently the U-boat suffered damage itself and was sunk.

Kovak wants to throw the German overboard, but many of the others object, particularly Connie (who can speak German) and Ritt. Kovac can't agree: 'The boat's too small right now for me and this German.'

After a vote on the matter, the survivors decide to allow the German to stay. Mrs Higgins is having great difficulty in dealing with the loss of her child. After they have buried the baby at sea, she tries to jump overboard herself. Eventually, under cover of darkness, she succeeds.

Ritt then seems to take charge of the group, organising the passengers so that they can survive in the middle of the ocean until they are rescued. Kovac and Joe build a sail, to help them propel the boat, hopefully in the direction of Bermuda. Unfortunately, Kovac and Joe are uncertain of the exact direction to head in. Connie and Ritt want to take the German's word on the correct way to head to Bermuda, but Kovac persuades the rest of the crew not to trust him – especially when Connie makes the German reveal that he was actually the captain of the U-boat.

Gus notices that his leg has become gangrenous. Alice is reluctant to operate, as she has never undertaken such a procedure before. The German claims that he was a surgeon before the war, and offers to perform the amputation. Gus is scared that if he loses his leg he will also lose his dancing-crazy girlfriend, but eventually realises that the operation is the only way to save his life. Connie gives Gus all of her brandy, which causes him to pass out before they begin the operation.

The amputation complete, the boat seems to be on a favourable course towards Bermuda with a good prevailing wind. Kovac is still disinclined to trust the German – as a captain, he would be certain to know exactly where other U-boats and supply ships are likely to be. Despite Kovac's misgivings, the consensus appears to be that they should follow the German's suggested directions. As a storm whips up, they discover that the German has actually been hiding a compass. At that moment, a huge wave sweeps Stan overboard. As the crew struggle to rescue him, the German assumes command, choosing that moment to reveal that he speaks perfect English and has understood everything they've been discussing. Although they manage to rescue Stan, they lose their rations, water and mast.

Willi the German seems to have taken command of the boat, the will to live slipping away from the others. The storm has blown them off course, and their only hope of survival is to be rescued by a German supply ship, which will presumably take them straight to a concentration camp. Gus, still weak from his operation, is even more desperate for a drink than the others. About to drink some seawater, he is stopped by Alice, who warns him that it will only make him thirstier. The tensions between the survivors start to mount, and they start to bicker and argue among themselves, and even the hope of a rainstorm turns into a bitter disappointment. Gus drinks the salty seawater, and begins to hallucinate. While all the others are asleep, Gus spots Willi drinking fresh water from a bottle he has concealed. Willi pushes the crippled and unstable Gus overboard, the others waking up only as they hear his final cries.

They confront Willi, eager to know why he didn't prevent Gus from 'committing suicide'. When they notice that Willi is sweating, they realise that he must have been drinking fresh water. They discover the concealed bottle, and realise that Gus's death wasn't suicide. Willi's cold-blooded response – 'to survive, one must have a plan' – is the final straw for the others, who round on the German, beat him senseless, then throw him overboard to drown.

Shocked and numbed by what they have just done – by what they have just become – the survivors react in very different ways. Stan and Alice, who have become very close over the previous few days, decide to get married if they survive long enough to get rescued. Connie tries to instil a bit of energy and self-worth into her comrades, using her precious Cartier bracelet as bait in an attempt to catch a fish for essential food and water. Just as they get a bite, Joe notices a ship on the horizon, and Connie loses her grip on her last possession as it sinks to the ocean floor. The ship is a German supply vessel, and they experience a combination of elation and despair. Just as the ship is about to pick them up, it is shelled by another ship, an Allied vessel. As the German ship tries to escape, it narrowly misses the lifeboat before being hit itself and sinking.

As the Allied ship heads towards them to pick them up, a survivor from the shelled German supply ship climbs into the boat. The German, who is barely older than a boy, pulls a gun on them. Ritt wants to throw the boy overboard, but when Connie and Joe manage to disarm him they see that the boy is terrified, expecting them to kill him then and there. Thinking about the losses they have sustained – Gus, Mrs Higgins, her baby, Willi – they spare the boy and wait for rescue.

ROOTS: Hitchcock originally wanted Ernest Hemingway, author of *The Old Man and the Sea* and *A Farewell to Arms*, to work on the script. When his efforts came to nothing, he persuaded the celebrated author John Steinbeck (*Of Mice and Men*) to work on a plot outline.

LEGACY: Remade as a sci-fi thriller by Ron Silver in 1993.

WHO'S WHO?: Hodiak was married to Anne Baxter of *I Confess*.

THE USUAL SUSPECTS: Hume Cronyn had earlier appeared in *Shadow of a Doubt*.

KILLER LINES: When Kovac notices Connie filming a baby's milk bottle floating past, he angrily retorts: 'Why don't you wait for the baby to float by and photograph that?'

Ritt neatly sums up the plight the survivors find themselves in: 'We're all sort of fellow travellers, in a mighty small boat on a mighty big ocean.

The more we quarrel and criticise and misunderstand each other, the bigger the ocean gets and the smaller the boat gets.'

Connie manages to put it more succinctly: 'Dying together's even more personal than living together.'

THERE HE IS!: Making a cameo appearance in a movie set in a boat in the middle of the ocean was always going to be tricky. Having briefly entertained the suggestion that he should float past the camera as a corpse, he changed his mind, realising it would simply make people laugh and shatter the tension. Instead he devised possibly his most ingenious appearance yet.

So keep an eye open for the moment when one of the characters is seen reading a newspaper. In an advertisement for the weight-loss product, Reduco, 'before' and 'after' pictures clearly show two images of Hitchcock, who had genuinely lost a huge amount of weight prior to filming *Lifeboat*.

AWARDS: *Lifeboat* was Oscar-nominated for Best Photography, Best Writing (Original Story) and Best Director. Tallulah Bankhead won a New York Film Critics' Circle Award for Best Actress.

THEMES AND MOTIFS: Survival of the fittest, the Nietzschean philosophy that led to the concept of the *Übermensch* ('superman'), is examined and deconstructed in depth here. Hitchcock shows that war can dehumanise anybody, even the sympathetic heroes of the film. We sympathise with the uncontrolled fury that overwhelms the survivors when they realise that Willi has killed Gus, but it's also easy to forget that they are murderers, plain and simple. The added fact that it's the sweet nurse, dedicated to saving lives, who snaps first makes the message all the more powerful.

There is hope, however, that democracy can survive. Hitch clearly shows his audience that the only way in which a more powerful enemy can be defeated is by putting aside petty differences in geographical boundaries and working together. The weary British are represented by the upbeat and chipper Stan, as well as the emotionally distraught Mrs Higgins, who has suffered so many losses that she is forced to give up. Americans of all different classes, backgrounds and races are able to work together – even Gus, who was born Schmidt but changed his name to Smith because of the war. In short, Hitchcock's message is that the Allies must never underestimate the intelligence and cunning of their enemies, and that the only way to win is to work together.

TABOOS: The black sailor 'Charcoal' – such a name would certainly be taboo today – expresses some surprise when the other survivors allow him to vote on their decisions. It's easy to forget that such a concept may not have been controversial in the least when the movie was made.

MUSIC: Aside from the opening and closing titles, there is no musical score for *Lifeboat*. This was partly due to the absurd concept that it would be difficult to dump an orchestra in the middle of the ocean – by the same train of thought, placing a film crew there might be somewhat difficult, too.

POSTER: 'Six men and three women – against the sea and each other'.

WHAT THE PAPERS SAID: The American critic Bosley Crowther argued: 'We would never in the world have believed that a film could have been made which sold out democratic ideals and elevated the Nazi superman. Mr Hitchcock and Mr Steinbeck failed to grasp just what they had wrought.' However, the reviewer in *The Times* had spotted the key argument that Hitchcock makes about the superiority of the 'master race'. 'It turns out that the captain is keeping up his strength and spirits by drinking water he has secreted, taking vitamin pills and setting a course by a concealed compass; in short, that he owes his supremacy to fraud and lies.'

COSTUME: During the studio filming, the set was visited by a female reporter, who was shocked and scandalised to notice that Talullah Bankhead wasn't wearing any underwear. When Hitchcock was asked if he could do anything about Bankhead's outrageous exhibitionism, he allegedly replied that he wasn't sure if it was a matter for the costume or hairdressing departments.

Nonetheless, the costume department does a sterling job of damaging and dirtying down the cast's outfits as the picture progresses. The importance of Connie's possessions – including her fur coat and Cartier bracelet – is effectively represented by Tallulah Bankhead's glamour.

TRIVIA: Many of the cast caught severe colds and chills from being doused with thousands of gallons of cold water for weeks on end. Tallulah Bankhead even ended up with a bout of pneumonia.

FINAL ANALYSIS: Riveting, disturbing and claustrophobic, *Lifeboat* could never be described as an easy ride. The darkest corners of the human condition are laid bare here: as viewers, we wonder if we would be capable of behaving as badly as the supposed heroes of the film do. The most shocking aspect of the beating and murder of the German captain Willi is that it's the characters who have protested against such an action who initiate the violence. We are forced to consider if war corrupts even the best and most noble of intentions – in short, if 'good' has to perform 'evil' acts in order to survive, does 'good' become inherently 'evil'? There are no easy answers here, providing us with one of the most nihilistic films Hitchcock ever produced. 8/10

Spellbound (1945)
(Working title: *The House of Dr. Edwardes*)

(B & W – 111 mins)

Produced by David O Selznick/Selznick International Pictures

Adapted by Angus MacPhail & Ben Hecht, based on the novel *The House of Dr. Edwardes* by Francis Beeding (pseudonym for John Leslie Palmer and Hilary Aidan St George Saunders)

Music composed by Miklós Rózsa
Photography: George Barnes
Costume Design: Howard Greer
Production Design: James Basevi
Film Editing: Hal C Kern & William H Ziegler
Special Effects: Jack Cosgrove
Dream Sequence: Salvador Dali
Sound: Richard Deweese
Art Director: John Ewing
Assistant Director: Lowell J Farrell
Set Decorator: Emile Kuri
Psychiatric Adviser: May E Romm

CAST: Ingrid Bergman (*Dr Constance Peterson*), Gregory Peck (*Dr Anthony Edwardes/John Ballantine*), Michael Chekhov (*Dr Brulov*), Leo G Carroll (*Dr Murchison*), Rhonda Fleming (*Mary Carmichael*), John Emery (*Dr Fleurot*), Norman Lloyd (*Garmes*), Bill Goodwin (*House Detective*), Steven Geray (*Dr Graff*), Donald Curtis (*Harry*), Wallace Ford (*Hotel Stranger*), Art Baker (*Lt Cooley*), Regis Toomey (*Sergeant Gillespie*), Paul Harvey (*Dr Hanish*).

UNCREDITED CAST: Jean Acker (*Matron*), Richard Bartell (*Ticket Man*), Harry Brown (*Gateman*), Joel Davis (*Younger John Ballantine*), Edward Fielding (*Dr Edwardes*), Teddy Infuhr (*Ballantine's Brother*), Victor Kilian (*Sheriff*), George Meader (*Railroad Clerk*), Matt Moore (*Policeman*), Addison Richards (*Police Captain*), Erskine Sanford (*Dr Galt*), Janet Scott (*Norma Kramer*), Clarence Straight (*Secretary at Police Station*), Dave Willock (*Bellboy*).

SUMMARY: Dr Constance Peterson works at an asylum, specialising in emotional disorders. The head of the asylum, Dr Murchison, is about to retire after recent accusations of senility, and there is much excitement among the other doctors when they learn he is to be replaced by Dr Anthony Edwardes, celebrated author of a number of authoritative texts on psychology. Dr Edwardes arrives and the other doctors are struck by how much younger he is than they expected. Certainly, he has an instant effect on Constance Peterson, who is taken by his strong good looks and charming disposition.

Constance's first suspicions about their new head arise at dinner on the first night, when he seems perturbed by grooves left by her fork on the tablecloth. Later that day, Edwardes sends a note to her asking her to help with a patient, Garmes, who has confessed to him that he murdered his father. However, Constance tells him Garmes is merely suffering from a guilt complex and expresses the belief that it probably stems from childhood jealousy that has managed to remain with him through adulthood. Edwardes seems interested by the case, even though, as Constance reminds him, he has seen many such cases before.

The other doctors comment on Edwardes's attention to Constance and mock her playfully, commenting on the way she blushes every time they mention his name. Late at night she sneaks to the library to read a copy of Edwardes's book *The Labyrinth of the Guilt Complex*, which, she notices, is signed by the author. She borrows the book, then enters Edwardes's room, where she finds him reading. She tells him she wants to discuss his book with him, but quickly confesses this is just an excuse to speak with him. He tells her he feels there's something between them too. As they kiss he notices the faint lines in her robe and seems strangely anxious about them, as he had earlier been about the fork grooves. He excuses himself, claiming he's been suffering from stress.

At that moment a call comes through, telling him that Garmes has tried to slit his own throat and that he requires instant surgery. Edwardes and Constance rush to be there for the operation, where Edwardes seems to have an episode and begins ranting about guilt complexes. Constance orders that he be taken back to his room. As she sits by his bedside, she compares the handwritten note he sent her about Garmes with the dedication in his book – the two styles of writing are completely different.

When he wakes, he once again apologises for his behaviour and Constance asks him who he really is. He tells her Edwardes is dead and that he took his place, but that he doesn't know his own identity, except that he suspects he's guilty of murder. He shows her a cigarette case inscribed with the initials 'JB.' She offers to help him remember what happened.

The secretary of the real Dr Edwardes comes to the institution. She has worked for him for five years, and confirms that the man they believed was Dr Edwardes is an impostor. She had been worried about him and came to the institution to find out what happened. She shows the other doctors a photo of the real Edwardes. Dr Murchison comes to the conclusion that the impostor is a paranoid amnesiac who must have murdered the original. When he brings in the police Constance tells them she suspected something was wrong. As Murchison leaves he hands her a note that has been slipped under Constance's door – it's from 'Edwardes', and it explains to her that he has decided to leave, and that he doesn't want to involve her in his problems. He signs the note 'J.B.' After much deliberation, she decides to follow him to the Empire Hotel in New York.

As she sits in the hotel lobby, a man pesters her. He's frightened off by the house detective. The detective boasts that he is very intuitive and claims he can tell things about her. He guesses that she's a schoolteacher looking for her husband after a quarrel. She plays along with him and asks for his help in finding her 'husband'. She gives him a description of 'Edwardes' and through this the detective helps her find the man's room number. Surprised that she has found him, 'Edwardes' tells her he doesn't want her to throw her career away because of him. She tells him she's not been able to work since he left, and that she's here as his doctor, not because of love. Despite this, they kiss passionately.

The confused man reads in a newspaper that the police are looking for a missing patient of the real Dr Edwardes and makes the assumption that he must be the wanted man. Constance refuses to believe he's responsible for Edwardes's disappearance, identifying his guilt fantasy with some event from his childhood. Constance then notices that her picture has been printed in the paper in connection with the investigation over Edwardes's disappearance and suggests they leave the hotel immediately. She decides that she needs help and takes 'Edwardes' to see her old tutor, Dr Brulov.

They arrive at Brulov's to find him being questioned by the police. He tells them that Edwardes took a patient on holiday (against Brulov's advice) in the belief that it would help him overcome his problems. Once the police have left, Constance introduces her latest patient as her new husband, 'John Brown'. Her tutor seems overjoyed at her news and sets up the spare room for the 'newly-weds'. Tired from their travelling, they retire for the evening.

The next morning, however, Dr Brulov forces Constance to come clean, having realised they are not married – they have no wedding rings and no luggage. He found 'John' sleepwalking in the middle of the night carrying a razor and managed to slip a sedative in a glass of milk to knock him out. He thinks that her companion is somehow linked to Edwardes's disappearance. He threatens to call the police, but Constance begs him not to; she believes a police investigation would ruin any chances for him to recover. She asks for his help in finding the truth and reluctantly he agrees.

Brulov tells his new patient he believes he's trying to hide something and that maybe his dreams might help him. He tells them about a dream that he keeps having in which he's playing cards at a table in what seems to be a gambling house with images of eyes all over the walls. A seminaked woman (who he says looks like Constance) comes over to his table. He deals the seven of clubs to a man with a beard. The man claims he's got 21 and turns his cards over – but the cards are blank, just like the face of the proprietor of the casino, who accuses the man of cheating.

Next he finds himself looking at a sloping roof and a man with a misshapen wheel, which he drops from the roof. Finally he's running pursued by something with a great pair of wings.

After relating his dream, 'John' looks out of the window to see that it is snowing and immediately suffers another anxiety attack. Constance realises that he's haunted by a memory of snow tracks. She believes Edwardes went skiing and took 'John' with him. The bearded man in the dream is presumably Dr Edwardes. The winged figure is herself. 'John' suddenly remembers that the place Edwardes took him to was called Gabriel Valley. She suggests that she, therefore, must take him to Gabriel Valley, despite his fear that he murdered Edwardes and that returning to the scene of the crime might trigger him to kill again. Constance is unperturbed; she doesn't believe he killed Edwardes.

She takes him skiing. As they ski they find themselves heading towards a precipice. 'John' is suddenly overcome by a memory from his childhood – it was snowing. There was a sloping wall and his brother was sitting at the bottom of it. 'John' had slid down the wall, accidentally knocking his brother off. His brother fell directly on to a railing and was impaled by the spikes, killing him instantly.

This has unlocked all his memories: his name is John Ballantine; he attended medical school and then entered the army; he was involved in a plane crash and, traumatised by the event, he'd sought help from Dr Edwardes, who was on vacation at the time. They'd gone skiing and it was at that precipice that he saw Edwardes fall to his death. He informs the police where to look for the body, but when they recover Dr Edwardes's corpse they discover a bullet wound and immediately arrest John for murder. Despite Constance's evidence at the trial, John is convicted of murder.

Returning to work, Constance is relieved when Dr Murchison offers her his support. He tells her that he knew Edwardes slightly and though he didn't like him he knew he was a brilliant man. Later, Constance is suddenly struck with a realisation – if Murchison knew Edwardes, then how could he have mistaken Ballantine for him? She remembers the card game in Ballantine's dream and the bearded man. She confronts Murchison and asks him to analyse John Ballantine's dream. He helps her clarify some of the finer details: The seven of clubs represents the 21 Club, which he and Edwardes had once been to, and that the proprietor is in fact himself. Constance suggests that the 'wheel' in the dream was probably the revolver used to kill Edwardes, and that it must still be in the snow with the killer's fingerprints all over it. Here Murchison disagrees with her – for the simple reason that the murder weapon is still in his possession, and as proof he points it directly at her. She realises that Murchison killed Edwardes because of professional jealousy. She knows she can get enough evidence against him, and notes that, while he could possibly find extenuating circumstances for the murder in the snow, he could not explain killing her. She leaves the room, telling him she intends to phone the police. Alone, Dr Murchison turns the gun on himself.

Freed at last, John marries Constance, with Dr Brulov's blessing.

CASTING: Selznick originally considered Joseph Cotton for Gregory Peck's role, with Dorothy McGuire, and later Greta Garbo for the cool psychonanalyst and Paul Lukas for the role awarded Leo G Carroll.

ROOTS: The opening caption, 'The fault . . . lies not in our stars but in ourselves', comes from Shakespeare's *Julius Caesar.*

Salvador Dali continued some of the visual themes he had constructed with Luis Buñuel on *Un Chien Andalou* (1929), such as the eyes being cut (a less horrific version of an image from Buñuel's film).

LEGACY: Rózsa's romantic score was surely the inspiration for John Williams when he wrote the famous love theme from the *Star Wars* trilogy – which is ironic considering the similarity between Dr Brulov and the Jedi Master, Yoda.

Color of Night (Richard Rush, 1994) stars Bruce Willis as a psychoanalyst trying to ascertain which of his colleague's patients is a murderer.

WHO'S WHO?: A solid, reliable leading man, Gregory Peck was equally at home as the earnest action hero – in films like *Duel in the Sun* (King Vidor, 1946), *Captain Horatio Hornblower* (Raoul Walsh, 1951), *Moby Dick* (John Huston, 1956) and *The Guns of Navarone* (J Lee Thompson, 1961) – or the protective father, as seen in his Oscar-winning performance as Atticus Finch in the film adaptation of Harper Lee's *To Kill a Mockingbird* (Robert Mulligan, 1962). In the late seventies, he appeared in two very dark films, *The Omen* (Richard Donner, 1976) – as the adoptive father of the antichrist – and the Nazi thriller *The Boys from Brazil* (Franklin J Schnaffer, 1978). He also appears in Hitchcock's *The Paradine Case.*

THE USUAL SUSPECTS: *Spellbound* marks the first of three collaborations with Hitchcock for Ingrid Bergman (see the box below). Leo G Carroll (*Dr Murchison*) can be seen in *Rebecca*, *Suspicion*, *The Paradine Case* and *North By Northwest*. Wallace Ford pops up in *Shadow of a Doubt*. Norman Lloyd appears in *Saboteur* and was the associate producer/director of *Alfred Hitchcock Presents* and *The Alfred Hitchcock Hour.*

KILLER LINES: 'Edwardes' confesses his feelings to Constance: 'As a doctor you irritate me. I sit here swooning with love and then suddenly you ask me a question and I don't like you any more. Do you have to sit there smiling at me like some smug, know-it-all schoolteacher?'

Dr Brulov helps Constance try to get over her lover's imprisonment:

'It is very sad to love and lose somebody. But in a while you will forget, and you will take up the threads of your life where you left off not so long ago, and you will work hard. There's lot's of happiness in working hard. Maybe the most.'

THERE HE IS!: Just short of 40 minutes in, Hitchcock is the first person to emerge from the lift at the Empire Hotel. He's carrying a violin case and smoking a cigarette rather daintily.

GOOFS: It is impossible to swivel your wrist 180 degrees while holding a gun. Also, the photos circulated by the police are obviously studio publicity photos – how many doctors have glamour photos taken of themselves?

MISOGYNY: Dr Peterson presumably studied for her doctorate like all her contemporaries, yet she's subjected to an almost constant stream of ridicule from her peers. Her old tutor Dr Brulov remarks within earshot of her that 'Women make the best psychoanalysts – till they fall in love. After that they make the best patients'; her colleague Dr Fleurot tells her she's emotionally repressed, claiming that kissing her is 'like embracing a textbook'; and, when Dr Murchison realises that she is close to curing her most troublesome patient as well as exposing the real killer, he sneers: 'You're an excellent analyst but a rather stupid woman.' It's no wonder she falls in love with one of her patients – he's the only person who offers her any support.

AWARDS: Won an Academy Award for Best Music for Miklós Rózsa, and was nominated for Photography, Special Effects, Best Supporting Actor (Michael Chekhov), Best Picture and Best Director. Ingrid Bergman won a New York Film Critics' Circle Award for her roles in both *Spellbound* and *The Bells of St. Mary's* (directed by Leo McCarey). Listed by the *New York Times* as one of the top ten movies of 1945.

THEMES AND MOTIFS: The concept of the transference of guilt rears its ugly head with the mysterious patient 'J.B.' tortured by guilt from his childhood, which allows him to assume the guilt for a crime he didn't commit. Additionally we overhear a conversation between two police detectives. One of them feels oppressed by his mother, who wants to move to Florida because of her rheumatism though he feels such a move would hurt his career.

MUSIC: Though for a modern audience Miklós Rózsa's score might appear overly sentimental and just a little over the top, it was a highly inspirational arrangement, creating motifs that have become accepted shorthand notations for psychological thrillers, notably the harps, violins and theremin combination.

Ingrid Bergman (1915–1982)

She was Sweden's leading actress when the producer David Selznick tempted her to Hollywood in 1938 to star in a remake of *Intermezzo* opposite Leslie Howard. She would become an international star with her appearance as Ilsa in the romantic World War Two drama *Casablanca* (Michael Curtiz, 1942) opposite Humphrey Bogart and she'd win her first Oscar for her role in *Gaslight* (Charles Boyer, 1944).

In 1945, Ingrid Bergman appeared in the first of three pictures for Hitchcock, *Spellbound*, followed by *Notorious* in 1946 and finally *Under Capricorn* in 1949. The same year she worked for Roberto Rossellini on *Stromboli*. Bergman would soon find herself scandalised after she left her husband, Dr Peter Lindstrom, for Rossellini. Unable to reconcile her private life with her virtuous screen image, Hollywood shunned her for over a decade. Thankfully, this attitude didn't last: in 1957 she won her second Oscar for *Anastasia* (Anatole Litvak) and in 1974 she received her third for her supporting role in *Murder on the Orient Express* (Sidney Lumet).

Bergman's health began to fail in the late 1970s, though she fought off cancer long enough to complete a TV miniseries, *A Woman Called Golda* (Alan Gibson, 1982), in which she portrayed the Israeli Prime Minister Golda Meir. The performance earned her an Emmy, her final honour. She died on 19 August, her birthday, aged 67.

TRIVIA: The dream sequence was designed by Salvador Dali, and was originally supposed to run for 20 minutes. It included a scene with Dr Peterson covered in ants. Only part of it was filmed, and even less of it ended up in the release version.

The shot where the audience sees the killer's view down a gun barrel pointing at Peterson was filmed using a giant hand holding a giant gun to get the perspective correct. Some frames were tinted red and hand-spliced into all the original prints.

The snow falling on John Ballantine and Dr Peterson during the skiing scene was actually cornflakes.

FINAL ANALYSIS: At many points during *Spellbound* we find ourselves watching with increasing incredulity that someone as intelligent as Constance (Bergman) could be so repeatedly stupid, fawning over her new boss, falling inexplicably in love with him, and then risking her career by getting emotionally involved with a patient. But then this is the thing that makes Constance so interesting – having been accused of not being emotional herself, she sees her chance and refuses to let go until the very end. It's such a shame that the object of her affection is so completely lacking in any appealing personality (though this could have something to do with Gregory Peck, whose sincere, earnest portrayal fails to elicit sympathy in the way it so often does in his other films).

As the summary above shows, this is a fairly convoluted story made no easier by some surreal and at times bizarre imagery. Of course there is the notorious dream sequence designed by Dali, and during the scene where Constance and the fake Dr Edwardes first kiss we're confronted with a series of white doors slowly opening – a none-too-subtle Freudian device to simulate the sex that the characters *aren't* actually having. The final dream sequence, though, where we see the young John Ballantine accidentally push his little brother on to some railing, stays in the mind far longer than any of the other superficial nonsense, being both visually arresting and playing upon our primal fears so heavily. And to think we thought he'd learnt his lesson about killing children with *Sabotage*. 6/10

Notorious (1946)
(Early working title: *Who Is My Love?*)

(B & W – 101 mins)

Produced by Alfred Hitchcock/RKO Radio Pictures, Inc./Selznick International Pictures

Written by Ben Hecht, inspired by the short story 'The Song of the Dragon' by John Taintor Foote

Original music: Roy Webb
Photography: Ted Tetzlaff
Costume Design: Edith Head
Film Editing: Theron Warth
Musical Director: C Bakaleinikoff
Set Decorator: Claude E Carpenter
Art Director: Carroll Clark, Albert S D'agostino
Assistant Director: William Dorfman
Production Assistant: Barbara Keon
Set Decorator: Darrell Silvera
Director of Photography, Second Unit: Gregg Toland
Sound: John E Tribby, Clem Portman, Terry Kellum
Special Effects: Vernon L Walker, Paul Eagler

CAST: Cary Grant (*TR Devlin*), Ingrid Bergman (*Alicia Huberman*) Claude Rains (*Alexander Sebastian*) Louis Calhern (*Paul Prescott*), Leopoldine Konstantin (*Madame Sebastian*), Reinhold Schüenzel (*Dr Anderson*), Moroni Olsen (*Walter Beardsley*), Ivan Triesault (*Eric Mathis*), Alex Minotis (*Joseph*), Wally Brown (*Mr Hopkins*), Gavin Gordon (*Ernest Weylin*), Charles Mendl (*Commodore*), Ricardo Costa (*Dr Barbosa*), Eberhard Krumschmidt (*Emil Hupka*).

UNCREDITED CAST: Fay Baker (*Ethel*), Candido Bonsato, Ted Kelly (*Waiters*), Eddie Bruce, Paul Bryan, Ben Erway, Donald Kerr, James

Logan, John Vosper, Emmett Vogan, Alan Ward (*Reporters*), Tom Coleman (*Court Stenographer*), Lester Dorr, Garry Owen (*Motorcycle Police*), Warren Jackson (*District Attorney*), Frederick Ledebur (*Knerr*), Frank Marlowe, Howard Negley, George Lynn (*Photographers*), Howard M Mitchell (*Bailiff*), Roman Nomar (*Dr Silva*), Fred Nurney (*Huberman*), Luis Serrano (*Dr Silva*), Dink Trout (*Court Clerk*), Charles D Brown (*Judge*), Herbert Wyndham (*Mr Cook*), William Gordon (*Adams*), Aileen Carlyle, Alameda Fowler, Beulah Christian, Leota Lorraine, Lillian West (*Women*), Richard Clark, Frank McDonald (*Men*), Antonio Moreno (*Señor Ortiza*), Bea Benaderet, Bernice Barrett (*Clerks*), Frank Wilcox (*FBI agent*), Harry Hayden (*Defence Counsel*), Patricia Smart (*Mrs Jackson*), Tina Menard (*Maid*), Virginia Gregg (*Clerk*), Peter von Zerneck (Rossner).

SUMMARY: After her father is imprisoned for treason, Alicia Huberman is desperate to escape the attention of the press and police, so she decides go on holiday with some friends. She throws a party for her last night in the USA, where a friend introduces her to a tall, dark stranger called Devlin. After her other guests have gone to sleep, a drunken Alicia takes Devlin for a drive. A highway patrolman pulls her over, but Devlin shows him some identification and the patrolman immediately backs off and leaves them alone. Realising Devlin must be a policeman himself, Alicia is furious. He offers to drive her home and when she resists he knocks her out.

She awakes the next morning with a hangover and an unwelcome Devlin still hanging around. He explains that he is a government agent and that he has been sent to make her an offer. They want Alicia to use her father's contacts to flush out a group of Nazi agents still at large in Brazil. Alicia initially refuses, saying she feels no allegiance to America, but Devlin plays her recorded conversations between her and her father that contradict her claims. Reluctantly, she agrees to help and cancels her holiday. On the way to Brazil, Devlin learns that Alicia's father committed suicide just before they left. When Alicia learns this she seems almost relieved, telling Devlin that at least she doesn't have to hate her father for what he was any more.

Awaiting orders, Devlin spends more time with Alicia and it becomes obvious to her that they are growing very close. She begins to resent Devlin's coolness and mocks him. Eventually they both cave in and become locked in a passionate embrace.

Devlin goes to see his superior, Captain Prescott, saying that he believes Alicia is insufficiently trained for the mission, but is surprised to learn that their intended target, Alexander Sebastian, is known to her – indeed he had once been in love with her. Returning to Alicia's apartment, Devlin explains the mission and tells her she must reacquaint herself with Sebastian and 'land' him. Almost in spite of Devlin, Alicia agrees to do as he says.

The next morning they make their way to a riding club, where they know they'll meet Alex Sebastian. As they ride past Alex and his companion, Alicia is disappointed that he doesn't recognise her, forgetting that the brim of her hat is obscuring her face. Devlin gives her horse a slight kick, sending it galloping off out of control. As Devlin anticipated, Alex races to save the woman and is evidently pleased to discover it's his one-time love. Alex and Alicia arrange to meet for dinner. Alex confesses that he is still in love with her and invites her to a party his mother is throwing the following night.

As Alicia arrives, she is given a frosty greeting by Alex's mother, Madame Sebastian, who questions Alicia about her father's trial. Alex 'rescues' her and introduces her to the other guests. As they sit down to dinner, Alicia notices that one of the guests, Emil Hupka, is in a highly agitated state, seemingly worried by a wine bottle. Alex manages to calm him down and the rest of the evening is uneventful. At the end of the night, Emil apologises for his early behaviour and goes to leave. Eric Mathis says he's leaving too and offers Emil a lift home.

Alicia and Devlin arrange to meet at the racetrack while Alex and his mother watch the race. She passes on the names of all the guests at the party and remarks casually on Emil's distressed state and says she hasn't seen the man since. Their talk moves on and soon it becomes apparent that Devlin is uncomfortable with what Alicia is prepared to do and they end up bickering. Alex strolls over and after Devlin has left tells Alicia that he has been watching her from afar and is concerned by Devlin's attentions to her. Wanting an affirmation of her love for him, he asks her to marry him.

While Alicia breaks this news to Captain Prescott and Devlin, Alex consults his mother. She is against the union, believing the woman has come to Rio with the sole intention of trapping her son. Alex, in a fury, tells his mother that she is being jealous and that he will marry Alicia in spite of her wishes.

After the briefest of honeymoons, the newly-weds return to the family home to find Madame Sebastian sulking in her bed. Alicia sets about arranging her things and begins to inspect the closet space. Finding a locked closet, she asks the butler, Joseph, if he can open it, and he tells her Madame Sebastian holds the key. When Alicia asks Alex for the key, she hears him rowing with his mother before he finally hands it over. He gives her the keys to all the doors except one – the one for the wine cellar.

Alicia and Devlin meet again and she tells him about the locked wine cellar. Remembering the party guest's suspicious behaviour over a wine bottle, Devlin suggests she get Alex to throw a party to give her a chance to look for the key to the wine cellar. It will also give the newly-weds a chance to show off their love in front of a spurned Devlin.

The night of the party, Alicia manages to steal the key from Alex's room without his noticing. During the party, she slips away and shows

Devlin where the wine cellar is. Snooping around, Devlin accidentally knocks a bottle off the shelf and is surprised to find what looks like sand inside. Scooping up a sample, he tidies up the best he can and makes to leave the cellar. Alicia hears Alex coming down the stairs and ushers Devlin through a back door into the garden. Realising they have been seen, Devlin forces himself on to Alicia and tells her to push him away. When Alex confronts her, Devlin apologises, claiming he's drunk and promptly leaves. Alex is furious, believing that Alicia led Devlin on. As Alicia returns to the party, Alex notices for the first time that the key to the wine cellar is missing from his keyring. When he wakes up in the middle of the night, Alex is surprised to find the key has mysteriously returned and begins to suspect Alicia. He goes down to the cellar and eventually finds a bottle misplaced, and is now convinced that Alicia is spying on him, with the help of Devlin. Unsure of what to do for the best, he consults his mother.

Alicia visits Captain Prescott again, who tells her that the sample Devlin found was not sand but uranium. He also says that Devlin is to be moved to Spain at his own request. When she meets Devlin again, he notices how distant she appears. She tells him she has a mild headache, but he thinks she is just hung over again. Annoyed that Devlin hasn't told her he's leaving, she returns the scarf he gave her on their first meeting and says goodbye.

Apparently concerned about Alicia's health, Alex asks his doctor to examine her. As he tries to reassure her he accidentally picks up her coffee cup, prompting the Sebastians to both jump up. Alicia suddenly realises they are plotting to kill her. She tries to escape to her room, but passes out before she gets there.

After a week with no contact from Alicia, Devlin decides to take matters into his own hands. He goes to the Sebastian mansion and tells the butler, Joseph, to inform Alex he's waiting for him. Alex is having a meeting with his fellow Nazi conspirators, who are aware they are being followed by American agents. This news worries Alex, and he is even more concerned when he hears that Devlin is in the house. Devlin makes his way to Alicia's room, where he finds her weak and broken. She tells him that the Sebastians know everything. They had Emil the party guest killed and have poisoned her. He confesses that he still loves her and that he will help her escape. He picks her up and is about to take her down the stairs when Alex discovers them. Devlin warns Alex that if he does anything to arouse suspicion he'll raise the alarm and tell his colleagues that he has been helping the American government all along. The two men help Alicia down the stairs and out to a waiting car, but once Devlin has got her and himself inside the car he slams the door and the car drives off, leaving Alex to face his now suspicious colleagues alone.

CASTING: As usual, Selznick had suggested Vivien Leigh for the female lead, and Hitch had wanted Ethel Barrymore for the role of Madame Sebastian. On the recommendation of Reinhold Schüenzel, who was to play Dr Anderson, they eventually settled on the German actress Leopoldine Konstantin, who had been a huge prewar star in her home country but was almost unknown in Hollywood.

ROOTS: Hitch's inspiration for *Notorious* came from three sources: from conversations he'd had with Jewish and German refugees he'd met in New York and from the story of the famous Dutch spy Mata Hari. Born Margaretha Geertruida Zelle, Mata Hari had started out as an exotic dancer and soon began to mix in the highest circles. Eventually she was used by the French government in World War One to socialise with German officers to see what information she might discover. When he approached David Selznick with the idea, he showed him the short story 'The Song of the Dragon' that he had cut from the pages of the *Saturday Evening Post* in 1921, which would eventually form the basis of the picture.

LEGACY: The scene where the inebriated Ingrid Bergman drives her car with Cary Grant as her passenger can be linked to *Suspicion*, *To Catch a Thief* and, most obviously, *North By Northwest*, where Grant is arrested for drunk driving. Likewise, the meeting between the CIA members is repeated in *North by Northwest* too. *Notorious* was rather unwisely remade for television in 1992, starring John Shea as Devlin, and it's one of a number of Hitch's films spoofed in *High Anxiety* (Mel Brooks, 1977) and was cut into the Steve Martin noir spoof *Dead Men Don't Wear Plaid* (Carl Reiner, 1982).

WHO'S WHO?: Claude Rains was the perfect villain, always able to make even the coldest of men seem sympathetic and untrustworthy at the same time. Notable roles include *The Invisible Man* (James Whale, 1933), the self-motivated Senator Paine in *Mr. Smith Goes to Washington* (Frank Capra, 1939) opposite the idealistic James Stewart, and in a career high, the charming Louis Renault in *Casablanca* (Michael Curtiz, 1942), which also starred Ingrid Bergman. Rains also appeared in five episodes of Alfred Hitchcock's television series.

Louis Calhern (*Prescott*) played the eponymous emperor in *Julius Caesar* (Joseph L Mankiewicz, 1953) opposite a young Marlon Brando.

THE USUAL SUSPECTS: Cary Grant makes his second of four appearances for Hitch (the other three being *Suspicion*, *To Catch a Thief* and *North by Northwest*). Ingrid Bergman starred in *Spellbound* and *Under Capricorn*.

KILLER LINES: A cynical Alicia says to Devlin: 'There's nothing like a love song to give you a good laugh.' When they arrive in Rio, she berates Devlin's lack of faith in her: 'Why don't you give that copper's brain of yours a rest? Every time you look at me, I can see it dwelling over its slogans. "Once a crook, always a crook". "Once a tramp, always a tramp". Go on. You can hold my hand. I won't blackmail you for it afterwards.'

After Alex asks his mother if she could possibly smile occasionally when addressing Alicia, she remarks: 'Wouldn't it be a little too much if we *both* grinned at her like idiots?'

And of course, Devlin's deeply ironic outburst after one of his fellow agents comments on Alicia's character: 'Miss Huberman is first, last and always not a lady. She may be risking her life, but when it comes to being a lady she doesn't hold a candle to your wife, sir, sitting in Washington playing bridge with three other ladies of great honour and virtue.'

THERE HE IS!: At the party in Alex Sebastian's mansion, we see Hitch walk over to a table, knock back a glass of champagne, then leave.

AWARDS: Oscar-nominated for Best Supporting Actor (Claude Rains) and Best Original Screenplay. Listed by the *New York Times* as one of the top ten movies of 1946.

THEMES AND MOTIFS: Note how many scenes are shot from Alicia's perspective or in a first-person viewpoint. The early scene where Devlin circles the hung-over Alicia is quite stylised, with the camera performing a 180-degree spin, and the later scene where Alicia begins to realise she's been poisoned has Madame Sebastian and her son fade into silhouette and blur in and out with a highly stylised special effect.

Also, the poison drink, a plot element found in both *Suspicion* and *Spellbound*, pops up here. As with the glowing glass in *Suspicion*, Hitch draws our attention to the poisoned drink by placing enormous coffee cups in the foreground of the shot.

A theme that would be explored more fully in *Frenzy* is that of the link between sexual desire and appetite. As the romance between Alicia and the repressed Devlin grows, they discuss their evening meal and nibble lovingly at each other's ears, but once Devlin has discovered she knows the man she must entrap he cannot eat the food she has prepared. This contrasts with Alex, who on being reunited with Alicia invites her to dinner and confesses that he still has 'the same hunger' for her.

A fine representative for Hitchcock's traditionally difficult parental relationships, the uncomfortably Oedipal link between mother and son Sebastian opens up a psychological can of worms surpassed only by *Psycho* fourteen years later. After Alex has been oppressed all these years by his overcritical mother, it's nevertheless understandable that, faced with the possibility that his wife might be an enemy agent, he runs straight to his mother – the only person he can really trust.

POSTER: With a subtle key motif, the poster exclaims: 'Notorious Woman of many Desires! Fateful Fascination! Bold Intrigue!' With such attractive leads, it justifiably proclaims: 'The screen's top romantic stars in a melodramatic masterpiece'.

THE ICE MAIDEN: As the critics noted at the time, never had an actress been so adored by the camera as Bergman was here: the way Tetzlaff photographs her to give her a luminescent quality, in the Sebastians' party, where her white gown glows through the darkness, and in her final scenes where Cary Grant is rendered almost invisible in shadow while she appears as if in a halo of light. The fact that Bergman is much taller than the average Hitchcock woman gives her an added air of dignity. She only barely looks up at the tall Grant while towering over the five-foot-seven Rains. It would be some time before Hitch would so lovingly portray femininity in the way he does here, empowering Bergman's Alicia only to take that power away stage by stage.

COSTUME: Bergman looks stunning, particularly in the luminous evening gown she wears to the Sebastians' party. As she stands framed against a huge dark doorway, she's positively glowing.

TRIVIA: Hitchcock claimed that the FBI had him under surveillance for three months because the film dealt with uranium. This is more than likely an exaggeration for publicity, though David Selznick did receive a letter from the FBI ordering him to submit any material depicting American intelligence agents to the State Department for approval before the film could be distributed overseas.

FINAL ANALYSIS: For many, this is Hitchcock's finest black-and-white picture. Skirting round the restrictions of the Hays Code by having Grant and Bergman nibble at each other, Hitchcock made cinematic history with an amazingly prolonged and lusty lovemaking scene. Both Grant and Bergman seem to hold back so much that they make the scene all the more emotional and passionate, and certainly this is Hitchcock's most glamorous pairing yet.

Braver still though is Rains's portrayal of Alex Sebastian as an almost likable Nazi. Like so many Hitchcock villains, he's cultured and extremely polite, even managing to keep his cool for appearances' sake when he catches his wife in the arms of another man. Admittedly, as the spurned husband he allows himself to be persuaded by his mother to poison his wife, which, as we note above, is interesting on a psychological level; but what's even more daring is that we slowly find ourselves caring for this monster, hoping that this known Nazi sympathiser will be able to escape both his colleagues and his tyrannical mother with the assistance of Devlin and Alicia. Just as our strange allegiances look like they'll be satisfied, Hitch tricks us once again as Devlin and Alicia drive off, leaving Alex faced with trying to decide between the lesser of two evils – the Nazis or his own mother. 8/10

The Paradine Case (1947)

(Working Titles: *Mrs Paradine Takes The Stand/The Lie/Heartbreak/The Grand Passion/ A Question of Life and Death/A Woman of Experience/A Crime of Passion/Bewildered/ Guilty?* and many more)

(B & W – 125 mins)

Produced by David O Selznick/United Artists/Vanguard Films Production/Selznick International Pictures

Written by James Bridie, Ben Hecht (uncredited), Alma Reville, David O Selznick based on the novel by Robert Hichens

Music: Franz Waxman
Photography: Lee Garmes
Costume Design: Travis Banton
Production Design: J McMillan Johnson
Film Editing: John Faure & Hal C Kern
Unit Manager: Fred Ahern
Assistant Director: Lowell J Farrell
Hair Stylist: Larry Germain
Set Decorator: Emile Kuri
Art Director: Thomas N Morahan
Set Decorator: Joseph B Platt
Scenario Assistant: Lydia Schiller
Special Effects: Clarence Slifer
Sound: James G Stewart & Richard Van Hessen

CAST: Gregory Peck (*Anthony Keane*), Ann Todd (*Gay Keane*), Charles Laughton (*Judge Lord Horfield*), Charles Coburn (*Sir Simon Flaquer*), Ethel Barrymore (*Lady Sophie Horfield*), Louis Jourdan (*Andre LaTour*), Alida Valli (*Mrs Maddalena Anna Paradine*), Leo G Carroll (*Counsel for the Prosecution*), Joan Tetzel (*Judy Flaquer*), Isobel Elsom (*Innkeeper*), John Williams (*Barrister*), John Goldsworthy, Lester, Patrick Aherne, Colin Hunter.

SUMMARY: Mrs Maddalena Paradine is arrested by police, who charge her with murdering her husband on 6 May 1946 by poisoning him. Her family solicitor, Sir Simon Flaquer, says that he will get one of his colleagues, the charismatic Anthony Keane, to defend her in her trial.

When Tony goes to visit Mrs Paradine in prison, he learns more about her background. Her husband, a former war hero, was blind and unable to look after himself. Mrs Paradine is worried that people will automatically assume that she married him for his money, then killed him, and is greatly comforted when Tony appears to support her completely. Tony's wife Gay is concerned that by taking on this new case they will not have enough time to go away on the anniversary holiday Tony had promised her. He reassures Gay that, despite the fact that his client is an attractive, mysterious woman, they will still be able to get away on holiday.

During further discussions about the case, Tony asks Mrs Paradine to confide in him about any possible embarrassing 'details' about her past that might undermine her case. She tells him that she is a woman 'who has seen a great deal of life', telling him about the men she has used and been used by during her early years. She tells a disturbed Tony that despite all of this she loved her husband, and he was aware of her history.

One night, when Sir Simon and Tony are discussing the case, Gay overhears her husband furiously defending Mrs Paradine from Sir Simon's accusations. Tony can't believe that Sir Simon believes Mrs Paradine to be guilty and little more than a common adventuress. The force of Tony's reaction leads Gay to believe that Tony may be falling in love with his client. When Sir Simon confides in his daughter Judy about his feelings on the case, Judy is deeply concerned. Gay is one of her oldest friends, and is worried that she will get hurt by Tony's infatuation. Judy is even more concerned when she hears that Tony is planning to travel to the Lake District, where the Paradines own a large country house, Hindley Hall. Judy guesses that Tony has become jealous of the Paradines' valet Andre LaTour, who it is rumoured had an affair with his mistress.

Gay is concerned about the state of her marriage, and asks if she can come to Cumberland with Tony, in lieu of their anniversary trip. Tony can see that his behaviour is deeply hurting his wife, and sincerely offers to abandon the case if it will ease her pain. Gay is relieved by this offer – she now knows that Tony is prepared to put her first, before his career and before Mrs Paradine. Convinced that Tony still loves her, she gives her blessing for him to go to Cumberland.

Arriving in the beautiful Cumberland countryside, Tony checks into his hotel and goes up to Hindley Hall the following day. Meeting both Andre and the housekeeper, Tony discovers little more about the case. Back in his hotel, Tony is surprised when LaTour comes to his room late that night. LaTour tells Tony that he believes Mrs Paradine is an evil woman, and that Tony is working on the wrong side in this case. Angered by LaTour's comments, Tony throws him out.

Back in London, Tony tells Mrs Paradine about his trip to Hindley Hall. She reacts badly, and during their heated discussion Tony admits that he has strong feelings for her. Some time later, Gay and Tony have a bitter argument about Mrs Paradine. Gay surprises Tony when she tells him that she wants Mrs Paradine to be found innocent of the charges, even though she hates her. Gay knows that Tony is in love with Mrs

Paradine, and is terrified that if she is executed Tony will for ever regret his lost love. She tells him. 'I want you to win this case. I want you to get her free.'

The trial begins, with Lord Horfield appointed as judge. LaTour is called to give evidence, and tells the court that he believes Mrs Paradine has lied in her evidence. Tony manages to completely discredit LaTour, revealing that not only did Colonel Paradine leave LaTour £3,500 in his will, but also that LaTour had used poison two years previously to put down the Colonel's dog. Mrs Paradine is furious with Tony and the way in which he has practically accused LaTour of murdering her husband. Later, during further intensive cross-examination by Tony, LaTour admits that he and Mrs Paradine did indeed have an affair. He hesitated in revealing the fact because he didn't want to discredit the name of his beloved former master.

Next day, during Mrs Paradine's testimony, the court is told that Andre LaTour has committed suicide in the cells. She cries out in horror at the news. Shaken by the death of her lover, she confesses to murdering her husband. When Tony tries to maintain control over her defence, she tells him that she doesn't care any more. 'What does it matter now? Andre's dead. The man I love is dead.' Tony, shaken to his very core, begs the jury and the court for their forgiveness and stands down as defence counsel. Later that night, Gay goes to comfort her husband in his moment of remorse, guilt and public shame. She reassures him that he will be able to resurrect his career, and vows to stand by him.

CASTING: Producing a movie version of *The Paradine Case* had long been an obsession of David O Selznick's. Over the years, practically every major Hollywood name had been linked to the film, including Joan and Lionel Barrymore, Diana Wynyard, Greta Garbo, Hedy Lamarr, Leslie Howard and Ronald Coleman.

WHO'S WHO?: Ethel Barrymore was one of the three legendary Barrymore siblings, along with her brothers Lionel and John. They appeared only in one film together: *Rasputin and the Empress* (Richard Boleslawski, 1932).

Louis Jourdan was born Louis Gendre or Gendice, and was one of the biggest screen stars in France when David O Selznick invited him to Hollywood to appear in *The Paradine Case*, his first English-speaking picture. He went on to star in *Gigi* (Vincente Minnelli, 1958) and the BBC TV adaptation of *Count Dracula* (1977), playing the Count.

(Known simply as 'Valli') Alida Valli appeared in *The Third Man* (Carol Reed, 1949), *The Cassandra Crossing* (George P Cosmatos, 1976) and Bernado Bertolucci's *1900* (1976).

Isobel Elsom would later win roles in *The Two Mrs Carrolls* (Peter Godfrey, 1947) and *The Ghost and Mrs Muir* (Joseph L Mankiewicz, 1947).

THE USUAL SUSPECTS: Ann Todd would play the eponymous Sylvia in an episode of *Alfred Hitchcock Presents*.

Gregory Peck had appeared earlier in *Spellbound*, and Charles Laughton portrayed an equally subtle role in *Jamaica Inn*.

John Williams makes his first appearance for Hitchcock in *The Paradine Case*. He would later return in *Dial M for Murder*, *To Catch a Thief* and several episodes of Hitch's TV show. Leo G Carroll can also be seen in *Rebecca*, *Suspicion*, *Spellbound*, and *North by Northwest*.

KILLER LINES: Gay explains to Tony that she wants her love rival to be found innocent and released: 'not for any noble reason, but because I want this business over and done with, and an end to your being part lawyer, part frustrated lover. If she dies, you're lost to me for ever. I know you'd go on thinking that you love her, you'd go on imagining her as your great lost love.'

THERE HE IS!: Getting off a train at the Cumberland station carrying a cello (see also his cameo in *Strangers on a Train*).

AWARDS: Best Supporting Actress Oscar nomination for Ethel Barrymore.

TABOOS: Mrs Paradine is portrayed as little more than a money-grabbing whore by the prosecution. That is perhaps a little unfair, particularly looking at the situation with today's values and morals. That said, it's still deeply unpleasant to contemplate a planned murder of a blind old man for financial gain – especially using common or garden poison that he drinks himself.

TRAILER: 'Presenting the most distinguished cast of stars in screen history. *The Paradine Case* starring Gregory Peck, Ann Todd (of "The Seventh Veil"), Charles Laughton, Charles Coburn, Ethel Barrymore, Louis Jourdan and Valli.'

A voice then adds: 'What manner of woman is Mrs Paradine? What is the truth about this woman around whom there raged such a violent storm of conflicting emotions?'

THE ICE MAIDEN: Valli's performance as Mrs Paradine is pretty good for a non-English speaker in her first Hollywood role. That said, she does lack much of the depth and subtlety that Ingrid Bergman for instance brought to her roles – this could largely be due to the somewhat limited scope of the part she has to play, however.

WHAT THE PAPERS SAID: The over-the-top Laughton commanded the greatest attention from the review in *The Times* on 17 January 1949: 'Mr Charles Laughton is, magnificently, the Judge – ripeness is all, ripeness and the relishing of it – and it is as well he is there to preside, for

Mr Peck is never quite convincing and Valli is content simply to exist and allow her loveliness to act her part for her.' Sounding almost like a viewer complaining to *Points of View*, the anonymous reviewer concludes that 'the film, for long stretches at a time is mercifully free of all musical accompaniment. A moderate Hitchcock: no more, no less.'

TRIVIA: An exact replica of the Old Bailey courtroom was constructed for the court scenes.

FINAL ANALYSIS: A somewhat predictable plotline mars a film that boasts some superb performances. Gregory Peck is vulnerable yet believable in a role that requires significant delicacy of touch in order to maintain the viewers' loyalty and interest. To judge by Tony's character from the script alone, it would be almost impossible to maintain any respect or sympathy. Tony places his marriage with Gay in jeopardy because of an unattainable infatuation with somebody he barely knows. As he is married to the most perfectly understanding, intelligent and emotionally mature wife in the whole of Hitchcock's work, this sort of silly adolescent behaviour doesn't make him any easier to sympathise with. **4/10**

Rope (1948)

(Colour – 80 mins)

Produced by Sidney Bernstein, Alfred Hitchcock/Transatlantic Pictures

Adapted by Hume Cronyn, with Arthur Laurents and Ben Hecht (uncredited), based on the play by Patrick Hamilton

Original music by Leo F Forbstein based on the theme 'Perpetual Movement No. 1' by Francois Poulenc
Photography: William V Skall, Joseph A Valentine
Costume Design: Adrian
Film Editing: William H Ziegler
Production Manager: Fred Ahern
Set Decorator: Howard Bristol
Colour Coordinator: Robert Brower
Camera Operator: Richard Emmons
Assistant Director: Lowell J Farrell
Art Director: Perry Ferguson
Camera Operator: Eddie Fitzgerald
Camera Operator: Paul Hill (credited as Paul G Hill)
Colour Consultant: Natalie Kalmus
Set Decorator: Emile Kuri
Gaffer: James Potevin (credited as Jim Potevin)
Sound: Al Riggs
Camera Operator: Morris Rosen
Make-up Artist: Perc Westmore

CAST: James Stewart (*Rupert Cadell*), John Dall (*Brandon Shaw*), Farley Granger (*Philip Morgan*), Sir Cedric Hardwicke (*Mr Kentley*), Constance Collier (*Mrs Atwater*), Douglas Dick (*Kenneth Lawrence*), Joan Chandler (*Janet Walker*), Edith Evanson (*Mrs Wilson, the housekeeper*), Dick Hogan (*David Kentley*).

SUMMARY: A man's protracted death scream is heard. David Kentley has just been strangled by two of his college friends, Brandon Shaw and Philip Morgan. Careful not to leave fingerprints, they use gloves and a rope to commit the crime. Brandon and Philip dump the corpse into a large open trunk in the middle of their living room, and slam the heavy lid shut. Brandon opens the curtains of the living room, to reveal a spectacular panoramic view across the skyline of Manhattan. The sun is starting to set on a perfect New York evening. Philip hides the gloves, and seems to be having some second thoughts about what they have just done.

Brandon clearly has fewer doubts about their actions, and is proud for having committed such a crime. The killers plan to dump David's body in the Hudson River in eight hours' time, when they head out of the city for the weekend. Brandon is enthralled by the fact that they still have the best part of the murder to come: they plan to throw a party for David's family and friends in the flat, and instead of serving dinner from the usual dining table Brandon intends to serve the food from the top of the large trunk in the living room. A final extra chill of excitement comes from the fact that the trunk has no lock, and that the guests could theoretically uncover the body at any moment.

Just as Mrs Wilson the housekeeper arrives to help the men prepare for the dinner party, Philip spots the rope sticking out of the trunk. Brandon yanks it clear, and, walking past Mrs Wilson with it in his hand, puts the 'ordinary, household rope' into the kitchen drawer. Mrs Wilson discusses the guest list for the party with Brandon, and is particularly delighted to hear that Rupert Cadell will be attending. Philip, on the other hand, is appalled, believing that Rupert – their old housemaster at prep school – is one of the few people who might be able to work out what it is they have done.

Kenneth Lawrence, another of Philip and Brandon's college friends, arrives for the party. He is uncomfortable when he discovers that his ex-girlfriend, Janet Walker, will be at the party too. Janet is now going out with the murder victim David Kentley, and is less than impressed with Brandon's malicious sense of humour when she arrives and sees Kenneth present. David's father, Mr Kentley, arrives next. His wife is sick in bed with a cold, so he has decided to bring his sister, Mrs Atwater, along instead. Mr Kentley is surprised that David hasn't yet arrived for the party, and the other guests begin to discuss the last time that they each saw him.

The final guest for the party arrives, Rupert Cadell. Rupert is pleased but somewhat bemused about why he has been invited, and even the unflappable Brandon begins to lose his cool a little in the presence of his old teacher and mentor, gaining a slight excited stutter. The food is served and Philip's strange aversion to eating chicken is revealed by the manipulative Brandon: Philip used to have a job strangling chickens, which he found deeply disturbing. The discussion moves on to the topic of murdering people, a concept that Rupert seems to approve of.

'Think of the problems it would solve,' he says. 'Unemployment. Poverty. Standing in line for theatre tickets . . .' When he is challenged about his beliefs by the shocked and offended Mr Kentley, Rupert firmly stands by them. His philosophy is that concepts of good and evil were created for average people – principally because they need a moral code to live by. Superior, more intellectually advanced citizens need not feel that such codes apply to them, because they don't need them. Brandon eagerly supports his former teacher's views.

Janet is becoming increasingly concerned about David's absence. The fact that he hasn't telephoned any of his family or friends adds to her fears, and makes her believe that Brandon has deliberately not invited David, just to cause trouble. Rupert becomes increasingly concerned about the situation, and takes the opportunity to question the nervous Philip on his own. Just when Philip starts to crack under Rupert's interrogation, Brandon walks back into the living room, carrying some books that he is giving to Mr Kentley. Philip stares in horror as he realises that Brandon has bound the books together with the rope he used to murder Mr Kentley's only child. Rupert spots Philip's reaction, and starts to form some very nasty suspicions.

A big discussion takes place among the partygoers as to David's whereabouts. While they are talking, Mrs Wilson has been clearing away all of the food from the top of the trunk. She is about to return some more books into the trunk with Rupert's assistance when Brandon tells her not to do it right now, and to return to finish the cleaning up tomorrow. The party disperses, with all of the guests heading home to their own fears about David's whereabouts. Rupert goes to the hall cupboard and puts on a hat that looks like his, but which is clearly too small. Looking inside the hat, he sees the initials 'DK' – David Kentley. He finds his own hat and leaves, clearly troubled.

Alone in their apartment at last, Philip and Brandon celebrate their success. They are planning to leave the city for a few days, disposing of the body in the river on the way. Brandon calls to the apartment valet to bring his car to the front of the building and, just as they are about to manhandle David's corpse out of the trunk, Rupert arrives at their door, apparently looking for his mislaid cigarette case. Philip panics, and Brandon shouts at him: 'I am not going to get caught, because of you or anyone else. Nothing is going to get in my way now!'

They let Rupert into the apartment, who starts to search for his cigarette case. Rupert miraculously 'finds' his cigarette case among the books on top of the trunk, and manages to challenge the egotistical Brandon into pouring him a drink. Rupert then engages the two of them in a verbal game of cat and mouse, trying to get them to give him proof of his suspicions. Brandon turns the tables and asks Rupert to suggest how he might have murdered David – if he were him. Rupert then walks through the entire murder plot, having guessed almost perfectly everything they've done. He then pulls the murder weapon out from his pocket, reducing Philip to hysterics. Philip grabs the gun that Brandon had previously loaded, and pulls it on both Brandon and Rupert. Rupert lunges for the gun and struggles with Philip for a while before it goes off. Now in control of the gun, Rupert opens the trunk and staggers back in horror at what he sees inside.

Rupert demands an explanation for what his former pupils have done. Brandon explains to Rupert that they took his theories and put them into practice. Devastated that his theories have been so twisted, Rupert fires a number of shots out of the apartment window, and waits with Philip and Brandon for the police to arrive. Philip and Brandon now have the luxury of realising that they will both probably be executed for what they have done.

CASTING: Hitchcock's original choice to play the smug ex-schoolteacher was Cary Grant, believing that he would be able to convey the air of intellectual superiority necessary for the part. When Grant fell through, Hitch offered the part to James Stewart, who up until that moment had always played whiter-than-white parts. Although Stewart claimed to have had a miserable time filming *Rope*, the role proved his versatility as an actor and did his long-term career no end of good.

For the role of the psychopathic bully boy Brandon, Hitchcock hoped that he would be able to utilise the services again of Montgomery Clift. However, as Clift was having severe problems in his private life about accepting his own homosexuality, he felt that accepting such a role would damage both his career and his own state of mind.

ROOTS: Based upon the 1929 play of the same name by Patrick Hamilton, which was in turn based upon a real-life incident. The Leopold–Loeb case, where two college friends murdered another of their number for the aesthetic thrill, shocked and scandalised the world. One of Shakespeare's least-known plays, *Titus Andronicus*, features an earlier attempt by a killer to serve a buffet to his victim's family. However, in *Titus Andronicus*, the family fail to realise that they are actually eating their missing relative.

WHO'S WHO?: James Stewart makes his Hitchcock debut here (see box). Constance Collier was the author of the play that became Hitchcock's *Downhill*.

THE USUAL SUSPECTS: Sir Cedric Hardwicke also appears in *Suspicion*. Farley Granger would return for *Strangers on a Train*, and Edith Evanson would play Rita in *Marnie*.

The original play was adapted by Hume Cronyn, who had appeared in *Lifeboat* as the sympathetic Stan.

ANIMAL CRUELTY: Thankfully not seen on screen, the tale of Philip's chicken-strangling job is a particularly unsettling one.

TRIVIA: The film was shot in a series of eight-minute continuous takes (the maximum amount of film that a camera could hold). Every eight minutes, the camera alternates between zooming in to a dark object and making a conventional cut (to allow a projector switchover in the theatre). Most of the props were on castors and the crew had to wheel them out of the way as the camera moved around the set. Despite the 'free-moving' sets, the rumble of the walls being moved during filming was clearly audible on the soundtrack. This resulted in the entire cast having to redub their own lines in post-production.

Hitchcock managed to shoot roughly only one segment per day. The last four or five segments had to be completely reshot because Hitchcock wasn't happy with the colour of the sunset.

A continuity error occurs quite early in the film when Philip cuts his hand quite badly when crushing a glass. Two minutes later he is having his palms read, and they appear completely unscathed.

KILLER LINES: Brandon discusses why his friend was the ideal person to murder: 'The good Americans usually die young on the battlefield, don't they? Well, the Davids of the world merely occupy space, which is why he was the perfect victim for the perfect crime.'

Rupert confronts his protégé, unable to cope with the knowledge of what he has created: 'Did you think you were God, Brandon?'

Mrs Atwater is patronised by Brandon without even knowing it. 'Do you know, when I was a girl, I used to read quite a bit,' she comments. 'We all do strange things in our childhood,' he quips.

THERE HE IS!: On a neon sign in the view from the apartment window.

THEMES AND MOTIFS: The question of the nature of the Nietzschean superman, discussed previously in *Lifeboat*, is readdressed here. In this case, it's a pair of successful, all-American boys who believe they are the *Übermenschen*, the supermen. Once again, it's their own hubris that brings about their destruction.

TABOOS: One element of the real-life case proved to be so much of a taboo that it never actually reached the final stage of the script. Although it's heavily implied in the finished film, the real relationship between the killers was a sexual one.

POSTER: 'Nothing ever held you like Alfred Hitchcock's Rope'/'It's his most nerve-stretching thriller!' Hitch's face dominated the poster, with a

James Stewart (1908–1997)

James Stewart, known to one and all as 'Jimmy', was one of cinema's best-loved leading men, thanks to his 'Everyman' appeal and his insistence on playing likable characters. From his first film, *The Murder Man* (Tim Whelan, 1935) opposite Spencer Tracy, to his last, the animated adventure *An American Tail: Fievel Goes West* (Phil Nibbelink, Simon Wells, 1991), he epitomised all the best qualities of a leading man, tough, yet capable of emotional outbursts and romance.

A graduate of Princeton University, Stewart earned the respect of his peers and his country by becoming the first movie star to enter into service for World War Two, a year before the bombing of Pearl Harbor. He eventually became a colonel, and earned the Air Medal, the Distinguished Flying Cross, the Croix de Guerre and seven battle stars.

His screen persona can be categorised by his collaborations with the idealist Frank Capra in films such as *You Can't Take it With You* (1938), *Mr. Smith Goes to Washington* (1939) and possibly his most celebrated work, *It's a Wonderful Life* (1946).

Stewart's first involvement with Hitchcock was not a happy one, with the technical difficulties of the production of *Rope* proving a strain for all involved. However, such was Stewart's enthusiasm for *Rear Window*, he accepted a percentage of the gross rather than a fee upfront and he starred in a further two Hitchcock pictures, *The Man Who Knew Too Much* and *Vertigo*.

small three-quarter-length picture of James Stewart and a noose making up the rest of the composition.

TRAILER: In one of the most innovative of all of Hitchcock's attention-grabbers, we are privileged to see the final meeting between David Kentley and Janet Walker. They discuss their plans to get married, and David rushes off. As David departs into the distance, we hear James Stewart's voice.

'That's the last time she ever saw him alive, and that's the last time you'll ever see him alive. What happened to David Kentley changed my life completely, and the lives of seven others. Janet Walker, Henry Kentley, the boy's father, his aunt, Mrs Atwater, his best friend, Kenneth Lawrence, the housekeeper, named Mrs Wilson, and the two who were responsible for everything, Brandon Shaw and Philip Morgan.' Essentially, the trailer acts as a prologue. The information contained within is not essential for the enjoyment of the movie, but it does add a charming extra dimension to David and Janet's relationship. By extension, it also makes the audience realise just how horrible a crime is about to be committed.

WHAT THE PAPERS SAID: One reviewer accuses Stewart of acting 'with a deceptive laziness which contrasts vividly with Mr Dall's neurotic intensity – intensity the more obvious the more it is disguised.'

FINAL ANALYSIS: Hitchcock attempts a very interesting experiment with *Rope*, but one that doesn't pay off in hindsight. It's easy to see why he thought that filming a play in as naturalistic a style as possible might work, but the only thing that the long, protracted takes achieves is to alienate the audience from any emotional involvement in what's happening. We feel as detached from the action as a member of the audience in the back row of the balcony – although we can see what's happening, it just doesn't affect us in any great way. With the luxury of some more close-ups, some rapid cutting between characters as they react to the events unfolding, *Rope* might have developed into a more involving tale.

Some of the performances too are a little bit forced, particularly the ever-disappointing Farley Granger. Constance Collier, though, is just superb as the boys' housekeeper. As with Stella in *Rear Window*, Mrs Wilson helps the audience to realise what a lot of pretentious intellectual twaddle is being spoken by some of the other characters. **6/10**

Under Capricorn (1949)

(Colour – 117 mins)

Produced by Sidney Bernstein & Alfred Hitchcock

Written by James Bridie, based on the novel by Helen Simpson

Music: Richard Addinsell
Photography: Paul Beeson, Jack Cardiff, Ian Craig, Jack Haste & David McNeilly
Costume Design: Roger K Furse
Production Design: Thomas N Morahan
Film Editing: AS Bates
Colour Consultants: Joan Bridge, Natalie Kalmus
Assistant Director: CR Foster-Kemp
Sound: Peter Hadford, AW Watkins
Make-up Artist: Charles E Parker
Set Decorator: Philip Stockford

CAST: Ingrid Bergman (*Henrietta Flusky*), Joseph Cotton (*Sam Flusky*), Michael Wilding (*Charles Adare*), Margaret Leighton (*Milly*), Jack Watling (*Winter*), Cecil Parker (*Governor*), Denis O'Dea (*Corrigan*), Harcourt Williams (*Coachman*), John Ruddock (*Mr Potter*), Olive Sloan (*Sal*), Bill Shine (*Mr Banks*), Victor Lucas (*The Reverend Smiley*), Ronald Adam (*Mr Riggs*), Francis De Wolff (*Major Wilkins*), GH Mulcaster (*Dr Macallister*), Maureen Delaney (*Flo*), Julia Lang (*Susan*), Betty McDermot (*Martha*).

SUMMARY: In 1831, some sixty years after the discovery of Australia, a new Governor arrives to supervise the colony of New South Wales. Cedric Potter, manager of the Bank of NSW, introduces himself to Charles Adare, the Governor's second cousin, and chats with him to make Adare feel welcome in his new country. Just then, Mr Flusky arrives to meet with Potter. Flusky is a very rich and influential man in the local area – despite being an ex-convict. Potter informs Adare that 'we do not discuss such matters in Sydney. A man's past is his own business. Out here, we let bygones be bygones.'

Flusky and Adare are formally introduced. Adare tells him that he has come to Sydney from the west coast of Ireland to make his fortune. Flusky seems slightly worried about this, but agrees to show Adare how to make money. He tells Adare about a piece of land that's for sale for £1,000. He wants Adare to buy it on his behalf, as he has already purchased as much from the crown as he is entitled to. Once the deal has been completed, Flusky decides to hire a newly arrived convict called Winter, who was deported for getting a girl pregnant.

As he leaves the office, a street hawker tries to sell Flusky a shrunken human head. Flusky knocks the hawker to the ground, and the hawker runs off accusing him of being a murderer. Flusky invites Adare to join him and some guests for dinner at his house that night, and gives him £100 for his troubles. Adare is driven to Flusky's house, Minyago Yugilla, which means 'Why Weepest Thou?' Many of the guests have turned up without their wives, all of whom seem to have been taken suddenly ill. Just as they are about to start dinner, Flusky's wife Henrietta – who he had said was also ill – enters the room, obviously drunk. Adare recognises Henrietta from back home in Ireland, and they begin to briefly reminisce. Flusky looks uncomfortable, both at their family connections, and also at Henrietta's behaviour.

After dinner, Adare and Flusky talk about Henrietta – specifically, about how much better she seemed to be when Adare knew her back in Ireland. Flusky tells him how Henrietta's family set him up for the death of her brother and got him transported to an Australian prison for seven years. Distraught at losing her new husband, Henrietta sold everything she owned and followed him, where she waited for him to be released. However, when Flusky was freed, their relationship never felt right, despite the wealth he amassed to make her happy. Flusky tells him that the main reason he invited him over to dinner was to see if interacting with an old friend might snap her out of her drunken melancholy.

When the Governor finds out about his cousin's land deal with Flusky, he is furious. He tells Adare that Flusky murdered Henrietta's brother Dermott and that he must pull out of the land deal, but Adare refuses.

Later, Adare visits Henrietta again in an attempt to cheer her up. He seems to be succeeding when Flusky returns home, at which point Henrietta's sparkle and life vanish and she goes to bed. Making another attempt, Adare takes her shopping. Looking more beautiful than she has done for quite a while, Henrietta tries to reassert her authority over the household staff, who have begun to run riot. When the housekeeper, Milly, confronts her with a large stack of empty alcohol bottles she recovered from her mistress's room, Henrietta flees in embarrassment. Adare tries to continue with his rehabilitation work, and climbs into Henrietta's room. He comforts her and puts her to bed – but only after Milly has observed their growing closeness.

Milly tells Flusky her suspicions about Adare and Henrietta's improper relationship. Flusky reluctantly accepts Adare's version of events and dismisses Milly from the household, putting Winter in charge. Winter is unable to control the rest of the staff, so Henrietta is forced to take control. She wins their trust through kindness and respect. Adare then passes an invitation to the Governor's Irish Society Ball to Flusky and Henrietta. Happy to see how much better his wife is becoming, Flusky gladly sends her and Adare to the party together. Milly, returning to the house to collect her belongings, makes several sarcastic comments about Henrietta and Adare to Flusky. She asks if she can stay the night in her old room before she starts her new job the next day, offering to bring Flusky 'something warm' in the night like she used to. Milly continues to plant malicious seeds in Flusky's mind that the friendship is much more than supportive and platonic.

Henrietta and Adare are the stars of the ball. The Governor is transfixed by her, and even forgets how angry he is with his cousin for a while. Flusky, furious about the imagined affair, gatecrashes the party and tries to take Henrietta home. Publicly humiliated, she flees back to her home, where she tells Adare that she is disgusted at her husband's behaviour, but that she still loves him dearly: 'Sam is part of me and I am part of Sam for ever and ever. It was long ago when I was very young that I learnt that, but it was true and nothing can change it.'

She admits to Adare that it was she who accidentally shot her brother, and then collapsed from the shock and guilt. By the time she regained consciousness weeks later, Flusky was already in chains and on his way to Australia. At that moment, Flusky returns home and sees Adare and Henrietta sitting closely together. He throws Adare out, who borrows Flusky's favourite horse to return to the governor's house. Seconds later, the horse stumbles and throws Adare, who returns to Minyago Yugilla and informs Flusky. In a blistering rage, Flusky walks outside and shoots his horse. He returns home and proceeds to shoot Adare too.

Adare is in hospital, with Henrietta anxiously waiting outside his room to check on his condition. The Governor tries to get Adare to make a statement implicating Flusky, but he refuses. Angry with his cousin, the Governor tells him that he will deport him back to Ireland as soon as he is well enough to travel. Henrietta then speaks at length to the Governor, confessing her guilt in shooting her brother. She goes home to Flusky and tells him that she will be sent back to Ireland to stand trial. Flusky is furious – 'I wasted the years I did for you. You've been fool enough to spill your story, so *you* pay for it this time, not me.' He thinks that Henrietta has set all this up, planning to return to Ireland with the soon-to-be-deported Adare. Upset and confused by her husband's allegations, Henrietta runs for comfort to the arms of Milly, who has returned to work at the house. Milly offers her a drink to help her settle down.

The doctor visits Henrietta, and is unable to believe how bad her condition has become. Milly is horrified to discover that Flusky still loves her and plans to return to Ireland too. Flusky visits Henrietta in her room, and it seems clear that she is beginning to lose her mind again. However, the grinning head she always sees on the end of her bed is actually real this time – Milly had planted it there to give her nightmares and drive her mad. She collapses by the bed, only to see Milly trying to remove it when she wakes up. She pretends to stay asleep and sees Milly pouring her entire bottle of sleeping draught into a brandy glass. When Milly tries to make her drink it, she screams for Flusky, who discovers that the jealous Milly has been undermining Henrietta's health for many years.

The Attorney General arrives and asks Flusky to corroborate his wife's confession. He refuses to send his wife home to hang, so the Attorney General tells Flusky that the Governor plans to issue a warrant for his arrest for the attempted murder of Adare. As an ex-convict, he will be sent back to the chain gang. Facing this terrible dilemma, Flusky and Henrietta fall into each other's arms. The next day, the police arrest Flusky and take him back to Sydney, followed by the loving Henrietta.

The Governor has deliberately avoided keeping Adare updated on the situation with Henrietta and Flusky, and when Adare discovers what has been going on, he backs up Flusky's version of events, saying that the shooting was an accident. Flusky is released, much to the Governor's disgust. Realising he has no future in Australia, Adare decides to go back to Ireland, and is waved off from the harbour by Flusky and Henrietta, who seem to be rebuilding their lives together.

CASTING: Hitchcock had planned to make *Under Capricorn* before *Rope*, but had to delay filming because the script wasn't ready and because he wanted to ensure Ingrid Bergman's involvement in the picture. Joseph Cotton was hired for the picture by arrangement with Hitch's old sparring partner, David O Selznick.

WHO'S WHO?: Jack Watling appeared in several British movies, including *Reach for the Sky* (Lewis Gilbert, 1956), and is the father of the actors Dilys, Deborah and Giles Watling.

THE USUAL SUSPECTS: Ingrid Bergman and Joseph Cotton both made their final Hitchcock appearances here. Michael Wilding would later reappear in *Stage Fright*. Cecil Parker was also in *The Lady Vanishes* as well as appearing in the *Alfred Hitchcock Presents* episode 'I Spy'.

ANIMAL CRUELTY: Flusky's shooting of his beloved horse is thankfully kept off screen.

THERE HE IS!: About five minutes into the movie in Sydney town square wearing a coat and a brown hat. Ten minutes later he is one of three men on the steps of Government House.

MISOGYNY: Henrietta is treated very well by her husband and old friend – it's the housekeeper who nearly finishes her off.

THEMES AND MOTIFS: Hitchcock stretches the limits of marital fidelity – already explored in *The Paradine Case* – much further here. He asks the question of just how far a married couple would go to protect each other. In this case, both Henrietta and Flusky seem prepared to go to their graves. The real stress that comes to bear on the relationship stems from guilt, primarily that of the death of Henrietta's brother. It is almost implied that Flusky's prison term and Henrietta's descent into madness are not enough penance to atone for their crime and for their guilt about that crime. It's only when they confess to both their initial crime and to their real love for each other that they are allowed to be forgiven.

TABOOS: Henrietta's alcoholism is dealt with painfully and in agonising detail. Although her problem is inextricably linked to her deteriorating mental state, it must have been shocking for 1940s audiences to see the glamorous Bergman staggering around and slurring her words.

POSTER: With an illustration of Joseph Cotton clutching at Bergman's face in what is half embrace, half strangulation, the copy boasts that 'Ingrid Bergman shows you the heights *and* depths to which a woman like this would go!'

TRIVIA: Hitchcock's old friend and former leading lady Carole Lombard (*Mr. and Mrs. Smith*) first introduced Hitchcock to an Aboriginal shrunken skull she had acquired in 1941, and had played a joke on Hitch by planting the head in the middle of his back garden. Although Lombard died at New Year 1941–2 in a plane crash, her wicked sense of humour recurs here in the use of a similar shrunken head utilised by the vengeful Milly to destabilise Henrietta.

With *Under Capricorn*, Hitchcock went to great pains to depict a Sydney of yesteryear, particularly in the fact that none of the residents have an Australian accent (which wouldn't develop for another fifty to a hundred years. This attention to detail extends as far as ensuring that none of the wine bottles had cobwebs from the cork spider as this specific spider did not arrive in Australia until well after the time when the movie was set.)

FINAL ANALYSIS: 'All along we've sacrificed ourselves for each other. There must be an end to it.' Having recently played Joan of Arc, it must have been a real disappointment for Ingrid Bergman to portray a dull alcoholic, especially when you consider the major problems in her private life at the time (the impending divorce from her husband and her marriage to Roberto Rossellini). In *The Third Man* and working for Orson Welles, Joseph Cotton is a charismatic actor. Even in *Shadow of a Doubt*, his performance has a certain spark about it. However, in *Under Capricorn*, both he and Bergman look as though they are incredibly bored by the whole thing.

This is likely to be attributable, in part, to Hitchcock's attempt to use the lengthy 'single-shot' technique in *Under Capricorn* that had proved so annoying to his actors in *Rope*. Although he doesn't adhere to the eight-to-ten-minute takes as rigidly as he had done in his previous movie, the restriction of the format still makes for dull viewing. The one major highlight of the film comes with Bergman's ten-minute-long confession scene, which is electrifying. Despite this, *Under Capricorn* is an unsatisfying experience, a Technicolor hybrid of *Wuthering Heights* and *The Thorn Birds* while utilising the least interesting aspects of both. **3/10**

the

HITCHCOCK

complete

films 1950–59

Stage Fright (1950)

(B & W – 110 mins)

Produced by Alfred Hitchcock/Warner Bros.

Based on the novel *Man Running* (aka *Outrun The Constable*) by Selwyn Jepson

Screenplay: Whitfield Cook, adapted by Alma Reville, additional dialogue by James Bridie

Director of Photography: Wilkie Cooper
Art Director: Terence Verity
Film Editor: Emard Jarins
Sound: Harold V King
Make-up Artist: Colin Garde
Production Supervisor: Fred Ahern
Music Composed by Leighton Lucas
Musical Supervisor: Louis Levy
Costume Design: Milo Anderson & Christian Dior (uncredited)

CAST: Marlene Dietrich (*Charlotte Inwood*), Jane Wyman (*Eve Gill*), Richard Todd (*Jonathan Cooper*), Michael Wilding (*Inspector Wilfred 'Ordinary' Smith*), Alastair Sim (*Commodore Gill*), Sybil Thorndike (*Mrs Gill*), Kay Walsh (*Nellie Goode*), Miles Malleson (*Bibulous Gent*), Hector MacGregor (*Freddie*), Joyce Grenfell (*Shooting Gallery Attendant*), André Morell (*Inspector Byard*), Patricia Hitchcock (*Chubby Banister*), Ballard Berkeley (*Sergeant Mellish*).

SUMMARY: A car races through the streets of London. The driver is a drama student, Eve Gill, who is helping her friend Jonathan Cooper escape from the police. As they drive, Jonathan confesses he has been having an affair with the renowned stage actress Charlotte Inwood. That afternoon, Charlotte turned up unexpectedly at his apartment – her dress was covered in blood and she was in some distress. Charlotte told him that she had killed her husband by accident during a row. She asked for his help, so he went to her apartment to collect some clean clothes for her and while he was there he decided to make the murder look like the tragic result of a break-in. Unfortunately Charlotte's maid Nellie saw him leave the apartment and now the police are on the lookout for him. Eve offers to let him hide out at her father's cottage by the sea. She also promises to help him destroy the incriminating dress.

Eve explains the situation to her father, who reluctantly agrees to help them as he realises she is infatuated with the fugitive. Considering the evidence, Eve's father suspects that Jonathan has been misled by Charlotte, and notices that the blood on the dress was smeared on deliberately, which means it might be an important clue to Charlotte's guilt. But when Jonathan realises Eve still has the dress he panics and throws it on to the fire. Eve tells her father she is determined to make Charlotte confess. The next morning, Eve sneaks away from the cottage, though her father, realising she would do such a thing, has left a note of encouragement and warning.

Eve goes to Charlotte's apartment and finds it guarded by police and swarming with reporters. When one of the detectives on the case goes to a pub for lunch, Eve follows him and engineers a situation to get him to talk to her. As they talk, Charlotte's maid, Nellie, enters, obviously enjoying the attention. She brags that, as she'll be 'the star witness', she's confident she'll be able to make money from the case when the time is right.

The detective gives Eve a lift home and they arrange to meet again the next day. On departing he finally introduces himself as Wilfred Smith, which Eve comments is a little 'ordinary' for a detective. She returns to the pub and, posing as a reporter, persuades Nellie to help her get the story from Charlotte's point of view. Nellie accepts, encouraged by a substantial bribe, and Eve rushes home to 'prepare' for the role.

The next day, Eve, as 'Doris Tinsdale', Nellie's sister, goes to see Charlotte, who is preparing for her husband's funeral. The actress isn't exactly mournful, being more concerned that she looks glamorous rather than grieving. As Charlotte instructs 'Doris' on her duties, Inspector Smith arrives to question Charlotte. Eve is petrified and hides in the next room. She listens as Charlotte tells the police that she feels personally responsible for her husband's death – she never realised just how obsessed Jonathan Cooper was with her. Once the police have left though, it becomes obvious to Eve that Charlotte has set Jonathan up to rid her of her husband so she can be with her manager, Freddie.

When Eve returns home, she finds Smith waiting for her, chatting politely with her mother. Her father is also there, and he quietly tells her that Jonathan has absconded from the cottage. Eve is due at the theatre to help Charlotte prepare for her first performance since the murder, so she makes her excuses and leaves. As 'Doris', she tells Charlotte that she fears 'that man' might return to kill them all, but Charlotte dismisses her concerns as silly. However, during the performance, Charlotte is horrified to see Jonathan lurking in the audience.

As he makes his way backstage, Eve hides and watches him enter Charlotte's dressing room. When Charlotte comes off stage, Eve warns her that she saw a man prowling about. Charlotte tells her she isn't needed for the rest of the night and sends her home, but Eve listens at the door and hears Jonathan and Charlotte talking. Charlotte casually thanks Jonathan for not exposing her, yet seems distant from him and he begins to realise he's been used. He lies to her, claiming he still has the bloodstained dress that he could still use against her. At that moment, Charlotte gets a curtain call and she leaves Jonathan hiding in her room. As she reaches the stage, Charlotte's manager Freddie tells her that the police have traced Jonathan to the theatre and asks 'Doris' to show the police detective to Miss Inwood's room. As they approach the room, Eve begins to talk loudly in order to alert Jonathan. Sure enough, when the detective begins his investigations, there is no sign of Jonathan anywhere.

Eve has been asked to help at a garden fête. Coincidentally, Miss Inwood is due to perform there to help raise money for an orphanage. Eve plans on exploiting the event as an opportunity to expose Charlotte's guilt and invites Inspector Smith along. But when she gets home she finds another visitor instead – Jonathan, who is chatting to her mother. With the help of her father, Eve manages to hide Jonathan away, though by now she realises that her feelings for him might be waning.

Smith calls for Eve and they take a cab to the fête. On the way he informs her that there's a new lead in the case – the police want to question Charlotte's maid, 'Doris Tinsdale'! Eve tries to sow the seeds of suspicion in Smith's mind by wondering aloud if Charlotte might have been responsible for the murder, but she soon becomes distracted by the realisation that she is falling in love with Smith.

At the fête, Eve leaves Smith with some friends as she sets off to work. As she approaches Miss Inwood's tent, she sees the maid, Nellie Goode, waiting for her. Nellie threatens her with blackmail, saying she'll expose Eve to both Miss Inwood and Inspector Smith. Eve agrees to give her more money, then phones her father and asks for his help once again. Her father arrives, pays Nellie off, then tells Eve he has an idea. He instructs her to ensure that Inspector Smith is positioned at the front of Miss Inwood's show, then goes off to win a doll on one of the stalls. He carefully cuts his hand, then smears blood across the doll's dress and bribes a small boy to take it to the front of the show tent. The trick has the desired affect. Charlotte sees the bloodied doll and panics. Smith also sees the doll and Charlotte's reaction. Eve's father's plan seems to be a success. Unfortunately, when 'Doris' is called up to help Charlotte, Eve is forced to reveal to Smith that she is Doris Tinsdale.

Later that afternoon, Eve tries to explain everything to Smith, who is understandably furious. Despite Eve's assurances that she loves him and not Jonathan, Smith feels betrayed. Just then, Eve's father reveals he has another idea . . .

At the theatre, Eve asks if she can speak to Charlotte in private. She tells her that she has come into possession of a bloodied dress of hers and doesn't know what to do. At first Charlotte feigns ignorance, but soon reveals her guilt when she says that she was in the room at the time of the murder but played no part in it. Nonetheless, just as Eve's father had predicted, Charlotte tries to buy Eve's silence. Charlotte is arrested by waiting policemen – they had hidden a microphone in the room and had heard every word of the conversation. At that moment, Jonathan is brought in, accompanied by two policemen. It seems Smith had telephoned Eve's house to warn Jonathan that the police were on their way. Jonathan bolted but was arrested by the officers, who had been waiting outside all along. Jonathan manages to escape and loses the policemen inside the theatre. He calls out to Eve from the shadows and leads her away to hide. Through the darkness, she hears her father shouting to her – he's just discovered that Jonathan has been accused of murder before, but that he managed to make it look like self-defence. Eve now realises Jonathan has lied to her the whole time. Charlotte may have been the provocation, but it was Jonathan who had killed Mr Inwood all along. Jonathan then tells her that he intends to plead insanity – and that he will kill her to improve his chances. Eve manages to calm him down and leads him towards the orchestra pit. Then she screams to the police, sending Jonathan into a panic. He runs across the stage. The police try to cut him off by dropping the iron safety curtain but it falls on him and kills him outright. A distressed Eve leaves with Smith.

TITLES: Projected across a safety curtain, which rises to reveal the City of London.

ROOTS: Parts of the film are inspired by the famous Thompson–Bywaters murder case, which took place in England in 1922. Edith Thompson had married an older man for security, but had fallen in love with Edward Francis Bywaters (known as Frederick), a twenty-year-old sailor. Thompson had written some playful letters to Bywaters, joking about how she might rid herself of her husband by killing him. One night, as Thompson and her husband Percy walked home, Bywaters appeared and picked a fight, during which Percy Thompson was stabbed. During the trial, Mrs Thompson's love letters were brought as evidence of her immorality and she was hanged along with her lover. Dietrich's character is almost certainly based on Edith Thompson, with Richard Todd as the manipulated Bywaters.

LEGACY: The idea of the false flashback was imitated in *The Usual Suspects* (Bryan Singer, 1996), where much of the evidence given is revealed in the final scene to have been made up by the only witness.

WHO'S WHO?: Marlene Dietrich was surely one of the greatest icons of the Silver Screen. Born in Berlin in 1901 as Marie Magdelene von Losch, Dietrich shot to fame in Josef Von Sternberg's *Der Blaue Engel* (aka *The Blue Angel*, 1930). Von Sternberg brought Marlene with him to Hollywood, where she won a six-picture deal that began with *Morocco* (1930). She became an 'overnight' sensation with her androgynous performance in top hat and tails that helped create the powerful, ambiguous yet beautiful figure that became legend. During World War Two, Dietrich declared herself vehemently opposed to the Nazi regime and her work for the war effort solidified her in the hearts of America and Europe. Postwar, Dietrich became one of the most powerful women in the film industry, and indeed she was one of very few people Hitchcock ever allowed to contribute to his on-set direction. After she returned to the stage and enjoyed a successful recording career, Dietrich's last performance came in 1978, when she played her last film role opposite David Bowie in David Hemmings's *Just a Gigolo*. After breaking her leg on stage, she gave up acting and became a virtual recluse until her death in Paris in May 1992.

Jane Wyman had just won an Oscar and divorced Ronald Reagan when she accepted the role of Eve Gill. Years later she would star in the glam soap *Falcon Crest*. Richard Todd is probably best known for his performance as Wing Commander Gibson in *The Dam Busters* (Michael Anderson, 1954).

Whether delivering the definitive portrayal of Scrooge in Brian Desmond Hurst's 1951 film of the same name, the eponymous detective, Poole, in *An Inspector Calls* (Guy Hamilton, 1954) or playing the headmistress of St Trinians (in full drag), Alastair Sim remained one of Britain's most popular actors until his death in 1976. A fellow St Trinians star, Joyce Grenfell, was admired for her witty one-woman stage show 'Joyce Grenfell Requests the Pleasure', a combination of monologues and songs.

Famous across the world as the Major in *Fawlty Towers*, Ballard Berkeley plays Smith's colleague, Sergeant Mellish. André Morell (*Inspector Byard*) played Professor Bernard Quatermass in the BBC TV sci-fi drama *Quatermass and the Pit*.

THE USUAL SUSPECTS: Michael Wilding played Charles Adare in Hitch's *Under Capricorn*. Patricia Hitchcock makes the first of three appearances in her father's films here (see also *Strangers on a Train* and *Psycho*). She would also appear in several episodes of *Alfred Hitchcock Presents*.

ANIMAL CRUELTY: After being arrested, Charlotte tells Sergeant Mellish that she once had a pet dog. It bit her, so she had it shot.

KILLER LINES: The commodore (Alastair Sim) observes his daughter's actions and says: 'Everything seems a fine acting role when you're stage-struck'. When Smith reprimands the commodore and asks him what sort of father he thinks he is, the commodore replies smugly: 'Unique. Quite unique.'

In the pub, one of the customers says: 'I heard they clocked him so hard that his false teeth went right across the room.'

THERE HE IS!: As Eve first approaches Charlotte's apartment to pose as her maid, Hitch walks past, turns, looks at her rehearsing her part and then walks away puzzled. Possibly his most scene-stealing cameo ever, it's hilarious.

THEMES AND MOTIFS: Like Hitchcock's 1930 thriller *Murder!*, *Stage Fright* takes a look at the acting profession and shows us how we all play 'roles' at some time. From the opening titles, where the safety curtain rises to reveal London, the aim is to hint at some kind of façade in everyday life: Jonathan plays the part of an innocent man and a spurned lover. Charlotte Inwood has to 'act out' her grief for her husband's funeral, completely devoid of any genuine emotion, and as she tries on her 'costume' she advises the dress fitter to allow the dress to reveal a little more cleavage and maybe work in a little colour.

Eve is forced to play a variety of roles to avoid being exposed. She's the eager *ingénue* desperate for her first big break and, as her father notes, 'Everything seems a fine acting role when you're stage-struck.' When she introduces herself to Charlotte as 'Doris Tinsdale', the new maid, she receives the reprimand, 'Not so loud, dear', as if she were rehearsing at the academy. Charlotte soon finds her a part, telling her to be ready to introduce the doctor when Charlotte gives her a cue by coughing. During this scene, Charlotte keeps forgetting her new maid's name, despite some prompting from Eve herself; and, when Eve hides in the next room to await the doctor's arrival, the ensuing action is filmed as if from the wings of a theatre. In two instances, Eve is beckoned to help Charlotte, but freezes to the spot for fear of revealing her alter ego to Inspector Smith – heavily suggesting the stage fright of the title.

Eve's father, the commodore, also involves himself in this sliding of the roles, starting out as a supportive father, nudging his daughter 'on stage' for her first role, as Charlotte's maid; later Eve tells her that she considers him to be her audience, and at the garden party he finally becomes the director, engineering the situation to provoke Charlotte to deliver an altogether more natural performance.

As in *Torn Curtain*, at vital moments the people on stage become like the audience: Charlotte sees Jonathan in the audience and becomes transfixed; later she again becomes the 'watcher' when she sees the soiled dress in the audience; and in her last 'big performance', protesting her innocence to Eve back in her dressing room, the police stand on stage waiting, listening intently.

Note also the garden party (which, depicting a typical English summer, is a downpour), where Hitch shows us a sea of black umbrellas, then focuses on just one, that of the blackmailer, Nellie Goode. Look for similar scenes in both *Rich and Strange* and *Foreign Correspondent*. In a reverse of the tracking shot down the stairs in *Frenzy*, Hitch shows Richard Todd, in the flashback, entering the house from outside. The camera follows him up the stairs and into Charlotte's room in one long shot.

MUSIC: Hitchcock doesn't insert a musical number just for the fun of it, and it's entirely relevant that he has Marlene Dietrich sing Cole Porter's 'The Laziest Gal in Town'. With words like 'It's not 'cause I shouldn't't/it's not 'cause I wouldn't't/And you know it's not 'cause I couldn't . . .' Hitchcock all but gives the surprise ending away – that she didn't in fact kill her husband. Was this because she's 'The Laziest Gal in Town', or just the most devious?

POSTER: With poster art depicting an innocent Jane Wyman and a sinister Richard Todd (rather giving the game away), the copy announces that 'The stage is set for Warner Bros.' most exciting hit yet!'

THE ICE MAIDEN: More as a parody of this category than a legitimate entry, we note that Marlene Dietrich is nevertheless glorious as the theatre madame. Hitch not only allowed her to direct the cinematographer Wilkie Cooper but gave her free rein with her costume, make-up and jewellery. As much high camp as high drama, Charlotte Inwood is a superb creation.

WHAT THE PAPERS SAID: *Stage Fright* was not well received on its release, with many feeling angered that Hitch should cheat them by presenting false evidence at the start. The reviewer for *The Times*, however, seemed to appreciate the finer comic touches of the film claiming it 'ceases to be a Hitchcock exercise in dramatic suspense and becomes instead a diverting comedy brilliantly served by its supporting cast . . . Mr. Hitchcock stages a come-back with an ingenious end which suggests that he dealt the opening hand with an unfair ace up his sleeve. Mr. Hitchcock, in not making a "typical" Hitchcock film, has made an exceedingly diverting one.'

FINAL ANALYSIS: It's truly surprising that *Stage Fright* remains a forgotten film in Britain. Perhaps because, like *Murder!*, it's a comedy posing as a thriller, some viewers might find it a little confusing, not helped at all by the superb twist in the tale, where we discover that events that we assumed had happened were reported to us by a most unreliable narrator. *Stage Fright* is probably the nearest Hitchcock ever came to high camp, with Dietrich rolling her eyes and vamping up her role supremely, Wyman playing down her American accent only to adopt one straight out of *My Fair Lady*, and Alastair Sim committing petty larceny by stealing every scene he's in.

As the **Themes and Motifs** section above shows, it is a film with a great deal of depth. But it's not 'depth' that interests Hitchcock – quite the reverse. Finally he has the chance to satirise the actors and actresses that he once declared should be treated like cattle, and gleefully exposes them as superficial, oversexed, backstabbing and completely self-obsessed. *Stage Fright* is the work of a director glad to be home after so long and he's determined to have fun while he's there. From the false flashback and the dizzying chase from the police that Jonathan describes at the beginning, to the melodramatic final act, it's one of the happiest murder mysteries ever made and certainly deserving of a much higher profile than it's had over the last fifty years. **9/10**

Strangers on a Train (1951)

(B & W – 100 mins)

Produced by Alfred Hitchcock/Warner Bros

Based on the novel by Patricia Highsmith

Screenplay: Raymond Chandler & Czenzi Ormonde, adapted by Whitfield Cook

Director of Photography: Robert Burks
Art Director: Edward S Haworth
Film Editor: William H Ziegler
Sound: Dolph Thomas
Set Decorator: George James Hopkins
Wardrobe: Leah Rhodes
Make-up Artist: Gordon Bau
Special Effects: Hans F Koenekamp
Production Associate: Barbara Keon
Musical Director: Ray Heindorf
Original Music: Dmitri Tiomkin

CAST: Farley Granger (*Guy Haines*), Ruth Roman (*Anne Morton*), Robert Walker (*Bruno Antony*), Leo G Carroll (*Senator Morton*), Patricia Hitchcock (*Barbara Morton*), Laura Elliot (*Miriam Haines*), Marion Lorne (*Mrs Antony*), Jonathan Hale (*Mr Antony*), Howard St John (*Captain Turley*), John Brown (*Professor Collins*), Norma Varden (*Mrs Cunningham*), Robert Gist (*Hennessy*).

UNCREDITED CAST: Ralph Moody (*Seedy Man*), Dick Wessel (*Bill*), John Doucette (*Hammond*), Howard Washington (*Waiter*), Edward Clark (*Mr Hargreaves*), Leonard Carey (*Butler*), Joel Allen (*Policeman*), Murray Alper (*Boatman*), John Butler (*Blind Man*), Roy Engel (*Policeman*), Tommy Farrell, Rolland Morris (*Miriam's Boyfriends*), Sam Flint (*Man*), Edward Hearn (*Sgt Campbell*), Harry Hines (*Man Under Merry-Go-Round*), J Louis Johnson (*Butler*), Louis Lettieri (*Boy*), Charles Meredith (*Judge Dolan*), Georges Renavent (*Monsieur Darville*), Odette Myrtil (*Madame Darville*), Monya Andre, Minna Phillips (*Dowagers*), Mary Alan Hokanson (*Secretary*), Edna Holland (*Mrs Joyce*), Janet Stewart, Shirley Tegge (*Girls*), Laura Treadwell (*Mrs Anderson*).

SUMMARY: On a train journey to Metcalf, his home town, a celebrity tennis player, Guy Haines, meets Bruno Antony, who declared himself a fan of Haines and seems to know a great deal about him through the social pages of the newspapers. He's aware that Haines is courting Anne Morton, the daughter of a senator, and soon works out that the reason he's travelling to Metcalf is to ask his estranged wife Miriam for a divorce. Guy tries to distance himself from the all-too-forward stranger, but Bruno is persistent and invites him to dine with him in his cabin. Bruno seems to be a bit of a dreamer, so Guy doesn't pay too much attention when the stranger shares with him a theory for the perfect murder. He illustrates the theory by suggesting that, if Guy's wife proved difficult, Bruno could murder her, then Guy could murder Bruno's father, whom Bruno obviously hates. Neither of them could be connected to the murder he committed because each lacks a motive, and of course they would have a cast-iron alibi. Guy humours him until the train nears his stop, when he politely makes his excuses and leaves, not noticing that he has left behind a monogrammed cigarette lighter which Bruno takes.

In Metcalf, Guy tells Miriam he'll grant her the divorce she's been pestering him for, but she tells him she's changed her mind. Now that his tennis career has taken off and he is mixing in sophisticated circles she wants a part of it. She threatens to go to the papers and ruin both him and his prospective father-in-law if he leaves her. Frustrated, Guy storms out.

Unbeknown to Guy, Bruno travels to Metcalf and traces Miriam Haines. He stakes out her house and follows her and two male companions to the fair. Miriam's companions take her to an island in the middle of a boating lake and she playfully hides from them. Alone, she is startled by Bruno, who swiftly strangles her. By the time her body is discovered, Bruno has already left the fairground.

At exactly the same time, Guy is on a train returning to Washington. He shares his carriage with a drunken professor and the two exchange pleasantries. Guy finally reaches his home to find Bruno waiting for him. He shows Guy his wife's glasses and explains he's killed her for him. Guy is horrified and is about to call the police when Bruno warns him that they're in it together, just as *they* planned on the train. Then Bruno reminds him of the other half of the plan – he expects Guy to kill Bruno's father for him. Convinced the man is mad, Guy tells him to go away and closes the door on him. As he enters his apartment he receives a call from his girlfriend, Anne, begging to see him.

Anne's father breaks the news of Miriam's death to Guy. Anne's younger sister tactlessly points out that, as he had wanted Miriam out of his life, the police will probably consider him as their prime suspect. Guy knows he has an alibi, and tells the Mortons about his train journey and the drunken professor. When he sees the police the next morning, he's pleased to hear they have traced the professor, but his happiness is short-lived when he learns that the man was so drunk he has no recollection of their ever meeting. The police release him pending further investigations and assign Officer Hennessy to watch him around the clock. Concerned about the likely disruption to his training, Guy considers pulling out of an upcoming tennis tournament, but Senator Morton encourages him to go about his life as if nothing had happened. This soon proves difficult: Bruno refuses to leave him alone, telephoning him, writing urgent letters to him and turning up wherever Guy is. Eventually Guy receives a key and a map of Bruno's father's house – and a gun.

Bruno invites himself to a party thrown by the Mortons. The man slowly works his way round the guests, acting charming and sharing some of his wilder theories with them. Two older women find themselves discussing with him his theory for the 'perfect murder' and try to decide the best way to go about it. Bruno recommends strangulation, and to illustrate his point he places his hands around the throat of one of the women. Just then, Barbara Morton walks into his line of vision and, noticing that she bears a passing resemblance to Miriam Haines, Bruno goes into a trance. He passes out, completely unaware that he has very nearly strangled the now hysterical old woman. Guy orders him to leave and escorts him to his car. Barbara, meanwhile, tells her sister that she saw the way Bruno looked at her – she's certain he thought he was strangling *her* instead. A thought suddenly occurs to Anne. She also recognises the similarity between her sister and Miriam and decides to confront Guy about the disturbed gatecrasher. Guy explains the situation to her, but insists he's unwilling to involve anyone else in his predicament.

Later that night, Guy telephones Bruno to say he'll go along with Bruno's plan. He takes the gun that Bruno sent him, goes to Bruno's house, and using Bruno's map he finds Mr Antony's bedroom. He tries to wake the sleeping figure and warns him about his son's murderous plan, but when the lights come on he sees Bruno lying in his father's place. Guy returns the key and the gun and begs him to get help, telling him he has no intention of playing a part in his scheme. Bruno feels cheated, having committed a murder he believes wasn't his to commit, and warns Haines he'll find a way to get even.

The next day, the morning of Guy's tennis match, Anne goes to visit Mrs Antony, hoping she might be able to stop her son, but the woman merely dismisses the affair as one of her son's practical jokes. Once his mother has left the room, Bruno appears and asserts that it was Guy who killed Miriam. Bruno claims Guy asked for his help in retrieving a lighter that he dropped during the murder. He tells Anne that, of course, he couldn't do it, as it would make him an accessory. Fortunately, Anne doesn't believe him and tells Guy what has happened. Guy realises that Bruno plans on putting the lighter on the island where Miriam was murdered to incriminate him. He realises he must get to Metcalf before Bruno, but that if he doesn't play in the tennis match the police will be alerted and then he'll have no chance. He banks on Bruno using the cover of darkness, reckoning that, as long as he can get the match over with quickly, he'll be able to get to Metcalf in time. He works out a plan with Anne and her sister.

Guy wins the match as expected and races to a waiting cab while Barbara creates a distraction by 'accidentally' letting her face powder fall open all over Hennessy. On the way to the station, Guy changes into a suit that Barbara had left for him on the cab's back seat. Guy's train leaves seconds before Hennessy arrives. The detective guesses where Guy is heading and calls ahead to the Metcalf police.

As the sun finally sets, Bruno makes his way through the fairground again. He takes his place in the boat queue, but there are more people than before, drawn to the island through morbid curiosity. As the queue slowly moves, the boatman recognises Bruno from the night of the murder and alerts the police. Bruno panics and tries to hide on a merry-go-round, but Guy sees him and jumps on too. Thinking the boatman is directing them to Guy, the police try to shoot him. A stray bullet hits the merry-go-round's operator and the ride goes spinning out of control. Clinging on for his life, Guy tries to wrestle the lighter from Bruno. The ride explodes, throwing Guy to safety, but Bruno is mortally wounded. As he dies, Guy manages to retrieve the lighter from his hand. He promises the police he'll explain everything in the morning, then phones Anne to tell her everything is finally OK.

CASTING: Hitchcock originally wanted William Holden, who had recently starred in Billy Wilder's *Sunset Boulevard*, for the role of the socialite tennis player but he was unavailable.

LEGACY: Remade as *Once You Kiss a Stranger* (1969) and *Once You Meet a Stranger* (1996) and was the inspiration for *Throw Momma from the Train* (Danny DeVito, 1987). Excerpts from the film were used to help complete *My Son John* (Leo McCarey, 1952) after the sudden death of Robert Walker.

THE USUAL SUSPECTS: Farley Granger appeared in *Rope*, and Hitchcock's daughter Patricia had small roles in *Stage Fright* and *Psycho* as well as appearing in several episodes of *Alfred Hitchcock Presents*. Leo G Carroll had small roles in *Rebecca*, *Suspicion*, *Spellbound*, *The Paradine Case* and *North by Northwest*.

KILLER LINES: 'I certainly admire people who do things,' declares Bruno. 'People who do things are important. Now *me*, I don't seem to do *anything*.'

When he finds Anne Morton at his house he apologises for her wasted journey: 'I'm afraid that Mother wasn't very much help, was she? Well, y'know, she hasn't been well for a long time – she's a little, how shall I say . . . confused. Poor Mother.' Compare this to Norman Bates's description of his mother in *Psycho*.

After Barbara Morton calls Guy's dead wife a 'tramp', her father reminds her that '. . . even the most unworthy of us has a right to life in the pursuit of happiness.' 'From what I hear she pursued it in all directions,' notes Babs, cattily.

THERE HE IS!: Ten minutes in, as Guy gets off the train, Hitchcock tries to get on, carrying a double bass.

AWARDS: Oscar-nominated for Best Cinematography.

THEMES AND MOTIFS: As with *Shadow of a Doubt*, *Strangers on a Train* is a play of doubles and opposites. Obviously we have the pair at the centre of the film, linked from the first scene by the two pairs of feet hurrying to catch the train. The murdered girl, Miriams, is linked to both Anne Morton, her rival for Guy's affections, and Anne's sister Barbara, who bears a slight facial similarity to her. There is also, surely, a link between Bruno's dotty mother and Mrs Cunningham, the equally trivial woman who almost loses her life at Bruno's hands.

Guy's life is made more difficult by two occasions where he feigns understanding, first with Bruno, who fails to realise Guy is merely being polite and of course remembers the conversation wrongly. Then, as Guy travels to Washington, he meets Professor Collins, who recognises immediately that Guy doesn't understand, but then fails to remember the conversation at all the next morning. This adds contrast to Bruno, who considers only his own point of view. This is shown in the way he identifies the subject in his mother's abstract painting as his father, and not, as she insists, St Francis. Note also how Bruno is multiplied as he murders Miriam Haines, doubly reflected by the two lenses in her glasses as they fall to the ground.

POSTER: One poster boasts: 'Alfred Hitchcock brings you 101 minutes of matchless suspense!' The accompanying artwork (included in our second picture section) shows a huge Hitchcock plucking the letter 'L' from the middle of the word 'Strangers', hinting at the 'Strangler' at the centre of the story. A more verbose poster talks of how the film 'begins with a train whistle and ends with shrieking excitement. Young American idol – a good looking stranger in search of sensation – and a girl in love. These are the people around whom Alfred Hitchcock spins his wonderful new web of suspense and surprise. WARNER BROS. brings a pounding new tempo to motion picture entertainment. It's off the beaten track!'

TRAILER: With a rather intimidating tone, a voice-over says: 'You had made the mistake of speaking to a stranger on a train. And now, wherever you go, whatever you do, you find yourself dominated by [Bruno's] evil presence.'

WHAT THE PAPERS SAID: 'Mr Robert Walker's extraordinary power of suggesting by minute indications an unbalanced mind is too terrifying to allow epigram to prevail over emotion.' *The Times*, 6 August 1951.

TRIVIA: The British and American versions of the film differ at three points. The American cut loses a few lines from Guy's first meeting with Bruno, as well as the shot where Guy collects the map before going to

Bruno's house. Conversely, the epilogue where a clergyman recognises Guy is missing from the British edit.

Hitchcock bought the rights to the original novel anonymously to keep the price down, and got them for just $7,500. Though Raymond Chandler is credited as the main author of the script, it was almost completely written by Czenzi Ormonde, who was credited as second author.

FINAL ANALYSIS: As tightly plotted as you could possibly get, *Strangers on a Train* is rightly admired as a Hitchcock classic. Robert Walker steals every scene as the creepy daydreamer who tries to entice a tennis player into a murder swap. Surprising for the time, Walker delivers a brave performance, playing up the homoeroticism with deep, meaningful looks at the rather dull Granger, his eyes rolling skyward in disappointment as he drapes himself casually across the furniture and almost seductively purrs. As usual, Hitch blames the parents, a disciplinarian father and a dotty mother who pampers her son, never taking him seriously and humouring him with his ridiculous plans to fly to the moon and blow up the White House. She dismisses him, claiming he's a 'naughty boy . . . but you can always make me laugh'. Like Uncle Charlie in *Shadow of a Doubt*, Bruno is a suave and charming villain, enjoying his role to the hilt. How more evil can a man be than to pop a child's balloon with a cigarette?

As great as Robert Walker is, he couldn't really fail acting opposite Farley Granger, who is as dull and stiff as he was in *Rope*. The real surprise here, though, is Patricia Hitchcock who, having enjoyed a minuscule role in her father's previous film, obviously relishes the much juicier part here as the tactless but enchanting Barbara.

Strangers on a Train does have a number of inescapable flaws at its heart. The reason why Guy Haines doesn't run straight to the police is far-fetched and quite unbelievable, as is the initial leap of logic that encourages Bruno to kill in the first place. None of this, however, manages to get in the way of a very smart, witty and atmospheric film. 8/10.

I Confess (1953)

(B & W – 95 mins)

Produced by Alfred Hitchcock/Warner Bros

Screenplay: George Tabori & William Archibald, based on the play *Nos Deux Consciences* by Paul Anthelme (pseudonym of Paul Bourde)

Director of Photography: Robert Burks
Art Director: Edward S Haworth
Film Editor: Rudi Fehr

Sound: Oliver S Garretson
Set Decorator: George James Hopkins
Wardrobe: Orry-Kelly
Production Supervisor: Sherry Shourds
Production Associate: Barbara Keon
Make-up Artist: Gordon Bau
Assistant Director: Don Page
Technical Adviser: Father Paul Lacouline
Musical Direction: Ray Heindorf
Music Composed and Conducted by Dmitri Tiomkin

CAST: Montgomery Clift (*Father Michael Logan*), Anne Baxter (*Ruth Grandfort*), Karl Malden (*Inspector Larrue*), Brian Aherne (*Willy Robertson*), OE Hasse (*Otto Keller*), Roger Dann (*Pierre Grandfort*), Charles Andre (*Father Millars*), Dolly Haas (*Alma Keller*), Ovila Légaré (*Villette*), Judson Pratt (*Murphy*), Gilles Pelletier (*Father Benoit*).

SUMMARY: In a district of Quebec, a German refugee called Otto Keller murders a local lawyer called Villette while in the process of robbing him. Keller works as a caretaker in a nearby church and has stolen a priest's cassock to use as a disguise. Panicked by his actions, Keller flees the murder scene and having removed and hidden the stolen cassock he confesses his sins to a young idealistic priest called Michael Logan. Keller knows that his confession absolves him and that Father Logan is forbidden from disclosing his guilt.

Keller's wife tells him he must maintain his normal duties to prevent suspicion. The next day he is due to tend Villette's gardens. Father Logan realises this and goes to Villette's house, where he finds crowds gathering. Inspector Larrue, the officer in charge of the investigation, tells Logan that Keller 'discovered' the body and phoned the police, and that he is now helping with their enquiries. Larrue notices that Logan seems concerned about something and later sees him meet a young woman who seems less than distraught at the news of Villette's death.

Larrue questions two schoolgirls who claim to have seen a priest leave Villette's house on the night of the murder. On this evidence, he dispatches officers to question priests in every rectory in the area, though he tells the Crown Prosecutor, Willy Robertson, that he already has a prime suspect. Keller learns that Father Logan is being questioned by Larrue and immediately jumps to the conclusion that Logan will betray him. Then he remembers that his wife still has the cassock that he wore on the night of the murder. He orders her not to wash it – he has an idea.

Back at the police station, Larrue is frustrated by Father Logan, who seems unwilling to answer his questions and offers little explanation as to why. But the little Logan has told him only adds to his suspicions that he is somehow connected to the murder, so Larrue informs Willy Robertson that he intends to arrest Logan for the murder.

The woman Michael Logan met is Ruth Grandfort, the wife of a respected politician. On learning that Logan is going to be arrested, she arranges to meet with him. She offers to tell the police the truth, that he was with her that night and couldn't have committed the crime, but Michael tells her that such an admission would only incriminate her. However, the police have seen the two together and Ruth is soon invited for questioning.

Accompanied by her husband, and in the presence of Michael, Ruth tells the police that she had been with Logan between 9 and 11 o'clock on the night of the murder and that she had not told her husband about the meeting. She reveals that she and Michael had been engaged some years earlier. She'd been desperately in love with him and was heartbroken when he left to fight in the war. Though at first he wrote regularly, the letters soon stopped and Ruth lost all contact with him. She eventually met Pierre Grandfort and married him despite the fact she still loved Michael. When Michael finally returned to Quebec, she met him at the port and they spent the day together. The next day they went for a walk and when a storm erupted they sought shelter in a nearby pagoda. There they were discovered by the owner of the pagoda, Villette, who recognised Ruth as Grandfort's wife. The lawyer greeted her as such, and that was how Michael discovered she was married. He ran away from her and some time later she discovered he'd accepted holy orders and been ordained as a Catholic priest. Years later, Villette began blackmailing her. He had found himself facing a tax scandal and was pressuring her to get her husband to help him. She refused but soon she was at breaking point and went to Father Logan for help. When she'd heard that Villette was dead, she'd been relieved – she was free.

Ruth's husband remains loyal to her and forgives her indiscretions, but tells her regretfully that he has learnt that her testimony has done more harm than good. Villette's autopsy has revealed that he could not have died earlier than 11.30 that night. By confirming that Michael left her at 11 o'clock and confessing their former relationship she has ruined his alibi and provided the police with the motive they were looking for.

The case comes to trial. With Keller's help, the police have found a bloodied cassock in among Logan's things. Keller also gives evidence, claiming he saw Logan on the night of the murder in a state of distress. Ruth is also forced to give evidence and to her shame she is unable to retract the written statement that she gave to the police, further incriminating the priest. Finally Logan gives his defence and disputes the evidence provided by Keller. Logan's words are chosen carefully to ensure each answer is totally honest without betraying the confidence of Keller's confessional. Fortunately for Michael, the jury finds him not guilty, though the judge, in discharging him, comments that he believes they have come to the wrong decision. As he leaves the court, Michael faces a hostile public, who jeer at him and demand he take off his collar. As the crowd jostle him, Otto's wife runs to aid him and shouts to the crowd that she knows he is innocent. Before she can say any more, however, Keller shoots her and runs away, pursued by the police.

Keller escapes to a theatre. When Larrue asks him about Villette, Keller shouts that Logan must have talked, that he is a coward, betraying the sacred trust of the confession. Michael walks slowly to him asking him to put the gun down. He goads Logan and in the process confesses his crime within earshot of the police. As he moves to shoot Michael he is gunned down. The frightened man begs for Michael's forgiveness. Michael reads him the last rites as the man dies in his arms.

CASTING: Originally contracted to play the role of Ruth was Anita Björk, recently acclaimed for her performance in *Miss Julie* (Alf Sjöberg, 1952). However, when she arrived in America with her lover and their child, Hitch was forced to recast the role to avoid upsetting the producer Jack Warner with a scandal. In her place, Hitch cast Anne Baxter, whom he had first seen back in 1939 when he did screen-tests with her for *Rebecca*.

ROOTS: Having been brought up in a Catholic household and educated by Jesuits, Hitchcock knew only too well the importance of the ritual of confession and was intrigued by the idea that a criminal could confess his crime to a priest and the priest would be duty-bound to protect his identity.

WHO'S WHO?: Hitchcock was not overly impressed with Montgomery Clift, a deeply insecure method actor who was dependent on both his acting coach and alcohol. Hitchcock was, however, intrigued by Clift's confused sexuality, having worked with a number of bisexual or homosexual men, including Ivor Novello and Charles Laughton.

Anne Baxter was married to John Hodiak, whom Hitch had cast in *Lifeboat*, and had won an Oscar the previous year for her part in *All About Eve* (Joseph L Mankiewicz, 1950). Karl Malden worked for Eliah Kazan on *A Streetcar Named Desire* (1951) and *On the Waterfront* (1954), though he is best known for co-starring with Michael Douglas in *The Streets of San Francisco*.

KILLER LINES: Cornered by the police, a dazed Otto Keller mourns the loss of his wife, saying: 'I loved her. It made me cry to see her work so hard, those poor hands, those beautiful hands.'

THERE HE IS!: He strolls along the top of a staircase during the opening titles.

THE MACGUFFIN: Like the secret codes and plans in other movies, the MacGuffin here is the information our hero possesses that the policemen want. That this information takes the form of a murderer's confession seems to baffle many non-Catholics, who find it hard to believe a man would risk imprisonment rather than break the confidentiality of this solemn Catholic ritual.

POSTER: With no indication of Montgomery Clift's role as a priest, the poster for *I Confess* depicts Clift and Baxter in a passionate embrace, and poses the question: 'If you knew what he knew, what would you do?'

WHAT THE PAPERS SAID: A generally unenthusiastic reception greeted *I Confess*, with the *Los Angeles Times* describing how 'The whetted knife of Hitchcock's direction blunts itself again and again on a ponderous, equivocal situation.' The London *Times* did reserve praise for Karl Malden, who 'as the police inspector who brings father Michael within the shadow of the noose, acts everyone else off the screen.'

COSTUME: As usual, Hitchcock had Anne Baxter's already blonde hair bleached to make it even fairer, and had the costumes that had been cut for Anita Björk altered to fit Baxter.

FINAL ANALYSIS: As noted in **The MacGufffin** above, the central issue here is whether one believes the sacred trust of the confessional is worth playing the martyr as thoroughly as Michael Logan does here. As with every other character in the piece, Logan's martyrdom seems to be as much motivated by selfish reasons as anything else. Larrue's ambition to catch the killer lets him make some rather callous decisions in his line of questioning. There is also Otto's desperation to avoid being hanged. Otto frames a priest for murder and shoots his wife to protect himself and once again the feeling seems to be that these foreign chaps just can't be trusted.

Michael's selfishness is much stranger. Does he join the priesthood on a petulant whim just to spite Ruth? Is he keeping Otto's secret just to prove he can, no matter how abominable Otto actually is? Why couldn't he at least hint at the fact that he knows who the killer is to persuade Larrue to look elsewhere? *I Confess* is a frustrating work, simply because, despite some marvellous cinematography (immediately identifiable as an old-school Warner picture) and strong acting (in particular Malden as the bulldog detective and Baxter as the lovelorn public figure, who both have trouble with letting things go), the overall impression is that we're not at all sure if we really care what happens to any of these people. We certainly don't want Otto to escape punishment; we couldn't care less about the oily Villette; and while Willy Robertson is a wonderfully trivial Crown Prosecutor, messing around with forks and balancing glasses of water on his head, it's almost too great an about-face for him to goad Ruth in court as he does, having established himself as a friend of her husband. Fans of Montgomery Clift might enjoy his introspective pouting and his oh-so-sincere inner conflicts before he hands himself over to the police. Everyone else will have long lost interest. **4/10.**

Dial M for Murder (1954)

(Colour – 105 mins)

Produced by Alfred Hitchcock/Warner Bros

Written by Frederick Knott, based on his play

Music composed by Dmitri Tiomkin
Director of Photography: Robert Burks
Film Editing: Rudi Fehr
Make-up Artist: Gordon Bau
Art Director: Edward Carrere
Assistant Director: Mel Dellar
Sound: Oliver S Garretson
Set Decorator: George James Hopkins
Wardrobe: Moss Mabry

CAST: Ray Milland (*Tony Wendice*), Grace Kelly (*Margot Wendice*), Robert Cummings (*Mark Halliday*), John Williams (*Inspector Hubbard*), Anthony Dawson (*Captain Swan Lesgate*), Leo Britt (*Storyteller*), Patrick Allen (*Pearson*), George Leigh (*Williams*), George Alderson (*First Detective*), Robin Hughes (*Police Sergeant*), Guy Doleman, Sanders Clark, Thayer Roberts (*Detectives*), Robert Dobson (*Police Photographer*), Sam Harris (*Man in Phone Booth*), Jack Cunningham (*Bobby*).

SUMMARY: Margot Wendice is entertaining an old friend from America, Mark Halliday. The last time Mark visited Margot her marriage had been in difficulty. They had an affair and on his return to America they continued to write to each other. Before her husband Tony comes home, Margot tells Mark that her relationship with her husband has improved dramatically. However, something happened that she thinks Mark should be aware of. She had destroyed all bar one of Mark's love letters, which she had kept in her handbag. Some time ago her handbag was stolen at Victoria Station, and though the bag was returned the letter was missing. Soon after, she received a blackmail note demanding money in exchange for her precious letter.

Tony returns home, and Margot introduces him to Mark. Tony tells Margot that he needs to complete some work and that, regretfully, he won't be able to join her and her friend in their planned trip to the theatre and insists they go on without him. To make up for this, he invites Mark to accompany him to a stag party the next evening. Margot and Mark, happy to be able to spend more time on their own, head off to the theatre.

With his wife out of the way, Tony telephones Captain Lesley, who has advertised that he is selling his car. Tony invites him to bring the car to his apartment, but when Lesley arrives Tony reveals the truth. He and

'Lesley'– or Swan Lesgate, to use his real name – had attended the same university, and Tony recalls that the man had been involved in a minor scandal and was forced to leave. By chance, Tony had seen Swan the previous year and has since discovered that Swan has a habit of seducing rich, lonely women and absconding with their savings.

Tony tells the stunned Swan that he has discovered that his wife is having an affair. He admits that, now he has given up his career as a professional tennis player, he is largely reliant on Margot's wealth, which unfortunately makes it difficult for him to divorce her and risk losing his sole source of income. When Swan asks Tony why he is revealing all of these embarrassing details, Tony plays his trump card. He uses his knowledge of Swan's crimes to force him to accept a proposition: for the sum of £1,000 he wants Swan to murder Margot.

The next evening, Tony and Mark go to the stag night. Remembering he has to make an important call, Tony makes his apologies and goes to a phone box. He calls his own home phone number. The ringing of the telephone wakes Margot, who gets out of bed, walks across the living room and picks up the receiver, unaware that the call was a signal to Swan, who steps out from behind a curtain, wraps a stocking around Margot's neck and proceeds to strangle her. She struggles and her hand closes around a pair of scissors lying on a nearby desk. She stabs her attacker, who falls to the floor dead.

Tony, who is still on the other end of the telephone, realises that his plan has gone awry. Thinking quickly, he tells Margot not to touch anything and rushes home from the stag party. Earlier that night he stole Margot's front-door key from her handbag and left it outside their apartment under the stair carpet so that Swan could let himself in. Realising that Swan must still have Margot's key on him, Tony searches the dead man's pockets, finds the key and places it in Margot's bag. Tony also plants the missing love letter in Swan's coat pocket, and only then does he phone the police.

Inspector Hubbard, the officer in charge of the investigation, jumps to the conclusion that Swan had discovered Margot and Mark's affair and had proceeded to blackmail Margo. He further believes that Margot deliberately invited Swan to the apartment, and had murdered him to protect the secret about her affair. Tony is shocked to discover these 'facts' and plays the role of the loyal, betrayed husband almost faultlessly.

Margot is tried for murder and found guilty. Mark is desperate to prove her innocence, but it seems that there is no way to prevent her imminent execution. The day before the hanging, Mark begs Tony to tell whatever lies he can in order to save his Margot's life. As a writer of scripts for TV, Mark has been trying to come up with another possible explanation for what has happened to Margot. The only thing that seems to make sense to him is that Swan had been hired by Tony to murder his wife, and that the attack went wrong. Mark argues that merely planning a murder would get Tony only a few years in jail – a lesser punishment than the death sentence awaiting Margot. Tony ridicules Mark's suggestion, claiming that no one would believe such an outrageous story.

At that moment, Inspector Hubbard arrives. Mark hides in Margot's bedroom, where he discovers a suitcase full of money – the remainder of the money Tony had meant for Swan. Mark believes that he has rumbled Tony, and tells the inspector his suspicions. Quick-witted as ever, Tony explains to the inspector that the money was actually Margot's – she had intended to use it to pay off Swan, but then killed him in a moment of panic. He adds that he realised what the money was for, but hid it until after Margot's trial, aware that if the jury knew about the money it would definitely convict her. Inspector Hubbard seems perfectly convinced by Tony's story, and tells Tony that it would be a good idea for him to collect his wife's belongings from the police station as soon as possible. While Tony is distracted, Hubbard swaps overcoats with him and leaves.

Tony eventually heads to collect Margot's things. As soon as he is out of sight, Hubbard lets himself back into the Wendices' apartment with the key he found in Tony's overcoat pocket. He phones the local police station, telling one of his officers to 'Start the ball rolling!'

Mark also returns to the apartment, determined to find out what's going on. He is delighted when Margot is escorted by police officers back to the apartment. He and Hubbard watch as Margot takes her key from her handbag and tries to let herself in, but it doesn't work. Instead Hubbard lets her in. Bewildered, Margot can't understand why the key didn't fit the lock and Hubbard explains that he now knows she is innocent of the crime, certain that her husband had plotted to murder her. The key in Margot's bag was in fact Swan's own house key. Tony had assumed that the key he found in Swan's pocket was the one he had left under the stair carpet, not realising that Swan had returned the key before entering the apartment. Sure enough, Hubbard finds Margot's key where Swan left it. He dispatches one of his officers to get Margot's handbag back to the station before Tony arrives to collect it.

Tony has realised he's got the wrong overcoat and heads up to the police station to get his own back from Hubbard. When he discovers that Hubbard isn't there, he collects Margot's handbag and returns home, planning on using Margot's key to let himself in, but of course 'Margot's key' doesn't work. It doesn't take long for Tony to work out his mistake. Retrieving the hidden key from under the carpet, Tony lets himself into the flat, where he is greeted by Inspector Hubbard, a bewildered Margot and Mark. He quickly realises that the game is up and helps himself to a large drink.

ROOTS: Once again, Hitchcock decided to make a film of a play, in this case Frederick Knott's highly successful *Dial M for Murder*, which had been a massive hit in both London and New York in 1952.

LEGACY: Remade for television in 1981, starring Angie Dickinson and Christopher Plummer. An Indian version, called *Aitbaar*, was made in 1985 and an updated version – based more closely on the original stage play – appeared in 1998 in the guise of *A Perfect Murder*, starring Michael Douglas and Gwyneth Paltrow.

WHO'S WHO?: Ray Milland's most famous performance was as an alcoholic writer in *The Lost Weekend* (Billy Wilder, 1945). Anthony Dawson (*Swan Lesgate*) played James Bond's sinister opponent Blofeld in two uncredited appearances in *From Russia With Love* (Terence Young, 1963) and *Thunderball* (Terence Young, 1965).

Patrick Allen (*Pearson*) is best known as a voice-over artist, most notably for the famous Barratt Homes adverts that saw him swooping into housing estates in a helicopter. Guy Doleman (*a detective*) was the first of many Number 2s in the classic 60s TV show *The Prisoner*.

THE USUAL SUSPECTS: Robert Cummings had previously played the dashing hero Barry Kane in *Saboteur*. John Williams had already turned up in *The Paradine Case* and would return later in *To Catch a Thief* in addition to several episodes of *Alfred Hitchcock Presents*. Grace Kelly makes her first of three appearances for Hitchcock here – see the box below.

KILLER LINES: Inspector Hubbard, to Mark, as he tries to explain the convoluted plot: 'They talk about flat-footed policemen . . . may the saints preserve us from the gifted amateur!'

THERE HE IS!: When Tony shows Swan the old reunion photo, Hitchcock can be seen seated on the left-hand side of the picture.

MISOGYNY: Swan's attack on Margot is very unpleasant, appearing more like a rape than a strangulation. The care and attention Hitch paid to this sequence – allegedly spending a quarter of the shooting time on this one scene – reinforces the view that Hitchcock was preoccupied with the beauty of death and suffering. And, yet again, Hitchcock chooses strangulation as his preferred method of dispatch for a beautiful blonde. However, it's the oft-quoted line 'There wasn't enough gleam to the scissors, and a murder without gleaming scissors is like asparagus without the hollandaise sauce: tasteless,' that encouragingly reveals that Hitchcock could be interested in other methods of dispatch as well.

TABOOS: Margot Wendice commits a serious moral sin for the audience of the early 1950s. Although she is trapped in a loveless marriage, she has an affair. Worse still, she doesn't appear to regret what she's done, and she seems to be actively considering starting the affair up again. With his Victorian Catholic sensibility, it's unsurprising that Hitchcock makes Margot suffer for her sins before she is allowed to be forgiven.

MUSIC: A very uneven score that sometimes manages to support the content of the film perfectly, and sometimes undermines dramatic moments with inappropriately bombastic or light-hearted movements.

POSTER: 'If a woman answers . . . hang on for dear life!'/'It holds you spellbound with suspense'/'Murder calling in 3D! The most famous Alfred Hitchcock movie of all time!' (1978 rerelease). Most posters showed a variation on the same artwork, depicting a blonde woman with one arm outstretched as a man attacks her and a telephone receiver dangles from the table. Some posters had the additional line, 'Is that you, darling?' coming from the phone's mouthpiece.

THE ICE MAIDEN: In her first film for Hitchcock, Grace Kelly makes an immediate and stunning impact. Although her performance here is perhaps less confident than her later roles in *Rear Window* and *To Catch a Thief*, Margot Wendice is still a sympathetic heroine. We really sympathise with her plight – initially in whether to choose her husband or her lover, later her bemused detachment when she realises she is soon to die for a crime she didn't commit.

WHAT THE PAPERS SAID: *The Times* viewed *Dial M for Murder* as a movie with an ingenious plot but a unique challenge to its director, in filming almost the entire picture on one set: 'The dependence of the film on words makes it unusually difficult for Mr Alfred Hitchcock to give the production as a whole his characteristic subtle touch.' The review goes on to add, 'The use of colour, too, hardly helps; the bright interior simply refuses to brood.'

COSTUME: Grace Kelly felt that her working relationship with the costume designer, Edith Head, was a particularly successful partnership. She gained Hitchcock's confidence when she convinced him that Margot would get up to answer the telephone wearing only her nightdress, rather than the heavy velvet robe he had suggested. Throughout the film, her costumes reflect her mood and behaviour: virginal white when with her husband; bright scarlet when in a passionate kiss with Mark (a 'scarlet woman', indeed!); then gradually becoming more and more drab as her hopelessness and sense of confusion increase.

TRIVIA: *Dial M . . .* was filmed and briefly released in 3-D and if you look carefully, you will notice that the finger dialling the fateful letter 'M' in the murder sequence is actually a huge wooden replica. It seems that the 3-D process didn't work when the camera focused in on small details, so Hitchcock had a massive telephone and finger built (similar to the hand he had constructed for *Spellbound*) to ensure that this important shot worked as effectively as possible. The movie was quickly released in a conventional, 'flat' version as the fad for 3-D movies ran its course. *Dial M for Murder* was reissued in 3-D in 1980 during a

Grace Kelly (1928–1982)

A former model and stage actress, Grace Kelly came to prominence with *High Noon* (Fred Zinnermann, 1952) and her Oscar-nominated role in *Mogambo* (John Ford, 1953). Kelly starred in three consecutive films for Alfred Hitchcock, who made brilliant use of her signature combination of cool, elegant charm and smouldering sensuality. In 1956 she married Prince Rainier of Monaco, becoming Her Serene Highness, Princess Grace of Monaco, and retired from acting. Though her collaboration with Hitchcock was brief, their friendship lasted until his death and her influence on the director was evident in the way he continued to remould his later actresses in her image. Grace Kelly died in a tragic car accident in 1982.

resurgence of interest in the gimmick, and fans can still see the attempted murder sequence in 3-D today, at the Alfred Hitchcock attraction at Universal Studios' Theme Park in Florida.

The 'M' that Tony dials refers to Maida Vale in North London, where the Wendices' apartment is located: in the 50s, different parts of London could be telephoned by prefixing the individual number with a code letter – in this case, 'M'.

FINAL ANALYSIS: An altogether more successful attempt at filming a stage play in a single set than *Rope* had been, *Dial M for Murder* is a colourful and entertaining romp that moves along at a very brisk pace. Ray Milland continues the Hitchcock tradition of making the villain the most interesting character in the movie, and, although our sympathies lie with Margot, it's Tony for whom the audience roots. We want his meticulous planning and preparation to be successful – it's by far the most premeditated murder in any of Hitchcock's films, having been planned by Tony for at least twelve months. Of course, no matter how intelligent a villain may be, it's always the little details that lead to their downfall. In Tony Wendice's case, it's his underestimation of Swan's intelligence – that he would immediately put the key back underneath the stair carpet – that proves his undoing. And it's even more satisfying that the equally intelligent and equally charming Inspector Hubbard manages to see through Tony's duplicity. 8/10

Rear Window (1954)

(Colour – 113 mins)

Produced by Alfred Hitchcock/Paramount Pictures

Written by John Michael Hayes, from a story by Cornell Woolrich

Original music: Franz Waxman, with additional music by
Friedrich von Flotow (from *Martha*)
Director of Photography: Robert Burks
Costume Design: Edith Head
Film Editing: George Tomasini
Assistant Director: Herbert Coleman
Set Decorator: Sam Comer
Special Effects: John P Fulton
Art Director: J Mcmillan Johnson
Technical Adviser: Bob Landry
Sound: Harry Lindgren, John Cope
Set Decorator: Ray Moyer
Colour Consultant: Richard Mueller
Art Director: Hal Pereira
Special Visual Effects: Irmin Roberts
Camera Operator: William Schurr
Camera Assistant: Leonard J South
Make-up Artist: Wally Westmore
1998 Reconstruction and Restoration: Robert A Harris
Producer, 1998 Restoration: James C Katz

CAST: James Stewart (*LB 'Jeff' Jeffries*), Grace Kelly (*Lisa Carol Fremont*), Wendell Corey (*Thomas J Doyle*), Thelma Ritter (*Stella*), Raymond Burr (*Lars Thorwald*), Judith Evelyn (*Miss Lonelyhearts*), Ross Bagdasarian (*Songwriter*), Georgine Darcy (*Miss Torso*), Sara Berner (*Woman on Fire Escape*), Frank Cady (*Man on Fire Escape*), Jesslyn Fax (*Miss Hearing Aid*), Rand Harper (*Honeymooner*), Irene Winston (*Mrs Thorwald*), Havis Davenport (*Newlywed*).

UNCREDITED CAST: Jerry Antes (*Dancer*), Barbara Bailey (*Choreographer*), Benny Bartlett (*Miss Torso's Friend*), Iphigenie Castiglioni (*Woman with Bird*), Marla English, Kathryn Grant (*Party Girls*), Bess Flowers (*Woman with Poodle*), Fred Graham (*Stunt Detective*), Len Hendry, Mike Mahoney (*Policemen*), Harry Landers (*Young Man*), Alan Lee (*Landlord*), Anthony Warde (*Detective*), Eddie Parker, Dick Simmons, Ralph Smiley.

SUMMARY: LB Jeffries, known to his friends as 'Jeff', is a successful magazine photographer who specialises in dangerous-sports photographs and foreign assignments. Jeff has broken his leg while trying to get a spectacular photo at a Grand Prix, and has been confined to his small New York apartment for the past seven weeks. He discusses his situation with Stella, the nurse sent to look after him by his insurance company. Stella disapproves of Jeff's principal pastime: his window looks out into an enclosed courtyard, almost entirely surrounded by apartment blocks, and he has taken to watching the lives and loves of his nearby neighbours, including a lonely woman (whom Jeff names 'Miss Lonelyhearts'), a composer and a salesman who has regular rows with his bedridden wife. Stella reminds him that 'Peeping Toms' used to have their eyes put out with a red-hot poker.

Stella also disapproves of Jeff's reluctance to marry his girlfriend Lisa. Jeff argues that Lisa's job as a fashion model and 'It Girl' isn't compatible with his high-risk career and the worldwide travel he needs to do.

Stella leaves, and Jeff spends some time watching his neighbours, but eventually he doses off. Early the same evening, he is woken up by a kiss from his girlfriend, Lisa. She has brought with her a sumptuous lobster dinner from one of New York's top restaurants, and is wearing an expensive *haute-couture* dress. Once again feeling insecure about his relationship, Jeff is barely polite to Lisa. She raises the subject again of Jeff's career and suggests that she could get him all the work he could ever need thanks to her connections. Jeff snubs her offer, ridiculing her idea by turning it back on her and noting how unlikely it would be for her to abandon her career and follow him around the world instead. Lisa leaves, her feelings hurt. Jeff begins to fall asleep in his wheelchair again, and is woken up by a piercing scream coming from somewhere outside.

Jeff happens to notice that a salesman who lives across the courtyard from him has left his apartment in the pouring rain several times through the night. Each time he carries his heavy suitcase of sample products with him, returning with it empty. Thinking little of it, Jeff finally falls asleep.

The next morning, Jeff notices some more suspicious activity. The salesman starts shooing a neighbour's pet dog away from one of his flower beds – a flower bed that looks as though it has already been disturbed. Jeff becomes curious when he sees the salesman cleaning the inside of his sample case, and scrubbing a saw and a large knife clean. Perhaps most damning of all is that the salesman's sick wife is nowhere to be seen. Jeff shares his suspicions with Stella, who gleefully joins in the speculation.

On her next visit to Jeff, Lisa does her best to make up with him. Despite her extremely provocative advances and glamorous nightwear, Jeff seems to be far more interested in the salesman and his missing wife. Lisa is not entirely convinced by Jeff's theories, but they soon notice the salesman tightly tying some ropes around a very large and heavy trunk and soon Lisa is as intrigued as Jeff and Stella.

Lisa discovers from the apartment block letterboxes that the salesman's name is Lars Thorwald. Stella and Jeff observe two parcel-post men arriving at Thorwald's apartment to collect the trunk. Stella dashes out of Jeff's apartment, but just misses seeing the name of the delivery firm. Jeff decides to contact a police friend of his, Tom Doyle, who is sympathetic, but dismissive of Jeff's theories. He can rebuff all of Jeff's accusations, citing witnesses who believe they saw Mrs Thorwald leaving with her husband on the night she disappeared. He has even retrieved a postcard from Thorwald's letterbox, which says, 'Arrived, feeling better, Anna.' Jeff is both embarrassed and disappointed, and Doyle leaves.

Later that night, Lisa arrives with a small overnight bag, clearly intent on staying over. They notice that Thorwald seems to be packing a large suitcase to leave. Their suspicions are raised again when Jeff notices that Thorwald has his wife's handbag. Lisa supports Jeff with her view that no woman would ever go away on a journey and leave her favourite handbag behind. Doyle pops in again to say that his colleagues have intercepted the mysterious trunk. All that was inside were Mrs Thorwald's clothes. Lisa and Jeff insist that this is suspicious, but Doyle is still adamant that they have no real evidence to support their murder theory. When Doyle adds that Mrs Thorwald signed the delivery note for the trunk, they both blank him and keep on watching Thorwald. Doyle leaves, unwilling to waste any more time.

Lisa changes for bed and unveils a glamorous silk nightgown. She closes the blinds in preparation for an intimate evening with Jeff. Suddenly, they hear a piercing scream. The owner of the overcurious dog has found it lying dead in the courtyard with its neck broken. Distraught, the woman shouts a tirade of abuse at her neighbours, all of whom look out of their windows or come on to their balconies to observe what is happening. All but one, that is – Thorwald doesn't react.

The next day, Jeff, Lisa and Stella observe Thorwald washing the walls of his bathroom down and come to the conclusion that he must have used his bath to dismember his wife's body. They also work out that the dog was sniffing around the flower bed because Thorwald had buried something there, which is why he killed it. They plan to wait until it gets darker before digging the flowerbed up, but are shocked to realise that Thorwald is packed and ready to leave. Jeff scribbles a note that reads: 'What have you done with her?' which Lisa pushes through Thorwald's door. Thorwald reads it, and hastens his packing. Jeff then telephones Thorwald's apartment, and tells the salesman that he wants to meet him immediately in the bar of the Albert Hotel in order to 'settle the estate of your late wife'. Thorwald leaves for the nearby hotel, and Lisa and Stella run down into the courtyard and begin digging up the garden, as Jeff keeps lookout for Thorwald.

Lisa and Stella gesture back up to Jeff that they can't find anything buried and, to Jeff's horror, Lisa decides to climb up the exterior fire escape and break into Thorwald's apartment through an open window. It's clear that she's looking for Mrs Thorwald's handbag. Stella returns to Jeff's apartment, where she notices the depressed 'Miss Lonelyhearts' about to take an overdose of pills and alcohol. She begs Jeff to call for the police. At the same time, Lisa seems to have found some evidence – she gestures to Jeff from across the courtyard that she has found some of Mrs Thorwald's jewellery. She is about to leave the apartment when Thorwald returns – distracted by Miss Lonelyhearts, Jeff had failed to see him coming. Instead of calling the police to help Miss Lonelyhearts, Jeff tells them that a man is molesting a woman in Thorwald's apartment. He can only watch in impotent horror as Thorwald finds

Lisa, starts violently shaking her, and turns out the light. Thankfully, at that moment the police arrive.

Lisa is explaining her breaking and entering to the police. As she does so, she turns her back to the window and holds her hands behind her back. She points to her hand – she is wearing Mrs Thorwald's wedding ring, surely the crucial evidence they need. Unfortunately, Thorwald observes the gesture and finally realises where his tormentor has been.

Lisa is led away by the police. Stella goes to the station to bail Lisa out, leaving Jeff alone in the apartment. He phones Doyle and tells him that Lisa has been arrested. Doyle agrees to come over at once. Jeff suddenly realises that Thorwald is nowhere to be seen, and that Thorwald now knows where he lives. Stuck in his wheelchair, Jeff can do little to protect himself. He grabs a handful of spare flash bulbs and backs his chair as far away from the door as he can. Thorwald enters the apartment. He moves forward to attack Jeff, but is temporarily dazzled by Jeff repeatedly firing his camera flash at him. The police and Lisa arrive at Thorwald's apartment from where they see Thorwald trying to tip Jeff out of his window. Jeff struggles to hold on to the window ledge, but loses his grip and plummets to the courtyard below.

Thorwald confesses to the police and takes them on a tour of the East River, where he has distributed some his wife's body parts. Some of her had indeed been buried under the flower bed, but, after the dog started digging around, he had moved it to a hatbox in his apartment.

Some time later, we see the lives of the residents of the apartment block again. The young composer and Miss Lonelyhearts have become close, thanks to the melody he played that prevented her suicide attempt. The owner of the murdered dog has acquired a new canine companion, and a newly married couple are having their first major row. Jeff, however, is not paying any attention to any of them. He is sitting in his wheelchair, both legs now in plaster, dozing peacefully with his back to the window. Lisa is sitting beside him, happily looking after her future husband.

CASTING: Hitchcock supposedly hired Raymond Burr to play Lars Thorwald because he could be easily made to look like his old producer David O Selznick, who Hitchcock felt interfered too much. James Stewart was so convinced this movie would be a hit that he agreed to receive a percentage of the film's profits rather than a salary. Supposedly, Grace Kelly had to choose between *Rear Window* and *On the Waterfront*, which was offered to her at the same time. The female lead in *On the Waterfront* was Eva Marie Saint, who of course later starred in *North by Northwest*.

ROOTS: The original short story, 'It Had To Be Murder' (published under Cornell Woolrich's pen name William Irish) was republished under the title 'Rear Window' after the film's release.

In 1933, Tony Mancini, a 26-year-old waiter, was acquitted of the murder of his mistress, whose body was found inside a trunk, in his flat. A second body was found the same year at a railway station. Jammed into the trunk, it was found to be missing its head and legs and was never identified, nor was the murderer ever found. In 1976, Mancini confessed to a newspaper that he had killed his mistress, but that he knew nothing about the other body.

LEGACY: Based mainly on Woolrich's original story, a television remake of *Rear Window* aired in the US in November 1998 on ABC. Christopher Reeve starred as a quadriplegic who engages in a cat-and-mouse game with a killer. Despite the fact that the Hitchcock estate owns the rights to the film, The *Los Angeles Times* reported that the owner of the Cornell Woolrich short story is still legally entitled to commercially exploit their property. This entitlement runs out in late 1999, which was the reason that the restored rerelease of the film was delayed for nearly two years.

The noted Hitchophile Brian De Palma has, of course, made his own versions of *Rear Window*: First in *Hi, Mom* (1970), a comedy in which Robert De Niro plays an amateur pornographer who uses his neighbours as his subjects, then in *Sisters* (1973), where Margot Kidder plays twins, one of whom is seen murdering her boyfriend by her neighbour. In *Body Double* (1984), which also has links to *Vertigo*, Craig Wasson spies on Melanie Griffith and witnesses what appears to be her murder. Other films that revolve around similar themes include *I Saw What You Did* (William Castle, 1965), in which teenage prank callers stumble across a murderer; Woody Allen's *Manhattan Murder Mystery* (1993), where Allen and Diane Keaton suspect their neighbour of killing his wife for the insurance; *Sliver* (Phillip Noyce, 1993), where William Baldwin uses an intricate CCTV network to spy on the residents of an apartment block; and *Dream With the Fishes* (Finn Taylor, 1997), starring David Arquette as a suicidal voyeur who develops an obsession with one of his neighbours. In *A Kiss Before Dying* (James Dearden, 1991), we actually get to see the killer, Matt Dillon, disposing of one of his victims by cutting the body up in a bath, then packing the remains in a trunk. Ugh.

Also, look out for a *The Simpsons* episode, 'Bart of Darkness', which not only features a similar plotline to *Rear Window*, but features a guest appearance by Jimmy Stewart, who still apparently lives in that same apartment. Of course, the fate that befalls Jeff is almost replayed by James Stewart in the opening moments of *Vertigo* – only this time, he manages to hold on!

WHO'S WHO?: Raymond Burr would gain worldwide fame in the mid-60s for his roles in the TV series *Perry Mason* and *Ironside*, where – somewhat spookily – he played a detective confined to a wheelchair.

THE USUAL SUSPECTS: Jimmy Stewart made his first Hitch appearance in *Rope*, and would later return for *The Man Who Knew*

Too Much and *Vertigo*. Grace Kelly was in the middle of her three-film sequence of *Dial M for Murder*, *Rear Window* and *To Catch a Thief*.

ANIMAL CRUELTY: The murder of the dog shows the extent of Thorwald's evil: 'I couldn't imagine any of you being so low as you'd kill a little helpless friendly dog,' cries the dog's owner in disbelief. 'The only thing in this whole neighbourhood who liked anybody. Did you kill him because he *liked* ya?'

KILLER LINES: As they begin to doubt their convictions, Lisa makes a telling observation: 'You know if someone came in here, they wouldn't believe what they'd see? You and me with long faces plunged into despair because we find out a man *didn't* kill his wife. We're two of the most frightening ghouls I've ever known.'

Stella complains to Jeff: 'We've become a race of Peeping Toms. What people ought to do is get outside their own house and look in for a change. Yes, sir. How's that for a bit of homespun philosophy?' Later, as Jeff tries to eat his breakfast, Stella speculates as to how Thorwald disposed of the body: 'Just where do you suppose he cut her up? Of course – the bathtub! It's the only place he could have washed away the blood . . .' Jeff looks queasy and puts down his fork and takes a swig of coffee, which he nearly chokes on as Stella adds: 'He'd better take that trunk away before it starts to leak . . .'

Jeff, to Doyle, discussing Lars Thorwald and his missing wife: 'Don't tell me – he's an unemployed magician entertaining the neighbourhood with his sleight of hand.'

THERE HE IS!: About an hour into the film, Hitchcock is briefly seen winding the clock in the songwriter's apartment. The songwriter is the real-life composer and vocalist Ross Bagdasarian Jr.

MISOGYNY: Having just witnessed one of the Thorwalds' fiery rows, Jeff tells his boss: 'If you don't pull me out of this swamp of boredom I'm gonna do something drastic . . . I'm gonna get married'.

AWARDS: Oscar-nominated for Best Cinematography, Screenplay, Sound and Best Director. Though John Michael Hayes won an award for the screenplay, Hitchcock received only a nomination for direction, despite the film's clear financial success. Listed as one of the American Film Institute's top 100 films of the decade (number 42), *Rear Window* has also been selected for preservation by the National Film Registry of the Library of Congress.

THEMES AND MOTIFS: Male and female gender roles are very important in *Rear Window*. Jeff is terrified of committing to a relationship with Lisa because she is too perfect, too feminine. He sees this as a challenge to his ultramasculine job, and can't reconcile the two.

In fact, for a large portion of the film, it looks as though their relationship is going to break down completely. It's only Lisa's determination that keeps it going.

But note how Jeff's perception of Lisa changes significantly when she assumes a more reckless, brave, 'masculine' role. He is scared for her, of course (not least because he, as the man, is unable to protect her from danger), but he is also transfixed. When she breaks into Thorwald's apartment, there is a sense of overwhelming pride in Jeff. The camera makes us believe that Jeff is finally falling back in love with Lisa again. When Lisa is seen to be in real peril, Jeff's impotent reaction shots are almost feminine – gasping and holding his hands to his mouth. Once the crime has been solved, we see Jeff back in his wheelchair, more helpless than he was before. However, he now has the brave Lisa, masculinised and able to protect him. She even literally 'wears the trousers' in their relationship. It's only when she's certain that he is asleep that Lisa is able to cast off her male-image and return to reading the fashion magazine she is really interested in.

Of course, the concept of voyeurism plays its part too. All of the major characters warn Jeff of the consequences of looking, despite the fact that his best friend Doyle is a detective and his girlfriend Lisa is a model used to being looked at by complete strangers. Even the 'moral' Stella, who vociferously objects to Jeff's hobby, admits to having spied on the Director of General Motors and his bathroom habits. This all fits neatly in with Jeff's occupation – he is of course a celebrated photographer, paid to see what others can't. As such, it's not surprising that his attention starts to wander. Perhaps Lisa ought to be grateful that Jeff obsesses on Thorwald and not the more obvious attractions of Miss Torso!

When it comes to voyeurism, few are greater perpetrators than movie directors themselves, revealing to audiences the innermost stories and feelings of other people's lives. It's clear that Jeff is a substitute figure for Hitchcock himself. Largely chairbound and immobile, Jeff's/Hitch's point of view is exactly what we as an audience end up seeing. Like his director, Jeff spends most of his time creating stories and names for the characters he sees. He even views them through a series of small movie-screen-shaped frames. It's also interesting to speculate how closely Jeff's feelings of inadequacy when confronted with the 'perfect' Lisa matched Hitch's own relationships with his glamorous stars, as well as with his own wife.

TABOOS: Doyle is slightly scandalised and more than a little envious of Jeff when he realises that Lisa – his girlfriend, not his wife – is planning to spend the night with him. As Lisa puts it when showing Jeff her glamorous nightdress, it's a 'preview of coming attractions'. The newly married woman appears to be naked in a scene when she comes to the window, though on closer inspection we realise she's actually wearing a snug-fitting skin-coloured bodice.

MUSIC: Franz Waxman's score recycles music from older scores of his, among them *A Place in the Sun* (1951) and *Elephant Walk* (1954). The song 'To See You is to Love You' is playing when Jeff toasts Miss Lonelyhearts. Another nice little touch is that the song 'Mona Lisa' (made famous by Nat King Cole) can be heard playing at the lively party while Jeff's Lisa moans at Doyle for not doing anything. As a very naturalistic film, it would be very inappropriate for the orchestra to strike up every few minutes. The lack of a score significantly adds to the tension in many of the scenes, particularly during Lisa's investigation of Thorwald's apartment. At times, you can even hear Jeff and Stella holding their breath!

POSTER (for 1962 rerelease): 'See it! . . . if your nerves can stand it after Psycho'.

TRAILER (again for 1962 rerelease): A voice-over introduces us to the 'scene of the crime' and shows us round some of the neighbours before James Stewart explains: 'First I watched them just to kill time, but then I couldn't take my eyes off them, just as you won't be able to . . .' The voice-over resumes, promising that : '. . . you won't be able to take your eyes off the glowing beauty of Grace Kelly, who shares the heart and curiosity of James Stewart in this story of a romance shadowed by the terror of a horrifying secret.'

THE ICE MAIDEN: For the single greatest example on celluloid of Hitchcock's ideal woman, you need look no further than Grace Kelly. She's stunning in *Dial M for Murder* and *To Catch a Thief*, but here in *Rear Window* she's simply unparalleled. All of the characteristics that sum up the Ice Maiden – cool, emotional restraint barely masking a passionate, energetic personality underneath; untouchable glamour; and an eventual unwavering support for our flawed hero – can be found here. Grace never looked better; her performance is little short of flawless; and that opening kiss must be the most enticing kiss in cinema history.

WHAT THE PAPERS SAID: The 11 October 1954 edition of *The Times* describes how Hitchcock plays a game with his audience: 'He plays fair – not an extra knave, let alone an ace, up his sleeve – and he plays skilfully, but he must be glad of the presence of some bright, amusing dialogue and of the help of the playing of Mr Stewart, in the major role, and of Miss Thelma Ritter and Miss Grace Kelly in minor ones.'

COSTUME: Edith Head's designs are flawless, particularly for Grace Kelly's Lisa. Her outfits are perfect for a glamorous fashion model, and in particular the use of colour is clever and effective. The colour of Lisa's outfits is often mirrored in those worn by Miss Torso and Miss Lonelyhearts – linking the three characters as fragments of the same potential woman/fate for Jeff.

TRIVIA: The set (Thorwald's apartment is on 125 W Ninth Street) contained 32 apartments. At the time it was the largest indoor set ever built at Paramount Studios. They were all constructed in the studio because real apartments couldn't be lit to Hitchcock's satisfaction. In reality, there is no 125 W. Ninth Street in Manhattan – it turns into Christopher Street before the numbering gets that high. The design of the apartment block seen in the film was based on a real apartment block which could be found on Christopher Street. The real-life stretch of road that can be seen behind the apartment block was also the location of the famous Stonewall gay-rights riots some fifteen years later.

Aside from a couple of shots near the end and the discovery of the dead dog, the entire film apparently originates from inside Jeff's apartment.

FINAL ANALYSIS: It could be argued that *Rear Window* struggles to overcome the limitations of yet another one-set film (like *Lifeboat* and *Rope*). It could be argued that very little actually happens, being made up of the suspicions and inferences of a very bored man. It could even be argued that *Rear Window* is Hitchcock's least dynamic picture of all.

Of course, to do so would be sheer madness, overlooking the fact that the film is a triumph because of those very limitations. It is far too easy to eulogise about how brilliant *Rear Window* actually is. The film's undoubted success and near-legendary reputation are simply due to the fact that all of the ingredients in the mix work so well together. Boasting an ensemble cast that are perfect for their roles, a script that sparkles with dozens of memorable lines, a stunningly innovative and realistic set and a director at the very peak of his powers, *Rear Window* just couldn't fail. Perfection. **10/10!**

To Catch a Thief (1955)

(Colour – 107 mins)

Produced by Alfred Hitchcock/Paramount Pictures

Written by John Michael Hayes, based on the book by David Dodge

Original music: Lyn Murray
Director of Photography: Robert Burks
Costume Design: Edith Head
Film Editing: George Tomasini
Second Unit Director: Herbert Coleman
Set Decorator: Sam Comer
Sound: John Cope
Process Photography: Farciot Edouart
Dialogue Coach: Elsie Foulstone
Special Effects: John P Fulton

Art Director: Joseph Macmillan Johnson
Photographer, Second Unit: Wallace Kelley
Set Decorator: Arthur Krams
Sound: Harold C Lewis
Assistant Director: Daniel McCauley
Colour Consultant: Richard Mueller
Art Director: Hal Pereira
Make-up Artist: Wally Westmore

CAST: Cary Grant (*John Robie*), Grace Kelly (*Frances Stevens*), Jessie Royce Landis (*Jessie Stevens*), John Williams (*HH Hughson*), Charles Vanel (*Bertani*), Brigitte Auber (*Danielle Foussard*), Jean Martinelli (*Foussard*), Georgette Anys (*Germaine*).

UNCREDITED CAST: John Alderson (*Detective*), René Blancard (*Inspector Lepic*), Lewis Charles (*Man with Milk in Kitchen*), Frank Chelland (*Chef*), William 'Wee Willie' Davis (*Big Man in Kitchen*), Dominique Davray (*Antoinette*), Guy De Vestel (*Detective*), Russell Gaige (*Mr Sanford*), Steven Geray (*Desk Clerk*), Michael Hadlow (*Monaco Policeman*), Gladys Holland (*Elegant French Woman*), Jean Hébey (*Mercier*), Bela Kovacs (*Detective*), Roland Lesaffre (*Claude*), Edward Manouk (*Kitchen Help*), Don Megowan (*Detective*), Louis Mercier (*Croupier*), Paul Newlan (*Vegetable Man*), Leonard Penn (*Monaco Policeman*), Otto F Schulze (*Chef*), Marie Stoddard (*Mrs Sanford*), Aimee Torriani (*Woman in Kitchen*), Philip Van Zandt (*Jewellery Clerk*), Martha Bamattre.

SUMMARY: In the South of France, a spate of late-night jewel robberies alarms the police. They immediately suspect John Robie, a man reputed to have been one of the most successful cat burglars ever. During the war he had been a hero of the French Resistance and now he lives in retirement in a villa in Nice. The police go to question him and after hearing their accusations he pretends to go to get changed and successfully escapes. After a brief chase through the hills, Robie gives them the slip and catches a bus to Cannes. There he visits Bertani, an old friend from the war who is now a restaurateur. Robie protests his innocence to him but Bertani warns him that many of his old colleagues believe he is guilty and feel he has let them all down. He soon sees evidence of this when he notices the looks that the kitchen staff give him.

Robie doesn't understand how someone could copy his style so closely, picking their victims so carefully and covering their tracks so carefully. He decides the only way he can prove his innocence is to catch the copycat thief himself. Bertani tells him that recently a man came to the restaurant and asked many strange questions regarding the jewellery of his patrons. Just then, the police arrive and Robie is helped to escape by a girl called Danielle, daughter of Foussard the head waiter.

They drive off in a speedboat. Danielle teases Robie, insisting on referring to his days as 'the Cat'. It seems she does not believe he is innocent either. Returning to shore, Robie speaks to Bertani by telephone. His friend tells him that a man has contacted him, and asked him to tell Robie to meet him at the entrance to the flower market in Nice.

At the flower market HH Hughson, a respectable-looking middle-aged man, introduces himself to Robie. He tells him that he is a representative of Lloyd's of London, who act as insurers for most of the wealthy locals. Bertani has told Mr Hughson that Robie is willing to offer a little help in recovering some of their losses. Hughson believes that only an honest man would be so foolish and agrees to give him a list of his wealthiest clients. At this point, Robie notices he's being followed and tries to escape but the police catch him.

Awaiting his court appearance, Robie tells Hughson that he has ten days to prove his innocence. They examine the list of clients to decide who is most likely to be at risk. Hughson confesses he's informed the police about their plan and was surprised that they thought it was a good idea, even if only because they believe Robie will make a mistake and expose himself as the thief. Looking at the list, Robie highlights the most likely person to be the ersatz Cat's next victim, Mrs Stevens, an American woman travelling with her daughter. Asking Hughson if he knows them, he informs him that coincidentally he's due to have dinner with them the following evening.

After their meal, Mrs Stevens drags Hughson and her daughter Frances to the casino. She sees John Robie at the table and soon invites him for a drink, evidently as a prospective suitor for her daughter. At the end of the evening, Robie escorts the women to their hotel rooms and as he says goodnight to Frances she kisses him passionately.

The next morning, as Robie visits the Stevenses, Hughson comes to tell them there's been another robbery. Mrs Stevens refuses to place her jewellery in the hotel safe, despite pleas from Mr Hughson. Frances invites John for a swim and the couple head to the foyer. As John drops off his room key, the concierge tells him there's a message for him – the note warns him he's used up one life and not to risk his remaining eight.

At the beach, Robie sees Danielle. She accuses him of being responsible for last night's robbery and warns him his old colleagues are planning to kill him rather than risk letting him continue his exploits. When he returns to collect his clothes he notices that the list of Hughson's clients that was in his jacket now has a wet thumbprint on it. Returning to the hotel, Frances offers to take him for a drive and be his tour guide for the duration of his stay. Noticing he is still under observation from the police, he accepts her offer. Along the way, he encourages her to speed in the hope that they might lose their tail. Eventually, Frances slows down – and tells him that she was aware they were being followed and that she knows he is John Robie, 'the Cat'. He claims she is mistaken but she is certain – she saw him swim ashore that first day, then two days later he appeared as 'Mr Conrad Burns, just over from America', even though he's evidently not an American. She noticed how he spoke only to her mother, never to her, and after reading about the newspaper reports of the Cat she put two and two together. Seemingly excited by the prospect of 'catching' a famous thief, Frances invites him to dinner.

At dinner she teases that he might want to use the upcoming costume ball as the perfect opportunity to steal any number of jewels. But her jokes turn to condemnation when her mother's jewels go missing. She immediately runs to search his room while he speaks to Mrs Stevens and confesses his true identity. Frances brings her mother the list of Hughson's clients as evidence of his guilt, but Mrs Stevens believes he is innocent – it turns out she cares little for the jewels as they were insured. When Frances opens the door to the police, John slips out and her mother covers for him by pretending to have never heard of him.

Robie arranges a meeting with Hughson to warn him that he's been staking out the house of the Silvers, a South American couple. He's seen someone else doing just the same and wants to use the Silvers to set a trap for whoever is posing as him. Unfortunately the trap backfires as Foussard and some other men from Bertani's restaurant are lying in wait. Robie manages to escape but not before Foussard falls to his death from a cliff top. The police misreport the event, claiming that the dead man was the cat burglar. Hughson is about to pay out on Mrs Stevens's claim and wants to be certain the return of her jewellery is not imminent. However, Robie informs him that the police have spread misinformation to prevent the robberies affecting the holiday trade, that Foussard had a wooden leg and was therefore incapable of committing the crimes, and that their real criminal is still at large.

The night of the costume ball every woman arrives wearing expensive jewellery. Frances and her mother are accompanied by Robie disguised as a canopy-bearer and wearing a face mask. He warns the women that the only unaccompanied men there will be policemen. Mrs Stevens asks Robie to fetch something for her and tactlessly addresses him by name within earshot of the police commissioner and a number of officers. Through the night they watch the bearer and Frances dance and when they eventually leave the party the police follow them – unaware that Hughson is now wearing the bearer's costume and that Robie has long left the party and is currently staking out the most likely property on the thief's list. It's not long before he sees a black-clad figure leave one of the houses via the rooftops. He slowly approaches but is seen and is forced to give chase. He captures and unmasks the thief – it's Danielle, who had provided the 'legwork' for her father's plans all along. The police see movement on the roof and train spotlights there as they try to shoot Robie down. As Robie tries to stop Danielle from escaping she slips. Robie manages to grab her hand and forces her to confess to the police down below that her father and Bertani had planned the robberies all along.

Back at Robie's villa, Frances tells him that he has her to thank for the police not gunning him down. She then confesses that she loves him and the couple embrace. It becomes clear to Robie that Frances is intent on staying – and that her mother will be moving in too.

TITLES: The opening titles roll across the backdrop of a travel agent's window (see also *The Man Who Knew Too Much*, 1934).

THE USUAL SUSPECTS: Cary Grant appears in *Suspicion, Notorious* and, with Jessie Royce Landis as his mother, *North by Northwest*. Grace Kelly completes her final picture for Hitchcock, having appeared in both *Dial M for Murder* and *Rear Window*. John Williams is also in *The Paradine Case* and *Dial M For Murder*, as well as several episodes of *Alfred Hitchcock Presents*.

ANIMAL CRUELTY: A minor point, but in the car chase at the very beginning the police car manages to brake as a flock of sheep blocks the way – and the sheep at the rear are visibly pushed forward.

KILLER LINES: 'I'm sorry I ever sent her to that finishing school,' says Jessie Stevens of her daughter. 'I think they finished her there!' Jessie later extols the virtues of bourbon over champagne: 'Why wait eighty years before you can drink the stuff? Great vineyards, huge barrels ageing for ever, poor little old monks running around, testing it just so some woman in Tulsa, Oklahoma, can say it "tickles her tongue"!'

HH Hughson asks Robie why he took up theft as a career. Robie replies honestly: 'To live better, to own things I couldn't afford, to acquire this good taste which you now enjoy and which I should be very reluctant to give up.' 'Oh, you mean you were frankly dishonest.' 'I try to be.'

THERE HE IS!: Nine minutes in, when Cary Grant gets on the bus, he sits between a cage containing two birds and Hitchcock. Grant stares at the director in surprise, as Hitch looks ahead, ignoring him. (On the video release of this, Hitchcock is almost completely excised thanks to that wonderful invention – the panned-and-scanned edit.)

AWARDS: Winner of the Best Cinematography Oscar, and nominated for Best Art Direction and Best Costume Design.

THEMES AND MOTIFS: The image of the black cat is exploited to the limit here. Black cats prowl the rooftops; one sits calmly in Robie's house clawing up the newspaper; Robie himself was once known as the Cat and when we first see him he's wearing a black-and-white-striped jumper (well, he is in France) and a red neckerchief that looks just like a pet's collar. See also **There he is!** above.

TABOOS: *To Catch a Thief* is riddled with innuendo. When Robie 'accidentally' drops a gambling chip down the front of a woman's dress, we see a lingering shot of her cleavage. The woman refuses to allow him to retrieve the chip (understandably), though when he explains it's a 10,000-franc chip she reluctantly takes him at his word and gives him the equivalent amount of her own chips as a pay-off, much to Mrs Stevens's amusement. The banter between Frances and Robie is particularly saucy and we challenge anyone to be able to suppress a smirk as Frances asks Robie if he fancies a leg or a breast – of chicken (see also **Final Analysis** below).

Jessie Stevens panders to Hitch's obsession with toilet humour. After her husband's death they discovered oil on their land. As they'd had an outside toilet, she quips that he 'never knew how close he came to twenty million barrels of oil'.

The police, who crash their car after swerving to avoid a roadhogging chicken, radio into base, shouting the word *'poulet'* – both 'chicken' and a term of abuse for policemen in French.

Robie claims he was a member of an American trapeze act and when the circus folded he put his agility to 'a more rewarding purpose'.

WHAT THE PAPERS SAID: Reporting on the Royal Film screening of *To Catch a Thief* that November, the reviewer for *The Times* noted how 'there is more wit than thrills, more humour than crime, more optimism (without false sentiment) than materialism. It is as good as a holiday in itself.'

FINAL ANALYSIS: Considering this was made during one of the most repressive eras of Hollywood, with the Hays Code still in force and everyone still sore after the McCarthy witch hunts, this is refreshingly light and shockingly suggestive. When Robie apologises for being so long with Danielle, Frances replies that she was surprised he wasn't 'a lot longer', and, when she invites him to 'hold them', we know full well he's not thinking of the diamonds she displays enticingly. Almost every line is exploited for double entendres and sexual innuendo, like the most sophisticated and relaxed *Carry On . . .* movie.

Throughout the film, Grant's masculinity seems to be undermined, in the way he trots downstairs, is watched almost lecherously by the beach attendant and quite clearly targeted by both Danielle and the Stevens women for seduction. It's quite refreshing to see Grace Kelly as the predator with someone like Grant as the object of desire. Though *To Catch a Thief* comes as something of a disappointment after *Dial M* and *Rear Window*, it's a sweet, entertaining distraction free of much of Hitchcock's traditional angst and repression. 7/10.

The Trouble with Harry (1955)

(Colour – 100 mins)

Produced by Alfred Hitchcock/Paramount Pictures

Associate Producer: Herbert Coleman

Written by John Michael Hayes, based on the novel by Jack Trevor Story

Original music: Bernard Herrmann
'Flaggin' the Train to Tuscaloosa': Lyrics by Mack David,
Music by Raymond Scott
Director of Photography: Robert Burks
Costume Design: Edith Head
Film Editing: Alma MacRorie
Set Decorator: Sam Comer
Special Photographic Effects: John P Fulton
Art Directors: John B Goodman, Hal Pereira
Assistant Director: Howard Joslin
Set Decorator: Emile Kuri
Sound: Harold C Lewis, Winston H Leverett
Colour Consultant: Richard Mueller
Make-up Supervisor: Wally Westmore

CAST: Edmund Gwenn (*Captain Albert Wiles*), John Forsythe (*Sam Marlowe*), Mildred Natwick (*Miss Gravely*), Mildred Dunnock (*Mrs Wiggs*), Jerry Mathers (*Arnie Rogers*), Royal Dano (*Calvin Wiggs*), Parker Fennelly (*Millionaire*), Barry Macollum (*Tramp*), Dwight Marfield (*Dr Greenbow*), Shirley MacLaine (*Jennifer Rogers*).

UNCREDITED CAST: Leslie Wolff (*Art Critic*), Philip Truex (*Harry Worp*), Ernest Curt Bach (*Chauffeur*).

SUMMARY: It's autumn in rural New England. A small boy, Arnie Rogers, is walking through the woods early one morning when he hears gunfire and goes to investigate. He discovers the body of a man, lying flat on his back in the middle of a clearing with a trickle of blood on his forehead. Arnie runs off just as Captain Albert Wiles arrives. He has been practising his gun technique, and automatically assumes that he has shot and killed the man. As the captain tries to hide the body, a local woman called Miss Gravely turns up. She is very sympathetic about his plight, and is quite happy to ignore what she's seen. She invites the captain to come over to her house for coffee and muffins.

Little Arnie returns with his mother Jennifer. Although she obviously recognises the dead man, Jennifer seems completely unfazed by his death, and takes her son back home. Two more passers-by encounter the corpse – a short-sighted and absent-minded doctor who trips over the body while reading a book, and a tramp who steals the poor man's shoes. Waiting in hiding for all of these passers-by to go, the captain nods off.

Sam Marlowe, a local artist, walks into Highwater village, planning to put another of his paintings up for sale at Mrs Wiggs's Emporium. Sam briefly chats to Mrs Wiggs's son Calvin, the deputy sheriff. Calvin is concerned about the gunfire he heard, and heads up into the woods to investigate. Inside the Emporium, Sam talks to Miss Gravely, who lets slip that she is expecting a 'gentleman caller' that afternoon.

Discovering the corpse, Sam sits down to sketch it. The captain wakes up and decides to confess to Sam that he accidentally killed the man. He asks Sam to help him bury the body, on the condition that they first check with Jennifer and little Arnie, to see if they are planning to report their discovery to the police.

While the captain has his date with Miss Gravely, Sam exchanges some flirty banter with Jennifer, and is shocked to discover that the corpse was in fact Harry Rogers, Jennifer's husband. She doesn't seem at all bothered by his death. She tells Sam about her tragic first marriage, losing her husband and then discovering that she was pregnant. Her husband's brother Harry decided to be noble and marry her, but after the wedding ceremony Harry abandoned her. She went back to live with her mother until Arnie was born, and then she and her son moved away. That morning he finally traced her. When she found him at her doorstep she whacked him with a milk bottle, and he staggered up to the forest where he presumably expired.

Later that afternoon, Sam and the captain go to bury the body. Deciding to say a few final words, the captain decides on 'Don't you ever show your face around here ever again.' Harry is finally laid to rest when the captain suddenly realises that he couldn't possibly have shot the man: he fired his gun only three times, and can account for each bullet. The captain therefore decides that they must dig Harry back up again, to check how he actually died. They fail to find any obvious injury on the body apart from the small mark on his forehead, so the number-one murder suspect now becomes Jennifer. In order to avoid becoming accessories to murder, Sam and the captain bury Harry again.

Miss Gravely visits the captain's house, where she admits to him that *she* murdered Harry. She was going for a stroll in the woods when he lurched out of the trees at her, so she hit him on the head with the metal heel of her hiking boot. She vows to go to the police and admit her *slight* involvement in his death – after the captain has dug the body up.

Sam and Jennifer are beginning to become close, despite her concern about Harry's death. Miss Gravely and the captain arrive, but are warned against confessing anything by Sam. He points out the publicity and intrusion that such an act would bring, and that it would also drag Jennifer's name through the papers. Miss Gravely, Sam, the captain and Jennifer decide to go up to the forest and bury Harry once more.

By now, night has fallen. As they walk back down the hill they are met by Mrs Wiggs, who is running excitedly towards them. She tells Sam that a millionaire wants to buy his pictures, and that he is waiting at the Emporium. It's true, and Sam ends up selling his artwork in return for gifts for all of his friends – strawberries every month for Jennifer, a cash register for Mrs Wiggs, a beauty parlour for Miss Gravely, and a Davy Crockett outfit for the captain. For himself, Sam secretly asks one thing of the millionaire, who says it can be easily arranged. The millionaire says he will return in the morning for the paintings, and will continue to buy them for as long as Sam continues to paint. Sam is particularly happy that Jennifer thinks he did the right thing, as he says he loves her and wants to marry her. She seems keen, but says she needs a little time to think about it.

Calvin returns home to his mother's store. He tells the group of amateur gravediggers that he found a pair of new shoes on a tramp, who says he took them from a corpse in the woods. Despite going to look for the body, he found nothing. The guilty parties quickly make their excuses and leave the Emporium. Just as Calvin is phoning the local police, he notes Sam's sketch of Harry's dead face. He's concerned that it matches the description of the corpse that the tramp gave him.

Jennifer agrees to marry Sam. Sam suddenly realises that they're not through with Harry. In order for them to marry, they are going to have to prove that Harry's dead. It looks as though they are going to have to dig the guy up again. They realise that they have to do it right now, before Calvin Wiggs gets the state police involved. So all four of them march up the hill again to dig Harry up. As they complete their task, the short-sighted local doctor wanders past again. They ask the doctor to look at the body and give them his opinion on how Harry died. He tells them it's quite impossible to do such an examination in the middle of the forest, and arranges to look at Harry at Jennifer's house later that night. They carry Harry back to Jennifer's house, where they wash and iron all of his clothes, to remove the mud and soil on them. Before they can dress him, Calvin Wiggs arrives. They manage to hide Harry's body in the bathtub from the slow-witted Calvin, who is convinced that Sam knows where Harry is.

The doctor confirms that Harry died from natural causes, and gets thoroughly confused by the convoluted story that Jennifer tells him about the various burials and exhumations that have taken place throughout the day. He leaves in a tizz. They decide to finish dressing Harry, and the next morning leave him where he was originally found for little Arnie to discover. As the young boy has difficulty in remembering the difference between 'today', 'tomorrow' and 'yesterday', they know he won't be taken seriously by the police if he tells them he first saw the body the day before.

ROOTS: Based on J Trevor Story's comical short novel, published in 1950. Hitch read the story and gave it to John Michael Hayes to adapt while he was still working on *To Catch a Thief*.

LEGACY: The movie *Weekend at Bernie's* (Ted Kotcheff, 1989) takes the initial idea of *The Trouble with Harry* one stage further. Two young men try to save their careers by pretending that their recently deceased boss is actually still alive. This in turn led to an even more unlikely sequel some years later. Also, the world's worst hotel manager discovered a body in one of his bedrooms in the hilarious episode of the TV series *Fawlty Towers*, 'The Kipper and the Corpse'.

WHO'S WHO?: John Forsythe played Blake Carrington in the glamorous soap *Dynasty* for over nine years, having previously been the oft-heard, never-seen Charlie in *Charlie's Angels*. He also appears in Hitchcock's *Topaz*.

Jerry Mathers would achieve major fame as Beaver in the American TV comedy series *Leave It to Beaver*. The legendary actress Shirley MacLaine makes her first screen appearance here. The sister of Warren Beatty, Shirley won Most Promising Newcomer (along with Kim Novak) at the Golden Globe Awards in 1955. Her later famous roles include *The Apartment* (Billy Wilder, 1960), *Sweet Charity* (Bob Fosse, 1969) and *Terms of Endearment* (James L Brooks, 1983), for which she won an Oscar.

THE USUAL SUSPECTS: Edmund Gwenn appears in *The Skin Game*, *Waltzes from Vienna*, and *Foreign Correspondent*. Bernard Herrmann, working for Hitchcock for the first time here, would compose the soundtrack for every Hitchcock film between this and *Marnie*, as well as being the 'sound consultant' for *The Birds*.

ANIMAL CRUELTY: The captain shoots and kills a rabbit, which little Arnie takes great pleasure in showing to all and sundry.

KILLER LINES: Miss Gravely, discovering the captain dragging Harry's corpse along the floor, delivers the phenomenally understated: 'What seems to be the trouble, Captain?' When they have tea later that day, the captain admires Miss Gravely's teacup. She tells him it was her father's until he died. 'I trust he died peacefully,' says a tactful captain, but Miss Gravely calmly tells him: 'He was caught in a threshing machine.'

THERE HE IS!: About twenty minutes in, walking past the limousine of a man looking at the paintings.

AWARDS: Shirley MacLaine was nominated for Best Foreign Actress by the British Academy of Film and Television (BAFTA).

TABOOS: Sam teases the captain about his date with Miss Gravely. 'Just think. You'd be establishing a precedent. Do you realise you'd be the first man to . . . cross her threshold?' 'Oooh, not too late, you know,' replies the captain. 'She's a well-preserved woman. Yes, well preserved.

Bernard Herrmann (1911–1975)

Bernard Herrmann scored a number of Orson Welles's radio shows before making the move west for *Citizen Kane* (1941). Almost immediately he became a highly sought composer of film scores.

Having tried to secure him for *Spellbound* in 1944, Hitchcock finally worked with Herrmann for the black comedy *The Trouble with Harry* in 1955. Herrmann went on to score all of Hitchcock's films for the next decade, including the hypnotic love themes for *Vertigo*, and the highly original strings accompaniment for *Psycho*, notably the much-imitated shrieks that helped the shower scene achieve its notoriety in movie history. But in the mid-60s, after completing the score for *Torn Curtain*, Herrmann was replaced by James Addison at the behest of the studio executives, effectively ending the partnership that had seen Hitchcock through his most successful and innovative period.

Herrmann died in 1976 after completing the jazz-inspired soundtrack for Martin Scorsese's *Taxi Driver*.

And preserves have to be opened some day . . .' Nothing like a healthy dose of innuendo to get over discovering a corpse, is there?

MUSIC: Infectious, light and amusing, Bernard Herrmann's first score for a Hitchcock film matches the mood of the movie perfectly. Individual themes are created for some of the characters, and the absurdity of the situations – while never mocked with 'silly' music – is highlighted in a tongue-in-cheek fashion.

POSTER: Accompanying a picture of the cast, who are staring at a clearly dead Harry, comes the sublime caption, 'The unexpected from Hitchcock!'

WHAT THE PAPERS SAID: The headline to the review in *The Times* describes Hitchcock as 'The Life and Soul of the Wake', before going on to add that the only reason we know that Harry was a rogue was 'because his irresistibly charming widow (Miss Shirley MacLaine) could not abide him.' The reviewer seems to take great pleasure in the naughtiness of the entire film: 'Though convention is all against it, and sometimes propriety too, the sheer absurdity of the proceedings carries the day.' He concludes by stating that 'the armchair detective will probably recall various loose ends in this story and actual inconsistencies, but . . . so long as he is in the cinema, he will merely take the fun as it comes.'

TRIVIA: Hitchcock bought the rights to the original novel anonymously for just $11,000. Its author Jack Trevor Story had worked with Hitch on *Champagne* (1928), playing the role of the Officer.

The opening title sequence sees a large number of cartoon birds looking down at the body of Harry. Hitchcock foreshadows his later movie with a much friendlier image here – seven years later, the birds would be seen to be feasting on the body.

The film finishes with the words 'The trouble with Harry is over'.

FINAL ANALYSIS: The trouble with *The Trouble with Harry* is that it simply doesn't hang together very well. Hitchcock intended to use the film as a template for the stories he planned to feature in his *Alfred Hitchcock Presents* TV series. However, it's far too drawn out – the first half being simply dull – and none of the cast seem to have any real enthusiasm for what they're doing. Shirley MacLaine, in her first film role, seems almost embarrassed by her lines, whereas poor, sweet Edmund Gwenn is simply too old and tired to inject the necessary life into what are some genuinely witty lines. *3/10*

The Man Who Knew Too Much (1956)

(Colour – 120 mins)

Produced by Alfred Hitchcock/Paramount Pictures

Associate Producer: Herbert Coleman

Written by John Michael Hayes, based on a storyline by Charles Bennett & DB Wyndham-Lewis

Music: Bernard Herrmann, with songs by Ray Evans & Jay Livingston
'Storm Cloud Cantata': Arthur Benjamin
Director of Photography: Robert Burks
Costume Design: Edith Head
Production Design: Sam M Comer, John B Goodman, Emile Kuri, Hal Pereira
Film Editing: George Tomasini
Art Director: Henry Bumstead
Technical Adviser: Abdelhaq Chraibi
Process Photography: Farciot Edouart
Special Effects/Special Photographic Effects: John P Fulton
Sound: Gene Garver, Paul Franz
Sound Recordist: Gene Garvin
Assistant Director: Howard Joslin
Set Decorators: Arthur Krams, Sam Comer
Colour Consultant: Richard Mueller
Art Director: Hal Pereira
Make-up Supervisor: Wally Westmore
Technical Adviser: Constance Willis

CAST: James Stewart (*Dr Ben McKenna*), Doris Day (*Jo McKenna*), Brenda De Banzie (*Mrs Drayton*), Bernard Miles (*Mr Drayton*), Ralph Truman (*Buchanan*), Daniel Gélin (*Louis Bernard*), Mogens Wieth (*Ambassador*), Alan Mowbray (*Val Parnell*), Hillary Brooke (*Jan Peterson*), Christopher Olsen (*Hank McKenna*), Reggie Nalder (*Assassin*), Richard Wattis (*Assistant Manager*), Noel Willman (*Woburn*), Alix Talton (*Helen Parnell*), Yves Brainville (*Police Inspector*), Carolyn Jones (*Cindy Fontaine*), Betty Bascomb (*Edna*), Leo Gordon (*Chauffer*), Patrick Aherne (*Handyman*), Lewis Martin (*Detective*), Louis Mercier, Anthony Warde (*French Policemen*), Richard Wordsworth (*Ambrose Chappell Jr*), George Howe (*Ambrose Chappell Sr*), Gladys Holland (*Bernard's Girlfriend*), Barbara Burke (*Assassin's Girlfriend*).

UNCREDITED CAST: Alexi Bobrinskoy (*Foreign Prime Minister*), Peter Camlin (*Head Waiter*), Abdelhaq Chraibi (*Arab*), Bernard Herrmann (*Conductor*), Ralph Neff (*Henchman*), Eric Snowden (*Special Branch Officer*).

SUMMARY: '*A single crash of cymbals and how it rocked the lives of an American family.*'.

In Marrakech, Dr Ben McKenna, his wife Jo and their son Hank make the acquaintance of a French businessman called Louis Bernard. Jo is concerned by the way Bernard seems to be asking her husband a lot of questions yet revealing very little about himself. Despite her reservations, she and Hank accept an invitation from the man to dinner. As Jo gets Hank ready for bed, Ben and Monsieur Bernard enjoy a drink. Jo asks the Frenchman what business he is in, a question he diverts with ease. Ben answers a knock at the door and finds a rather shifty-looking man who explains he has come to the wrong room and apologises for the intrusion. This seems to prompt Bernard's memory, for he suddenly remembers that he has forgotten a prior engagement and excuses himself.

Ben and Jo decide to go out anyway and go to a traditional Moroccan restaurant. Jo notices that another couple, a man and a woman, seem to be paying them far too much attention. The woman introduces herself as Mrs Drayton and explains that she recognises Ben's wife as the famous singer Jo Conway. Ben invites the couple to join them and soon they're all chatting like old friends. The Draytons invite the McKennas to join them in a trip to the market the next morning. At that moment, Louis Bernard walks in with a beautiful young woman. Angered at being snubbed by the Frenchman, Ben accepts the Draytons' offer, unaware that they are being watched by Bernard and his companion.

The next day, the McKennas and the Draytons trawl the streets of Marrakech, watching the street entertainment and looking at the many market stalls. A disturbance in one of the town squares distracts their enjoyment. Ben watches as a Moroccan man slowly lumbers towards him, trying to grasp something behind him – he's been stabbed in the back. He collapses into Ben's arms and it's only when Ben sees the brown greasepaint on his own hands that he realises the 'Moroccan' is Louis Bernard in disguise. The Frenchman pulls Ben close to him and with his dying breath whispers a warning to him: 'A statesman is to be killed . . . assassinated . . . in London, soon. Tell London . . . Ambrose Chapel . . .'

Ben quickly writes down the man's words as the police arrive to investigate. They wish to question Ben and Jo, so Mrs Drayton offers to take Hank back to the hotel while her husband accompanies the McKennas to the police station. The chief of police seems unwilling to believe that Ben and the dead man were not well acquainted, despite Ben's assurances that they had met only twice before. It comes as a complete surprise to the McKennas to learn that Louis Bernard was a known agent of the Deuxieme Bureau, the French equivalent of the FBI. They believe he had come to Morocco to obtain information and that he was killed to prevent the information being passed on. At that moment, a telephone call comes through for Ben.

Taking the call in another room, Ben is stunned to hear a mysterious voice warning him that if he says one word of what he learnt from Bernard his son will be in serious danger. Ben asks Drayton to return to the hotel to make sure his wife and Hank arrived back safely. He then composes himself and calmly collects Jo from the police chief's office. On their return to the hotel, Ben learns that Drayton has already checked out and begins to fear the worst. He bullies Jo into taking a sedative before breaking the news to her.

They make the journey to London, where they are greeted by crowds of Jo's loyal fans – and an inspector from CID. He introduces them to Buchanan of Special Branch, who tells them that Bernard had been sent to Marrakech to investigate a plot to assassinate an ambassador. Regretfully, Ben can tell him only that their son has been kidnapped and that he is unwilling to take the risk of assisting him in his enquiries. As in Marrakech, a telephone call comes through for Ben – another reminder to keep silent.

The McKennas arrive at an apartment that has been arranged for them by a friend. Ben scours the telephone book to find an Ambrose Chapel and finds that there's a taxidermist of that name nearby. He telephones the man and arranges to meet him at his premises. Just as he departs, some of Jo's friends turn up. Ben makes his apologies and leaves his wife to entertain them, but then Jo realises that Ambrose Chapel is a place, not a person. Checking the address in the phone book, she leaves her bemused friends with a message for Ben and rushes off. Ben's search was inevitably fruitless and he returns to the apartment just as Jo telephones him to say that she has found the right place.

They enter Ambrose Chapel during a mass and immediately recognise

Mr and Mrs Drayton, posing as a vicar and his wife. Unfortunately, Mrs Drayton sees them too and alerts her husband. Ben sends Jo to fetch help while he sits the service out. Drayton announces to his surprised congregation that he has decided to curtail the mass to allow them to contemplate the joys of God's love and the chapel quickly empties. Ben immediately starts shouting Hank's name. From somewhere in the chapel, he hears his son cry out to him seconds before Ben is knocked unconscious by one of Draytons' hired thugs.

Jo tries in vain to contact Buchanan at Scotland Yard, but she's told that he has left for a performance at the Albert Hall that evening. Jo makes a snap decision and heads off to find him. Arriving just before the performance, Jo examines the sea of faces in the lobby. A man walks deliberately towards her. She recognises him as the man who came to their room 'by mistake' in Marrakech. Slowly he leers: 'You have a very nice little boy, *madame*. His safety will depend on you tonight.' He then walks up the stairs to take his seat in a reserved box.

Meanwhile Ben wakes up to find himself locked inside the church. With no obvious way out, Ben climbs a bell rope and escapes via the roof.

Jo hears the performance begin and is drawn into the hall. She sees Buchanan seated to one side of a foreign ambassador. On the opposite side of the hall sits the strange man. Ben arrives and sees Jo standing in the doorway. She explains the situation and he sprints up a flight of stairs in an attempt to alert Buchanan. As the music builds to a crescendo, Jo sees the strange man pull out a gun. He aims it at the ambassador and slowly prepares to shoot. Jo lets out a shattering scream just as the assassin takes his one chance of a shot at his target. The distraction knocks the assassin's aim and the ambassador is merely wounded. The police corner the assassin, who tries to make his escape by climbing from box to box. He loses his footing and crashes to the floor, breaking his neck and dying instantly.

The ambassador comes to thank Jo for saving his life and invites her to the embassy. Ben and Jo reluctantly tell their entire story to Buchanan, who in turn informs them that one of his contacts claims he saw their boy being smuggled through a back door of the embassy by the Draytons. Ben suggests they accept the ambassador's invitation to the embassy.

It's not long before the famous Jo Conway is asked to sing for the ambassador and she chooses a song she knows her son is familiar with. Up in an attic room, Hank is alone with Mrs Drayton. They hear the music from down below and Hank instantly recognises his mother's voice. Tired and distressed by the kidnapping, Mrs Drayton encourages the boy to whistle along to attract someone's attention. Downstairs, both Ben and Jo hear their son's whistle. Jo continues to sing as Ben takes advantage of the distraction to search the embassy. He eventually finds Hank, but just as they make to leave Mr Drayton returns. It seems the ambassador was betrayed by a member of his own government who is furious that the Draytons have brought the child to the embassy. Drayton has returned with instructions to kill the boy. Instead, Drayton decides to use Ben and Hank as human shields, holding them at gunpoint until he is able to escape. As they walk down a long flight of stairs, Ben manages to trip Drayton, who falls, accidentally triggering the gun and shooting himself.

Reunited at last, the McKennas return to their apartment to introduce their friends to their son Hank.

ROOTS: Hitchcock had almost remade his 1934 British classic in the early 40s when he first joined David O Selznick in Hollywood. With the storyline relocated to South America, the idea was abandoned after the plot became too bogged down in the politics of Brazil.

We should also note the similarity between the Albert Hall sequence and the assassination of American President Abraham Lincoln, who was shot in a theatre by John Wilkes Booth in 1865.

LEGACY: *The Man Who Knew Too Much* is one of those titles that tend to pop up all over the place – we've traced it to episodes of the British sitcom *2 Point 4 Children*, the *Simpsons* episode 'The Boy Who Knew Too Much' (in which Bart has to decide whether to give evidence in a murder trial, even though it will prove he played hooky from school), a strip in *Judge Dredd* comic and a book by Dick Russell about the assassination of John F Kennedy.

Frantic (Roman Polanski, 1988) has Harrison Ford in search of his kidnapped wife, which is also the basis for the Kurt Russell thriller *Breakdown* (Jonathan Mostow, 1997). Less subtle is the Bill Murray comedy *The Man Who Knew Too Little* (Jon Amiel, 1997), concerning mistaken identity and international espionage. 'Ambrose Chapel' is the name given to a CIA agent in the episode of *The X Files* entitled 'Colony', and the ubiquitous Brian De Palma is, at the time of writing, preparing to direct a movie called *Ambrose Chapel*, something he first discussed nearly a decade ago.

WHO'S WHO?: Doris Day was born Doris von Kappelhoff in 1924. She performed successfully as a band singer and starred in her first film in 1948. She had an extremely successful film career throughout the 50s and 60s in romantic comedies (often alongside Rock Hudson) and musicals such as *Pillow Talk* (Michael Gordon, 1959), *Move Over Darling* (also Gordon, 1963) and *Calamity Jane* (David Butler, 1953). She hosted *The Doris Day Show* on TV from 1968 to 1973. Today she is an animal-rights activist, and the founder of the Doris Day Animal League.

Appearing in his first American role here, the Austrian dancer and actor Reggie Nalder terrified a generation as the vampire Barlow in the

TV adaptation of Stephen King's *Salem's Lot* (Tobe Hooper, 1979). Caroline Jones (who appears as one of Jo's friends) achieved worldwide fame as Morticia Addams in *The Addams Family* TV series.

THE USUAL SUSPECTS: James Stewart also stars in *Rope*, *Rear Window* and *Vertigo*. Bernard Herrmann also composed the soundtracks for all of Hitchcock's films from *The Trouble with Harry* to *Marnie*, as well as being the 'sound consultant' for *The Birds*. In *The Man Who Knew Too Much* he can be seen conducting the orchestra during the Albert Hall sequence.

THERE HE IS!: In the Moroccan marketplace watching the acrobats with his back to the camera just before the murder.

MISOGYNY: Ben McKenna forces his wife to give up her career for the sake of his (see **Themes and Motifs** below). During their trip to the market, Ben worries that he and Jo might be about to have one of their 'monthly rows', suggesting that Jo suffers from PMT. If this wasn't bad enough, Ben forces his wife to take a sedative before he tells her about Hank's kidnapping, which seems like such an abuse of his power as a doctor that only an actor as popular as James Stewart could possibly get away with it.

AWARDS: Won Academy Award for Best Song: 'Whatever Will Be, Will Be (Que Sera, Sera)' by Ray Evans and Jay Livingston.

THEMES AND MOTIFS: The events in both this and the original version appear to be an attack on complacency. But whereas in 1934 it was Jill Lawrence who was forced to learn the lesson 'Don't take your daughter for granted', the 1955 remake revolves around Ben's acceptance of the sacrifices his wife has made for him: she gave up her career for him, something that he takes for granted. He tells Louis Bernard that he's called his wife 'Jo' for so long 'nobody knows her by any other name'. But, as we see on her return to London, her fans still remember her as Jo Conway.

It's also a parody of the ignorant American tourist, as shown by young Hank's ignorance of the French delicacy of snails – inviting Louis Bernard to tuck into the ones in their garden back home – and his confusion when he accidentally knocks the veil from the head of a Muslim wife. In this scene, note the blonde tourist wearing shades and the way she stares at the veiled woman whose veil reveals only her eyes.

MUSIC: Though Hitchcock deliberately drops the incidental music for a few scenes – relying on the 'natural' sounds of Marrakech for the market scenes and heightening the suspense of the footsteps that Ben hears as he approaches the taxidermist – *The Man Who Knew Too Much* is the nearest he ever came to attempting a musical since the unsuccessful

Waltzes from Vienna from his British era. In addition to the tense Albert Hall segment (which lasts twelve minutes without a single word of dialogue), we have the uneasy singalong sequences where Doris Day sings to her son. For some, this seems like pandering to Day's fame as a singer and popular star of a number of hit musicals. But we challenge anyone to watch this film and *not* join in with 'Que Sera Sera', especially in the emotional reprise towards the end of the film.

POSTER: 'A little knowledge can be a deadly thing!' warns the poster, with an attractive montage combining the hand of a gunman with worried portraits of Stewart and Day and a diminutive cymbalist waiting to deliver the all-important cymbal crash.

TRAILER: What seems like a musical interlude with Doris Day is interrupted by a gunshot. 'You're right. That was a gunshot you heard,' explains Jimmy Stewart. 'That was the signal that brought all the trouble out in the open.' Stewart is surprisingly chatty, describing his part in Alfred Hitchcock's new picture and filling in a little background detail: 'Hitchcock took us thousands of miles away from Hollywood to Marrakech, which is right in the centre of the North African trouble area. And that was just the beginning. From there we flew to London, for backgrounds of a whole strange series of events that ended up that final night in the great concert hall, where the cue for murder was one single crash of the cymbals.' The trailer ends with 'Storm Cloud Cantata', the music from the Albert Hall sequence.

WHAT THE PAPER'S SAID: The *Times* reviewer notes that 'in spite of colour, wide screen devices and even louder sound, the Hitchcock technique has not changed greatly since the days of 1934 when the first *The Man Who Knew Too Much* was a high water mark of British production . . . The quality of acting, after all, is less good, the story is neither better nor worse, and the direction does nothing to prove the value of a film director repeating his work.'

COSTUME: Doris Day sports both the tightly bound blonde spiral hairstyle and the lime-green suit so favoured by Hitchcock in *Vertigo* and *The Birds*.

TRIVIA: The plot calls for a man to be discovered as 'not Moroccan' because he was wearing black make-up. The make-up artists couldn't find a black substance that would come off easily, and so they painted the fingers of the other man white, so that he would leave pale streaks on the other man's skin.

This film was unavailable for decades because its rights (together with four other pictures of the same period) were bought back by Hitchcock and left as part of his legacy to his daughter. They've been known for a long time as the infamous 'five lost Hitchcocks' among film buffs, and were rereleased in theatres around 1984 after a 30-year absence. The others are *Rear Window, Rope, The Trouble with Harry* and *Vertigo*.

It was during the making of this film that Hitchcock finally joined his wife in becoming an American citizen.

FINAL ANALYSIS: As we noted for the 1934 original, critics are divided as to which version is the better. Many criticise this remake for its glossiness; the Vista-Vision, the colour; the location footage and – heaven forbid! – the songs. In contrast, the original is altogether more sophisticated, wittier and closer to the spirit of Hitchcock's 'true' genius.

And to these critics we have but one word – rubbish!

Proving beyond a doubt that remakes can, occasionally, improve upon the original, *The Man Who Knew Too Much* is superior on almost every level; even the celebrated Albert Hall sequence, which is an almost exact reworking of a scene from the original, is somehow tighter, even more tense yet – strangely – longer here. Also lifted from the original is a scene where Drayton plays a segment of music to the assassin to show him his cue to shoot his target. But, where Peter Lorre was charming and attractive in his evil, Bernard Miles's Drayton is all the more effective because he is so ordinary, leaving the theatrical villainy to Reggie Nalder as the creepy assassin. Best of all, though, is Doris Day, whose Jo McKenna is a vast improvement on Edna Best as the fraught mother in search of her child, as is shown by the way the story is restructured to allow Day to take a much more active role in the action.

There is, however, one small flaw in this otherwise exceptional drama: like grit under a contact lens, little Hank McKenna is extremely irritating, and reminds us of the tragic Stevie in *Sabotage*, but for all the wrong reasons. Hitchcock learnt a difficult lesson with that particular child, and so it's probably just a little mean-spirited of us to have been hoping for a slightly more downbeat ending than the gleeful family reunion that concludes this film. **9/10**

The Wrong Man (1956)

(B & W – 105 mins)

Produced by Alfred Hitchcock/Warner Bros/First National Pictures Inc.

Associate Producer Herbert Coleman

Written by Maxwell Anderson & Angus MacPhail
Based on the novel *The True Story of Christopher Emmanuel Balestrero* by Maxwell Anderson

Music: Bernard Herrmann
Director of Photography: Robert Burks

Film Editing: George Tomasini
Make-up Artist: Gordon Bau
Sound: Earl Crain Sr
Technical Adviser: George Groves
Set Decorator: William L Kuehl
Assistant Director: Daniel McCauley
Technical Adviser: Frank D O'Connor
Art Director: Paul Sylbert

CAST: Henry Fonda (*Manny Balestrero*), Vera Miles (*Rose Balestrero*), Anthony Quayle (*Frank O'Connor*), Harold Stone (*Lt Bowers*), John Heldabrand (*Tomasini*), Doreen Lang (*Ann James*), Lola D'Annunzio (*Olga Conforti*), Robert Essen (*Gregory Balestrero*), Dayton Lummis (*Judge Groat*), Charles Cooper (*Detective Matthews*), Norma Connolly (*Betty Todd*), Esther Minciotti (*Mama Balestrero*), Laurinda Barrett (*Constance Willis*), Nehemiah Persoff (*Gene Conforti*), Kippy Campbell (*Robert Balestrero*), Richard Robbins (*Daniell*), Peggy Webber (*Miss Dennerly*).

UNCREDITED CAST: Charles Aidman (*Jail Medical Attendant*), Sammy Armaro, John Truax, Allan Ray (*Suspects*), Barry Atwater (*Mr Bishop*), Michael Ann Barrett (*Miss Daily*), John C Becher (*Liquor Store Proprietor*), Henry Beckman (*Prisoner*), Ray Bennett (*Policeman*), Harold Berman (*Court Stenographer*), Mary Boylan (*Curious Customer*), Paul Bryar (*Interrogation Officer*), Ed Bryce, Charles J Guiotta, Thomas J Murphy (*Court Officers*), John Caler (*Soldier*), Leonard Capone (*Court Clerk*), Paul Carr (*Young Man*), Gordon Clark (*Police Attendant*), William Crane, Josef Draper (*Jurors*), Spencer Davis (*Prisoner's Lawyer*), Mel Dowd (*Nurse*), Richard Durham, Chris Gampel, Mike Keene, Maurice Wells, Frank Schofield (*Department of Correction*), Olga Fabian (*Mrs Mank*), Bonnie Franklin (*Young Girl*), Earl George (*Delicatessen Proprietor*), Natalie Priest (*Delicatessen Proprietor's Wife*), Cherry Hardy, Elizabeth Scott (*Waving Women*), Don McGovern (*Waving Man*), Will Hare (*McKaba*), William Hudson (*Police Lieutenant from 110th Precinct*), Anna Karen (*Miss Duffield*), Barbara Karen, Tuesday Weld (*Giggly Girls*), David Kelly, Clarence Straight (*Policemen*), Werner Klemperer (*Dr Bannay*), Walter Kohler (*Manny's Felony Court Lawyer*), William LeMassena (*Sang*), Alexander Lockwood (*Emmerton*), Maurice Manson (*District Attorney*), Donald May (*Arresting Patrolman*), Marc May (*Tomasini's Assistant*), John R McKee (*Police Attendant*), Dallas Midgette (*Customer at Bickford's*), Silvio Minciotti (*Mr Balestrero*), Pat Morrow (*Young Girl*), Daniel Ocko (*Felony Court Judge*), Frances Reid (*Mrs O'Connor*), Maria Reid (*Spanish Woman*), Rossana San Marco (*Mrs Ferraro*), Penny Santon (*Spanish Woman*), Helen Shields (*Receptionist*), Otto Simanek (*Mr Mank*), Oliver Stacey, John Stephen, Rhodelle Heller, (*Stork Club Customers*), Dan Terranova (*Mr Ferraro*), Emerson Treacy (*Mr Wendon*), Don Turner (*Detective*), John Vivyan (*Detective Holman*).

SUMMARY: *'The early-morning hours of January the fourteenth, nineteen hundred and fifty-three, a day in the life of Christopher Emanuel Balestrero that he will never forget.'*

It's the end of the night at the Stork Club in New York City, and the house band are packing away their instruments. The double-bass player, Manny Balestrero, takes a subway train home to his wife Rose and his two children. Rose and Manny discuss the forthcoming dental surgery that she is going to need. The cost of the procedure – some $300 – is worrying her a lot. Manny agrees to go to his insurance office that afternoon, to see if he can borrow some money against Rose's insurance policy. At the insurance office, the counter staff think that Manny is the same man who held them up at gunpoint some months earlier. They call the police, who act quickly. Just as Manny arrives home, they take him in for questioning, promising that it 'won't take long'. They drive Manny to a number of nearby stores that were also robbed at gunpoint by the same man.

At the police station, Manny is questioned about his finances, which are in a fragile condition. The police read out loud the words written on the hold-up note handed to the insurance-office clerks by the gunman. Manny writes them down – not only is his handwriting similar, but he makes an identical spelling mistake. He is then put into an identity parade, where two of the clerks from the insurance office positively identify him. Manny is fingerprinted and searched. Protesting that he still hasn't told his wife where he is, Manny is locked up for the night.

Rose and his family are concerned about Manny's whereabouts. Rose eventually tracks him down by phone to the police station. She is told that Manny will be appearing in court the next day. His court appearance is very brief, and he is committed to stand trial by a grand jury in a month's time, with bail set at $7,500. Manny spends an unsettling night in Long Island prison before his family can raise the money to get him released.

Manny and Rose discuss their case with their lawyer Frank O'Connor. O'Connor advises them that the best way to prove his innocence is to find an alibi for the two dates that the robberies took place. The Balestreros go back to a hotel they were staying in on the first of the dates, where the two owners recognise them. However, although the owners remember that Manny and Rose were staying at their hotel, they cannot provide an alibi for the precise time of the robbery. Manny remembers playing cards at the time that the robbery took place, and with the help of the hotel register tries to track down his playing partners. When he discovers that two of the three have died, and realises that it's difficult to track down the other, the stress begins to show on Rose. She blames herself for everything that's happening to Manny, as it was because of her dental work that Manny went to the insurance office in the first place.

Manny then remembers that on the date of the second robbery he had a large, visible abscess on his tooth. This wasn't mentioned by any of the robbery victims, and can be confirmed by his dentist. Despite O'Connor's attempts to encourage Rose, she seems to be slipping further and further into depression. O'Connor advises Manny to get professional help for his wife, who by now isn't eating or sleeping. When Manny tries to talk to her, Rose snaps. She strikes Manny on the forehead and breaks the mirror on her dressing table. She realises that she needs help, telling her husband that 'you'll have to let them put me somewhere'. Manny seeks help from a psychiatrist, who recognises that Rose needs to be committed to a sanatorium to help her recover. Manny drops Rose off at her new home, but by now she barely even recognises him.

At the trial, things don't appear to be going well for Manny. The prosecution claims that he needed to rob the money to pay off gambling debts, and he is again positively identified by one of the robbery victims. However, one of the jurors stands up in the middle of the trial and protests about the amount of detail he is being asked to listen to. This forces the judge to announce a mistrial, meaning that they will have to wait for another date for the case to be heard again.

At home, Manny and his mother pray for strength and for luck in the case. Manny is playing at the Stork Club when he gets a message to report to the police station. It transpires that a man has been arrested while holding up another store – and that the man looks very like Manny. When the robbery victims identify this new suspect, Manny is released. He goes to see Rose in the hospital to tell her the good news, but she is still withdrawn and tells him to leave.

An epilogue states that Rose walked out of the sanatorium two years later, completely cured, and that the family moved to Florida, where they still live happily.

ROOTS: Although the movie was based on a true story, Hitchcock deliberately left out some of the information that pointed to Manny's innocence to heighten the tension. The 'happy' ending, with Rose recovering from her breakdown, was added to the film at the insistence of the studio. In reality, Rose Balestrero never fully recovered from the experience.

The true story was adapted by Herbert Brean in an article called 'A Case of Identity', which appeared in *Life* magazine in June 1953, some six months after Manny went through his real-life nightmare. Herbert Brean sold a movie treatment of his article to Warner Brothers at the same time.

LEGACY: Martin Scorsese claims the subjective viewpoint of the camera for the scene in the insurance office was his inspiration for the directorial style of his own 1976 film *Taxi Driver*.

WHO'S WHO?: Henry Fonda is one of the true greats of cinema. His most famous roles in his movie career, which spanned almost 50 years, include Abraham Lincoln in *Young Mr Lincoln* (John Ford, 1939); Tom Joad in *The Grapes of Wrath* (John Ford, 1940); and Norman Thayer in *On Golden Pond* (Mark Rydell, 1981), for which he won the Best Actor Oscar. He is the father of the famous actors Jane and Peter Fonda.

Anthony Quayle is another famous movie face. He appeared in *Ice-Cold in Alex* (J Lee Thompson, 1958) and *The Guns of Navarone* (J Lee Thompson, 1961).

THE USUAL SUSPECTS: Vera Miles can be seen in *Psycho*. She was Hitchcock's first choice for the role of Madeleine Elster in *Vertigo*. He first spotted an episode of *The Coca-Cola Playhouse*. Hitchcock rapidly signed her to a five-year, three-picture contract, fully expecting her to be the 'new Grace Kelly'.

Bernard Herrmann once again provides the soundtrack. Doreen Lang would return to play Cary Grant's secretary in *North by Northwest* and the distressed mother in *The Birds*.

KILLER LINES: Lieutenant Bowers offers Manny less than convincing reassurance: 'An innocent man has nothing to fear.'

Rose, on the verge of total collapse, is forced to spell out how bad their situation has become: 'Don't you see? It doesn't do any good to care. No matter what you do, they'll get it fixed so that it goes against you. No matter how innocent you are, or how hard you try, they'll find you guilty.' She believes that the only way to protect her family is to hide away from reality: 'We'll lock 'em out and keep 'em out.'

THERE HE IS!: Narrating the film's prologue, the only time he actually spoke in any of his films.

THEMES AND MOTIFS: 'The theme of the innocent man accused' reaches its peak both here and in the soon-to-be-produced *North by Northwest*. Hitchcock examines this theme in extreme close-up, detailing the effect of such a mistake on both the man himself and his wife (as he would do later in *Torn Curtain*).

POSTER: The poster featured the following challenge: 'If you don't believe that this weird and unusual story actually happened, see the records at Queens' County Court, Apr. 21, 1953. Indictment #273 S2 "The Balestrero Case." '

TRAILER: 'Twenty-five steps down into a subway and for the first time he doesn't come home that night'. 'For the first time Alfred Hitchcock goes to real life for his thrills! It's all true and all suspense – the all-round biggest Hitchcock hit ever to hit the screen! Warner Bros. present HENRY FONDA and VERA MILES and the exciting city of New York in Alfred Hitchcock's "The Wrong Man" . . . somewhere . . . somewhere there must be the *right* man!'

THE ICE MAIDEN: Vera Miles makes a stunning debut here, proving that she is one of the most accomplished and perceptive actresses ever to appear in a Hitchcock movie. She portrays Rose Balestrero with a subtlety and depth that most actresses would envy. In particular, the sequence where Rose finally snaps and strikes Manny is superb – the audience can really empathise with her plight as the hopelessness of her situation overwhelms her.

WHAT THE PAPERS SAID: *The Times'* film critic, Maxwell Anderson, reviewed *The Wrong Man* on 25 February 1957. 'Mr Hitchcock, for the first hour at any rate, chills the blood by following, for him, a new recipe and one which proves effective.' Anderson is less impressed by the movie once Manny has been released on bail: 'There are few tricks with the camera; no surprises created by the unexpected in the cutting or by visual shocks in the narrative.'

TRIVIA: The 'right' man (the real culprit) can be seen several times during the film: outside the Stork Club, in the Victor Moore arcade and near one of the liquor stores where the police take Manny.

FINAL ANALYSIS: An interesting departure for Hitchcock, but one that works very well indeed. The grim first half of the picture is almost hypnotic – we find ourselves as bemused by the tragic chain of circumstances as Manny and his family are. Hitch uses many of the tricks he has picked up over the years to hammer home the emotional impact of the situation, not just on Manny, but most tellingly on Rose. In particular, the use of shadow and restrained lighting makes the entire city of New York feel like one huge prison, with 'bars' of darkness regularly seen to slice across characters' faces. When Manny is put behind literal bars for his night in prison, we really feel as if we were in there with him.

However, it is with the performances of the two leads that much of the credit for the success of *The Wrong Man* must lie. Henry Fonda delivers a heart-rending portrayal of a man who refuses to allow the mistakes of society to alter his basic humanity and respect for others. His air of bewilderment about how such a miscarriage of justice could take place, and why it is happening to him, is perfectly measured, avoiding the nasty stench of oversentimentality that many other actors might resort to. Vera Miles, in her first major film role, acquits herself admirably.

This is a deeply unsettling film, one that remains in the mind long after the final frame. As a searing indictment of the need of many people to convict someone – anyone – of a crime, it does make you worry about whether such a miscarriage of justice could ever happen to you. The fact that the case is true makes it hit home hard. The added poignancy of the fact that Rose Balestrero never really recovered from her ordeal makes the film almost unbearable. 8/10

Vertigo (1958)

(Working titles: *From Among the Dead/Illicit Darkening . . .* and many others)

(Colour – 128 mins)

Produced by Alfred Hitchcock/Alfred J Hitchcock Productions/Paramount Pictures

Associate Producer: Herbert Coleman

Written by Samuel A Taylor & Alec Coppel
Based on the novel . . . *d'Entre les Morts* by Pierre Boileau and Thomas Narcejac

Original music: Bernard Herrmann
Director of Photography: Robert Burks
Costume Design: Edith Head
Film Editing: George Tomasini
Title Designer: Saul Bass
Art Director: Henry Bumstead
Set Decorator: Sam Comer
Process Photography: Farciot Edouart
Special Sequence: John Ferren
Special Effects: John P Fulton
Process Photography: W Wallace Kelley
Sound: Winston H Leverett, Harold C Lewis
Hair Stylist: Nellie Manley
Conductor: Muir Mathieson
Assistant Director: Daniel McCauley
Set Decorator: Frank R McKelvy
Colour Consultant: Richard Mueller
Art Director: Hal Pereira
Make-up Artist: Wally Westmore
1996 Reconstruction and Restoration: Robert A Harris
Producer, 1996 Restoration: James C Katz

CAST: James Stewart (*John 'Scottie' Ferguson*), Kim Novak (*Madeleine Elster/Judy Barton*), Barbara Bel Geddes (*Marjorie 'Midge' Wood*), Tom Helmore (*Gavin Elster*), Henry Jones (*Coroner*), Raymond Bailey (*Scottie's Doctor*), Ellen Corby (*Manageress of McKittrick Hotel*), Konstantin Shayne (*Pop Leibel*), Lee Patrick (*Older Mistaken Identification*).

UNCREDITED CAST: John Benson (*Salesman*), Margaret Brayton (*Ransohoff's Saleslady*), Paul Bryar (*Captain Hansen*), Roxann Delman (*Ransohoff's Model*), Mollie Dodd (*Beautician*), Carlo Dotto (*Ernie's Bartender*), Joanne Genthon (*Carlotta Valdez*), Don Giovanni (*Salesman*), Roland Got (*Maître D' at Ernie's*), Fred Graham (*Death Fall Officer*), Buck Harrington (*Elster's Gateman*), June Jocelyn (*Miss*

Woods), Miliza Milo (*Saleswoman*), Julian Petruzzi (*San Francisco Flower Seller*), William Remick (*Jury Foreman*), Jack Richardson (*Escort*), Bruno Santina (*Waiter at Ernie's*), Nina Shipman (*Younger Mistaken Identification*), Dori Simmons (*Middle-Aged Mistaken Identification*), Ed Stevlingson (*Inquest Attorney*), Sara Taft (*Nun*), Isabel Analla, Jack Ano.

SUMMARY: Scottie Ferguson, a police detective, is chasing a suspect over the rooftops of downtown San Francisco when he slips and ends up dangling by his fingertips from a fragile gutter. One of his uniformed colleagues reaches to help him, but Scottie can only watch helplessly as the cop falls to his death.

Some weeks later, Scottie discusses his future career options with his former girlfriend Midge. He has resigned from the police, concerned that his vertigo (a fear of heights) might cause the death of another innocent person. Scottie receives a phone call from an old friend, Gavin Elster. Elster has heard of Scottie's accident and retirement, and wants to hire him for some private detective work. Elster is deeply worried about his wife Madeleine, who seems to be living under the malevolent influence of the spirit of her great-grandmother, Carlotta Valdes. Carlotta was a deeply unhappy woman who committed suicide at the age of 26 – the age that Madeleine is now. Elster is worried that Madeleine will kill herself, too.

Scottie begins to trail Madeleine, in order to keep an eye on her and uncover her movements. Madeleine seems to be in a kind of trance, wandering from a florist's shop to Carlotta's graveside, to a gallery where she sits motionless for hours in front of her ancestor's portrait. Continuing his surveillance, Scottie observes Madeleine going into the McKittrick Hotel. The owner tells him that Madeleine regularly spends time there, but that her name is actually Carlotta Valdes. The more he follows her, the more Scottie seems to be falling in love with Madeleine. Midge and Scottie do some research, and discover that the hotel is actually the old house in which Carlotta lived many years before.

The next day, Scottie once again follows Madeleine, this time to the promenade underneath the Golden Gate Bridge. He watches in horror as Madeleine throws herself into San Francisco Bay. Scottie dives into the water and fishes her out, unconscious. He drives her back to his apartment, undresses her and puts her in his bed. When Madeleine wakes up later that day, she claims to have no memory of what happened at all, so to save her feelings Scottie tells her that she merely slipped and fell into the water. There appears to be a growing mutual attraction between the two of them, and they decide to spend the next day together.

Madeleine breaks down and confesses to Scottie that she is being haunted by terrible dreams of Carlotta and of a mysterious convent-like place that seems to be in Spain. She is convinced that Carlotta's influence will kill her. From her description, Scottie realises that the convent is in fact San Juan Batista, a Spanish mission located some 100 miles south of San Francisco. The strange dreams and memories are therefore completely explicable – Madeleine has probably been there before. Scottie decides to take her there, in order to cure her fears. The place is indeed the same as in her nightmare. The distraught Madeleine confesses her love for Scottie and dashes up the rickety staircase inside the mission's bell tower. Scottie, stricken once again by paralysing vertigo, manages to get only halfway up the tower when he hears a terrible scream. Through a window, he sees Madeleine's body fall from the top of the tower on to the adjacent roof below.

At the inquest into Madeleine's death, Elster is cleared of all responsibility in not reporting his wife's mental instability to the authorities. Scottie, however, is damned by the coroner for his 'weakness' directly causing the death of two innocent people – first the policeman, now Madeleine. This is the final straw for Scottie, who suffers a mental breakdown. Completely catatonic, he is hospitalised for over a year, visited regularly by a devoted yet helpless Midge.

On his recovery and release from hospital, Scottie spends his days wandering San Francisco's streets, a broken man. Everywhere he sees women who remind him of Madeleine. One day, he happens across a voluptuous brunette who bears a startling resemblance to the cool blonde Madeleine. He follows her back to her hotel and starts to question her. The woman, Judy Barton, is seemingly bemused, scared and fascinated by Scottie's attention, and agrees to meet him in an hour for a drink. As soon as Scottie leaves, Judy grabs a suitcase and starts packing. She hesitates, seemingly torn between a need to run and a desire to stay. She sits down and starts to write a letter to Scottie.

In the letter, Judy confesses her involvement in Gavin Elster's plot to murder his wife. An actress, Judy was spotted by Elster and hired because of her resemblance to his wife Madeleine. In fact, Scottie never even met the real Madeleine – he was chosen specifically by Elster to 'protect' the phony Madeleine because of his vertigo. Elster knew that Scottie would never be able to climb the staircase inside the bell tower at San Juan Batista, so Judy was primed to tell Scottie about a dream where she died at the place. Elster was already waiting at the top of the tower with the real Madeleine's body when Judy and Scottie arrived. Judy's impulsive act of running up the tower was nothing of the sort – as she reached the top of the stairs, Elster threw his wife's body from the top of the tower. This was the body that Scottie saw fall, not Judy/Madeleine, the woman Scottie had fallen in love with. Judy ends the letter by admitting that she actually fell in love with Scottie, and had been hoping to see him again one final time.

Judy tears the letter up and goes to meet Scottie, hoping that he will fall in love with her as Judy, not as the fake Madeleine. Unhappily, though, Scottie's obsessive behaviour with Judy and the late Madeleine gets more and more worrying. He buys Judy an identical dress to the one she wore on the day that 'Madeleine' died. He insists that she dye her hair blonde, and, when she returns to his apartment looking identical to Madeleine, Scottie's obsession is complete. They kiss passionately as the 'star-crossed lovers' are reunited.

Scottie and Judy are getting ready to go to dinner when he notices that she is wearing the same necklace that Madeleine was wearing when she died. He realises that Judy and Madeleine must be the same person, but says nothing. He suggests that they go for a drive in the country before dinner, and heads towards San Juan Batista. Judy is nervous at first, almost hysterical by the time they arrive. The furious Scottie manhandles Judy up the bell tower, blurting out his suspicions. Judy confirms her role in the plot, but pleads her love for him and the wish to be forgiven. At the top of the tower, the power of their twisted love for one another triumphs, and they share a passionate embrace. At that moment, the shadowy figure of a nun rises up next to them, startling Judy. She stumbles backward and plummets to her death, leaving a shell-shocked Scottie to stare down from the top of the tower, his vertigo replaced by an altogether greater horror . . .

CASTING: Having invested so much effort in presenting Vera Miles as his new 'Grace Kelly', it was with both disappointment and a sense of betrayal that he learnt she was pregnant (by her husband, the *Tarzan* actor Gordon Scott) and was therefore unavailable to star in *Vertigo*. Hitch took this as a personal and deliberate insult, as she had already completed screen tests and costume fittings for the role as well as commissioning a portrait of Carlotta Valdes with Miles's likeness. There is a body of opinion that suggests that Vera Miles was relieved to lose the role, as she was deeply uncomfortable at being 'remodelled' by Hitch into his perfect Ice Maiden.

ROOTS: The film is based upon the novel . . . *d'Entre les Morts* ('From Among the Dead') by Boileau and Narcejac. The story was allegedly written specifically for Hitchcock (although he denied this in his famous conversation with Truffaut) after the authors heard that he tried to buy the rights to their previous novel *Les Diaboliques*, losing out to Henri-Georges Clouzot, who filmed it in 1954.

Hitch's lifelong obsession with making a movie version of the play *Mary Rose* almost reached fruition with *Vertigo*. *Mary Rose*, a ghost story written by the *Peter Pan* author JM Barrie, is a story about a girl who vanishes without explanation, then returns to the world many years later looking not a day older.

The line 'the Chinese say that, once you've saved a person's life, you're responsible for it for ever' has little basis in Chinese legend. However, it was also the premise for the novel *Gallowglass* by Ruth Rendell (writing as Barbara Vine).

The Greek legend of Pygmalion (adapted by George Bernard Shaw and later immortalised as the musical *My Fair Lady)* tells of a man remodelling a woman in his own desired fashion.

Finally, an early gothic novel saw a scientist trying to remake another woman in the image of his dead wife – Mary Shelley's *Frankenstein*.

LEGACY: Hitchcock invented the famous combination of forward zoom and reverse tracking shot to convey the sense of vertigo to the audience. The view down the mission stairwell cost $19,000 for just a couple of seconds of screen time. The 'dolly out/zoom in' technique is now used in many, many films and TV series, but its most famous moment comes in Steven Spielberg's *Jaws* (1975), when Roy Scheider's character Brodie suddenly realises that the shark is attacking bathers on the beach.

Kim Novak later appeared for a year in the glossy American soap opera *Falcon Crest*. She played almost exactly the same role(s) in *Falcon Crest* as she had in *Vertigo* – an actress pretending to be somebody who had already been murdered.

Though the true legacy of *Vertigo* is far too great to be assessed here, we've selected just a few of the more obvious tributes: *Psycho III* (Anthony Perkins, 1986); *A Kiss Before Dying* (James Dearden, 1991); *Basic Instinct* (Paul Verhoeven, 1993); *Twelve Monkeys* (Terry Gilliam, 1996); Mel Brooks's *High Anxiety* (1997); Brian De Palma's *Sisters* (1973), *Obsession* (1976), *Body Double* (1984) and *Snake Eyes* (1998).

WHO'S WHO?: Kim Novak – real name Marilyn Novak – had previously appeared in *The Man With the Golden Arm* (Otto Preminger, 1955), and *Pal Joey* (George Sidney, 1957) opposite Frank Sinatra. She had no idea that she was the second choice to play Madeleine/Judy until she was told about Vera Miles's screen tests by an interviewer in 1980. Kim largely retired from acting at the end of the 60s, but has enjoyed occasional acting roles since, such as in *The Mirror Crack'd* and the TV series *Falcon Crest* (see **Roots** above). She now enjoys photographic nature studies, and lives on a farm with her vet husband and some llamas.

Barbara Bel Geddes (Midge) will be remembered mainly for her epic stint in *Dallas* as Miss Ellie. Strangely enough, in *Dallas*, Miss Ellie was also played by another actress (Donna Reed) for a short while before Bel Geddes returned to play the part.

Ellen Corby made numerous appearances in the TV series *Alfred Hitchcock Presents* and made a significant contribution to *The Addams Family*, playing Lurch's mother. But it is for her Emmy-winning role as Grandma in the epic frontier series *The Waltons* that most viewers will remember her. Another *Alfred Hitchcock Presents* regular, Raymond Bailey (*Scottie's Doctor*), played Milburn Drysdale, the overstressed bank manager, in *The Beverly Hillbillies*.

THE USUAL SUSPECTS: Tom Helmore (*Gavin Elster*) also appeared in *The Ring* (1927) and *Secret Agent* (1936). This would also prove to be

Jimmy Stewart's last appearance for Hitch, despite the fact that he begged to be allowed to have the lead in *North by Northwest*. Bernard Herrmann again provides the soundtrack, and Saul Bass makes the first of three major contributions for Hitchcock with the spellbinding title sequence.

KILLER LINES: Scottie, to Judy, talking about Elster: 'He made you over, just like I made you over – only better. Did he train you? Did he rehearse you? Did he tell you exactly what to do, what to say?'

Scottie reveals some of the key themes of the film when talking to Madeleine about the giant felled sequoia tree: 'It's true name is *Sequoia sempervirens*: always green, ever living.'

THERE HE IS!: About eleven minutes in, wearing a grey suit walking past Gavin Elster's shipyard.

MISOGYNY: There's little physical violence towards women shown on screen in *Vertigo*, but it's what happens off screen and in the mind that really leaves a nasty taste in the mouth. It's easy to miss the fact that Elster must have broken the real Madeleine's neck before throwing her corpse off the top of the bell tower.

Scottie's unpleasant voyeurism towards Madeleine during the early stages of the film is unsettling, but this is nothing compared with the brutal emotional rape he subjects Judy to. Judy submits to Scottie's unhealthy desires in order to please him, as she has fallen in love with him. Hardly an empowering statement of the independent nature of womankind. Even the normally sensible Midge seems to be scared of losing 'her' Scottie to the glamorous new stranger Madeleine, so she paints a picture of herself as Carlotta in order to remake herself in Madeleine's image. When she realises that the portrait has hurt both Scottie and herself, she defaces the artificial image and throws her paintbrush at her reflection in the window, implying that she is unhappy being herself and *not* being Madeleine.

It's testament to the quality of the performances and direction in the film that the dramatic conclusion to the film, where Scottie drags and pushes the terrified Judy up the precarious bell tower, doesn't come across as being too distasteful.

AWARDS: Oscar-nominated for Best Art Direction and Best Sound. *Vertigo* is listed as one of the American Film Institute's top 100 films of the decade (number 61) and selected for preservation by the National Film Registry of the Library of Congress.

THEMES AND MOTIFS: Treachery, betrayal and play-acting are key elements of *Vertigo*, but it's Scottie's obsession and descent into madness that really catches Hitch's eye. An obsessive relationship with a dead woman would form the keystone of *Psycho*, some two years later.

TABOOS: It's not going too far to suggest that Scottie is a necrophiliac. Calling a dead lover back to life by giving another woman an erotic makeover is kinky at best, sick at worst.

MUSIC: Bernard Herrmann provides one of the most beautifully romantic scores ever heard as a film soundtrack. The sweeping romance of the film is perfectly matched by the epic and timeless images it underscores, and the haunting main theme is still justifiably famous, having been used recently in a TV advert for Ford cars, featuring *The X Files*' David Duchovny.

POSTER: 'Alfred Hitchcock engulfs you in a whirlpool of terror and tension!'/'He Thought His Love Was Dead, Until He Found Her in Another Woman . . . See Kim Novak and James Stewart, Teamed For the First Time on the Screen in the Year's Outstanding Suspense Tale.' The bizarre image on the poster – of a male figure surrounded by swirling, confusing lines – is finally comprehensible in the final shot of the film when Scottie assumes the same pose.

THE ICE MAIDEN(S): It has been said that Hitchcock was unimpressed with Kim Novak's performance in *Vertigo*. Interviewed by the columnist Hedda Hopper, Hitch said: 'It was very hard for me to get what I wanted from her, since Kim's head was full of her own ideas.' The irony of Scottie and Judy's remodelling is hard to miss.

Nonetheless, to a modern audience, Novak's performance in *Vertigo* is breathtaking. As both Madeleine and Judy, Novak brings a raw, atavistic passion that is rarely visible in Hitch's other Ice Maidens. The blonde Madeleine is sultriness personified, particularly in the scenes in Scottie's apartment, where the electricity bouncing between the two leads is almost visible. Their first touch is particularly primal. As a story about a makeover, Hitchcock was actually extremely successful in 'making over' Novak, despite what he might have thought himself. Judy's painful transformation into Madeleine is agonising to watch, particularly the sequences where they are shopping for grey suits, and where Scottie forces Judy to put her newly dyed hair up into the swirling bun worn by Madeleine. It's Novak's performance that carries these scenes, and as viewers we are transfixed. In reality, Novak actually plays three roles – Madeleine, Judy, and Judy pretending to be Madeleine. Each performance is clearly different and carried off to perfection.

Barbara Bel Geddes gets to play a virtual photocopy of Doris Day's role in *The Man Who Knew Too Much* – a more homely and sensible version of the traditional Hitchcock Ice Maiden. In *Vertigo*, however, the crucial difference is that the Jimmy Stewart doesn't want his pretty best friend to be his wife – he wants the mystery, romance and danger of the stunning Novak. The audience clearly sees that Scottie would be happier with the ever-loving Midge, if only he could rid himself of his obsession with Madeleine.

WHAT THE PAPERS SAID: In her review of the 1984 rerelease of the film for the *New York Times*, Janet Maslin describes how: 'An astonishing burst of applause greeted the penultimate moments of *Vertigo* . . . at the performance I saw last week – astonishing because, only seconds later, the film's real ending left the audience gasping in disbelief. Those who had cheered the happy-looking near-finale must not have seen *Vertigo* before. They must have been caught off-guard by this film's stubborn, single-minded intensity, and by its uncharacteristic (for Hitchcock) reluctance to please.'

COSTUME: Once again, Hitchcock reveals that his image of an ideal woman (and, of course, Scottie's) is that of an elegant blonde woman dressed in a snugly fitting grey suit, her hair carefully arranged in a precise swirl (similar outfits are worn by Doris Day in *The Man Who Knew Too Much* and Tippi Hedren in *The Birds*).

TRIVIA: The film was unavailable for decades because its rights (together with those of four other pictures of the same period) were bought back by Hitchcock and left as part of his legacy to his daughter Pat. They were known for a long time as the infamous 'five lost Hitchcocks' among film buffs, and were rereleased in theatres around 1984 after a 30-year absence. The others are *The Man Who Knew Too Much*, *Rear Window*, *Rope*, and *The Trouble with Harry*.

San Juan Batista, the Spanish mission that features in key scenes in the movie, doesn't actually have a bell tower – it was added with trick photography. The mission originally had a steeple but it was demolished following a fire.

The screenplay is credited to Alec Coppel and Samuel A Taylor, but Coppel didn't write a word of the final draft, credited purely for contractual reasons. Taylor read neither Coppel's script nor the original novel, but worked solely from Hitchcock's outline of the story.

Hitchcock reportedly spent a week filming a brief scene where Madeleine stares at a portrait in the Palace of the Legion of Honour just to get the lighting right.

An addition to the ending was made for some European countries due to certain laws prohibiting a film from letting a 'bad guy' get away at the end of a film. In the new ending, after Scottie looks down from the bell tower (the original ending) there is a shot of Midge sitting next to a radio listening to reports of police tracking down Gavin Elster. As Midge turns off the radio the news flash also reports that three Berkeley students got caught bringing a cow up the stairs of a campus building. Scottie enters the room, looks at Midge plainly, and then looks out of a window. Midge makes two drinks and gives one to Scottie. It ends with both of them looking out of the window. This ending can be found on the restoration laserdisc.

FINAL ANALYSIS: Many thousands of words have been written over the years in praise of *Vertigo*, considered by most critics to be

Hitchcock's finest hour. Whole books have spent hundreds of pages examining its intricate plot, the convoluted journey Boileau and Narcejac's story took to make it to the big screen. Still others have examined the impact the film had on its stars, Jimmy Stewart and Kim Novak. It would be facetious for us to comment in any great depth about *Vertigo* when many more influential and respected critics have, in a sense, already said everything there is to say.

Nonetheless, *Vertigo* is, quite simply, a stunning and astonishing masterpiece. More than any other Hitchcock film, *Vertigo* rewards repeated rewatching. There is so much depth and confidence to this twisted story that Hitch unfolds that it simply cannot be appreciated on a first viewing. It's unremittingly gloomy – Hitchcock's view of the nature of male–female relationships offers the viewer little hope of redemption or, at the very least, a happy ending. Despite this, or rather because of this, *Vertigo* feels like the most 'grown-up' film that Hitchcock ever made. **10/10**

North by Northwest (1959)

(Working titles: *Breathless/In a Northwesterly Direction/The Man in Lincoln's Nose*)

(Colour – 136 mins)

Produced by Alfred Hitchcock/Metro-Goldwyn-Mayer
Associate Producer: Herbert Coleman

Written by Ernest Lehman

Original Music: Bernard Herrmann
Director of Photography: Robert Burks
Production Design: Robert F Boyle (credited as Robert Boyle)
Film Editing: George Tomasini
Title Designer: Saul Bass
Hair Stylist: Sydney Guilaroff
Colour Consultant: Charles K Hagedon
Special Effects: Lee LeBlanc, A Arnold Gillespie
Set Decorator: Frank R McKelvy (credited as Frank McKelvy), Henry Grace
Recording Supervisor: Franklin Milton
Art Directors: Merrill Pye, William A Horning
Assistant Director: Robert Saunders
Make-up Artist: William Tuttle

CAST: Cary Grant (*Roger Thornhill*), Eva Marie Saint (*Eve Kendall*), James Mason (*Philip Vandamm*), Jessie Royce Landis (*Clara Thornhill*), Leo G Carroll (*Professor*), Josephine Hutchinson (*Handsome Woman*),

Philip Ober (*Lester Townsend*), Martin Landau (*Leonard*), Adam Williams (*Valerian*), Edward Platt (*Victor Larrabee*), Robert Ellenstein (*Licht*), Les Tremayne (*Auctioneer*), Philip Coolidge (*Dr Cross*), Pat McVey, Ken Lynch (*Chicago Policemen*), Edward Binns (*Captain Junket*).

UNCREDITED CAST: Stanley Adams (*Lieutenant Harding*), Andy Albin (*Farmer*), Ernest Anderson (*Porter on 20th Century*), Malcolm Atterbury (*Man at Prairie Crossing*), Baynes Barron (*Taxi Driver #2*), John Beradino (*Sergeant Emile Klinger*), Sara Berner (*Telephone Operator*), Taggart Casey (*Shaving Man*), Bill Catching (*Attendant*),Walter Coy (*Reporter*), Jimmy Cross (*Taxi Driver #1*), Jack Daly (*Steward*), John Damler (*Lieutenant*), Lawrence Dobkin (*Cartoonist*), Tommy Farrell (*Elevator Operator*), Jesslyn Fax (*Woman*), Sally Fraser (*Attendant*), Paul Genge (*Lieutenant Hagerman*), Ned Glass (*Ticket Seller*), Len Hendry (*Lieutenant*), Bobby Johnson (*Waiter*), Madge Kennedy (*Housewife*), Doreen Lang (*Maggie*), Alexander Lockwood (*Judge*), Frank Marlowe (*Taxi Driver, Dakota*), Nora Marlowe (*Housekeeper*), James McCallion (*Plaza Valet*), Maura McGiveney (*Attendant*), Carl Milletaire (*Hotel Clerk*), Howard Negley (*Conductor on 20th Century*), Maudie Prickett (*Plaza Maid*), Ralph Reed (*Bellhop*), Harry Seymour (*Waiter*), Robert Shayne (*Larry Wade*), Doris Singh (*Indian Girl*), Olan Soule (*Assistant Auctioneer*), Helen Spring (*Bidder*), Harvey Stephens (*Stockbroker*), Harry Strang (*Assistant Conductor*), Dale Van Sickel (*Ranger*), Susan Whitney (*Attendant*), Frank Wilcox (*Weitner*), Robert B Williams (*Patrolman Waggonner*), Carleton Young (*Fanning Nelson*).

SUMMARY: A New York advertising executive, Roger O Thornhill, is on his way to meet some of his colleagues for his regular after-work drinks in the Plaza Hotel. After giving his secretary his final instructions for the day, he meets his colleagues. Just at that moment, a bellboy in the hotel announces that he has a message for a Mr George Kaplan. Roger beckons the bellboy over, planning on sending a telegram himself. However, Roger has been observed by two sinister-looking thugs, who jump to the fairly obvious conclusion that he is George Kaplan. Holding Roger at gunpoint, the thugs escort him out of the Plaza Hotel and into a waiting car.

The bewildered Roger is driven to the country mansion of Lester Townsend. He is escorted into the library, where he meets an intimidating gentleman who insists on calling him George Kaplan. The gentleman – whom Roger assumes to be Lester Townsend – says that he is 'a great admirer' of Kaplan's work. 'Townsend' tries to get 'Kaplan' to cooperate with his plans and rattles off a list of destinations that he knows Kaplan is going to be visiting in the next few days – the Plaza Hotel, then going on to Chicago and finally Rapid City, South Dakota.

When the sinister gentleman repeatedly presses him for information, Roger again tells him that his name is not Kaplan and he doesn't know what on earth is going on. 'Townsend' gets his associate Leonard and the two thugs to hold Roger down and pour an entire bottle of bourbon down his neck. They then set him loose in a stolen car on the clifftop roads heading back to New York. Roger, completely drunk, tries his best to control the vehicle and only narrowly manages to avoid a fatal accident. He brings the car to a halt and is arrested by the police – observed by the thugs who have followed him.

When Roger has sobered up the next morning, he tells the local judge that he was kidnapped and forcibly intoxicated by Lester Townsend and his staff. Suprisingly, he isn't believed, so he and the police return to the Townsend mansion. There, 'Mrs Townsend' warmly greets Roger and explains to the detectives that they held a party there the night before. She adds that they knew that Roger had drunk too much, but believed that he had ordered a taxi back to New York. She then tells the police that her husband could corroborate the story, but that he is due to address the United Nations General Assembly that afternoon!

Roger and his mother return to the Plaza Hotel, hoping to locate the real George Kaplan. They discover that Kaplan does indeed have a room booked at the Plaza, and manage to coerce the receptionist into giving them the key to the room. When both the maid and the valet believe that Roger is Kaplan, he realises that no one at the hotel has ever actually seen the man. At that moment, the phone rings. Roger answers it, and is shocked to hear the voice of one of the two thugs, calling from the hotel lobby. He grabs his mother and bundles her into a crowded lift, but the thugs follow them in. He realises that his life is in real danger and barely manages to evade the thugs thanks to a naive yet telling remark from his mother. He jumps into a taxi and heads for the United Nations building. At the reception desk, he says his name is George Kaplan and that he wants to speak to Lester Townsend. Roger is surprised when Townsend arrives and turns out to be a different man from the sinister gent he met at the mansion. As Roger explains what has been happening to him, Townsend gasps and collapses, a large knife sticking out of his back. A nearby photographer quickly snaps Roger holding the knife, and Roger makes a break for freedom, realising he is now on the run.

At a secret government intelligence bureau, Roger's situation is being discussed by a roomful of agents. They are aware that an innocent man has been mistaken for a nonexistent individual, created to protect the identities of their genuine agents. 'George Kaplan' had been created to help stop the smuggling of government secrets out of the USA by Philip Vandamm and his associates. Roger has now become a useful decoy, and the chairman of the discussions, the Professor, proclaims that they can do nothing to protect him.

Having discovered that 'Kaplan' has moved on to Chicago, Roger decides to follow him, in the hope of clearing his name. This proves increasingly difficult, as his photograph has been printed in the newspapers and the police are actively searching for him. Roger boards a train to Chicago at Grand Central Station. He bumps into a beautiful blonde woman, who assists him in evading the police. Some time later, he meets the same woman again in the dining car, where she introduces herself as Eve Kendall and flirts outrageously with him. Eve shocks Roger by admitting that she knows exactly who he is and what he's done – despite this, she says that she likes him and will hide him from the police. Concealed in Eve's sleeper compartment, Roger discovers the magnitude of her hospitality. As they are snuggling up for the night, Eve gets a porter to pass a note to the fake 'Townsend', who is in a nearby compartment with his companion Leonard. 'What do I do with him in the morning?' the note reads.

Arriving at Chicago, Roger disguises himself as a porter and carries Eve's bags off the train and past the waiting police. While Roger is getting changed and shaved, Eve speaks to Leonard. When Roger returns, she lies to him and tells him that she's phoned the hotel and spoken to Kaplan, who has agreed to a meeting at the Prairie Stop on Highway 41. Roger takes a bus to a deserted road in the middle of nowhere, lined with enormous cornfields. There is no sign of Kaplan, and Roger is about to give up and go home when a crop-dusting plane suddenly attacks him. He tries to take cover in the cornfield, but is forced to make a run for it when the plane dumps its load of choking white powder on him. He flags down a passing gasoline truck, at which point the crop duster crashes into it and explodes. A crowd of onlookers arrive, and Roger steals one of their trucks to make his escape.

Finally arriving at Kaplan's hotel in Chicago, Roger is shocked to discover that not only had Kaplan checked out before Eve allegedly phoned him, but that Eve is in fact staying there too. He goes to her room, where she is shocked and happily surprised to see him. Despite this, she tells him to leave, and never to try to see her again. Roger follows her to an auction house, where he sees her sitting alongside the phoney 'Townsend' and Leonard: 'The three of you together. That's a picture only Charles Addams could draw.' 'Townsend' confirms that his real name is Philip Vandamm, and he congratulates 'Kaplan' on his performance as the innocent man on the run. Once again, Roger protests that he isn't play-acting.

'The only performance that'll satisfy you is when I play dead.' 'In your very next role. You'll be quite convincing, I assure you,' replies Vandamm.

Having successfully bid for an antique sculpture, Vandamm leaves with Eve. Roger attempts to follow, but is blocked by Leonard and the two thugs. Realising that once again his life is in peril, he causes a disturbance at the auction and is arrested by police, who escort him out of the room, all the while being observed by the Professor. Instead of taking Roger to the local police station, they escort him to Chicago

Airport. There, he is greeted by the Professor, who explains that Kaplan never really existed. The Professor tells Roger that he knows Vandamm is trying to flee the USA with a microfilm full of secrets the following evening. He asks him to continue to pretend to be Kaplan for another 24 hours. Eve is in fact a US government agent, working undercover as Vandamm's 'moll'. Eve's obvious genuine attraction for Roger has placed her life in grave danger, so the Professor and Roger must travel to Rapid City, where Vandamm lives, near to the Mount Rushmore national monument.

Roger, pretending finally to be George Kaplan, arranges to meet Vandamm in the cafeteria at the base of Mount Rushmore. He offers not to report Vandamm's location to his superiors in exchange for Eve being allowed to stay with him. Vandamm refuses, and in a moment of apparent rage, Roger grabs Eve. She pulls a gun and shoots Roger, who collapses to the floor, apparently dead. Eve runs outside and drives off alone, leaving the stunned Vandamm and Leonard to wait, not wanting to get arrested themselves. Roger isn't dead, however. The shooting had been set up to convince Vandamm of Eve's loyalty, and to give him a reason not to leave her behind. The Professor arranges for Eve and Roger to briefly meet in the middle of the forest. She apologises for lying to him, but tells him that she must go back to Vandamm's house now and continue with her job. Roger is furious with the Professor for his insistence that she leave the country with Vandamm. He manages to escape from the Professor's protective care and rushes to Vandamm's house, intent on stopping her from leaving.

Overhearing a conversation between Vandamm and Leonard, Roger discovers that they are planning to throw Eve out of the plane after they take off. He further discovers that the microfilm is hidden inside the statue Vandamm bought at the auction. Just as the plane arrives on the concealed landing strip behind the house, Roger manages to alert Eve to the imminent danger facing her if she steps on board the aircraft. Unable to avoid her fate, Eve is escorted by Vandamm and Leonard to the plane. Just as she is about to get on board, Roger causes a distraction by driving a car dangerously close to them. Eve grabs the statue from Vandamm and jumps into the car. Discovering that the gates to Vandamm's estate are locked, the couple try to escape on foot, closely followed by Leonard and another of Vandamm's henchmen. They discover that they are now at the top of the sculptures of ex-US presidents' faces on Mount Rushmore. Realising that they have no other way to go, they begin a treacherous descent. Roger is attacked by the thug, who during the scuffle slips and falls to his death. Leonard attempts to kill them both, but is instead shot by a policeman. The Professor arrests Vandamm, and Roger manages to rescue Eve, who is hanging from a ledge by her fingertips.

Some little while later, Roger and the new Mrs Thornhill take the train back to New York on their honeymoon.

CASTING: James Stewart was eager to star in *North by Northwest*, but Hitch believed that the poor box-office returns for *Vertigo* were because Stewart 'looked too old'. MGM wanted Gregory Peck, but Hitchcock cast Cary Grant. Similarly, Hitch managed to get his first choice of Eva Marie Saint rather than the studio's preferred choice of Cyd Charisse.

ROOTS: It's impossible to ignore the impact that many of Hitchcock's previous movies had on *North by Northwest*. It continues the arc of 'innocent-man-on-the-run' pictures that goes from *The 39 Steps* through to *Saboteur*, and would later be adapted for elements of *Torn Curtain*.

Vandamm's cliff-top mansion mimics the style of the innovative architect Frank Lloyd Wright, which adds to the suggestion that Vandamm has successfully adopted the image of a sophisticated American by his appreciation of one of their great eccentrics.

LEGACY: The detective series *Remington Steele* revolved around the idea of a female detective who invents a male partner to give her credibility, but is then surprised when the fictional male partner turns up and takes over investigations. Remington Steele was played by the future James Bond, Pierce Brosnan. In one episode, Steele goes in search of a 'George Kaplan' and sets sail for 'two miles offshore, north by northwest'.

It could also be argued that Roger Thornhill's adventures were reflected and absorbed into the movie character of James Bond, who appeared on screen three years later in *Dr No*. The Bond movies tend to be glamorous travelogues, with a beautiful and mysterious woman who may (or may not) be a double agent, a charming villain and an outrageous stunt sequence, usually filmed on a building or location of international fame.

While we're at it, one can attribute pretty much every 'man-on-the-run' or action film since 1960 to *North by Northwest*.

WHO'S WHO?: Martin Landau has been acting for over thirty years, having starred in the TV series *Mission: Impossible* and *Space: 1999*, as well as appearing in such films as *Crimes and Misdemeanors* (Woody Allen, 1992) and *Ed Wood* (Tim Burton, 1994), for which he won the Best Supporting Actor Oscar for his uncanny impression of the classic horror-movie actor Bela Lugosi.

James Mason is best known for his parts in *The Boys from Brazil* (Franklin J Schaffner, 1978), opposite Gregory Peck; *A Star is Born* (George Cukor, 1954); as Brutus in *Julius Caesar* (Joseph L Mankiewicz, 1953); with Margaret Lockwood in *The Wicked Lady* (Leslie Arlis, 1945); and alongside the terrifying Reggie Nalder (*The Man Who Knew Too Much* – remake) in the TV movie of Stephen King's *Salem's Lot* (Tobe Hooper, 1979).

THE USUAL SUSPECTS: Leo G Carroll can also be seen in *Rebecca*, *Suspicion*, *Spellbound*, and *The Paradine Case*. Jessie Royce Landis had earlier played Grace Kelly's mother in *To Catch a Thief*. She must have been somewhat surprised at being cast as Cary Grant's mother in *North by Northwest*, as she was actually younger than Grant! Bernard Herrmann also composed the soundtracks for *The Trouble with Harry*, *The Man Who Knew Too Much*, *Vertigo*, *Psycho* and *Marnie*, as well as being the 'sound consultant' for *The Birds*. Saul Bass (titles designer) also provided innovative titles for *Vertigo* and *Psycho*, and is credited with storyboarding *Psycho*'s shower scene.

KILLER LINES: Vandamm, on discovering Eve's treachery: 'This matter is best disposed of from a great height. Over water.'

Roger's mother, chatting in the lift to Vandamm's thugs: 'You men aren't really trying to kill my son, are you?'

Vandamm, to Roger, in the auction room: 'Has anyone ever told you that you overplay your various roles rather severely, Mr Kaplan? First, you're the outraged Madison Avenue man who claims he's been mistaken for someone else. Then you play a fugitive from justice, supposedly trying to clear his name of a crime he knows he didn't commit. And now you play the peevish lover, stung by jealousy and betrayal. Seems to me you fellows could stand a little less training from the FBI and a little more from the actors' studio . . .'

THERE HE IS!: Missing a bus at the end of the opening titles.

THE MACGUFFIN: Everyone is trying to stop Vandamm from leaving the country with his microfilm of secrets, but, to be honest, neither the audience nor Hitchcock could care less about them.

AWARDS: Listed as one of the American Film Institute's top 100 films of the decade (number 40).

THEMES AND MOTIFS: The Innocent Man on the Run – again. However, the real theme of *North by Northwest* is acting and false pretences. Roger Thornhill has to pretend to be George Kaplan. Philip Vandamm pretends to be Lester Townsend. Eve Kendall pretends to love Vandamm, and then pretends to love Roger in order to please Vandamm. She then falls in love with Roger, and has to pretend to Vandamm that she has no feelings for Roger. In short, everything and everyone in *North by Northwest* is a fake. Even the precious antique is empty – just a cover for international spy secrets. When Roger admits that the 'O' in his name stands for 'nothing', he's admitting that he literally stands for nothing – he has no interest in the politics that the other characters are willing to die for. In his everyday life, Roger writes advertising copy, creating a spin on the truth to get the desired result.

TABOOS: The flirting between Eve and Roger is utterly disgraceful, revealing a degree of sexual innuendo rarely seen outside the average

Carry On . . . film, or *To Catch a Thief*, for that matter. When Eve asserts that she's 'a big girl', Roger can't help but comment: 'Yeah, and in all the right places.'

MUSIC: Bernard Herrmann produces yet another winner, a rip-roaring and exciting score that adds to the breathless pace of the film as a whole. The title theme is superb, underpinning several key moments throughout the movie, such as the drunken car hurtling along the cliff tops and the final pursuit across Mount Rushmore. Even more effective is the complete absence of music in the crop-dusting attack. The silence reinforces Roger's isolation, and the fact that he truly is lost in the middle of nowhere. This particular sequence is practically silent, reminding us that Hitchcock began his career before 'talkies' ever began. He lets the image tell the tale completely, using the visual images to convey far more than dialogue ever could. A perfect example of when his interest in 'pure cinema' shines through.

As an additional little joke, near the start of the picture, when Roger enters the Plaza Hotel, an orchestra can be heard playing the melody 'It's a Most Unusual Day'. It certainly turned out to be an unusual day for Roger.

POSTER: 'From the killer plane in the cornfield to the cliff-hanger on George Washington's nose, it's suspense in every direction!' 'Only Cary Grant and Alfred Hitchcock ever gave you so much suspense.'

THE ICE MAIDEN: Eva Marie Saint makes a stunning Ice Maiden, mixing professional detatchment with a burning passion for our hero. Eve is forced to enter into a relationship with Vandamm – an act that many people might find distasteful at best, impossible at worst. Despite all of this, she maintains a level of dignity, elegance and sophistication that is a pleasure to behold.

Eva Marie Saint is neither as warm as Grace Kelly nor as hard as Kim Novak nor as fragile as Tippi Hedren. Despite this, she displays many of the characteristics of all of the above. In modern cinema, Eve is a part that could so easily be reduced to that of a common tart, but Saint gives her an air of intelligence and vulnerability that present-day scriptwriters and casting directors could learn from.

WHAT THE PAPERS SAID: On Thursday 15 October 1959, the *Times* review of *North by Northwest* was somewhat mixed: 'A new Hitchcock film is not, perhaps to-day the occasion it once was. *North by Northwest* . . . is an expert bit of film-making, a smooth and not unsubtle piece of entertainment, but it is difficult to throw off the impression that we have seen it before. And, in a sense, we have. There is much in the story itself that recalls Mr Hitchcock's free and curious version of *The 39 Steps* . . .

'Yet, set down in cold blood, all this seems ungrateful, for *North by Northwest* remains consistently exciting and enjoyable, and Mr

Hitchcock proves that he has still a few new tricks to shake down from his capacious sleeve.'

TRIVIA: Hitchcock had severe trouble in gaining permission to film in the places he needed to. He was forced to smuggle a concealed camera into the lobby of the United Nations in order to film Cary Grant's arrival. When the press discovered that Hitchcock had asked to shoot footage on the Mount Rushmore National Monument, they were scandalised. One newspaper editor even suggested that Hitchcock should go back to Britain and make a movie about someone climbing over the Queen's face.

Awards: Oscar-nominated for Best Art Direction, Best Film Editing, Best Screenplay Written Directly for the Screen. Selected for preservation by the National Film Registry of the Library of Congress.

As the title of the film is *North by Northwest*, it's interesting to note that Roger Thornhill appears on the left side of the screen for almost the entire movie, usually in the top left of the frame. It has been suggested that the title is a misquote from *Hamlet* – 'I am mad but north-northwest' – but Hitchcock denied this played any part in the naming of the film. Thornhill's direction of travel is consistently in a northwesterly direction, and he even travels from Chicago to Mount Rushmore on Northwest Airlines.

FINAL ANALYSIS: *North by Northwest* is rightfully acclaimed as Hitchcock's greatest comic thriller. Although it is merely a reworking of some of his previous movies a quarter of a century after he first filmed them, on this occasion all of the ingredients in the recipe come together to create something really special. Here, he succeeds on every possible level – acting, writing, use of colour, atmosphere, music. The list is endless.

Roger Thornhill is essentially a distillation of the character that Cary Grant wanted to portray through his movies. Everything seems so effortless for Roger that we as an audience hardly ever question that he could ever be in real danger – after all, it's Cary Grant, not Roger Thornhill, that we are watching here. Roger Thornhill is an advertising executive who runs his own company called ROT. He's shallow, and keeps protesting to Vandamm that he has no more depth to him. It's the agents on both sides who enable Roger to realise that he's capable of so much more – a late spiritual awakening.

James Mason plays the perfect Hitchcock villain – more charming, sophisticated and witty than any previous bad guy. Even when Vandamm is arrested, he decries the use of real bullets by the police as 'not being sporting', as if to him the whole thing were nothing more than a game.

As a light-hearted breather between the angst of *Vertigo* and *Psycho*, *North by Northwest* is a welcome relief, and an unqualified success. It just took him 25 years to get the formula right. **10/10**

the complete

HITCHCOCK

films 1960–76

Psycho (1960)

(B & W – 109 mins)

Produced by Alfred Hitchcock/Shamley Productions

Screenplay: Joseph Stefano, based on the novel by Robert Bloch

Music: Bernard Herrmann
Director of Photography: John L Russell
Art Director: Joseph Hurley & Robert Clatworthy
Set Decorator: George Milo
Unit Manager: Lew Leary
Edited by George Tomasini
Costume Supervisor: Helen Colvig
Make-up Supervision: Jack Barron & Robert Dawn
Hair Stylist: Florence Bush
Special Effects: Clarence Champagne
Sound Recording: Waldon O Watson & William Russell
Assistant Director: Hilton A Green
Title Designer/Pictorial Consultant: Saul Bass

CAST: Anthony Perkins (*Norman Bates*), Vera Miles (*Lila Crane*), John Gavin (*Sam Loomis*), Martin Balsam (*Milton Arbogast*), John McIntire (*Sheriff Chambers*), Simon Oakland (*Dr Richmond*), Vaughn Taylor (*George Lowery*), Frank Albertson (*Tom Cassidy*), Lurene Tuttle (*Mrs Chambers*), Patricia Hitchcock – credited as 'Pat Hitchcock' (*Caroline*), John Anderson (*California Charlie*), Mort Mills (*Highway Patrolman*), Janet Leigh (*Marion Crane*).

UNCREDITED CAST: Francis De Sales, Sam Flint (*Officials*), George Eldredge (*Chief of Police*), Frank Killmond (*Bob Summerfield*), Ted Knight (*Prison Guard*), Ann Dore, Margo Epper, Mitzi (*'Mother'*), Jeanette Nolan, Paul Jasmin, Virginia Gregg (*Voice of 'Mother'*), Helen Wallace (*Customer in Sam's Store*), Marli Renfro (*Janet Leigh's double*).

SUMMARY: Marion Crane is tired of waiting for her debt-ridden lover, Sam Loomis, to earn enough money for them to wed. When her employer entrusts her with $40,000, Marion decides to steal the money and run away to be with Sam. Having driven for almost a day and a half, she begins to feel tired. As her vision becomes obscured by a heavy rainstorm she decides to find somewhere to stay for the night.

Through the dark rain she stumbles across the Bates Motel – small and shabby and overshadowed by an old house perched on a steep hill. The proprietor, Norman Bates, is a lonely, nervous young man who appears to be completely dominated by his bedridden mother. Norman makes some supper for Marion and the two engage in an awkward conversation. As they talk, Marion realises that stealing the money was a

big mistake and begins to regret her rash actions. She thanks Norman for
his hospitality and returns to her room. Resolving to return home and
face the consequences, she works out how much of the stolen money she
has left. She undresses and showers. As she washes herself, a female
figure wielding a knife pulls back the shower curtain and stabs Marion to
death. Minutes later, a shocked and repulsed Norman runs down from
his house and sees the body slumped on the bathroom floor. He carefully
clears the room of all evidence, places the body inside the boot of
Marion's car and pushes the vehicle into a nearby swamp.

The following week, Sam Loomis receives visits from Marion's sister
Lila and a private detective called Arbogast, both looking for his
girlfriend. Sam is horrified to hear that Marion is wanted for the theft of
$40,000. As Sam and Lila try to work out what to do, Arbogast begins
to ask questions at all the local hotels. Eventually, he reaches the Bates
Motel, where Norman's behaviour arouses his suspicions. Calling Sam
and Lila from a phone box, Arbogast tells them that he believes Norman
knows where Marion is and suspects Norman's invalid mother might be
able to help him. He returns to the motel and begins to search the house.
He makes his way upstairs, where he is startled by a female figure who
rushes at him with a knife. He falls backward down the staircase and hits
the bottom with a thud. As he lies in a daze the figure stabs him
repeatedly.

Back at the store, Sam and Lila tire of waiting for Arbogast to return.
They decide to ask the local sheriff for advice and tell him of Arbogast's
suspicions regarding Norman's mother. But the sheriff tells them that
Mrs Bates died over ten years earlier. Determined to find the truth, Sam
and Lila book into the Bates Motel as a married couple. Norman is
obviously annoyed by their presence and Sam distracts Norman, asking
him about the stolen money, while Lila searches the house. Norman
begins to grow nervous as Sam's questions turn into an interrogation and
in frustration he smashes a vase over Sam's head and knocks him out.

Having searched the rest of the house, Lila makes her way down into
the fruit cellar. In the gloom she discovers Mrs Bates sitting in a rocking
chair. She reaches forth and turns the woman to face her – a rotting
corpse stares back at her. Suddenly, another woman enters the cellar
holding a knife. Sam enters just behind her and the two struggle. As Lila
stares in horror it becomes apparent that the 'woman' is Norman
wearing a wig and dress. Slowly he weakens and collapses to the floor in
a silent scream.

Norman is committed and, later, a psychologist explains to Sam and
Lila that Norman was suffering from a split personality stemming from
his guilt over murdering his mother and her lover ten years ago. He
blames his 'mother' for the subsequent murders of Marion, Arbogast and
two girls who had been reported missing, and like any good son he saw it
as his duty to cover up for her. In fact, he has developed a psychological
obsession with trying to keep the memory of his mother alive: he stole

her body and preserved it, bought a wig, dressed up in her clothes, sat in her chair and spoke in her voice. But now the battle is finally over – Mrs Bates has won.

CASTING: Considered for the role of Marion were Eva Marie Saint, Piper Laurie, Martha Hyer, Hope Lange, Shirley Jones and, briefly, Lana Turner. For Sam, Hitch wanted Stuart Whitman, but the strict budget persuaded him to settle for John Gavin, whom Hitch would take to calling 'the Stiff' behind his back. Also in the running were Cliff Robertson, Tom Tryon, Leslie Neilson, Brian Keith, Tom Laughlin, Jack Lord, Rod Taylor (*The Birds*) and Robert Loggia. Loggia would eventually play the role of Norman's doctor in *Psycho II*. Hitch claimed that he was considering Judith Anderson – Mrs Danvers from *Rebecca* (1940) – and Helen Hayes for the role of Mrs Bates, prompting Norma Varden (Mrs Cunningham in *Strangers on a Train*) to enquire whether she was also in the running. 'I am afraid not. What a pity!' Hitch replied cruelly.

In reality, he chose three women to play Mrs Bates: Ann Dore played the silhouetted figure approaching the shower curtain, Margo Epper played her for scenes involving physical contact with Marion, and a stunt actress called Mitzi played her for the scenes inside the Bates house. For Mrs Bates's dialogue, Hitchcock used Paul Jasmin, a friend of Anthony Perkins and well-known mimic, to suggest a masculine quality behind the voice. He then spliced and mixed in words spoken by the actresses Jeanette Nolan and Virginia Gregg to create the unique voice. Gregg would later provide the voice of Mrs Bates in the two sequels.

ROOTS: Robert Bloch's original novel was inspired by the true events surrounding the Wisconsin mass murderer Ed Gein. The logo used for the movie posters was the one designed by Tony Palladino for the book's first print. Edward Hopper's painting *House by the Railroad* possibly inspired the Bates mansion, which is also reminiscent of the one seen in the *Addams Family* cartoons by Charles Addams. Saul Bass claims the final shot of Norman was a nod to the famous painting *Whistler's Mother* by James Abbott McNeill Whistler. *Les Diaboliques* (Henri-Georges Clouzot, 1954) was, like Hitch's *Vertigo* (1959), based on a novel by Pierre Boileau and Thomas Narcejac, and bears many similarities to *Psycho*: a murder in a bathroom, an overinquisitive detective, and a marketing campaign that advised patrons to view the film only from the beginning and not to spoil the ending for others. The swinging light bulb, as used to illuminate Mrs Bates's final unveiling, comes from *The Picture of Dorian Gray* (Albert Lewin, 1945), while the idea of a split personality of distinctly different characters can be traced back to Robert Louis Stevenson's *The Strange Case of Dr Jekyll and Mr Hyde*.

LEGACY: *Psycho* spawned the sequels *Psycho II* (Richard Franklin, 1983), and *Psycho III* (Anthony Perkins, 1986), the prequel/sequel TV movie *Psycho IV: The Beginning* (Mick Garris, 1991), and the spin-off TV movie *Bates Motel* (Richard Rothstein, 1987), starring Bud Cort as Alex, an old friend of Norman's from the asylum. There's also the 'Psycho Experience' at the Universal Studios Tour in Florida, which cost $20 million to build, and features a combination of live actors, clips from the movie and a specially created film segment starring Anthony Perkins. And, try as we might, we can't forget Gus Van Sant's controversial shot-for-shot 1998 remake, which starred Vince Vaughan as Norman and Anne Heche as Marion.

Psycho was, of course, the film that single-handledly kick-started the whole slasher-flick genre, notably *The Texas Chainsaw Massacre* (Tobe Hooper, 1974), *Halloween* (John Carpenter, 1978), *Friday the 13th* (Sean S Cunningham, 1980), and *Scream* (Wes Craven, 1997), along with a whole slew of sequels. See also *Don't Look Now* (Nicholas Roeg, 1973), Roman Polanski's *Repulsion* (1965) and *Frantic* (1988), *Fatal Attraction* (Adrian Lyne, 1987), and the Brian De Palma films *Sisters* (1973), *Carrie* (1976), *Dressed to Kill* (1980), *Body Double* (1984) and *Raising Cain* (1992). You can also trace the legacy of *Psycho* in Thomas Harris's novels *Red Dragon* and *The Silence of the Lambs* (which featured the mass murderer Hannibal Lector, as well as two serial killers with obsessions about mothers), and the stylish Generation X novel *American Psycho* by Brett Easton Ellis.

Psycho was one of many Hitchcock movies spoofed in Mel Brooks's *High Anxiety* (1977), though possibly the most impressive homages, as ever, appear in *The Simpsons*. The character Principal Skinner is bullied by his rarely seen mother and seems to live in the Bates house, and in the episode 'Itchy and Scratchy and Marge', Homer is attacked with a pencil by his daughter Maggie in an almost shot-for-shot parody of the shower scene.

WHO'S WHO?: Anthony Perkins was being groomed as a sex symbol for the more intelligent teenage viewer before *Psycho* came along. Though he resented the way his career suffered after playing the transvestite Norman, he would return to the role for *Psycho II*, *Psycho III*, which he also directed, and the TV prequel *Psycho IV: The Beginning* (which had a sense of irony about it that Hitch would have loved!). Perkins died of an AIDS-related illness in 1992 while preparing for a further *Psycho* sequel.

Janet Leigh had appeared in more than thirty films since her debut in *The Romance of Rosy Ridge* (Roy Rowland, 1947) and was one of the best-known Hollywood actresses thanks to both her versatility and her much-publicised marriage to the heart-throb Tony Curtis. She went on to star alongside Frank Sinatra in *The Manchurian Candidate* (John Frankenheimer, 1962), but soon after *Psycho*'s release her career appeared to stall. She appeared alongside her daughter, Jamie Lee Curtis, in *The Fog* (John Carpenter, 1980) and in an ironic cameo in *Halloween*

H20 (Steve Miner, 1998). Leigh provided a unique insight into her involvement in Hitch's most famous film in her book *Psycho: Behind the Scenes of the Classic Thriller*, published in 1995.

John Gavin played Julius Caesar in Stanley Kubrick's *Spartacus* (1960) and narrowly missed out on playing James Bond after George Lazenby bowed out. He would later play Cary Grant in the TV biopic *Sophia Loren: Her Own Story* (Mel Stuart, 1980). He began carving out a political career when he became president of the Screen Actors' Guild in 1971 and was later appointed Ambassador to Mexico by Ronald Reagan. Martin Balsam played the foreman of the jury in *Twelve Angry Men* (Sidney Lumet, 1957) and appeared in both the original *Cape Fear* (J Lee Thompson, 1962) and the remake (Martin Scorsese, 1991).

THE USUAL SUSPECTS: Vera Miles (*Lila Crane*) also appeared in *The Wrong Man* and the *Alfred Hitchcock Presents* episodes 'Revenge', 'Incident at a Corner' and 'Don't Look Behind You'. She also re-created the role of Lila (now Lila Loomis) for *Psycho II*. Patricia Hitchcock appeared in two of her father's earlier films, *Stage Fright* and *Strangers on a Train*. Lurene Tuttle (*Mrs Chambers*) had previously worked with Hitch on a radio adaptation of his film, *The Lodger*. Mort Mills (*the Highway Patrolman*) would later play the farmer in *Torn Curtain*.

Bernard Herrmann composed the soundtracks for *The Trouble with Harry*, *The Man Who Knew Too Much* (1956), *Vertigo*, *North by Northwest*, and *Marnie*, as well as being the 'sound consultant' for *The Birds*.

Saul Bass provided the awe-inspiring titles for *Vertigo* and *North by Northwest*, and is credited with storyboarding *Psycho*'s shower scene (see the box below).

ANIMAL CRUELTY: A woman customer in Sam's store asks the assistant about an insecticide and asks him if it will be painless for the insects, noting that 'death should always be painless'. This scene comes immediately after Marion's murder. And of course, we have the famous closing lines as 'Mother' declares: 'I hope they are watching. They'll see. They'll see, and they'll know, and they'll say, "Why, she wouldn't even harm a fly"!'

KILLER LINES: Marion (to Caroline, the secretary): 'Headaches are like resolutions – you forget them as soon as they stop hurting.'

Norman tells Marion cryptically: '. . . my mother, uh . . . what is the phrase? She isn't quite herself today,' and later excuses her behaviour by saying that 'She just goes a little mad sometimes. We all go a little mad sometimes.'

THERE HE IS!: About four minutes in wearing a cowboy hat outside Marion's office, this being the earliest possible opportunity he had to get the obligatory in-joke out of the way. In Gus Van Sant's remake, a Hitch-alike can be seen at the same point in the movie, reprimanding Van Sant.

THE MACGUFFIN: A little matter of $40,000. Oh, and Marion herself becomes the MacGuffin from the second act onward.

GOOFS: As the film was shot around Christmas 1959, some of the Phoenix location footage showed decorated windows (still visible in the scene where Marion sees her boss crossing the road in front of her). To account for this, Hitch inserted the captions at the beginning of the film, even though it's obviously high summer and no reference is made to the season anywhere in the movie. As many ophthalmologists wrote to point out to Hitch, Marion's irises should have been dilated, not contracted, when she died (a point Hitch remembered when he made *Frenzy* in 1972).

MISOGYNY: Marion's co-worker, Caroline, claims that her mother's doctor gave her tranquillisers the day of her wedding.

As Marion drives to Fairvale, she imagines a conversation between Lowery and Cassidy, with Cassidy claiming: 'I ain't about to kiss off forty thousand dollars! I'll get it back, and if any of it's missing I'll replace it with her fine, soft flesh!' This idea seems to amuse Marion.

AWARDS: Winner of Golden Globe Award for Best Supporting Actress (Janet Leigh). Oscar-nominated for Best Art Direction, Best Cinematography, Best Director and Best Supporting Actress (Janet Leigh). *Psycho* has been selected for preservation by the National Film Registry of the Library of Congress, and in 1998 it was listed as one of the American Film Institute's top 100 films of the century (number 18).

THEMES AND MOTIFS: *Psycho* contains many symbolic references to birds. The film begins in Phoenix, has two characters with the surname Crane and the Bates Motel's parlour is filled with Norman's stuffed birds: a pheasant sits in front of him; an owl, wings spread for take-off, hovers above his head. A raven – a bird that preys on carrion (Marion?) – is also there. There are bird pictures on the walls of the motel rooms (note how Norman accidentally knocks one of two bird prints off the wall when he discovers Marion's body). As Norman and Marion chat, he describes the town gossips who 'cluck their thick tongues and shake their heads', and he observes that Marion eats 'like a bird'. Taking into account Hitchcock's East End background, we can possibly see his ironic use of the word 'birds' to mean 'women', particularly in the scene where Norman explains his hobby to Marion: 'I don't really know anything about birds. My hobby is stuffing things – you know, taxidermy. And I guess I'd just rather stuff birds because I hate the look of beasts when they're stuffed . . . I think only birds look well stuffed because – well, because they're kind of passive to begin with.'

Psycho was also the film that confirmed in the public's mind what many psychologists had been saying for years – that it's all your mother's fault. Certainly *Psycho* has the bleakest view of the family in any of Hitch's films. In the novel it explains how Marion thinks she's an old maid because of the years she spent nursing her mother; Sam is trapped by both his father's debts and his ex-wife's alimony; Norman is still traumatised and sexually repressed as a consequence of years of mistreatment at the hands of his mother. See also **Misogyny** above.

Note also the many mirrors that appear in the film, a device in Victorian literature often used to reflect the soul or inner thoughts of a character: Marion checks herself in a compact at the office, and again checks her appearance in a bedside mirror the moment she finally decides to abscond with the money; she spends most of her journey to Fairvale looking nervously into her rear-view mirror; the patrolman's eyes are covered by shades that reflect Marion's guilt-ridden face back at her; she counts the money in front of the washroom mirror at the car showroom; and when Lila searches the Bates house she is startled by her own reflection in a full-length mirror.

TABOOS: Prior to this, no Hollywood movie had required an actress of Leigh's standing to be in such a state of undress, nor had lovemaking as explicit as *Psycho*'s first scene. The shot of Marion flushing the toilet is believed to be the first such shot in American cinema history. Note how Lila is obscured by Sam in the scene where she crouches over the toilet bowl and discovers the scrap of paper. Note also how Norman can't bring himself to even say the word 'bathroom'.

The Board of Censors expressed concern over a number of scenes in the script. An early draft had Marion telling Mr Cassidy that she intended spending the weekend in bed, with Cassidy joking crudely that bed is the 'only playground that beats Las Vegas!' This was softened to a comment about Las Vegas being the 'playground of the world'. Also of concern was Norman's observation that 'a son is a poor substitute for a lover', which the censors interpreted as suggestion of incest. However, Hitch managed to keep this line in. When the board saw the final film, a request was made to remove a few frames from the shower scene as they claimed one of Janet Leigh's nipples was visible. Hitch had already removed one shot, where Marion's bare buttocks were visible, so he simply resubmitted the same cut of the movie, on the assumption that the censors either wouldn't notice or wouldn't bother checking it again.

MUSIC: The composer Bernard Herrmann elected to use only strings for *Psycho*'s score, because he felt he could complement the black-and-white photography with 'black-and-white noise'. The effect of this is quite disorientating – strings are the usual accompaniment for love scenes, yet if one considers how stringed instruments are played the physical movement of the bow is almost akin to a stabbing motion. Ironically, Hitchcock considered not having a score for much of the movie, but the headstrong Herrmann prepared one anyway. From the tuneless, atmospheric melancholy of the lovers' illicit meeting and the frantic chase motif, to the now legendary murder theme, the whole effect is oppressive, unsettling and genuinely terrifying. *Psycho*'s music is so powerful it has become an automatic signifier throughout popular culture, and arguably is one of only two film soundtracks – the other being John Williams's shark theme for *Jaws* (1976) – that *everybody* knows.

POSTER: 'A new – and altogether different – screen excitement!!!'/'Don't give away the ending – it's the only one we have!'/'The screen's master of suspense moves his camera into the icy blackness of the unexplained!'

TRAILER: The specially filmed trailer consists of the director giving us a tour of the sets for the movie, beginning in the courtyard of the Bates Motel. 'In this house, the most dire horrible events took place,' he teases. He hints at the two murders, saying that 'the victim, or should I say victims, hadn't any conception as to the type of people they would be confronted with in this house. Especially the woman, she was the weirdest.' As he reaches the bathroom of cabin No. 1, Hitch says vaguely: 'You should have seen the blood. The whole, the whole place was . . . Well it's . . . it's too horrible to describe. Dreadful.' As the tour comes to a close, Hitch is interrupted by Marion screaming in the shower – except here it's actually Vera Miles posing as Leigh in a very brief clip. The final captions warn that *Psycho* is 'the picture you MUST see from the beginning . . . Or not at all! For no one will be seated after the start of Alfred Hitchcock's greatest shocker – PSYCHO'.

SELLING THE FILM: Hitchcock prepared a handbook for cinema managers called 'The Care and Handling of *Psycho*'. He issued clocks for theatre lobbies to remind audiences of the starting times, with a message from the director: 'It is required that you see PSYCHO from the very beginning. The manager of this theatre has been instructed at the risk of his life not to admit to the theatre any persons after the picture starts. Any spurious attempts to enter by side doors, fire escapes or ventilating shafts will be met by force. The entire objective of this extraordinary policy, of course, is to help you enjoy PSYCHO more.' Hitch also instructed managers that, after the film had finished, the lights should remain down for at least 30 seconds to allow 'the suspense of *Psycho* [to be] indelibly engraved in the minds of the audience', and ordered that the film must never be followed by a newsreel or short film.

THE ICE MAIDENS: Janet Leigh's performance in the opening scene is considerably hotter than anything we get from the other Hitch women, as she tries in vain to elicit any kind of response from John Gavin. Her frosty reaction to Cassidy's salty flirtation is spot on, and the way Marion and Norman appear to be bonding helps make what follows all the more horrific. Vera Miles, however, is more in the traditional mould of the untouchable blonde we'd expect from Hitch, despite the horrifically plain and unflattering clothes she's forced to wear. It's a shame Hitch allowed old resentments to undermine what is a confident performance from his one-time replacement for Grace Kelly.

WHAT THE PAPERS SAID: Possibly due to the fact that there were no press screenings before the film's release, many of the critics were openly hostile to *Psycho*. A mean-spirited reviewer for *The Times* all but gave away the ending and, somewhat missing the point, claimed that 'Psycho is neither so horrifying nor so surprising as might have been expected, and there are scenes and lines of dialogue which inspire the wrong kind of laughter'. Bosley Crowther of the *New York Times* called it 'a blot on an honourable career', though he would later revise his opinion and list it as one of the top ten films of the year.

Some critics were insightful enough to see that Hitch had another hit on his hands. 'There can be no gainsaying the fact that the film will grip audiences from beginning to end,' claimed the reviewer for *Box-Office* magazine, 'and because the effect cannot be shaken off immediately at its conclusion, word-of-mouth is guaranteed. Each bit of action and dialogue fits neatly into place as the plot unfolds. The first murder comes so suddenly that it staggers the viewer.'

COSTUME: Helen Colvig and her assistant Rita Riggs had worked for Hitch on his TV show but this was their first feature film. On Hitch's suggestion, Marion Crane's underwear was white when in the hotel room with Sam, and black in subsequent scenes after the robbery. According to Rita Riggs, Hitch had a feeling this would add to the idea of the 'good girl/bad girl' idea. All of Marion's clothes came off the peg from the West Coast Store, and only Anthony Perkins was allowed to choose his own wardrobe as he felt certain clothes might make his neck look long. A long-time collaborator, Edith Head, created Vera Miles's particularly dowdy wardrobe to Hitch's instructions. Riggs also had to provide a way of preserving Leigh's decency in the shower scenes, and came across the idea of using moleskin patches, which were then glued in place.

TRIVIA: Hitchcock bought the rights to the novel anonymously from Bloch for just $9,000. He then tried to buy as many copies of the novel as he could to keep the ending a secret. The titles for the film cost $21,000. Total production costs were little more than $800,000, because

Making a Killing – *Psycho*'s Shower Scene

One of cinema's most infamous sequences began shooting on 18 December 1959 and continued until 23 December. The shooting was delayed twice, once when Janet Leigh was suffering from a head cold and once because it coincided with her period.

For a shot right at the water stream, the crew had to block off the inner holes on the shower head so that the water sprayed past the camera lens. Rumour has it that Hitchcock arranged for the water to suddenly go ice-cold when the attack started. However, this is probably apocryphal, as it has been disputed by most of the parties present at the time.

After testing the sound generated by stabbing a number of different fruits, Hitch selected the sound of a stabbed casaba (a Turkish melon) for the sound effects to be used in the movie. The 'blood' seen in the shower was actually chocolate sauce.

Hitch used shots of Leigh's head, face, hands and midriff, but all the other shots were Marli Renfro, a nude model Hitch had hired to spare Leigh the discomfort of performing naked. Leigh was fitted for contact lenses for the final corpse shot, but in the finished film the close-up of Marion's dead body is a freeze-frame. Alma Reville apparently saw the original version and told her husband that she could see Leigh blink, so he changed it. Note how, in the finished scene, a droplet of water hangs from Janet Leigh's hair until the circling of the camera steadies out and begins to pull back, which is where the frame is unfrozen.

In 1973, Saul Bass claimed that he not only storyboarded the shower scene, but was actually allowed to direct it. He'd already mocked up a short reel to prove that the scene could be done in montage, and he said that as it was such a time-consuming scene that Hitch stepped aside and let him call the shots. Hitch himself claimed that, although he'd hired Bass to storyboard Arbogast's murder, he ended up not using his montage. He never publicly acknowledged Bass's involvement in the earlier murder. Janet Leigh and others reject Bass's claims. 'Saul Bass was there for the shooting,' Leigh clarifies, 'but he never directed me.'

'The shower was a baptism,' wrote Janet Leigh, 'a taking away of the torment from her mind. Marion became a virgin again. [Hitchcock] wanted the audience to feel her peacefulness, her kind of rebirth, so that the moment of intrusion is even more shocking and tragic.'

After the film's release Hitchcock received an angry letter from the father of a girl who refused to have a bath after seeing *Les Diaboliques* (1954) and now refused to shower after seeing *Psycho*. Hitchcock sent a note back simply saying: 'Send her to the dry cleaners.'

he used the production crew from his TV series, yet the film had earned more than $15 million in its first year.

To hide the fact that he was working on the movie, Hitch was photographed next to a camera slate carrying the name 'Wimpy'. This has led people to mistake this for a working title for the movie. The only working title used was the production number – 9401.

The record Lila discovers in Norman's bedroom, 'Eroica' (aka Beethoven's 3rd symphony), was originally composed as a tribute to Napoleon in 1804, though after the Frenchman declared himself Emperor Beethoven changed the dedication, claiming it was 'composed to celebrate the memory of a great man'.

Some prints of the original theatrical version showed subliminal shots of Mother's skull as Norman sinks Marion's car and in the final shot of Norman, but as Hitch began to lose confidence with the project he decided to remove the images from some of the prints. Only the second appearance of the skull remains on the video releases.

FINAL ANALYSIS: 'A boy's best friend is his mother.' Though *Psycho* is probably the film Hitch is most identified with, this is more likely to do with the enormous hype the film received than the actual content of it. It is a brave, ground-breaking movie, but it has dated slightly in the intervening years; the epilogue, where Dr Richmond explains the plot to Sam and Lila (and, by implication, the thicker elements of the audience) is painfully long and drawn out, and Simon Oakland is obviously just showing off his complete lack of psychiatric training. Most of the other performances, however, are fine. John Gavin is by no means as bad as Hitch believed, and Martin Balsam is his usual, reliable self. Of course, Anthony Perkins steals the film with a delicate, subtle and sympathetic performance that, unfortunately, was so good it ruined his career. But, despite the technical brilliance of the shower scene, the best moment of the film is the suddenness and the savagery of the second murder – truly horrific and likely to make first-time viewers jump even today! 8/10

The Birds (1963)

(Colour – 119 mins)

Produced by Alfred Hitchcock/Alfred J Hitchcock Productions/Universal Pictures

Written by Evan Hunter, based on the story by Daphne du Maurier

Director of Photography: Robert Burks
Costume Design: Edith Head
Production Design: Robert F Boyle
Film Editing: George Tomasini
Bird Trainer: Ray Berwick
Assistant Director: James H Brown
Hair Stylist: Virginia Darcy
Production Manager: Norman Deming
Special Effects: Dave Fleischer
Electronic Sound Effects: Remi Gassmann
Special Effects: Lawrence A Hampton
Special Photographic Adviser: Ub Iwerks

Set Decorator: George Milo
Title Designer: James S Pollak
Wardrobe Supervisor: Rita Riggs
Assistant to Mr Hitchcock: Peggy Robertson
Sound: William Russell, Waldon O Watson
Sound Consultant: Bernard Herrmann
Electronic Sound Effects: Oskar Sala
Make-up Artist: Howard Smit
Script Supervisor: Lois Thurman
Pictorial Design: Albert Whitlock

CAST: Tippi Hedren (*Melanie Daniels*), Rod Taylor (*Mitch Brenner*), Jessica Tandy (*Lydia Brenner*), Suzanne Pleshette (*Annie Hayworth*), Veronica Cartwright (*Cathy Brenner*), Ethel Griffies (*Mrs Bundy*), Charles McGraw (*Sebastian Sholes*), Ruth McDevitt (*Mrs MacGruder*), Lonny Chapman (*Deke Carter*), Joe Mantell (*Travelling Salesman*), Doodles Weaver (*Fisherman*), Malcolm Atterbury (*Al Malone*), John McGovern (*Postal Clerk*), Karl Swenson (*Drunk*), Richard Deacon (*Man in Elevator*), Elizabeth Wilson (*Helen Carter*), Bill Quinn (*Farm Hand*), Doreen Lang (*Mother in Café*), Morgan Brittany (*Schoolchild*).

SUMMARY: Melanie Daniels, a rich and glamorous socialite, is looking round a San Francisco pet shop. She is hoping to collect the mynah bird she has ordered for her aunt, but is disappointed to discover that it hasn't arrived yet. While the manager telephones the suppliers, a handsome customer arrives at the shop and seems to mistake Melanie for one of the staff. He asks for some lovebirds for his sister's birthday and Melanie plays along, showing him a number of birds she clearly knows nothing about. He has the upper hand though – he reveals that he knows who she is: he saw her in court the previous year when he acted as the prosecuting counsel who got Melanie convicted for breaking a plate-glass window during a practical joke. Having recognised her the moment he walked into the shop he thought she might benefit from a taste of her own medicine. Melanie is furious, but also intrigued. She makes a note of the man's licence plate as he drives away, and tracks down his name – Mitchell Brenner – and address through one of the reporters at her father's newspaper. Melanie orders a pair of lovebirds and arranges to collect them early the next day.

Melanie goes to Mitch's apartment to deliver the lovebirds, but is told by one of Mitch's neighbours that he has gone home to Bodega Bay for the weekend. She drives the 60 miles north up the coast road with the two birds to the bay, a small, remote fishing village. She asks for directions at the local post office and the clerk points out the Brenner house on the opposite side of the bay. The clerk tells Melanie that Mitch lives there with his mother Lydia and his much younger sister. To complete her surprise, Melanie goes to the local school to learn the name of Mitch's sister. There she meets a schoolteacher, Annie Hayworth, a single woman in her late twenties who lives alone in a house adjoining the school. It becomes clear to Melanie that Annie has an emotional connection to Mitch. Having learnt the sister's name, Melanie inscribes a card 'To Cathy' and makes her way across the lake by motorboat.

Melanie cuts the engine on the motorboat and paddles ashore to avoid being noticed. She then creeps into the house and places the birds in the middle of the living room before making her escape back to the boat. She paddles some distance out into the bay before stopping to observe Mitch's reaction. When Mitch discovers the cage, he dashes out of the house to look for his mysterious benefactor. With the aid of a pair of binoculars, Mitch spots Melanie in the boat heading back to the town. Almost impressed at her nerve, he jumps into his truck, drives into the town and waits for her on the jetty as the smug Melanie slowly pilots her boat towards its mooring.

A lone seagull swoops down from the sky without warning and strikes a startled Melanie on the head. Mitch helps her ashore, and takes her to the nearby Tides Restaurant to give her some first aid. While Melanie is resting, Mitch asks her what she is really doing in Bodega Bay. She lies, claiming that she was planning to visit her old friend Annie Hayworth, and as such it wasn't a big deal to deliver the lovebirds to Cathy at the same time. Mitch's mother, Lydia, arrives at the restaurant, and seems to take an immediate dislike to Melanie. Despite this, Mitch invites Melanie to dine with them that evening. Remembering that Annie Hayworth had a room to let, Melanie heads back to the school to freshen up.

Melanie arrives at the Brenner house for dinner, and is greeted by Cathy, clearly delighted by her present of the lovebirds. The evening goes well, and Cathy invites her new friend to attend her birthday party the following afternoon. Returning to Annie's, Melanie and her temporary landlady compare notes on Mitch. Annie tells her she dated Mitch some four years previously, and actually moved from San Francisco to Bodega Bay to be near him. Although their relationship eventually ended, thanks to some interference from the overprotective Lydia, Annie claims that their friendship is now stronger than ever. Just as Melanie is about to go to bed, the women hear a loud bang on the front door. Looking outside, they discover a dead seagull, which had obviously flown straight at the door.

At Cathy's birthday party the next day, Melanie and Mitch seem to be growing closer, and Mitch tries to persuade her to stay in Bodega Bay for another day. Melanie is undecided, keen to return to the civilisation of San Francisco. As Cathy and her friends play a game of blind man's buff, a huge flock of seagulls swoops down from the skies and attacks them. The adults manage to get the children indoors before they are badly injured, and the birds quickly disperse. Later that evening, Melanie is again having dinner with the Brenners when, without warning, a swarm of sparrows erupts from the chimney into the living room. Mitch manages to open the front door and the birds eventually either die or find their own way out of the house. Arriving at the house to survey the damage, the sheriff is more than a little sceptical about Lydia and Mitch's description of the way in which the birds attacked them. A little shocked herself, Melanie agrees to stay over in Bodega Bay another day.

Early the next morning, Lydia takes Cathy to school and then drops in on one of her neighbours. His house has been wrecked and eventually she stumbles across his corpse lying on the floor, his eyes apparently pecked out by birds. Hysterical, Lydia manages to get home, where she alerts Mitch. While Mitch heads off with the sheriff to investigate the mysterious death, Melanie stays with Lydia, who is now very worried about Cathy's safety. At Lydia's request, Melanie goes to the school to check.

Melanie waits outside until the lessons finish. She smokes and watches absently as a bird flies across the sky. Observing the bird as it glides down to rest, Melanie is suddenly aware of the hundreds of birds that have amassed on the fences and climbing frames right behind her. She runs into the school to warn Annie, and they try to escort the children down the hill from the school into the town centre. However, the instant the children leave the building, the crows take to the air and chase them down the road, pecking and clawing at the youngsters' hands and faces. Melanie and Annie manage to get the children to safety, and as before the birds quickly disappear.

Melanie heads to the Tides Restaurant, where she has a discussion with an eccentric old woman, an ornithologist who flatly disputes Melanie's account of the attacks. Mitch and the sheriff arrive at the restaurant. The sheriff still has difficulty believing that the attacks are deliberate or planned. Meanwhile, outside a seagull dive-bombs a man filling his car up with petrol, knocking him out. From inside the diner, Melanie watches in horror as the petrol slowly trickles towards another man about to light a cigarette. Distracted by the cries of warning from the diner, the man burns his fingers on a match, which then falls to the floor and ignites the petrol stream, blowing up his car, him and the petrol station in a spectacular fireball. Melanie and some of the other customers rush out of the restaurant to help the wounded, but the smoke and fire have attracted still more birds. Melanie seeks cover from attack in a phone booth, and hides inside her glass cage as hundreds of gulls swarm towards her. Mitch rescues her from the booth just as the attack begins to subside.

Mitch and Melanie go to collect Cathy, who stayed with Annie after the attack on the schoolhouse. As they approach the house they see Annie's inert body lying just outside her front door. She's been pecked to death. Cathy is safe indoors – the terrified girl tells them that Annie saved her by throwing her indoors, but only at the cost of her own life. They drive back to the Brenner house and board all of the windows and doors shut. Listening to the radio, they realise that the outside world has little idea of the scale or seriousness of the attacks. They wait in the house in silence.

Suddenly, an all-out attack begins. Gulls start to smash through the boarded-up windows, and Mitch struggles to tie the shutters back into place as the birds peck savagely at his hands. Holes begin to appear in the front door, which Mitch also blocks off with a dressing mirror. Just as the lights fail, the attack dies down.

Later that evening, Lydia, Mitch and Cathy have fallen asleep in the living room. Melanie, still awake, hears a noise upstairs and goes to investigate. She steps into one of the bedrooms and notices an enormous hole in the ceiling looking right out through the roof. From nowhere she is overcome by a chittering mass of beaks and beating wings. The attack seems relentless and she collapses to the floor, blocking her own exit. By the time Mitch and Lydia manage to rescue her, Melanie is deeply traumatised, and although they manage to stem the bleeding from most of the physical wounds, Mitch realises that Melanie needs to get to a hospital quickly. He goes outside to collect Melanie's car, and carefully picks his way through an eerily still flock of birds, which have roosted on the floor, on the garage, and everywhere for miles around. Mitch taxis the car up to the front door of the house and helps his mother, sister and a near-catatonic Melanie into the vehicle. They drive off, surrounded on all sides by many millions of birds, all watching and waiting in silence.

CASTING: Hitchcock first spotted Tippi Hedren in a commercial for Sego, a diet drink. For the purposes of her screen test, Tippi Hedren reprised Ingrid Bergman's role from *Notorious* opposite Martin Balsam, as well as a few sequences from *To Catch a Thief* and *Rebecca*. Hitchcock purportedly had to destroy this footage afterwards, because he no longer held the rights to the originals. Evan Hunter suggested that Anne Bancroft would be ideal for the part of Annie Hayworth, but Hitch didn't want any additional established actors in the cast, aside from Jessica Tandy, as they would have diverted much of his budget away from the special effects he needed.

ROOTS: The original Daphne du Maurier short story was about a Cornish farmer and his wife whose cottage is attacked by birds. Evan Hunter recalls that the only elements Hitch was keen to retain from the dialogue-free story were the title and the basic concept of birds attacking people. In April 1960, Hitchcock read of a flock of birds which flew down the chimney of a house in La Jolla, California. This reminded him of the du Maurier short story he'd acquired the rights to some years earlier. A year later, on 17 August 1961, fog caused migrating birds in their millions to fly inland, causing major devastation to the town of Santa Cruz, where Hitch had filmed *Shadow of a Doubt*. Hitch owned a house in the region and asked to be sent a copy of the local paper. Within a year of the second incident, shooting had commenced on *The Birds*. On the first day of filming, 22 March 1962, the *Los Angeles Times* reported that a hawk had attacked children in Victoria Park until local police shot it down.

The Production Designer, Robert Boyle, claimed to have been inspired by Edvard Munch's *The Scream* – the famous painting of a distorted figure screaming silently over a backdrop of desolate farmland. This can be seen most clearly in the framing of Lydia's flight from Dan Fawcett's farm and the montage of shots of Melanie watching the ensuing inferno at the Tides Restaurant.

Tippi Hedren's entrance in the first scene is a nod to the advert that originally brought her to Hitchcock's attention. In both, Hedren turns to acknowledge an off-screen wolf whistle, though in the advert the whistle comes from her character's son, evidently impressed with the effects the diet drink has had on her figure. Hitch also suggested that the drunk at the Tides owed more than a little to the Irish playwright Sean O'Casey (*Juno and the Paycock*).

LEGACY: *The Birds* couldn't avoid the inevitable dodgy sequel, spawning the TV movie *The Birds II: Land's End* (Rick Rosenthal – credited to Alan Smithee, 1994), but its legacy isn't all bad. In another movie made some thirteen years later, a series of vicious animal attacks on a small fishing town created the phenomenon of the summer blockbuster movie, thanks to Steven Spielberg's *Jaws* (1975). The final attack on the house is clearly an influence on *Night of the Living Dead* (George A Romero, 1969). In transferring Stephen King's novel *The Dark Half* to the screen in 1991, George Romero would again borrow from *The Birds* for the climactic scene where the villain is dissected, piece by piece, by a parliament of crows.

John Carpenter's *The Fog* (1979) not only features a sequence where people are barricaded into a room, fighting off an attack from outside, but also name-checks Bodega Bay on several occasions. Bird attacks feature in *Damien: Omen II* (Don Taylor, 1978), most memorably when an unfortunate journalist meets a particularly messy demise thanks to the combined efforts of a raven and a juggernaut.

A smart tribute to *The Birds* can be found in the *Simpsons* episode 'A Streetcar Named Marge'. Homer tries to rescue his baby daughter Maggie from a crèche full of sinister-looking babies, all of which are making strange clucking noises with their dummies. Homer carefully picks his way through them on tiptoes, mimicking Mitch's final escape from the house. Just to drive home the point, the next scene of the episode sees a cartoon version of Hitch walking in the background with two poodles, re-creating his cameo from the start of the film (see **There he is!** below).

WHO'S WHO?: Hedren would never really escape the Hitchcock legacy. She starred in his next feature, *Marnie* (1964), and appeared in both a remake of *Shadow of a Doubt* and a sequel to *The Birds*, both for television. Hedren is the mother of the actress Melanie Griffith, whom she appeared alongside in *Pacific Heights* (John Schlesinger, 1990).

Very much the rugged action hero, Rod Taylor was an Australian, born in Sydney in 1930. Prior to *The Birds*, he had already starred in *The Time Machine* (George Pal, 1960) and provided the voice of Pongo in Disney's much-loved *One Hundred and One Dalmations* (Clyde Geronimi and Hamilton Luske, 1961). Also faking an American accent was the English actress Jessica Tandy (*Lydia Brenner*), who was, of course, best known for her lead role in *Driving Miss Daisy* (Bruce Beresford, 1989). She was married to the actor/writer Hume Cronyn (*Lifeboat, Shadow of a Doubt, Rope*) for over 50 years, until her death in 1994.

As an adult, Veronica Cartwright (*Cathy Brenner*) played Lambert, one of the first victims of the horrific acid-dripping monster in *Alien* (Ridley Scott, 1979) and the cherry-stone-spewing victim of Jack Nicholson's Devil in *The Witches of Eastwick* (George Miller, 1987).

The screenwriter Evan Hunter (real name Salvadore Lombino) was the author of the book *The Blackboard Jungle*, later made into one of the first 'teen peril' movies in the 50s, and had written the short story that became the *Alfred Hitchcock Presents* episode 'Vicious Circle'. He also writes as Ed McBain, under which name he created the '87th Precinct' series of novels.

THE USUAL SUSPECTS: Doreen Lang plays Ann James in *The Wrong Man*, a small role in *North by Northwest* and the distressed mother in *The Birds*.

ANIMAL CRUELTY: Tippi Hedren had to endure an entire week of live birds being flung at her by stage hands, to create the illusion of the final attack. Some birds were even tied to her clothes so they wouldn't fly away. The filming was allegedly called to a halt, when one of them left a deep gash on the lower lid of Hedren's left eye.

KILLER LINES: In search of lovebirds for his sister, Mitch tells Melanie that as she's only eleven he 'wouldn't want a pair of birds that were too demonstrative . . . at the same time I wouldn't want them to be too aloof either. Do you happen to have a pair of birds that are just "friendly"?'

'I have never known birds of different species to flock together,' claims the ornithologist at the diner. 'The very concept is unimaginable. Why, if that happened, we wouldn't have a chance. How could we possibly hope to fight them?'

THERE HE IS!: At the start of the film, just as Melanie enters the pet shop, Hitch leaves with his two dogs, Geoffrey and Stanley, on leads.

THE MACGUFFIN: Both the characters and we, the audience, are driven to know why the strange and uncharacteristic attacks occur, but if any of us expect Hitchcock to provide explanation we'll be sorely disappointed. There is some speculation, such as the hysterical mother at the restaurant who accuses Melanie of bringing some kind of evil to the town. Maybe she's right. After all, we know she's an agent of chaos prone to practical jokes that often backfire on her, and she seems to be at the centre of many of the attacks. Considering the way the feathered fiends amass as Melanie smokes with abandon and when the petrol station burns, could this be a commentary on mankind's pollution of the environment? We suspect Hitchcock's own explanation, that Melanie represents 'complacency', is more telling than may at first appear. Though the birds' 'motivation' is not a MacGuffin, more a double bluff, it adds weight to the theory that Hitch was more concerned about the technical perfection of the film than in plugging the major plot hole in its premise.

MISOGYNY: It's no coincidence, surely, that, during her first visit to the Tides Restaurant, Hitchcock frames Tippi Hedren against a sign that reads: PACKAGED GOODS SOLD HERE.

THEMES AND MOTIFS: Putting aside the 'birds' motif that Hitchcock had already exploited more subtly in *Psycho*, the film continues his obsession with watching, or, more accurately, seeing. Both Melanie and Annie confirm their understanding with the words 'I see', and significantly it's the vulnerability of the eyes that makes us so squeamish while watching *The Birds* – a vulnerability that Hitchcock exploits when Lydia discovers the sightless corpse of Dan Fawcett and again when Melanie is attacked towards the end of the film. Note, during the attack on the schoolhouse, the broken glasses of the fleeing child, an image also found in *Strangers on a Train*; and then there's Mitch's choice of barricade during the attack on his home – a cabinet with a long mirror, which reflects his image back at him as he props it against a doorway as if the attack is forcing him to look at himself – which of course it does, as no character survives the film without undergoing a great deal of self-reassessment.

There's also the theme of the relationship between a mother and her son, which also featured in Hitch's previous film. Unlike that of the Bateses, Lydia and Mitch's relationship involves a greater sense of loneliness. Like Madame Sebastian in *Notorious*, Lydia clings to her son for fear of abandonment, and, though he, like Alex Sebastian, tries to rebel, ultimately he can't bring himself to leave his mother alone.

TABOOS: Though obviously it's an extension of the issue discussed above, Lydia is disgusted by rumours she's heard about Melanie cavorting naked in a fountain while in Rome.

MUSIC: There is no music score for the film, just a carefully modulated series of shrieks and cries at the right moment. Nonetheless, Hitch employed the services of Bernard Herrmann to supervise the electronic noises. If anything, this adds to the overall unsettling effect of the movie, with the artificiality of the birdsong making their actions even more 'out of character'.

POSTER: 'Suspense and shock beyond anything you have seen or imagined!'/'It could be the most terrifying motion picture I have ever made! . . . and remember, the next scream you hear may be your own.' Another poster for the movie declared, seemingly ungrammatically: 'THE BIRDS IS COMING!', irritating English teachers nationwide. The main artwork for all of the advertising depicts a blonde woman being savaged by birds in silhouette. Often mistaken for Tippi Hedren, this is in fact taken from a still of Jessica Tandy.

TRAILER: Hitch delivers a lengthy ironic lecture on our feathered friends, the birds, and explains exactly what they have to be grateful to us for – feathered hats, gourmet meals, gilded cages and so on. Just as his lecture comes to an end, Tippi Hedren bursts in and screams: 'They're coming!'

THE ICE MAIDEN: Tippi Hedren makes an exceptionally good impression in her first major acting role. It's clear to see exactly what Hitchcock saw in the beautiful young woman – elegance, determination, and yet a fragile nature that was easy to hurt and control. Her acting ability is a great deal better than many critics have suggested, and any actress who would willingly subject herself to such a gruelling ordeal as filming the final bird attack has to gain our respect and admiration.

WHAT THE PAPERS SAID: *The Times*, on 29 August 1963, was enthusiastic in its praise. 'It is in general brilliantly handled. The old master's skill at starting from the ordinary, only to drop us terrifyingly into the extraordinary has seldom been better deployed.' However, the critic was less kind on Tippi Hedren: '. . . another of those cool-but-sizzling-underneath blondes that Mr Hitchcock delights to feature in his films, is less appealing than many; one takes the point that she is not meant to be a very agreeable character, but at least the qualities she does have might come over more vividly.'

COSTUME: Hitchcock had a particular penchant for his leading ladies to be dressed in either grey or green suits, and here Tippi Hedren looks cool, refined and elegant in her pale-green outfit. As Melanie has only one costume for most of the film, it's left to the outrageous fur coat in the early San Francisco scenes to convey some of the wealth and glamour that Melanie was undoubtedly used to. It's quite ironic that Tippi Hedren became such a staunch animal-rights campaigner!

TRIVIA: The film does not finish with the usual 'THE END' title because Hitchcock wanted to give the impression of unending terror. A final shot of the Golden Gate Bridge covered in birds was abandoned due to cost.

Hedren's daughter Melanie Griffith claims that as a child she was traumatised by a gift Hitchcock gave her during the filming – a doll of her mother in a coffin, which Hitchcock intended as a joke.

Hitch appeared on the front cover of the 1 February 1963 edition of *Time* magazine with a raven on his head and one on each shoulder, his arms outstretched apologetically.

FINAL ANALYSIS: A poetic nightmare, *The Birds* is another of those films that are remembered for a couple of key scenes. Indeed for the first 45 minutes we almost forget that we're watching 'the most terrifying film' Hitchcock has ever made, as we revel in the gentle romantic comedy unfolding between Melanie and Mitch. But when the first attack comes it comes swiftly and without warning, and is therefore much scarier. As we note above, the lack of a traditional music score adds to the apocalyptic atmosphere: in the scene where Melanie is trapped in the attic with a swarm of pecking birds the soundtrack is almost deathly silent, punctuated by a few frightened gasps and the dull beating of a hundred pairs of wings; when Lydia discovers the eyeless body of Dan Fawcett the silence is almost deafening.

The cast are uniformly excellent. Rod Taylor's macho hero is the epitome of masculinity – strong, brooding and tied to his mother's apron strings. Jessica Tandy manages to shine, despite coming so soon after the most influential 'mother' in cinema history (*Psycho*), with a character who controls her son's life in a much more subtle way. But the true stars here are the birds themselves, whether pecking relentlessly at fingers or simply perching on fences, watching the humans as they await their next assault. With a combination of hand-puppets and live birds, it's amazing that it still manages to be unsettling nearly 40 years on. **9/10**

Marnie (1964)

(Colour – 130 mins)

Produced by Alfred Hitchcock/Geoffrey Stanley Productions/Universal Pictures

Screenplay by Jay Presson Allen & Evan Hunter (uncredited), based on the novel by Winston Graham

Director of Photography: Robert Burks
Production Design: Robert Boyle
Assistant Director: James H Brown
Unit Manager: Hilton A Green
Edited by George Tomasini
Miss Hedren's and Miss Baker's Costumes Designed by Edith Head

Miss Hedren's Hairstyles created by André of Paris
Pictorial Design: Albert Whitlock
Sound Recording: Waldon O Watson & William Russell
Make-up: Jack Barron, Howard Smit & Robert Dawn
Hair Stylist: Virginia Darcy
Assistant to Mr Hitchcock: Peggy Robertson
Set Decorator: George Milo
Script Supervisor: Lois Thurman
Camera Operator: Leonard South
Costume Supervisor: Vincent Dee
Women's Costumes: Rita Riggs
Men's Costumes: James Linn
Music Composed by Bernard Herrmann

CAST: Tippi Hedren (*Marnie Edgar*), Sean Connery (*Mark Rutland*), Diane Baker (*Lil Mainwaring*), Martin Gabel (*Sidney Strutt*), Louise Latham (*Bernice Edgar, Marnie's mother*), Bob Sweeney (*Cousin Bob*), Milton Selzer (*Man at Track*), Mariette Hartley (*Susan Clabon*), Alan Napier (*Mr Rutland*), Bruce Dern (*Sailor*), Henry Beckman (*First Detective*), S John Launer (*Sam Ward*), Edith Evanson (*Rita*), Meg Wyllie (*Mrs Turpin*).

SUMMARY: Mark Rutland, a businessman, visits a client, Sidney Strutt, who has recently been embezzled by his secretary, Marion Holland, to the tune of $9,967. Strutt is able to give a vivid description of the woman to the police, down to her blue eyes and black wavy hair. In a hotel room in another town the raven-haired Marion Holland becomes platinum-blonde Margaret Edgar. She places the stolen money in a railway deposit box, then throws the key down a grid. She books into a hotel, then goes to the stables to ride her beloved horse, Foreo.

The woman then returns to her childhood home to visit her mother. Her mother, who greets her as 'Marnie', is looking after a neighbour's child, Jessie Cotton. Marnie spies some bright-red gladioli which spark something in her. She replaces them instantly with white chrysanthemums. Marnie's mother seems to pamper young Jessie, a fact that leads Marnie to ask her mother why she never loved her as much as she obviously loves her neighbour's child. That night, Marnie sleeps in her own room but is awoken by a nightmare, a recurring dream that has troubled her since childhood.

Returning to the city as the brunette Mary Taylor, Marnie looks for employment. She gets a job as a payroll clerk at Rutland and Co. – thanks to the intervention of the proprietor, Mark Rutland. As 'Mrs Taylor' becomes acquainted with her work, Mark's sister-in-law Lil arrives to take Mark for lunch. Lil is the sister of Mark's late wife, and has now more or less become part of the Rutland family. As Marnie works, she accidentally drips red ink on her white blouse. She seems unnaturally upset by this and rushes to the bathroom.

Later, Marnie notices how her manager Mr Ward keeps locking and unlocking a drawer – her colleague Susan explains that it's because he can never remember the combination to the safe, so he's locked it away so he can always find it.

Mark Rutland asks Marnie to work overtime one Saturday afternoon. She reports to his office and is surprised when he asks her to type up a zoological paper he's written. He tells her that before taking over his father's company he'd trained as a zoologist, specialising in instinctual behaviour. As she works, he watches her keenly. A sudden thunderstorm alarms her; she becomes frozen with terror, despite Mark's reassurances. The storm blows a tree through the office window, sending a display of Mark's late wife's artefacts crashing to the floor. Marnie clings to Mark, petrified, and he kisses her. The storm ends and Marnie is apologetic, embarrassed by her overreaction. Mark offers to drive her home. He turns the radio on and, noticing her avid interest in the racing results, invites her to accompany him to the races.

Marnie appears to have a knack of picking winners though she herself never gambles. A man approaches her, addressing her as 'Peggy Nicholson'. She assures him he is mistaken and Mark tells the man to leave. Marnie then asks to visit the paddock to see a horse called Telepathy. She's like an excited child until she sees that Telepathy's jockey is wearing red and white silks. Suddenly she cools towards the horse, making an excuse about its being 'wall-eyed'. Mark finds her puzzling, and asks her casually if she had a tough childhood. She becomes evasive, turning his questions back on him. She asks to leave, but Mark notes that the track is open for another month and suggests that if her luck in picking winners holds out she might make him a rich man.

He takes her to meet his father, who seems immediately taken by her. She's also properly introduced to Lil, who treats her like a member of staff. Mark takes her to the stables, where he kisses her and asks her to stay with him the following weekend.

The following Friday, as everyone finishes work, Marnie hides in the ladies' bathroom until she's certain everyone has left. She creeps out and makes her way to the company safe. Using a stolen key she unlocks the drawer that contains the safe's combination, helps herself to its contents and leaves.

She returns to her former life, her hair a platinum blonde once again. She again visits the stables to ride her favourite horse, Foreo – which is where Mark finally catches up with her. Back at her hotel room she returns some of the money she stole, and hands over a key and registration slip to a post-office box where Mark will be able to find the remaining money. She claims that she acted on impulse to help her run away from a troublemaking cousin called Jessie. She explains that after her mother's death she lived with a family friend until the friend died, leaving her some money in her will. After the money ran out she was forced to get a job.

Mark knows she's lying. He reveals that he had recognised her from when she worked for Strutt, Mark's tax consultant. When she came to him for a job he was curious and decided to wait to see if she would rob from him too. She begs him to let her go, but he claims that if he does that he'll be criminally and morally responsible. He wants to help and understand her and says that he's already replaced the money and decided on a course of action. He tells her she will return home with him. They will claim they had a lover's quarrel and that she left him but that he managed to bring her back. They will marry before the week is out and then go on a cruise. He confesses that it's his misfortune to have fallen in love with a thief and a liar. He makes sure she understands: it's either him or the police.

As the newly-weds leave for their honeymoon, Lil tells Mark's cousin that the wedding ring alone cost $42,000 plus tax. The cousin works out that in the space of just one week Mark has worked his way through $70,000 for a 'meagre, furtive little wedding'. That evening, Lil snoops around Mark's study and finds a checklist in his handwriting. She notices a list of things to do that includes a reminder to 'pay off Strutt'.

On the cruise, Mark lavishes flowers upon his new bride and tries to pamper her, but to no avail. She is withdrawn and when he kisses her she pulls away from him, swearing that if he touches her again she'll kill herself. She cries that she can't stand the thought of a man – any man – touching her. Mark suggests she might see a psychiatrist, a suggestion she doesn't take kindly to.

Over the next few days Mark tries to engage Marnie in conversation, but she appears neither interested nor receptive to his efforts. In frustration, Mark forces himself on her. In the early hours of the morning, Mark wakes to find himself alone. He makes a frantic search of the ship and eventually finds Marnie face down in the ship's swimming pool. He drags her to safety and revives her.

On their return home, Marnie locks the door to her bedroom and shuns Mark. The next morning, Mark decides to give her tutelage on how to at least act out the role of a dutiful wife. He tells her he's paid off Strutt anonymously to prevent the police coming for her. Later that day, Mark returns with a gift for her – Foreo, her horse. For the first time she seems genuinely grateful to him and rides off around the Rutland estate. Lil confides in Mark that she overheard his earlier conversation with Marnie and offers to help him in any way she can. Mark says she can help by befriending Marnie. She then tells him that Marnie has lied to him – she overheard her speaking to her mother on the phone, contradicting her earlier claims that she was dead. Mark dismisses this as one of Marnie's jokes to get back at Lil's meanness, but secretly he's disappointed. He hires a private detective to investigate, and the man comes back with startling information: not only is Marnie's mother alive and residing in Baltimore but she once stood trial for murder when Marnie was a small child.

Hearing her cry out in the night, Mark enters Marnie's room. She is having another nightmare and crying out to someone who she believes is hurting her mother. When she wakes, she tells Mark she has no idea what the dream could mean. She says she hears three taps, followed by her mother's voice telling her to get out of bed, but she doesn't want to leave her bed as it's too cold and 'they' will hurt her. Mark questions her more, but Marnie resorts to mocking his amateur psychology. She jokingly suggests they play a game of word association. At first she treats the game frivolously, but, when it begins to take on a deeper psychological relevance, she finds herself sobbing in Mark's arms begging for help.

Mark decides to throw a party and leaves Lil in charge of the invitations. Marnie appears completely at ease and confident until she sees that one of the guests is none other than Mr Strutt. Mark apologises to her, though he didn't invite the man. Marnie realises it must have been Lil. She begs Mark to allow her to hide but Mark encourages her to face him off. Mr Strutt recognises Marnie immediately and subtly hints as much, though Marnie with good grace denies having ever met him. Lil watches on, admiring the situation she's engineered, until she hears Mark tell Mrs Strutt that he's known Marnie for four years, long before his first wife died.

Within five minutes, Marnie has excused herself, rushed upstairs and packed her bags, terrified that Strutt will call the police and have her arrested. Mark tries to reassure her by saying he'll resort to blackmail and cut off Strutt's business interests if he dares speak of her past crime. If Strutt's silence can be bought, Mark reasons, what can the police do? But Marnie then admits that she embezzled more people than just Strutt – four others, totalling more than $150,000. She's desperate for him to let her escape, but Mark shows her two other alternatives. They could hire a lawyer and a psychiatrist and offer a voluntary confession (though that would mean going public); or they could privately visit each and every victim of her crimes and offer to pay them off as he has done with Strutt. Having laid out the plan so clearly, he orders her to attend the hunt the next day so that she's out of the house when Strutt arrives.

At the hunt, Marnie rides splendidly until the moment when the hounds corner and savage a fox. She rides off on her own, pursued by Lil. Having ridden in a daze she suddenly becomes aware that Foreo is heading towards the wall of a farm. The wall is too high for him to jump and as Foreo leaps his back legs catch the edge of the wall. Marnie is thrown clear but the horse is seriously wounded and screeches in agony. Marnie runs to the nearby farmhouse and demands to borrow a gun to put the horse out of its misery.

Mark is trying to persuade an unwilling Strutt to see his point of view. Lil telephones Mark to let him know what has happened to Marnie and he abruptly terminates his meeting with Strutt. He eventually finds his wife in a trance-like state in the process of robbing the company safe again. He watches as she tries to take the money but something seems to be holding her back. Mark decides enough is enough – he takes her to Baltimore to see her mother.

They arrive at Marnie's home during a thunderstorm and Marnie enters another trance. Mark helps her into the house and introduces himself to the baffled Mrs Edgar as Marnie's husband. He tells her Marnie isn't well; in fact, he says, she hasn't been well since Mrs Edgar had what she's always referred to as her 'accident'. He insists she tell Marnie what happened all those years ago; she owes it to Marnie to explain why she is so terrified of men. He tells her that he had read the transcripts from her murder trial and is all too aware that she used to earn her living as a prostitute – the murder victim had in fact been a client of hers. Mrs Edgar attacks him and as they struggle they hear a shrill, childlike voice cry out for him to 'let my momma go'. Marnie regresses and soon her memories come flooding back: a client of her mother's had called one stormy night; he knocked three times on the door and Marnie had been taken out of bed by her mother and made to lie on a couch. She'd started crying, frightened by the storm. The man touched her as if to comfort her, but when her protective mother pulled him off her he attacked her. The frightened child grabbed a fire poker and beat the man across the head, killing him. Her mother had taken the blame in court and never spoke of that night again.

Having blanked her mother's sacrifice from her memory, Marnie realises how much her mother had done for her. She tells Mark that she wants to admit her guilt and face the consequences, but he promises he'll sort things out for her. She then tells him she wants to stay with him and they leave for home together.

CASTING: Even as he was sculpting Tippi Hedren for stardom, Hitchcock was still desperate to tempt Grace Kelly to make her screen comeback in the title role, but the people of Monaco were not happy with the idea of their princess being an actress, particularly one playing a compulsive thief.

LEGACY: A tribute to the celebrated safe-robbery scene appears in, of all things, *The Exorcist III* (aka *The Exorcist: Legion*, William Peter Blatty, 1990), where, from one end of a hospital corridor, we watch a nurse go about her duties in silence until the scene's horrific conclusion.

WHO'S WHO?: Tippi Hedren starred in Hitch's previous film, *The Birds* (1963). A former Mr Universe contestant (placed third in 1953), Sean Connery is, for many, the only true 007. Having played James Bond in seven films, Connery is now regarded as one of the world's most powerful and respected actors. He won an Oscar for his role as an Irish-American cop in *The Untouchables* (Brian De Palma, 1987) and is a keen golfer and supporter of the Scottish National Party.

Diane Baker (*Lil Mainwaring*) later played Senator Ruth Martin, mother of the abducted girl in *The Silence of the Lambs* (Jonathan Demme, 1991).

THE USUAL SUSPECTS: *Marnie* is Tippi Hedren's second and final film for Hitchcock. After an incident during which Hitchcock allegedly made advances towards his star the two fell out. By the end of the film, it's said, Hitchcock was communicating with Hedren through an intermediary.

Also performing his last credited duties for Hitchcock was Bernard Herrmann, who had written the scores for all of his films since *The Trouble with Harry*. See *Torn Curtain* for an explanation of the dispute that led to the break-up of their collaboration.

Bruce Dern (*the sailor*) later starred in *Family Plot*; Edith Evanson appeared in *Rope*.

ANIMAL CRUELTY: In addition to the distressing scene where hounds maul a captured fox, which is followed by Marnie being compelled to kill her beloved horse to end its suffering, the film carries a none-too-subtle theme of hunting: Marnie mocks Mark's unrequited proposal by accusing him of treating her as 'some kind of animal you've trapped'. 'That's right, you are,' Mark says, 'and I've caught something really wild this time, haven't I? I've tracked you and caught you and, by God, I'm going to keep you.'

KILLER LINES: When Marnie ponders how Mark has made his money, he explains smugly: 'Nothing ever happens to a family that traditionally marries at least one heiress every other generation.'

Mrs Edgar tells her daughter that she'd always hoped she could bring her up 'decent'. 'Decent?' Marnie cries, 'Oh, Momma, you surely realised your ambition: I certainly am "decent". Course, I'm a cheat, and a liar and a thief, but I *am* decent.'

THERE HE IS!: Five minutes into the film. As Marnie walks along a hotel corridor, Hitchcock steps from one of the rooms and looks directly at the camera guiltily.

MISOGYNY: For many, *Marnie* is the noose by which Hitchcock hangs himself, containing what is up to now the most controversial scene of his career, where Mark forces himself on to the 'frigid' Marnie. As the screenwriter Evan Hunter recalls, this was a scene that Hitchcock had been obsessing about for months prior to filming, telling Hunter that 'When [Mark] "sticks it in her" I want the camera right in her face.' Hunter's refusal to write the scene was, he believes, the reason he was later replaced by Jay Presson Allen, the woman who had successfully adapted *The Prime of Miss Jean Brodie* for the stage.

Marnie later spurns Mark's advances, crying: 'Men! You say "No, thanks" to one of them and bingo! You're a candidate for the funny farm. It would be hilarious if it weren't pathetic!'

Mark has a curious line in compliments, telling Marnie that his father judges people by scent: 'If you smell anything like a horse, you're in.'

POSTERS: The film was billed as 'Alfred Hitchcock's suspenseful Sex Mystery', which says it all, really.

TRAILER: As with *Psycho* and *The Birds*, *Marnie*'s trailer was like a mini *Alfred Hitchcock Presents* episode of its own. Introducing himself in the traditional genial manner, Hitch explains that '*Marnie* is a very difficult picture to classify. It is not *Psycho*, nor do we have a horde of birds flapping about and pecking at people willy-nilly. We do have two very interesting human specimens, a man and a woman. One might call *Marnie* a sex mystery, that is if one uses such words. But it is more than that.' Knowing the content of the film, dealing with frigidity, marital rape and murder, we can see that Hitchcock's flippant puns about Mark having to 'probe' her and apply 'mouth-to-mouth resuscitation' are quite distasteful.

THE ICE MAIDEN: This really is Hedren's moment of glory as the last of the cool blondes who so epitomise Hitchcock. She appears in one of the best examples of Hitchcock's suspense technique (the tense safe robbery with the cleaner mere feet away and Marnie's subsequent barefoot escape from the office), and from her first magical appearance, rinsing the dye from her hair in a hotel bathroom, she is rarely off the screen for the entire picture. Finally, having fallen for the nobility of Bergman, the warmth of Kelly and the complexity of Novak, Hitchcock found a woman who would yield to his total control yet hold so much of herself just beneath the surface. Hedren excels as this complicated woman desperate for love, yet unable to allow anyone close, and we can't help but feel that Hitchcock's appropriation of the total credit of her success in both *Marnie* and *The Birds* (claiming he controlled her every facial expression) is more than a little discourteous.

TRIVIA: The production company created for the film, Geoffrey Stanley, was named after Hitchcock's pet dogs.

FINAL ANALYSIS: Like the character it examines, *Marnie* is a work of both beauty and betrayal. Hitchcock's use of colour – notably the key colour of red, but also the vivid greens and yellows that we saw back in *Vertigo* – creates the effect of a surreal fairy tale, as if what we see is as much a façade as the identities Marnie picks up and drops with regularity. It's a work of love that is suddenly made ugly by the rape that lies at the centre of the tale. A man capable of great subtlety lets himself down with an act of brutality that fails to ellicit sympathy for either of the characters involved. Coupled with the behind-the-scenes issues that caused Hitchcock to lose interest in the film almost overnight (as mentioned above and detailed in, among others, Donald Spoto's *The Dark Side of Genius*), one can't help feeling a little disappointed by such a blot against the Master's traditional restraint. But, despite this, *Marnie* is a supremely crafted film, a masterpiece that confuses as much as enthrals. 8/10.

Torn Curtain (1966)

(Colour – 119 mins)

Produced by Alfred Hitchcock/Universal Pictures

Written by Brian Moore

Original music: John Addison
Director of Photography: John F Warren
Costume Design: Edith Head
Production Design: Hein Heckroth
Film Editing: Bud Hoffman
Art Director: Frank Arrigo
Assistant Director: Donald Baer
Make-up Artist: Jack Barron
Unit Production Manager: Jack Corrick
Costume Supervisor: Grady Hunt
Set Decorator: George Milo
Hair Stylist: Lorraine Roberson, Hal Saunders
Assistant to Mr Hitchcock: Peggy Robertson
Recording Director: William Russell
Camera Operator: Leonard J South
Script Supervisor: Lois Thurman
Sound: Waldon O Watson
Pictorial Designs: Albert Whitlock

CAST: Paul Newman (*Professor Michael Armstrong*), Julie Andrews (*Sarah Sherman*), Lila Kedrova (*Countess Luchinska*), Hansjörg Felmy (*Heinrich Gerhard*), Tamara Toumanova (*Ballerina*), Wolfgang Kieling (*Hermann Gromek*), Ludwig Donath (*Professor Gustav Lindt*), Günter Strack (*Professor Karl Manfred*), David Opatoshu (*Jakobi*), Gisela Fischer (*Dr Koska*), Mort Mills (*Farmer*), Carolyn Conwell (*Farmer's Wife*), Arthur Gould-Porter (*Freddy*), Gloria Gorvin (*Fraulein*).

SUMMARY: On board a cruise ship sailing down the Osterfjord in Norway, the passengers – mostly delegates at an international nuclear-physics conference – are all doing their best to fight off the freezing temperatures. For Professor Michael Armstrong and his assistant Sarah Sherman, this means staying in bed and discussing their forthcoming marriage. On their arrival in Copenhagen the couple check into a hotel, and as Michael showers Sarah answers a phone call for him from a book store that apparently has a book waiting for him. She decides to collect the book for him, and with the help of Professor Manfred, one of her East German colleagues from the conference, she manages to trace the bookshop, where she collects a carefully wrapped first edition.

She surprises her lover with the book, and Michael appears more than a little shocked. He dashes into a toilet and unwraps the book. It clearly indicates a code letter – the greek symbol pi (π), which is the codename for someone he is apparently meant to contact. At lunch, Michael drops a bombshell on Sarah: he will be leaving for Stockholm that evening, instead of delivering his keynote address to the conference. He acts very coldly and dismissively towards Sarah, and in effect breaks off their engagement, telling her she should head straight back to the United States. Upset, Sarah goes to the concierge to book her ticket home, only to discover from him that Michael bought a one-way ticket to East Berlin, not Stockholm.

The plane is en route to Berlin by the time Michael realises that Sarah has followed him. He is furious, and tells her she should get the first plane back home. As the plane lands, Sarah is shocked to see that Professor Manfred is also on the plane. Manfred is shocked to see Sarah as well, and confronts Michael, who reassures him that the woman knows nothing of their plans.

At the press conference that the East Germans have arranged, Sarah is stunned to hear Michael announce his decision to defect to the East. He reveals that the US government has cut funding for his research into the development of an *anti*-nuclear missile. He believes such a project is more important than national boundaries, and tells the crowd he is here to offer his services to the University of Leipzig.

Back at their hotel, a bewildered Sarah confronts Michael, accusing him of being a traitor, and begs him to return with her to the US. Michael decides to go for a walk, pursued by his personal 'assistant' Gromek. He goes to the Berlin museum where he successfully shakes off Gromek before jumping into a taxi, which takes him to a farmhouse in the middle of nowhere. Michael is met by the farmer's wife, and, after drawing the symbol π on the floor, she points to her husband out in the fields. Michael is in fact working as a double agent and meets the farmer – also an American agent – to learn that his next contact is a doctor called Koska, who will help Michael to escape once he has the information he needs. The escape, however, will be a great deal more dangerous now with Sarah to look after.

As Michael walks back to his waiting taxi, he sees Gromek pull up on a motorbike. He darts inside the farmhouse, and lies, unconvincingly, to Gromek, claiming the farmer's wife is a distant relative. Gromek has, however, seen the symbol in the dust outside and knows that Pi is an organisation for helping spies to escape. As he tries to telephone for assistance, Michael realises he's left with little choice but to commit murder. With the wife's help he grabs the determined Gromek and eventually they kill him by holding his head inside a gas oven. The woman gestures to Michael that she will bury Gromek and his motorbike in the fields nearby, and Michael takes the taxi back to Berlin.

Sarah has agreed to stay with Michael in East Germany, so Security Chief Gerhard arranges for them to travel on to Leipzig. He assigns them another 'assistant' after the mysterious disappearance of Gromek. At the University of Leipzig, Michael is walking down a flight of stairs on his way to meet Professor Lindt when he trips and falls. He is taken to the university medic, who turns out to be Dr Koska, his next contact. Koska admits that she deliberately tripped Michael up in order to be able to speak to him in private, and warns him that he has very little time to speak to Professor Lindt before the couple are due to be smuggled out of the country.

Michael reluctantly explains the truth to Sarah about his 'defection'. He had planned to wait until he had stolen the secrets from Lindt and was therefore ready to escape, but the authorities seem to be closing in on them hour by hour. That evening, Dr Koska tells them he and Sarah must be at her surgery by 10 the next morning to begin their escape. Professor Lindt joins Michael and Sarah for a drink, and the two men enjoy a light-hearted intellectual debate. They arrange to continue the discussion at 9.30 the next morning.

Lindt invites Michael to his workroom, where they try to outsmart each other with a series of equations. Michael plays up his ignorance by challenging Lindt's ego and in frustration the professor eventually reveals his all-important formula. Just then, the university's Tannoy system announces that Michael is to be arrested immediately on suspicion of espionage, and Lindt realises he has been tricked. Michael makes his escape and finally meets up with Koska and Sarah. The doctor shows the couple on to a bus owned by Pi. Although it follows the official route to Berlin so as not to alert the authorities, the passengers are all members of Pi. The journey is extremely perilous, with army roadblocks, terrorists trying to hijack the bus, and the ever-present threat that one of the genuine buses on the route might catch up with them. One of the 'passengers', Mr Jacobi, gives Michael their next point of contact, a man in the post office on Freidrichstrasse, but, just as they reach journey's end, the bus is pulled over by the police, forcing the occupants to flee from a hail of bullets.

At the post office they manage to speak to their contact just as the police arrive. Finally, they are met by 'the farmer', who tells them they are to be smuggled out of East Germany in the clothes baskets of a Czechoslovakian ballet company, which is leaving by boat for Sweden the next day. The couple take their seats at the ballet, waiting for a signal from one of the backstage crew. But they are recognised by the star performer, a prima ballerina who had arrived in Berlin on the same aeroplane as Michael and Sarah. During the performance she manages to alert the authorities and soon the security forces block all of the exits. Realising that they are trapped, Michael shouts 'fire!' and causes a stampede for the exits. Taking advantage of the confusion, Michael and Sarah meet their final contact, who hides them in the costume baskets.

Next day, the boat is pulling into the docks of Sweden. Recalling a previous escape attempt, the ballerina screams to the security forces to shoot the baskets, claiming they contain spies. The baskets are riddled with bullets. However, Sarah and Michael have already escaped to the dockside, where they are immediately offered political sanctuary.

CASTING: The casting decisions for *Torn Curtain* were largely taken out of Hitchcock's hands by Universal. Although Paul Newman and Julie Andrews were the biggest stars in Hollywood at the time, Hitch was uncomfortable about sharing top billing with anyone. He was allegedly still less happy about Julie Andrews's involvement, believing that the audience would be unable to see her as anything other than Mary Poppins, and that they would be expecting the picture to be a musical. According to Hitch himself, the two stars cost over $1.8 million of the film's $5 million budget. As he believed that the two stars were terribly miscast, this is undoubtedly one of the reasons he lost interest in the movie so much.

ROOTS: Hitchcock really wanted to make a movie based around the infamous Burgess and Maclean spy case. He had thought about it several times before, but, during early discussions on *Torn Curtain*, he decided that the most interesting part of the story would be to investigate the emotional impact on Burgess's wife when she discovers that her husband is a traitor. Of course, the recent near-cataclysm of the Cuban Missile Crisis a few years earlier provided a sensible rationale for Michael's desire to complete his research into an antimissile system.

WHO'S WHO?: Paul Newman has gained some notoriety, having established 'Paul Newman's Own', a brand of salad dressings. Newman is married to the actress Joanne Woodward, and his most celebrated roles include Eddie Felson in *The Hustler* (Robert Rossen, 1961), the eponymous *Cool Hand Luke* (Stuart Rosenberg, 1967), and Butch Cassidy opposite Robert Redford in *Butch Cassidy and the Sundance Kid* (George Roy Hill, 1969). He won an Oscar for re-creating his role from *The Hustler* in *The Color of Money* (Martin Scorsese, 1986). Newman also appeared in a little-known Hitchcockesque comedy thriller, *The Prize* (Mark Robson, 1963), playing a Nobel Prize-winning author pursued by spies in a cross between *Foreign Correspondent* and *North by Northwest*.

The eternally virginal Julie Andrews may have gained her reputation from such musicals as *Mary Poppins* (Robert Stephenson, 1964), *The*

Sound of Music (Robert Wise, 1965) and *Thoroughly Modern Millie* (George Roy Hill, 1967), but she also starred in a number of her husband Blake Edwards's more risqué films, such as his adaptation of the cross-dressing *Victor/Victoria* (1982) and the sex comedy *The Man Who Loved Women* (1983) opposite Burt Reynolds.

After playing the famer's wife in *Torn Curtain*, Carolyn Conwell would later appear in a *much* less violent film – *The Boston Strangler* (Richard Fleischer, 1968).

THE USUAL SUSPECTS: Mort Mills (*the farmer*) also appeared in *Psycho*.

KILLER LINES: Gromek, the East German with the curious line in Americanisms, arrests Michael with the words: 'It's the Big House for you, Professor!'

THERE HE IS!: Early in the film, Hitchcock sits in a hotel lobby in some discomfort as a baby, sitting on his knee, appears to soil itself.

THE MACGUFFIN: The Gamma 5 secrets that Michael is desperate to get his hands on occupy his interest for much of the film, but have little impact on the movement of the plot or our emotions. At first, we care about the poor unfortunate Sarah; about finding out just why Michael has defected; and about discovering what's really going on. Towards the end, all we care about is a primitive emotional response – will they escape?

THEMES AND MOTIFS: Treachery, betrayal and the man on the run – all classic Hitch themes utilised to fairly average effect here.

TABOOS: Michael breaks the ultimate taboo in the early 60s – he seems to be defecting to the enemy! There are also several comments about premarital sex. Sarah claims that she doesn't want to be the only 'common-law wife' living on the university campus, and is determined that Michael make an 'honest' woman of her.

MUSIC: *Torn Curtain* was scored by the Oscar-winning composer John Addison, who turned in a fun, if unremarkable, soundtrack. The most memorable segment is the theme that accompanies the lengthy bus sequence. It's the type of movie theme that tends to stick in the memory rather more than it ought to. Bernard Herrmann wrote the original score, but Universal Pictures executives convinced Hitchcock that they needed a more upbeat score. Hitchcock and Herrmann had a major disagreement, the score was dropped and they never worked together again. For many years, Herrmann's score was believed to have disappeared, but it was recently rediscovered and is currently available on CD. Herrmann's approach to *Torn Curtain* differed wildly from

Addison's. The graphic murder of Gromek – completely silent in Addison's version – is accompanied by a highly dramatic orchestral piece, which either adds to or detracts from the power of the scene, depending on your point of view.

POSTER: A fairly literal, if effective, image of a tear reveals portraits of Newman and Andrews with the strapline: 'It tears you apart with suspense!'

TRAILER: A cheesy voice-over announces: 'The acknowledged master of the unexpected, Alfred Hitchcock, thrusts you into his new world of suspense.' 'Paul Newman and Julie Andrews find love in danger and danger in love behind Alfred Hitchcock's *Torn Curtain*.'

THE ICE MAIDEN: Falling very much into the Doris Day mould of Hitchcock heroines, Julie Andrews makes a fairly creditable foray into acting in 'grown-up' films. Sarah is a quite emancipated young woman, a nuclear physicist in her own right, and not just a jumped-up secretary as she so easily could have been. The main weakness in her character is that she is not particularly interesting. We sympathise with her plight, but can't get particularly excited about anything that happens to her. With a few more facets to her character and performance, we might have been able to believe in the peril facing Sarah. As both Julie Andrews and the role she plays are so darned nice, it's hard for us to believe that anybody could possibly be mean to her.

WHAT THE PAPERS SAID: The review by an unnamed critic in *The Times* was more positive than many of its contemporaries, while acknowledging that *Torn Curtain* is essentially flawed in many ways: 'Paul Newman and Julie Andrews are . . . pretty wasted on pasteboard roles, since both are better as actors than as straight star-personalities. All the same, the film remains great fun for most of its length, and it would be silly to let regret for what it might have been and is not blind us to the considerable advantages of what it actually is.'

COSTUME: It's quite difficult to get enthusiastic about drab, Eastern-bloc costumes, which account for the vast majority of everything we see. Countess Luchinska's faded glamour, though, is another matter entirely. Her aspirations towards capitalist excess are clear from her multicoloured silk scarf, sunglasses and outrageous feathered hat. The ballerina is regularly dressed all in black, wearing feathers – watching and waiting from on high in her final scene like a sinister human crow. Once again, Hitch's bird obsession comes through!

TRIVIA: The scene where Gromek is killed was written to show how difficult it really can be to kill a man, and the finished version in the film proves this fact to unsettling – and perhaps darkly humorous – effect.

When Hitch was being interviewed by Truffaut in 1967, he showed his interrogator a complete scene that he cut from the finished print of *Torn Curtain*. The scene involved Michael bumping into a factory worker who turns out to be the brother of Gromek, whom he has earlier killed. To add insult to injury, the brother was also played by Wolfgang Kieling, this time wearing a moustache and wig.

THE FINAL ANALYSIS: *Torn Curtain* is certainly too long – about twenty minutes could easily be cut, and, surprisingly, there are also probably a couple of suspense sequences too many, in particular the post-office scene, which adds little to the film as a whole, despite being immensely entertaining. Nonetheless, it's quite a neat summary of what has gone before, updated for the sixties audience. Yet another spy story, *Torn Curtain* benefits from being the first Hitchcock movie where the threat is actually named – the Eastern bloc – as opposed to a generic, vaguely European menace. As a consequence, the film lacks a 'frontman' for the cause, like Peter Lorre in *The Man Who Knew Too Much* or James Mason in *North by Northwest*, but gains in the process by having the danger all around them: people who have previously helped them turn out to be on the side of the 'bad guys', such as the taxi driver, and when they eventually do meet up with someone willing to help – the gloriously daffy old countess – both the characters and the audience are wary of trusting her.

The key scene in *Torn Curtain*, and the one we imagine gave Hitchcock the most excitement, is the brutal murder of Gromek. It is genuinely nasty, going so far over the top as to be almost comical in its excess. The bus escape, too, is both tense and frustrating: we know full well which buttons Hitchcock is pushing yet we're unable to resist reacting to them – the Hitchcock equivalent of Pavlov's dog experiments perhaps? For these manipulative elements alone, *Torn Curtain* is much more enjoyable than its reputation might suggest. **7/10**

Topaz (1969)

(Colour – 127 mins)

Produced by Alfred Hitchcock/Universal Pictures

Associate Producer: Herbert Coleman

Screenplay: Samuel A Taylor, based on the novel by Leon Uris

Film Editor: William H Ziegler
Photographic Consultant: Hal Mohr
Sound: Waldon O Watson & Robert R Bertrand
Unit Production Manager: Wallace Worsley
Assistant Directors: Douglas Green & James Westman

Special Photographic Effects: Albert Whitlock
Set Decorations: John Austin
Script Supervisor: Trudy Von Trotha
Make-up: Bud Westmore & Leonard Engelman
Hair Styles: Larry Germain & Nellie Manley
Assistant to Mr Hitchcock: Peggy Robertson
Camera Operator: William Dodds
Men's Costume Supervisor: Peter Salcutti
Cuban Technical Adviser: JP Mathieu
French Technical Adviser: Odeth Ferry
Director of Photography: Jack Hildyard
Costume Design: Edith Head
Fashioned in Paris by Pierre Balman
Production Designer: Henry Bumstead
Music Composed and Conducted by Maurice Jarre

CAST: Frederick Stafford (*André Devereaux*), Dany Robin (*Nicole Devereaux*), John Forsythe (*Michael Nordstrom*), John Vernon (*Rico Parra*), Karin Dor (*Juanita de Cordoba*), Michel Piccoli (*Jacques Granville*), Philippe Noiret (*Henri Jarre*), Claude Jade (*Michele Picard*), Michel Subor (*François Picard*), Per-Axel Arosenius (*Boris Kusenov*), Roscoe Lee Browne (*Philippe Dubois*), Edmon Ryan (*McKittreck*), Sonja Kolthoff (*Mrs Kusenov*), Tina Hedström (*Tamara Kusenov*), John Van Dreelen (*Claude Martin*), Don Randolph (*Luis Uribe*), John Roper (*Thomas*), Lew Brown (*The American Official*), Roberto Contreras (*Munoz*), Carlos Rivas (*Hernandez*), George Skaff (*Rene d'Arcy*), Sándor Szabó (*Emile Redon*), Roger Til (*Jean Chabrier*), Lewis Charles (*Mr Mendoza*), Anna Navarro (*Mrs Mendoza*).

SUMMARY: On holiday in Copenhagen, Kusenov, a Russian official, leaves the Russian Embassy with his wife and daughter, passes through the security gates and goes for a walk around the town, followed by three government agents. The Kusenovs join a tour party being shown round a pottery factory. Kusenov's daughter deliberately breaks an ornament and is taken into an office out of sight of the agents, where she manages to make a phone call to their contact, an American agent called Michael Nordstrom. Nordstrom tells her to lead her family to a nearby department store, where he is able to snatch them from under the very noses of the agents and drive them to safety. Nordstrom then takes them by aeroplane to Washington, DC. Having secured political asylum for himself and his family, Kusenov engages the American agents in a face-off. He claims his defection does not automatically guarantee he is willing to trade secrets. They threaten to hand him over to the Russian Embassy but he points out that to do so would ruin the possibility of future defectors coming to America. They test him, asking him if the word 'topaz' means anything to him. He claims it doesn't.

Meanwhile, the agents at the French Embassy in Washington summon André Devereaux, one of their top agents, and demand to know why he knows nothing about the defection of the Russian official. Devereaux is surprised to learn that their Paris office knew about this first, and speculates that someone at the Russian office must have told them.

The next day they ask Kusenov about the situation in Cuba. He tells them there must be over 5,000 Russians working there as technicians, both military and civilian. Though he doesn't know anything concrete about the agreement between Cuba and Russia, Kusenov tells them that Rico Parra, the leader of the Cuban government, visited Russia recently to draw up a trade pact. Though Parra would never allow anyone to see the treaty, Kusenov believes the assistance of Parra's secretary, Luis Uribe, can be bought – but not by the Americans.

Devereaux's daughter arrives in New York. At the hotel the Devereauxs are surprised to see Nordstrom, who is an old friend of theirs, waiting for them in their hotel room. Nordstrom asks Devereaux for his help in contacting Uribe for the treaty. Devereaux refuses, knowing that his wife is desperate for him to avoid being dragged into Cold War politics. Nordstrom asks him to get one of his people to make the short taxi ride to Harlem where Rico and his followers are staying, and photograph the papers. Devereaux concedes and as Nordstrom leaves he spells out to him that he must appear to be acting alone – the mission must not be traced back to the Americans.

Devereaux visits Dubois, a black undercover agent who works from a florist's in Harlem. He explains the plan and shows him a sketch of Uribe. Dubois manages to make contact with Uribe and gains access to Rico Parra's hotel by posing as a reporter. He manages to gain an interview with Rico by suggesting he is racist. Rico explains that his country does not have colour bars but doesn't wish to speak with the American press after the reportage they have given to Cuba. Dubois explains he does not represent the American newspapers and asks if he can photograph Rico waving to the citizens of Harlem. Rico consents. He stands out on the balcony and as Dubois takes his picture Uribe steals the case containing the treaty. Dubois thanks Rico for his time and leaves, then heads for Uribe's room.

Rico notices the case is missing. His secretary tells him Uribe took it and Rico is immediately suspicious. He breaks down Uribe's door to find Dubois in the process of photographing the treaty. Dubois escapes via a window and manages to pass the camera on to a waiting Devereaux before reaching his shop as if nothing had happened.

Devereaux's wife Nicole learns he's going to Cuba and tells him that the wife of one of his friends told her he was having an affair with another woman, specifically Juanita de Cordoba, a member of the Cuban underground. But her suspicions are correct; he warns her of the danger of discussing sensitive political issues with her friends and denies the accusation. But the minute he reaches Cuba he heads for Juanita de Cordoba, who has been his mistress for some time. He brings with him some highly advanced espionage equipment, including remote-controlled cameras and a Geiger counter.

Juanita employs the Mendozas, members of her staff, to help her in her espionage to get shots of the port. They pretend to be picnicking on the hillside overlooking the port. However, a soldier sees them and opens fire on them. Eventually they are captured.

The next morning, Devereaux prepares to return home. The house boy has hidden tape recordings inside the spools of a typewriter, information about the Russian troops miniaturised and placed inside a microdot on one of the keys, and frames of film tucked inside the wrappings around the razor blades. Juanita gives him a journal as a parting gift and she and Devereaux say a tearful goodbye.

The Mendozas are tortured by Rico's soldiers. Close to death and clutching the body of her murdered husband, Mrs Mendoza finally caves in and tells Rico she was working for Juanita. He goes there with troops to search the house. There they uncover the dark room used to develop the film. Reluctantly Rico accepts that Juanita is a traitor and shoots her dead.

Devereaux meanwhile leaves Cuba unharmed. On the plane, he looks mournfully at the journal Juanita gave him and notices something uneven in the binding. He slashes the cover and finds some microfilm. On returning to Washington he learns that the French Embassy have learnt of his actions and that he must return to Paris to report to the Director General. Nordstrom apologises for involving him in his government's plans and as recompense he tells him their Russian defector has identified where the leaks in Paris have come from.

Kusenov tells him about 'Topaz'. 'Topaz' is a code name for a group of French officials who work for the Soviet Union. The head of the ring, known as Columbine, is unknown to Kusenov: he always dealt with the second in command, Henri Jarre, whom Devereaux knows. The Americans fear the Russians may learn that they are on the move and train their Cuban missiles at every major city in America. They must identify the leak and ask him to learn the truth about Topaz.

On returning to Paris, Devereaux meets secretly with a number of officials, including Jarre and a senior official by the name of Jacques Granville, who warn him he will face a full board of enquiry if he doesn't pass on the information he learnt for the Americans. He tells them he cannot do this as he believes someone is passing secrets back to the Russians. He asks them if they have ever had any links with the spy ring known as Topaz. It doesn't appear to register with anyone, so he tells them the name of the defector, Kusenov. Jarre tells him that the KGB reported that Kusenov died over a year ago and that this defector must therefore be a diversion on the part of the Americans.

Jarre visits Jacques Granville in secret and Granville reprimands him for lying about the defector being dead, believing this will alert Devereaux to their activities with Russia. Granville is expecting company and ushers Jarre out, and, soon after Jarre departs, Nicole Devereaux arrives. In retribution for her husband's infidelity she has entered into an affair with Granville.

Jarre agrees to be interviewed about his role in Nato by a young journalist called François Picard. As they talk, the young man sketches Jarre. When the interview veers towards Jarre's knowledge of the Russian defection Jarre realises that the interview is not for a newspaper. The young man reveals that he is Devereaux's son-in-law. He offers him the opportunity for him to leave the country in exchange for information, but Jarre refuses to cooperate. As François telephones Devereaux the young man is attacked and the line goes dead. Devereaux and his daughter rush to Jarre's office to find Jarre dead and François missing. They return to their apartment seconds before François who managed to escape from Jarre's killers with only a small bullet wound. As Nicole listens in horror to her son-in-law's story she is compelled to confess to Devereaux that she knows the traitor he is looking for – Jacques Granville.

The political situation is worsening. The US consider bombing raids on Cuba's known missile bases. Nordstrom comes to Paris for a peace conference. Devereaux meets him at the airport to warn him that Granville will also be attending. At the conference Nordstrom informs the other attendees of his suspicions regarding Granville and the man is ousted from the assembly. Disgraced, Granville goes home and shoots himself. Soon after, the missile crisis in Cuba is resolved.

TITLES: A huge banner depicting the three faces of communism (Lenin, Stalin and Marx) presides over a huge military procession of missiles and soldiers, the square awash with red. A title card informs us: 'Somewhere in this crowd is a high Russian official who disagrees with his government's display of force and what it threatens. Very soon his conscience will force him to attempt an escape while apparently on a vacation with his family.'

CASTING: The Associate Producer Herbert Coleman had advocated that Hitchcock should try for some big international names, suggesting Yves Montand and Catherine Deneuve. Hitchcock, Coleman believed, resented being told what to do, and so passed on both stars. According to the screenwriter Samuel Taylor, Karin Dor was cast at the last minute. Claude Jade had been recommended to Hitchcock by his fellow director François Truffaut, who had recently completed a lengthy series of interviews with his hero.

ROOTS: A rarity for Hitchcock, *Topaz* is inspired by the true story of the political crisis that emerged between the French, American, Russian and Cuban powers in 1962.

Rico paraphrases Hamlet's famous soliloquy when he refers to 'The journey from which no traveller *ever* returns' (see also 1934 version of *The Man Who Knew Too Much*).

WHO'S WHO?: The celebrated French actor Philippe Noiret played Alfredo in the Oscar-winning *Cinema Paradiso* (Giuseppe Tornatore, 1988).

Roscoe Lee Browne played Saunders, Benson's replacement, in the spoof sitcom *Soap*.

THE USUAL SUSPECTS: John Forsythe also appeared in *The Trouble with Harry*. The bird trainer Ray Berwick (*The Birds*) was hired for the scene where a gull was required to fly over.

THERE HE IS!: Just under 30 minutes in, at the airport, a nurse pushes Hitchcock along in a wheelchair until he is greeted by another man. Hitchcock instantly stands up and the two walk off together.

THE MACGUFFIN: The early MacGuffin of the trade pact between Cuba and Russia is quickly dispensed with, leaving only the small matter of the relevance of the film's title – a ring of French agents working as spies for Russia.

POSTER: The strapline boasts: 'Hitchcock takes you behind the actual headlines to expose the most explosive spy scandal of this century!'

TRIVIA: On 3 May 1968, after the American President announced that he would not be running for a second term in office, Hitchcock arranged a press conference. 'I'm here to announce that I'm going to run [long pause] . . . a picture, in about a year.'

Madeleine Carroll (*The 39 Steps*, *Secret Agent*) lived in the cul-de-sac that contained Michel Piccoli's apartment in the film. Hitchcock declined her invitation to dinner.

The location filming in Paris was slightly delayed when André Malraux, the French Minister of Culture, withdrew the crew's shooting permit as he felt the film was anti-French. Hurried negotiations between the American and French embassies ensued and the problem was sorted.

After preview audiences found the original ending to the film risible, Hitchcock was forced to refilm the climax. In the original version Devereaux and Granville stage a duel with pistols in an empty stadium, but as the duel begins Granville is assassinated by a Russian sniper. Hitchcock held on to the original footage and after his death his daughter Pat donated the shots to the American Academy of Motion Pictures Arts and Sciences.

As was traditional, Hitchcock paid special attention to the death scene of Juanita. Hitch had fine threads attached to the bottom of Karin Dor's robe so that when she fell to the ground the threads could be pulled to give the impression of a flower unfolding.

THE FINAL ANALYSIS: It's overly complicated, sprawling and completely lacking in any likable characters, and the over-riding feeling is that there's no reason why we should care. Maybe in 1968, merely five years after the Cuban Missile Crisis, this might have been of more interest, but we doubt it. This is one of those films where it's obvious the director has found himself with a mess on his hands with no idea how to deal with it. Hitchcock sometimes tackled projects he lost interest in, but this is one of a very few of his films that are just plain boring from the start. **2/10.**

Frenzy (1972)

(Colour – 116 mins)

Produced by Alfred Hitchcock/Universal Pictures

Associate Producer: William Hill

Screenplay: Anthony Shaffer

Based on the novel *Goodbye Piccadilly, Farewell Leicester Square* by Arthur La Bern

Original music: Ron Goodwin
Director of Photography: Gilbert Taylor (credited as Gil Taylor)
Film Editor: John Jympson
Assistant Director: Colin M Brewer
Production Manager: Brian Burgess
Production Design: Syd Cain
Art Director: Robert W Laing (credited as Bob Laing)
Set Dresser: Simon Wakefield
Hairdresser: Patricia McDermott (credited as Pat McDermott)
Make-up Artist: Harry Frampton
Special Photographic Effects: Albert Whitlock
Casting: Sally Nicholl
Assistant to Mr Hitchcock: Peggy Robertson
Wardrobe Supervisor: Dulcie Midwinter
Sound Editor: Rusty Coppleman
Sound Recordist: Gordon K McCallum
Sound Mixer: Peter Handford
Continuity: Angela Martelli
Camera Operator: Paul Wilson

CAST: Jon Finch (*Richard Blaney*), Barry Foster (*Bob Rusk*), Barbara Leigh-Hunt (*Brenda Blaney*), Anna Massey (*Barbara 'Babs' Milligan*), Alec McCowen (*Chief Inspector Oxford*), Vivien Merchant (*Mrs Oxford*), Billie Whitelaw (*Hettie Porter*), Clive Swift (*Johnny Porter*), Bernard Cribbins (*Felix Forsythe*), Michael Bates (*Sergeant Spearman*), Jean Marsh (*Monica Barling, Brenda's secretary*), Madge Ryan (*Mrs Davison*), Elsie Randolph (*Gladys*), John Boxer (*Sir George*), George Tovey (*Mr Salt*), Jimmy Gardner (*Hotel Porter*), Noel Johnson, Gerald Sim (*Men at Bar*).

UNCREDITED CAST: Bunny May (*Barman*), June Ellis (*Barmaid*), Robert Keegan (*Hospital Patient*), Rita Webb (*Mrs Rusk*), Geraldine Cowper (*Girl in Crowd*).

SUMMARY: A serial killer is at work in London's West End, nicknamed the 'Necktie Murderer' after his habit of strangling his victims with ties which he leaves dangling round their necks. On the morning that another victim is found floating in the Thames, a barman, Dick Blaney, helps himself to a drink before starting work. The landlord catches him and accuses him of theft. Blaney is ex-RAF with a short temper and a great deal of pride and insists he was about to pay for the drink. Dick's girlfriend Babs tries to arbitrate but the landlord clearly dislikes him and sacks him on the spot. Dick visits his best friend, a smartly dressed greengrocer called Bob Rusk, who offers him a place to stay and a racing tip, which Dick later regrets not backing when it comes in first.

Dick goes to a pub round the corner and downs a few double brandies before deciding to visit his ex-wife, Brenda, who ironically runs a dating agency. Dick is deliberately argumentative with Brenda, who sends her secretary for an early lunch to avoid a scene. Gradually Dick calms down and the two go out to dinner. Realising that he's fallen on hard times, Brenda offers to lend Dick some money but his pride stops him from accepting and he causes another scene. Having walked out on both his job and his home above the pub, Dick spends the night at a dosshouse. In the middle of the night he catches a tramp going through his pockets and is surprised to see the tramp apologetically returning money to Dick's pocket that hadn't been there earlier. He realises that Brenda must have slipped a few notes into his pocket while he wasn't looking.

The next afternoon, while her secretary is out to lunch, Brenda receives a visit from Dick's friend Bob Rusk, though he is using the name William Robinson. Brenda is immediately dismissive of him, knowing full well that 'Mr Robinson' wants girls only of a certain kind. She tells him her agency cannot cater for his tastes but the man refuses to listen, telling her that she is his kind of woman. Slowly he corners her and to her terror begins to rape her. It's not until he removes his tie that she realises the danger she's in but by then it's already too late. He wraps his tie around her neck and chokes her to death.

Rusk leaves the partly clothed body in her office and locks the door behind him. He leaves seconds before Dick rounds the corner and walks up the stairs to Brenda's office. The door is locked so Dick leaves. Brenda's secretary, Monica, returns from lunch and discovers her employer's body. Having caught a glimpse of Dick as he exited the building, she is able to give the police a detailed description of the 'suspect'.

Unaware of the trouble he's about to find himself in, Dick meets Babs and takes her to an expensive hotel, explaining that he won some money on a horse. He arranges to have his jacket deloused after his night at the dosshouse and hands it over to the porter. Downstairs the next morning, the hotel receptionist reads aloud the newspaper's description of a man wanted in connection with another necktie murder and she realises that it matches their new guest. The porter calls the police, who burst in too late to catch Dick, who has also read the paper and absconded with Babs.

Dick reassures Babs that he had nothing to do with his ex-wife's death, but he realises that there is most likely enough circumstantial evidence to make him the most likely suspect. During his divorce, Dick allowed Brenda to claim spousal abuse just to hurry things along. A voice calls out his name and Dick immediately makes to escape until he realises it's his old friend, Johnny Porter. Johnny knows Dick of old and, having read the newspapers with disbelief, he willingly offers Dick a place to hide. Babs returns to work late for her shift and after another row with the landlord she resigns. Leaving the pub, she realises that she too is now homeless. A voice from behind her asks her if she's looking for somewhere to stay; she's relieved to see it's Bob and gladly accepts his kind offer. As he shows her up to his room, Bob tells her that she's his kind of girl . . .

Under cover of darkness, Bob carries Babs's dead body, wrapped in a potato sack, out to a delivery truck in the market and dumps her among the sacks of potatoes. He returns to his flat and it's only then that he notices he's lost his monogrammed tiepin and realises it must be with Babs's corpse. He rushes back to the market and climbs into the back of the truck just as it drives off. The truck makes its way up the motorway as Bob unwraps the corpse to find the tiepin lodged in Babs's tightly clenched fist. Rigor mortis has already begun to set in and Bob is forced to snap the body's fingers to retrieve the pin. The truck driver stops off at a roadside café and Bob makes his escape. The driver returns to the truck, and it's many miles before he's alerted by some policemen to some spillage from the back of his vehicle. As he breaks to a halt, the naked body falls out of the truck on to the road.

The newspapers are quick to report this latest killing and on his wife's orders Johnny regretfully has to tell Dick to leave. Dick goes for help to Bob, who immediately says he can stay at his place, but Dick walks into a trap – Bob has tipped off the police, who quickly arrest Dick. At the Old Bailey, Dick is sentenced to life imprisonment, thanks largely to Bob having planted incriminating evidence on him. As he's taken down to the cells, Dick protests his innocence, now certain that Bob is the real killer.

Inspector Oxford of Scotland Yard, the officer in charge of the murder investigation, sits alone in the courtroom mulling over Dick's accusation. Though the evidence from Bob Rusk and Monica Barling suggests that Dick is indeed the killer, Oxford is now not certain. At home, he discusses the case with his wife, who expresses her belief that Blaney cannot be guilty of the crimes. She can't believe that a man would commit a crime of passion against his ex-wife so long after their divorce. Oxford visits the Blaney dating agency to speak to Monica, the secretary, and shows her a photograph of Rusk. She identifies him as 'Mr Robinson' and tells Oxford that he had approached them with an interest in women with masochistic tendencies. Though they told him they couldn't help him he kept coming back.

In prison, Dick deliberately falls down a flight of stairs and is taken to hospital. Meanwhile, Oxford learns that the driver of the truck where Babs's body was found made only one stop, at a roadside café, before the discovery of the body. Furthermore, a waitress at the café gives a positive identification that places Rusk at the café that night, and confirms that his clothes were covered in what looked like soil – which Oxford realises was almost certainly from the potatoes in the truck. Oxford prepares to arrest Rusk, only to learn that Dick Blaney has escaped from the hospital.

Dick makes his way to Rusk intent on killing him, figuring he might as well commit the crime he's been convicted of. He enters Rusk's flat and beats the sleeping figure in Rusk's bed with an iron bar. He pulls back the sheets to discover the strangled body of a woman, one of Bob's ties wrapped tightly round her throat. Oxford enters the flat and as the bewildered Blaney tries to explain they hear a noise from outside. Oxford hides behind the door and watches as Rusk enters, dragging a heavy trunk into the room. Oxford closes the door behind him and Rusk realises he is trapped at last.

ROOTS: *Frenzy* contains an eclectic mix of references: handing some fruit to Dick, Bob quotes Mae West's line from *I'm No Angel* (Wesley Ruggles, 1933), when he tells Babs to 'peel me a grape'; the speaker at the beginning quotes the line 'Bliss was it in that dawn to be alive' from William Wordsworth's *The Prelude*, Book XI; as Bob Rusk begins his attack on Brenda Blaney she quotes Psalm 91 ('Thou shalt not be afraid of the terror of the night . . .'); Dick signs himself and Babs into the hotel as 'Mr and Mrs Oscar Wilde' – Wilde was arrested in a hotel for acts of gross indecency. On the wall of Bob Rusk's appartment hang two portraits by the South African artist Vladimir Tretchikoff depicting strangely coloured women.

In an early pub scene, one of the customers makes a connection between the 'Necktie Murderer' and John Reginald Halliday Christie, who was hanged in 1953 for the rape and murder by strangulation of at least six women. Additionally, the final scene is inspired by the arrest of Dr Hawley Harvey Crippen who, after killing his nagging wife, boarded the SS *Montrose* with a woman friend, Ethel Le Neve, under pseudonyms. In the first arrest of its kind, Inspector Dew of Scotland Yard telegraphed ahead, then followed them on a faster boat so that he could greet Dr Crippen in person with the words 'Dr Crippen, I presume'.

Back in 1966, along with the writer Howard Fast, Hitch had prepared a screenplay for a film successively known as either *Frenzy* or *Kaleidoscope*, about a homosexual psychopath, but the idea was rejected by the executives at Universal, who, according to Fast, felt that Hitch's pictures 'were known for their elegant villains, and that here was an impossibly ugly one'. Apart from the psychopathic central character, this has little to do with the *Frenzy* he eventually filmed.

WHO'S WHO?: The Liverpudlian writer Anthony Shaffer was also the scribe behind *Sleuth* (Joseph L Mankiewicz, 1972) and *The Wicker Man* (Robin Hardy, 1972). His twin brother, Peter, wrote *Equus* (Sidney Lumet, 1977) and the Oscar-winning screenplay for *Amadeus* (Milos Forman, 1984).

Having appeared in the Hammer movies *The Horror of Frankenstein* (Jimmy Sangster – no relation – 1970) and *The Vampire Lovers* (Roy Ward Baker, 1970), and starred in the incredibly bloody *Macbeth* (Roman Polanski, 1971), Jon Finch must have appeared to Hitchcock to have been perfect for *Frenzy*, being one of the most disturbing films Hitch ever made.

The character actor Alec McCowan (*Inspector Oxford*) played 'Q' in the unofficial Bond movie *Never Say Never Again* (Irvin Kershner, 1983) and one of the 'clients' in *Personal Services* (Terry Jones, 1987).

Barry Foster played TV's Van Der Valk in the detective series of the same name. Clive Swift (*Johnny Porter*) plays the long-suffering Richard Bucket in the sitcom *Keeping Up Appearances*. Jean Marsh (*Monica, Brenda's secretary*) is best remembered for creating *Upstairs Downstairs* (in which she also played Rose) and *The House of Elliot*, though she also appeared in the TV version of the movie *9 to 5* as Roz.

Michael Bates (*Sergeant Spearman*) starred in the first three series of *Last of the Summer Wine*, though he's more familiar as the Indian bearer Rangi Ram in *It Ain't Half Hot, Mum*.

Billie Whitelaw similarly carved a niche for herself in bloody movies, having played the replacement nanny in *The Omen* (Richard Donner, 1976) and Violet Kray, the mother of the East End's most infamous twins, in *The Krays* (Peter Medak, 1989).

Barbara Leigh-Hunt and Anna Massey are familiar faces from a number of television costume dramas: Leigh-Hunt played Catherine Parr in *The Six Wives of Henry VIII* (Warris Hussein, 1970) and made her film debut in *Frenzy*; Massey appeared in, among many others, two TV adaptations of *Rebecca* as Mrs Danvers sixteen years apart, as well as *The Pallisers* (1977) and *The Mayor of Casterbridge* (1978).

THE USUAL SUSPECTS: Elsie Randolph, who worked for Hitch way back in 1932 on *Rich and Strange*, appears as Elsie, the receptionist at the Coburg Hotel.

KILLER LINES: Inspector Oxford has a number of choice lines. When his subordinate comes to bring him news he says the man is 'positively glutinous with self-approbation', and, when he finally catches the killer red-handed, he observes with heavy irony: 'Mr Rusk, you're not wearing your tie.'

Maisy the barmaid says, rather too keenly, that the Necktie Murderer is reputed to rape his victims first, prompting one of her customers to comment: 'I suppose it's nice to know every cloud has a silver lining.'

Another customer, Sir George, laments the lack of a decent series of sex murders recently, noting how it's good for tourism: 'Foreigners somehow expect the squares of London to be fog-weaved, full of hansom cabs and littered with ripped whores.'

THERE HE IS!: In the first moments of the film in the crowd, wearing a bowler hat, he is the only one not applauding the speaker.

MISOGYNY: Not surprisingly there's a great deal of offensive dialogue here, mostly from Bob Rusk: 'Half of 'em haven't even got their heads screwed on right,' he tells a passing policeman, 'let alone knowing when they've been screwed off.' He's also of the belief that 'There are some women who ask for everything they get.'

THEMES AND MOTIFS: *Frenzy* opens with a sequence not unlike that at the start of *The Lodger*, with a murder victim being discovered on the banks of the Thames, and features yet another staircase that leads off from the ground floor and curls to the left (*The Lodger*, *Shadow of a Doubt*, *Psycho*). Hitch examines the tradition of linking food with sexual desire in greater depth than before. Early on, the landlord of the Globe reprimands Babs, pointing out: 'This is Covent Garden, not the Garden of Love' – a clear reference to the Garden of Eden, at the centre of which is Bob Rusk, the purveyor of (forbidden) fruit.

Note how Rusk hides the body of one victim in the Thames, where, as we hear at the start, men used to fish for trout; a second, that of Brenda, is left with its tongue hanging out in a grotesque parody of someone licking their lips; and another body is thrown into a truck filled with potatoes.

Finally, we have Inspector Oxford, who chooses mealtimes to discuss the case in great detail with his wife, always with a horrific culinary concoction created from the discarded remains of animals (birds' claws, pigs' trotters).

AWARDS: One of Hitch's most successful films in the last decade, it was nominated for Golden Globe Awards for Best Director, Best Picture and Best Screenplay.

TABOOS: In the speech at the beginning, Hitch indulges in childish innuendo, with the speaker referring to 'brown trout' floating down the river in the same breath as referring to the effluent being dumped there. We then hear him euphemising about foreign bodies just as we see an Asian woman followed by a shot of the first dead body. The language in *Frenzy* is coarser and bluer than in any other of his films, with Bob Rusk betting on a horse called 'Coming Up' and frequent use of the word 'bastard'.

As in *Psycho*, an unmarried couple go to a hotel and are forced to adopt a fake name (premarital sex was still a taboo in 1972!), and the porter nudge-nudges with 'Can I get you anything from the pharmacy?' – possibly one of the first references to condoms in cinema.

Frenzy also marks the only time Hitchcock filmed a nude scene, with a model standing in for Anna Massey's naked stroll across the hotel room.

POSTER: The strapline is simply a rewording of the usual superlatives: 'From the Master of Shock, a shocking masterpiece – a deadly new twist from the original Hitchcock!'

TRAILER: In a teaser trailer, Hitchcock once again adopts the (now defunct) *Alfred Hitchcock Presents* approach. We see him shopping for ties. When asked by the salesman if he has a preference, he says: 'They're for a friend of mine. He uses them to strangle women.' He then boasts that '*Frenzy* will get you by the throat.'

In the final trailer, Hitch rehashes the framework of *Psycho*, giving us a tour of the location for each murder. He first appears in a most unusual way, floating on his back along the Thames (thanks to a specially crafted dummy – a trick he'd first suggested but later dismissed for his cameo in *Lifeboat*). He informs us that 'Rivers can be very sinister places, and in my new film, *Frenzy*, this river, you may say, was the scene of a very horrible murder.' He moves on to the alley outside Blaney's Dating Agency and from there to Covent Garden Fruit Market. 'I've heard of a leg of lamb,' he says, 'but never a leg of potatoes.'

TRIVIA: Hitchcock pays a possible tribute to John Galsworthy (writer of *The Skin Trade*), when he has Bob Rusk (Barry Foster) live as a tenant in the very building occupied by Galsworthy's regular publishers, Gerald Duckworth & Co. Ltd, 3 Henrietta Street, Covent Garden. This was also the one-time home of Clemence Dane, co-author of the play that inspired Hitchcock's *Murder!*.

FINAL ANALYSIS: Back on home turf in more ways than one, *Frenzy* is possibly Hitch's most negative, brooding and repellent depiction of the human condition. The murder of Brenda Blaney is so cold, so utterly nasty, that it's often cited as evidence of the director's sadism and misogyny, yet the scene where Babs is led up to Bob's flat is so tender, almost coy, as the camera follows the couple up the stairs, watches them go through the front door, then pulls back, as if witnessing Rusk's handiwork once is more than enough. It's almost as if he's embarrassed to put us through this again, considering how he's built her up as a loyal and loving woman who commands our respect and deep sorrow when she is inevitably killed. The entire scene is a perfect example of Hitchcock's subtlety: by dropping all noise from the soundtrack, then slowly bringing up the roar of a busy city as we get outside, he ensures that we'll be all too aware that, unlike with the previous murder, even if Babs did manage to scream, no one would be able to hear it.

Of course, this doesn't mean we can claim Hitch is sentimental in any way here. Having been so delicate about her death, he surely doesn't expect us to feel any emotional attachment to a corpse, so he plays with us again, almost daring us to want Bob Rusk to rescue the incriminating pin from the dead body's grasp, knowing we'll cringe as he snaps each finger deliberately, certain we'll cringe again as Mrs Oxford snaps breadsticks when referring to it later. The Oxfords are one of Hitch's all-time greatest double acts, allowing the inspector to discuss the case away from the confines of a police station with his wife, who serves him the most appalling meals.

Fans of Hitchcock's earlier films might find this all too much to bear, with his least appealing hero and most sadistic villain, and lacking his traditional cool, elegant women in favour of something less glamorous and more believable. It's ugly, it's manipulative, and it's the last great work of the Master. 9/10

Family Plot (1976)
(Working titles: *One Plus One Equals One/Deception*)

(Colour – 121 mins)

Produced by Alfred Hitchcock/Universal Pictures

Written by Ernest Lehman, based on the novel *The Rainbird Pattern* by Victor Canning

Original music: John Williams

Director of Photography: Leonard J South
Costume Design: Edith Head
Production Design: Henry Bumstead
Film Editing: J Terry Williams
Sound: James R Alexander, Robert L Hoyt
Make-up Artist: Jack Barron
Second Assistant Director: Wayne A Farlow
First Assistant Director: Howard G Kazanjian
Set Decorator: James Payne
Assistant to Mr Hitchcock: Peggy Robertson
Sound Editor: Roger Sword
Script Supervisor: Lois Thurman
Production Manager: Ernest B Wehmeyer
Special Effects: Albert Whitlock
Production Illustrator: Thomas J Wright

CAST: Karen Black (*Fran*), Bruce Dern (*George Lumley*), Barbara Harris (*Blanche Tyler*), William Devane (*Arthur Adamson*), Ed Lauter (*Joseph Maloney*), Cathleen Nesbitt (*Julia Rainbird*), Katherine

Helmond (*Mrs Maloney*), Warren J Kemmerling (*Grandison*), Edith Atwater (*Mrs Clay*), William Prince (*Bishop*), Nicholas Colasanto (*Constantine*), Marge Redmond (*Vera Hannagan*), John Lehne (*Andy Bush*), Charles Tyner (*Wheeler*), Alexander Lockwood (*Pastor*), Martin West (*Sanger*).

SUMMARY: Having harboured a family secret for many years, Julia Rainbird is tortured by guilt. In desperation, she consults a psychic, a young woman who calls herself 'Madame Blanche'. During a séance, Blanche enters a deep trance and through her spirit guide appears to make contact with Miss Rainbird's sister. Miss Rainbird is soon convinced of Blanche's psychic ability and believes that the young woman is her last hope for peace of mind. She tells her that many years ago her sister Harriet gave birth to a son. To avoid a scandal, the child was whisked away and adopted. Julia knows she does not have long to live and is desperate to ensure the child receives his fair share of the Rainbird legacy. She offers to pay Blanche $10,000 if she can use her special ability to trace her nephew with enough discretion to preserve the Rainbird family's good name.

Leaving the Rainbird estate, Blanche is picked up by her boyfriend, George Lumley. George is an out-of-work actor currently driving cabs to earn a living. Blanche tells George about the $10,000 on offer, but he's reluctant to believe they can find the heir with so little to go on.

As George drives along the road, a female figure steps out in front of the car, causing George to brake suddenly. The woman has long blonde hair, is dressed in a long black coat and is wearing shades. Barely acknowledging George, she crosses the road to the gates of a nearby complex. She makes the guard aware she's carrying a gun and silently makes her way to the main building. Inside, she hands a note to some men, who ask her for reassurance that a 'Mr Constantine' is still alive. She points her gun towards them and they hand over a large diamond. The woman then makes her way to a waiting police helicopter. She points at the pilot's compass to direct him until they reach her destination. The mystery blonde steps out of the helicopter and heads into the trees to where she can see a flashing signal. The pilot eventually follows her into the woods, where he sees the comatose figure of Mr Constantine.

The blonde, Fran, is collected by her partner Arthur Adamson. As she removes her six-inch heels and her wig, she and her partner laugh at the thought of the police looking for a tall blonde woman instead of a brunette of average height. They drive to their hideout, a large detached house with a cellar that contains a hidden wall, which in turn reveals a soundproofed cell.

Meanwhile, Constantine is telling the police and the FBI about his imprisonment. He's unable to give them much information, apart from the fact that his kidnappers were a man and a woman.

After a bit of amateur sleuthing, George manages to trace the daughter of the Rainbirds' chauffeur. Though her father died many years ago, the woman remembers a friend of his, Harry Shoebridge, who moved from the area soon after he and his wife adopted a baby boy. Sadly, she recalls that the whole family died in a house fire, and suggests that George visit the Barlow Creek cemetery to find out if this was indeed the case. At the cemetery, George finds two gravestones side by side; it certainly looks like the entire Shoebridge family – father Harry, mother Sadie and their son Edward (1933–50) – all died at the same time. The gravedigger can't explain why the child is buried in a separate grave from that of his parents, or why Edward has a brand-new gravestone. George feels he's stumbled on to something, but the gravedigger walks away. George then goes to talk to a local stonemason, who begrudgingly checks through his records. He finds an entry that reveals Edward's stone was eventually laid in 1965, though he suspects it was a commemorative stone, as Edward's body was never actually found. The mason also remembers that the second stone was paid for in cash by a slightly balding fellow in his late twenties, driving a tow-truck.

At the office of the Registrar of Births and Deaths, George is told that there is no death certificate for Edward, but an application for a death certificate was denied in 1965 due to lack of supportive evidence. The request was made by one Joseph Maloney of Barlow Creek. George goes to Maloney's gas station, and questions him about Edward Shoebridge. Maloney feigns ignorance, despite the offer of money. George tells Maloney that he thinks that Edward Shoebridge is still alive, and leaves him to contemplate matters. As George drives away, Maloney notes down his licence plate.

Adamson is working in his jewellery shop when Maloney turns up unexpectedly. He tells him that a man has been asking around about his past. Maloney has traced the car to 'Madame Blanche', and he is worried that, if Adamson's secret is uncovered, his will be too; although it was Eddie who locked his parents in their house, it was Maloney who set the house on fire as per Adamson's orders. Adamson tells Maloney to return home to Barlow Creek, and let him handle the matter. That night, Adamson and Fran wait in a car across the road from Blanche's house, and after overhearing her argue with George the criminals leave, reasonably confident the couple know nothing about Adamson's ransom scheme.

Blanche visits Julia Rainbird, who believes she has identified what could be an important lead. She remembers that the parson who baptised the baby had promised to keep track of the child's whereabouts. This 'parson' is now Bishop Wood, so George pays him a quick visit. The bishop is in the middle of a service, and George waits respectfully at the back of the cathedral. Coincidentally, the Bishop is the intended victim of Fran and Adamson's next ransom. In a daring bid, they manage to inject the Bishop with a sedative while he is at the altar and smuggle him out of the cathedral, leaving a ransom note inside a prayer book.

As they drive back to their hideout, Fran tells Adamson that she saw George at the cathedral and wonders if 'Madame Blanche' could be a genuine psychic – a possible explanation of how George could know where to find them. Adamson is unconcerned, having made a prediction of his own that the couple will soon suffer a fatal accident.

Maloney phones Blanche, inviting her and George to meet with him in order to give some information on the whereabouts of Eddie Shoebridge in exchange for $200. They both head up to the rendezvous, a café in the mountains, but when Maloney fails to show they decide to leave. They drive off back down the mountain roads, little knowing that their car's brake cables have been cut. George struggles to keep the car on the road, hindered by a hysterical Blanche. George eventually swerves the car away from the cliff edge off the side of the road. The car crashes to a halt, upturned and badly damaged. They begin to walk back down the main road when Maloney pulls up in his car. Suspecting the mechanic had something to do with their 'accident', they decline a lift. Maloney drives on up the road, turns the car around and speeds straight at them. They leap for cover and watch as Maloney's truck plummets down the cliff face and explodes.

George attends Maloney's funeral and tries to question his widow. The distressed woman confesses that Eddie Shoebridge no longer exists. With the help of her husband he moved to the city to become Arthur Adamson. In anger, she kicks down the fake gravestone of Edward Shoebridge.

George's absence from work has been noticed and he apologetically tells Blanche that he can't help her with her investigation. She decides to go off on her own, searching the city for every 'A Adamson' she can find. She eventually finds Adamson's jewellery store and from there she obtains his home address. After leaving a message with one of George's colleagues, she goes off to tell Mr Adamson the good news about his legacy.

Adamson and Fran are in the process of returning the Bishop in exchange for another hefty ransom. As they transfer the sedated man to their car they hear their doorbell ringing. They ignore it and make to drive off, but they open their garage door to find Blanche standing in their driveway. The enthusiastic woman finally gets to tell Adamson that he is the sole heir to the Rainbird fortune. He's relieved to realise that she has no idea about the kidnappings and is about to arrange a later meeting with the woman when the sleeping body of Bishop Wood slumps out of the car door. Blanche has seen far too much and Adamson sedates her.

George finally receives Blanche's message and races round to Adamson's house, where he finds Blanche's car abandoned outside Adamson's driveway. Immediately suspicious, George breaks into the house via a skylight. He searches the house and eventually finds the drugged Blanche. Adamson and Fran return from the drop-off with a brand-new diamond. George carefully follows Adamson through the house down into the hideout. Thanks to the quick reactions of Blanche, who has been merely faking unconsciousness, George manages to free her and trap the kidnappers inside the cell. Happy to have resolved the mystery, George is suddenly worried by Blanche, who seems to be in a trance. Led by her spirit guide, she finds the stolen diamonds, which have been in full view all of the time – hanging from a crystal chandelier in Adamson's hallway. George is amazed and impressed by the realisation that Blanche's psychic powers are real, while Blanche smiles to herself.

TITLES: As the opening credits roll we see a crystal ball resting on a red velvet backdrop. Images from a lava lamp disperse to form the face of Barbara Harris mid-séance.

CASTING: Executives at Universal attempted to lure Hitchcock into hiring bigger stars for the key roles, such as Liza Minnelli as the fey spiritualist. Nonetheless, Hitch wouldn't budge from the 'low-budget' cast he had, tired of having big names forced upon him by the studios. Roy Thinnes (perhaps best known for his long-running role as Peter Vincent in the TV series *The Invaders*) was originally hired to play Arthur Adamson, but Hitchcock was apparently dissatisfied with his performance and replaced him one month into the filming. The veteran actress Lilian Gish reportedly phoned Hitchcock, eager to audition for the part of Julia Rainbird. However, Hitch had already settled on his preferred choice, Cathleen Nesbitt.

LEGACY: Joel Schumacher's *8mm* (1999) also starts with an old, wealthy widow employing a discreet investigator (Nicolas Cage) to search for a missing person and avert a scandal. Similarly, the investigator finds himself embroiled in the schemes of a criminal.

WHO'S WHO?: Karen Black appeared in nearly twenty films before *Family Plot*, including an Oscar-nominated role in *Five Easy Pieces* (Bob Rafelson, 1970) and *The Great Gatsby* (Jack Clayton, 1974), though possibly her most unusual role is that of 'Joanne' the transsexual in *Come Back to the Five and Dime, Jimmy Dean, Jimmy Dean* (Robert Altman, 1982).

The character actor Bruce Dern had worked with Hitchcock before, playing the sailor in *Marnie*. He starred in *Silent Running* (Douglas Trumbull, 1971) and, with Karen Black, appeared as Mia Farrow's husband in *The Great Gatsby*. He is the father of the actress Laura Dern and ex-husband of Dianne Ladd.

Barbara Harris starred in the Disney movie *Freaky Friday* (Gary Nelson, 1977), in which she swaps bodies with her daughter, played by Jodie Foster. More recently, she played John Cusack's drugged-up mother in *Grosse Pointe Blank* (George Armitage, 1997).

William Devane played Greg Sumner in the *Dallas* spin-off *Knots*

Landing for nearly a decade, and Katherine Helmond (*Mrs Maloney*) would later find fame as Jessica Tate in the spoof sitcom *Soap*. Nicholas Colasanto (*Constantine*) went on to play the similarly dazed barman, 'Coach', in the early seasons of *Cheers*.

John Williams is one of the most celebrated composers in modern film, having created some of the most recognised film music ever. His filmography includes the *Star Wars* and *Indiana Jones* trilogies, the Christopher Reeve *Superman* movies, *Close Encounters of the Third Kind* and *E.T. – The Extra-Terrestrial*.

THE USUAL SUSPECTS: A mention here for the costume designer Edith Head, who worked on over three hundred movies in her long career, including eleven of Hitchcock's.

KILLER LINES: Adamson grins at a bewildered Maloney: 'Isn't it touching that a perfect murder has kept our friendship alive for all these years?'

Fran, speaking to Adamson, reveals her worries about their relationship: 'I thought I fell in love with you because I need some stability in my life.' 'Well I guess you're just a bad judge of character,' comes the reply.

THERE HE IS!: When George visits the Registrar of Births and Deaths, about forty minutes in, Hitchcock lurks behind a frosted-glass door; his silhouette can be seen through the glass and he appears to be arguing with a woman.

THE MACGUFFIN: The diamonds are a perfect MacGuffin here, being the thing that the villains want that the heroes are completely unaware of. Only at the end, when they realise why Adamson wants them dead, do they finally learn his prime motivation.

AWARDS: Barbara Harris was nominated at the Golden Globe Awards for 'Best Motion Picture Actress in a Musical/Comedy'.

TABOOS: Forty years earlier, Julia Rainbird helped her sister Harriet find a home for her illegitimate baby to preserve the family name. Such desperation for respectability is in contrast with the dialogue between Blanche and her common-law husband George: when he tells Blanche that they're in for an evening of passion, he says that she'll not have to worry about his performance as she'll see 'a standing ovation'. And, when he later complains about Blanche always having him by the 'crystal balls', Blanche snaps: 'Leave your crystal balls out of this, George!'

POSTER: A clever montage of images trapped inside the black silhouette of Karen Black, accompanied by a crystal ball containing Hitchcock's distorted face. The copy reads: 'From the devious mind of Alfred Hitchcock, a diabolically entertaining motion picture,' joking that 'There's no body in the family plot.'

TRAILER: The short version of the trailer opens to the accompaniment of Hitchcock's theme tune, 'Funeral March of a Marionette.' A voice-over announces that 'Alfred Hitchcock is involved in a family plot.' Hitch himself pops up, renouncing such a *'grave* insult'. He then tells us that there's a medium in the family plot, as well as a thief, a kidnapper, and a con man. 'But who,' Hitch asks 'is *buried* in the family plot?'

In a longer trailer, we see a clip of Julia Rainbird offering a young woman $10,000. 'That's Madame Blanche, a medium,' says Hitch. 'Being a master spiritualist myself, I can assure you that Madame Blanche is a fake.' Hitch then dabbles with a little fortune telling: 'I see a name strangely familiar. [the name "Alfred Hitchcock" appears on screen]. I see a title. ["Family Plot"]. The implication is quite grave . . .' He introduces the stars and finishes with a clip from the car chase, cutting as a car careers off the edge of the cliff: 'Poor Madame Blanche. I've grown very fond of that girl. Are you all right, Madame Blanche?'

WHAT THE PAPERS SAID: On Friday 20 August 1976, the *Times* reviewer noted that 'because it's played for light comedy going on farce, *Family Plot* risks being pigeon-holed as a frolic, a minor work in the old master's canon. Time, I guess, may well accord it a central place.' He goes on to add that 'what is most characteristic and charming in the film is a show-off relaxation, an easy demonstration of how it all should be done.'

TRIVIA: The movie didn't receive its name until just days before the final shoot. Hitchcock jokingly claimed during the production that the film could be titled *Alfred Hitchcock's Wet Drawers* and it would still be a hit.

In a spooky coincidence, the last films of Hitchcock and Bernard Herrmann were released in Britain in the same week; Herrmann died just hours after completing the score for Martin Scorsese's *Taxi Driver*.

FINAL ANALYSIS: More than anything, Hitchcock loved a joke at the expense of others. Although he'd spent his career being famed for his suspenseful thrillers, many of his broad comic touches are often forgotten. How fitting, therefore, that Hitch surprises us all, following his most brutal thriller with such a gentle comedy. Far closer to an old-fashioned screwball comedy than a thriller, *Family Plot* plays its audience along from the word go: we see a cool ice maiden who's revealed to be a brunette wearing a wig; we play witness to an intricate crime only for the police to draw a complete blank straight away; and a suspenseful high-speed drive along a cliff top throws a whole convoy of cars, juggernauts and motorbikes at the petrified driver, only for the road to empty the second his car comes to a halt.

Of course, Hitchcock can't resist playing on our primal fears and after lulling us into a false state of security presents us with the attack on Blanche with the hypodermic needle. Just the tiniest flecks of blood and yet it's as effective and unsettling an image as those from any number of bloodthirsty murders.

Family Plot was never intended to be Hitchcock's last film, as the last entry in this book shows. But it's perhaps a much more suitable final bow than we suspect *The Short Night* might have been. Blanche's final wink to the camera is a sweet touch, leading the audience to wonder whether it's all been a trick, or whether the star really does have the talent we've been led to believe. And of course, lest you need reminding, there *is* only one star in an Alfred Hitchcock production. **8/10**

The Short Night
(Unfinished)

SUMMARY: Gavin Brand, a British spy working for the Soviets, stages a daring escape from Wormwood Scrubs, the London prison, with the help of an accomplice, Ian Brennan. Brennan agrees to help him reach Finland, where his wife and children are waiting for him. Brennan takes him to a safe house and leaves him alone with a young woman called Rosemary. The woman tells him she will help him escape by hiding him inside the boot of her car while she drives through Europe. But Brand misunderstands her presence – he believes she is his 'reward' for staying silent for the last five years. She resists him and in the struggle he strangles her.

An American agent is dispatched to stake out the island off the coast of Finland where it's believed Brand's wife and children still live. There he will wait until Brand shows up and then kill him. He makes the acquaintance of the spy's wife and they fall in love, though she remains ignorant of his true identity and of his mission. Now she must face a dilemma: whether to escape to Russia with her husband or to start a new life with the American agent.

ROOTS: Based on both Kirkbride's novel *The Short Night* and *The Springing of George Blake* by Sean Bourke, which told of the notorious spy George Blake who, after escaping from Wormwood Scrubs, was helped by London gangsters to escape to Russia.

CASTING: Hitchcock had, according to François Truffaut, approached Catherine Deneuve and Walter Matthau to play the leads, though towards the end he was believed to be considering Liv Ullmann and Sean Connery.

FINAL ANALYSIS: Hitch's last project was, perhaps, the most important one he ever undertook, for trying to get this spy story to the screen allowed him to entertain the fantasy that he was both still working and well enough to work, despite evidence to the contrary. In truth, Hitchcock was seriously ill, and certainly far too ill to travel to Finland for the required location filming. Alma, his wife and long-time collaborator, was also housebound, requiring constant nursing, and the prospect of being separated from her for however long it would take to complete filming would have been unthinkable.

Though his friends and colleagues knew he would not complete the project they still offered him their support. Ernest Lehman, who had scripted *North by Northwest*, felt that their recent work on *Family Plot* wasn't good enough to be remembered as the Master's last work and, for this reason, was encouraged enough to collaborate with Hitch on the new screenplay. But Hitchcock began to fixate on the idea of a graphic rape scene, as he had done years earlier with *Marnie*, and Lehman found he could no longer pretend the film would see completion. David Freeman, the noted script doctor, playwright and scenarist, was brought on board, but he too found Hitchcock distracted, happier to share anecdotes and memories of happier times than work. Freeman's screenplay would later see publication as part of his book *The Last Days of Alfred Hitchcock*.

We include *The Short Night* in this collection over all other unrealised projects as an indication of what might have been had Hitchcock's death not robbed us of the most manipulative, innovative and entertaining film-maker of the century.

the **HITCHCOCK** complete

the teleplays

In 1940, CBS found they needed to find something to fill in for the popular *Lux Radio Theater* programme while it was off the air for the summer. They decided to use this as an opportunity to try out a few pilot shows – one-off episodes designed to test audience reaction before committing to the production of a complete series. One such show was *Suspense*, and Alfred Hitchcock was signed to direct it on his condition that the producers also allowed him to promote his latest film, *Foreign Correspondent*.

For his first radio broadcast, Hitchcock chose to adapt Mrs Belloc Lowndes's *The Lodger*, a novel he'd filmed in 1926 to great success. To play the eponymous lodger, Hitchcock hired Herbert Marshall, who was currently appearing as the villainous Stephen Fisher in *Foreign Correspondent*. Playing the housekeepers were Edmund Gwenn, a regular Hitchcock collaborator since *The Skin Game*, and Lurene Tuttle, who would later play the sheriff's wife in *Psycho*. Typically perverse, Hitchcock chose to withhold the play's ending, forcing thousands of outraged listeners to bombard the station with complaints about how they felt cheated. The strategy might have worked had it not been for the following week's play, 'Duffy's Tavern', a light-hearted comedy that was awarded a prime-time slot later that year. *Suspense* would eventually become a series two years later, but without involvement from Hitchcock.

Hitchcock's appetite had been whetted by the experience, though, and in 1945 he approached ABC with a pilot for a series called *Once Upon a Midnight*. As before, the intention was to feature a different story each week, and the pilot episode, 'Malice Aforethought', would be based on a story by Francis Iles, whose *Before the Fact* Hitchcock had filmed as *Suspicion* some years earlier. Hitchcock cast Hume Cronyn (*Shadow of a Doubt*, *Lifeboat*), and again employed the trick of holding back the ending, telling the listeners to tune in the following week. However, ABC remained unimpressed and rejected the pilot.

Meanwhile the ever-popular *Suspense* transferred to television, where it enjoyed an equally successful run for a number of years.

In 1955, Hitchcock was approached by Lew Wasserman and other executives from MCA with a mind to producing a television show under the banner of *Alfred Hitchcock Presents*. A number of similar anthology series already existed in addition to *Suspense*, such as *Pepsi-Cola Playhouse* and *Kraft Television Theater*. In signing up for his own television show, Hitchcock would not only provide a regular, high-profile means to promote his cinematic works, but would also sign one of the most lucrative contracts in the television industry, receiving just short of $130,000 for minimal involvement. Additionally, he would retain the rights to each show after initial broadcast.

Heading Hitchcock's new company, Shamley Productions (named after his old home in England), would be his former assistant, Joan

Harrison, who was appointed executive producer of the show. She was joined by Norman Lloyd, a former actor who had worked with Hitchcock on *Saboteur* and *Spellbound*, and had since become a director himself. He became associate producer and joined Hitchcock as one of the regular directors.

Each programme would begin with the distinctive theme music, an arrangement of Gounod's 'Funeral March of a Marionette', which would play over a graphic of a Hitchcock caricature, designed by Hitchcock himself. The episodes would feature a prologue and epilogue by Hitchcock, which was scripted by the playwright James Allardice. Allardice managed to capture perfectly the playfully lugubrious persona that Hitchcock had cultivated over the years, allowing him to share a world view as twisted as that of Charles Addams's celebrated cartoons in the *New York Times*. Each introduction would see Hitchcock in an electric chair, wearing a noose or in some other unusual situation, while waxing lyrical about some morbid notion of his that had a loose connection with the story that would follow. Often as not, these presentations were merely an opportunity for Hitchcock to goad the sponsors, something unheard of at the time. He introduced one sponsor slot by saying: 'Our story tonight is about a man called Perry. It follows after a minute called "Tedious".' The clear implication was that Hitchcock, like his audience, resented advertising, even though he acknowledged its necessity.

Such an irreverent attitude won the audiences over and soon *Alfred Hitchcock Presents* was one of the most popular television shows ever. It managed to attract many top-notch performers, such as Charles Bronson, Walter Matthau, Steve McQueen and Joanne Woodward, as well as giving directors like Robert Altman and William Friedkin their first big break. It also gained critical acclaim, winning two Emmys and gaining seventeen Emmy nominations over its record-breaking ten-year run.

The format changed slightly over the years, moving to NBC in 1960 and becoming *The Alfred Hitchcock Hour* in 1962. It ran for a further three seasons, with increasingly less involvement from Hitchcock as time went on. Eventually, Hitchcock tired of the format and the show came to a suitably unnatural conclusion in the summer of 1965 with an episode entitled 'Off Season'.

In 1985 *Alfred Hitchcock Presents* was resurrected through a combination of 'colourised' footage from Hitchcock's original presentations with new colour episodes. Some were remakes of the original stories, some new tales in a similar vein. This new series ran for four years before it too ended.

Alfred Hitchcock Presents

*Episodes directed by Alfred Hitchcock

1ST SEASON 1955–56
(broadcast on CBS)
'Revenge'*
'Premonition'
'Triggers in Leash'
'Don't Come Back Alive'
'Into Thin Air'
'Salvage'
'Breakdown'*
'Our Cook's a Treasure'
'The Long Shot'
'The Case of Mr. Pelham'*
'Guilty Witness'
'Santa Claus and the 10th Avenue
   Kid'
'The Cheney Vase'
'A Bullet for Baldwin'
'The Big Switch'
'You Got to Have Luck'
'The Older Sister'
'Shopping for Death'
'The Derelicts'
'And So Died Riabouchinska'
'Safe Conduct'
'Place of Shadows'
'Back for Christmas'*
'The Perfect Murder'
'There Was an Old Woman'
'Whodunit?'
'Help Wanted'
'Portrait of Jocelyn'
'The Orderly World of Mr. Appleby'
'Never Again'
'The Gentleman from America'
'The Babysitter'
'The Belfry'
'The Hidden Thing'
'The Legacy'
'Mink'
'Decoy'
'The Creeper'
'Momentum'

2ND SEASON 1956–57
'Wet Saturday'*
'Fog Closing In'
'De Mortuis'
'Kill With Kindness'
'None are So Blind'
'Toby'
'Alibi Me'
'Conversation Over a Corpse'
'Crack of Doom'
'Jonathan'
'A Better Bargain'
'The Rose Garden'
'Mr. Blanchard's Secret'*
'John Brown's Body'
'Crackpot'
'Nightmare in 4'
'My Brother Richard'
'Manacled'
'Bottle of Wine'
'Malice Domestic'
'Number 22'
'The End of Indian Summer'
'One for the Road'
'The Cream of the Jest'
'I Killed the Count' (1)
'I Killed the Count' (2)
'I Killed the Count' (3)
'One More Mile to Go'*
'Vicious Circle'
'The Three Demons of Mr. Findlater'
'The Night the World Ended'
'The Hands of Mr. Ottermole'
'A Man Greatly Beloved'
'Martha Mason, Movie Star'
'The West Warlock Time Capsule'
'Father and Son'
'The Indestructible Mr. Weems'
'A Little Sleep'
'The Dangerous People'

3RD SEASON 1957–58
'The Glass Eye'
'The Mail Order Prophet'
'The Perfect Crime'*

'Heart of Gold'
'The Silent Witness'
'Reward to Finder'
'Enough Rope for Two'
'The Last Request'
'The Young One'
'The Diplomatic Corpse'
'The Deadly'
'Miss Paisley's Cat'
'Night of the Execution'
'The Percentage'
'Together'
'Sylvia'
'The Motive'
'Miss Bracegirdle Does Her Duty'
'The Equalizer'
'On the Nose'
'Guest for Breakfast'
'Return of the Hero'
'The Right Kind of House'
'Foghorn'
'Flight to the East'
'Bull in a China Shop'
'The Disappearing Trick'
'Lamb to the Slaughter'*
'Fatal Figures'
'Death Sentence'
'Festive Season'
'Listen! Listen!'
'Post Mortem'
'The Crocodile Case'
'A Dip in the Pool'*
'The Safe Place'
'The Canary Sedan'
'Impromptu Murder'
'Little White Frock'

4TH SEASON 1958–59
'Poison'*
'Don't Interrupt'
'The Jokester'
'The Crooked Road'
'The Two Million Dollar Defense'
'Design for Loving'
'A Man with a Problem'
'Safety for the Witness'
'Murder Me Twice'
'Tea Time'
'And the Desert Shall Blossom'
'Mrs. Herman and Mrs. Fennimore'

'Six People, No Music'
'The Morning After'
'A Personal Matter'
'Out There – Darkness'
'Total Loss'
'The Last Dark Step'
'The Morning of the Bride'
'The Diamond Necklace'
'Relative Value'
'The Right Price'
'I'll Take Care of You'
'The Avon Emeralds'
'The Kind Waitress'
'Cheap Is Cheap'
'The Waxwork'
'The Impossible Dream'
'Banquo's Chair'*
'A Night With the Boys'
'Your Witness'
'The Human Interest Story'
'The Dusty Drawer'
'A True Account'
'Touche'
'Invitation to an Accident'

5TH SEASON 1959–60
'Arthur'*
'The Crystal Trench'*
'Appointment at Eleven'
'Coyote Moon'
'No Pain'
'Anniversary Gift'
'Dry Run'
'The Blessington Method'
'Dead Weight'
'Special Delivery'
'Road Hog'
'Specialty of the House'
'An Occurrence at Owl Creek Bridge'
'Graduating Class'
'Man from the South'
'The Ikon of Elijah'
'The Cure'
'Backward, Turn Backward'
'Not the Running Type'
'The Day of the Bullet'
'Hitch Hike'
'Across the Threshold'
'Craig's Will'
'Madame Mystery'

'The Little Man Who Was There'
'Mother, May I Go out to Swim?'
'The Cuckoo Clock'
'Forty Detectives Later'
'The Hero'
'Insomnia'
'I Can Take Care of Myself'
'One Grave Too Many'
'Party Line'
'Cell 227'
'The Schwartz-Metterklume Method'
'Letter of Credit'
'Escape to Sonoita'
'Hooked'

6TH SEASON 1960–61
(**transfers to NBC**)
'Mrs. Bixby and the Colonel's Coat'
'The Doubtful Doctor'
'Very Moral Theft'
'The Contest for Aaron Gold'
'The Five Forty-Eight'
'Pen Pal'
'Outlaw in Town'
'Oh, Youth and Beauty'
'The Money'
'Sybilla'
'The Man With Two Faces'
'The Baby Blue Expression'
'The Man Who Found the Money'
'The Changing Heart'
'Summer Shade'
'A Crime for Mothers'
'The Last Escape'
'The Greatest Monster of Them All'
'The Landlady'
'The Throwback'
'The Kiss Off'
'The Horse Player'*
'Incident in a Small Jail'
'A Woman's Help'
'Museum Piece'
'Coming, Mama'
'Deathmate'
'Gratitude'
'A Pearl Necklace'
'You Can't Trust a Man'
'The Gloating Place'
'Self Defense'
'A Secret Life'

'Servant Problem'
'Coming Home'
'Final Arrangements'
'Make My Death Bed'
'Ambition'

7TH SEASON 1961–62
'The Hat Box'
'Bang, You're Dead'
'Maria'
'Cop for a Day'
'Keep Me Company'
'Beta Delta Gamma'
'You Can't be A Little Girl All Your Life'
'The Old Pro'
'I Spy'
'Services Rendered'
'The Right Kind of Medicine'
'A Jury of Her Peers'
'The Silk Petticoat'
'Bad Actor'
'The Door Without a Key'
'The Case of M.J.H.'
'The Faith of Aaron Menefee'
'The Woman Who Wanted to Live'
'Strange Miracle'
'The Test'
'Burglar Proof'
'The Big Score'
'Profit Sharing Plan'
'Apex'
'The Last Remains'
'Ten O'Clock Tiger'
'Act of Faith'
'The Kerry Blue'
'The Matched Pearl'
'What Frightened You, Fred?'
'Most Likely to Succeed'
'Victim Four'
'The Golden Opportunity'
'The Twelve Hour Caper'
'The Children of Alda Nouva'
'First Class Honeymoon'
'The Big Kick'
'Where Beauty Lies'
'The Sorcerer's Apprentice'

The Alfred Hitchcock Hour

1ST SEASON 1962–63
(broadcast on CBS)
'A Piece of the Action'
'Don't Look Behind You'
'Night of the Owl'
'I Saw the Whole Thing'*
'Captive Audience'
'Final Vow'
'Annabelle'
'House Guest'
'The Black Curtain'
'Day of Reckoning'
'Ride the Nightmare'
'Hangover'
'Bonfire'
'The Tender Poisoner'
'The Thirty First of February'
'What Really Happened'
'Forecast: Low Clouds and Coastal
    Fog'
'A Tangled Web'
'To Catch a Butterfly'
'The Paragon'
'I'll Be the Judge, I'll Be the Jury'
'Diagnosis: Danger'
'The Lonely Hours'
'The Star Juror'
'The Long Silence'
'An Out for Oscar'
'Death and the Joyful Woman'
'Last Seen Wearing Blue Jeans'
'The Dark Pool'
'Dear Uncle George'
'Run for Doom'
'Death of a Cop'

2ND SEASON 1963–64
'A Home Away from Home'
'A Nice Touch'
'Terror in Northfield'
'You'll Be the Death of Me'
'Blood Bargain'
'Nothing Ever Happens in Linvale'
'Starring the Defense'
'The Cadaver'
'The Dividing Wall'

'Goodbye, George'
'How to Get Rid of Your Wife'
'Three Wives Too Many'
'The Magic Shop'
'Beyond the Sea of Death'
'Night Caller'
'The Evil of Adelaide Winters'
'The Jar'
'Final Escape'
'Murder Case'
'Anyone for Murder?'
'Beast in View'
'Behind the Locked Door'
'A Matter of Murder'
'The Gentleman Caller'
'The Ordeal of Mrs. Snow'
'Ten Minutes from Now'
'The Sign of Satan'
'Who Needs an Enemy?'
'Bed of Roses'
'Second Verdict'
'Isabel'
'Body in the Barn'

3RD SEASON 1964–65
'The Return of Verge Likens'
'Change of Address'
'Water's Edge'
'The Life and Work of Juan
    Diaz'
'See the Monkey Dance'
'Lonely Place'
'The McGregor Affair'
'Misadventure'
'Triumph'
'Memo from Purgatory'
'Consider Her Ways'
'The Crimson Witness'
'Where the Woodbine Twineth'
'The Final Performance'
'Thantos Place Hotel'
'One of the Family'
'An Unlocked Window'
'The Trap'
'Wally the Beard'
'Death Scene'

'The Photographer and the Undertaker'
'Thou Still Unravished Bride'
'Completely Foolproof'
'Power of Attorney'

'The World's Oldest Motive'
'The Monkey's Paw – A Retelling'
'The Second Wife'
'Night Fever'
'Off Season'

Alfred Hitchcock Presents (1980s version)

Pilot Movie Incorporating:
'Incident In A Small Jail'
'Man From The South'
'Bang! You're Dead'
'An Unlocked Window'

1ST SEASON 1985–86
'Revenge'
'Night Fever'
'Wake Me When I'm Dead'
'Final Escape'
'Night Caller'
'Method Actor'
'Human Interest Story'
'Breakdown'
'Prisoners'
'Gigolo'
'The Gloating Place'
'The Right Kind Of Medicine'
'Beast In View'
'Very Happy Ending'
'The Canary Sedan'
'Enough Rope For Two'
'The Creeper'
'Happy Birthday'
'The Jar'
'Deadly Honeymoon'
'Four O'Clock'
'Road Hog'

2ND SEASON 1987
'The Initiation'
'Conversation Over A Corpse'
'Man On The Edge'
'If The Shoe Fits'
'The Mole'
'Anniversary Gift'

'The Impatient Patient'
'When This Man Dies'
'Specialty Of The House'
'The Final Twist'
'Tragedy Tonight'
'World's Oldest Motive'
'Deathmate'

3RD SEASON 1988
'Very Careful Rape' (VCR)
'Animal Lovers'
'Prism'
'A Stolen Heart'
'Houdini On Channel 4'
'Killer Takes All'
'Hippocritic Oath'
'Prosecutor'
'If Looks Could Kill'
'You'll Die Laughing'
'Murder Party'
'Twist'
'User Deadly'
'Career Move'
'Full Disclosure'
'Kandinsky's Vault'
'There Was A Little Girl . . .'
'Twisted Sisters'
'The 13th Floor'
'Hunted' (Part One)
'Hunted' (Part Two)

4TH SEASON 1988–89
'Fogbound'
'Pen Pal'
'Ancient Voices'
'Survival Of The Fittest'
'The Big Spin'

'Don't Sell Yourself Short'
'For Art's Sake'
'Murder In Mind'
'Mirror, Mirror'
'Skeleton In The Closet'
'In The Driver's Seat'
'Driving Under The Influence'
'In The Name Of Science'

'Romance Machine'
'Diamonds Aren't Forever'
'My Dear Watson'
'Night Creatures'
'The Man Who Knew Too Little'
'Reunion'
'South By Southeast'

References

HITCHCOCK ON THE WORLD WIDE WEB

A number of different websites have provided us with invaluable resources for this book. The following addresses were correct at the time of going to press and we are indebted to the various webmasters whose hard work and dedication we salute here:

ADVERTISING HITCHCOCK: The site owner Martin Dawber hosts a well-designed and easy-to-use site containing an exhaustive collection of posters from across the world.
http://www.geocities.com/Hollywood/Cinema/2434/

THE MACGUFFIN WEB PAGE: Alfred Hitchcock scholars meet here! Administered by Ken Mogg, this is the official site for *The MacGuffin Journal*, containing subscription details for the journal as well as offering a refuge for those fans of Hitchcock who long for serious intellectual debate, with essays, links to other sites and a regularly updated journal of the editor's thoughts and opinions.
http://www.labyrinth.net.au/~muffin/

THE DEFINITIVE HITCHCOCK LINKS PAGE: Another superb resource, John Couke's site contains over 120 links grouped into relevant categories. An excellent place to start.
http://www.interlog.com/~couke/index.html

THE MASTER OF SUSPENSE: We are indebted to Patrik Wikström, whose site contains transcripts of the many trailers that promoted Hitchcock's films. There's also a superb reference guide to the TV shows, which was invaluable to us in the compilation of the episode titles.
http://www.geocities.com/SunsetStrip/Towers/7260/hitch.html

Bibliography

Alfred Hitchcock and the Making of Psycho, Stephen Rebello (Marion Boyars, 1998). ISBN 0-7145-3003-4.

The Art of Alfred Hitchcock, Donald Spoto (Anchor Books, 1992). ISBN 0-385-41813-2.

The Art of Looking in Hitchcock's Rear Window, Stefan Sharff (Proscemium Publishers, Inc., 1997). ISBN 0-87910-087-7.

BFI Film Classics: The Birds, Camile Paglia (BFI, 1998). ISBN 0-85170-651-7.

The Complete Films of Alfred Hitchcock, Robert A. Harris and Michael S. Lasky (Citadel, 1993). ISBN 0-8065-1464-7.

The Dark Side of Genius: The Life of Alfred Hitchcock, Donald Spoto (Plexus, 1994). ISBN 0-85965-213-0.

Hitchcock, François Truffaut (Simon & Schuster, 1985). ISBN 0-671-60429-5.

Hitchcock on Hitchcock: Selected Writings and Interviews, Alfred Hitchcock and Sidney Gottlieb (Faber & Faber, 1997). ISBN 0-571-19136-3.

Me and Hitch, Evan Hunter (Faber & Faber, 1997). ISBN 0-571-19306-4.

Vertigo: The Making of a Hitchcock Classic, Dan Auiler (Titan Books, 1999). ISBN 1-84023-065-7.

Picture Credits

BLACK-AND-WHITE SECTION
1. The Ronald Grant Archive
2. The Ronald Grant Archive
3. The Kobal Collection
4. The Ronald Grant Archive
5. The Kobal Collection
6. The Kobal Collection
7. The Ronald Grant Archive
8. The Kobal Collection
9. The Ronald Grant Archive
10. The Kobal Collection
11. The Kobal Collection
12. The Ronald Grant Archive

Psycho
First picture: The Kobal Collection
Second picture: The Kobal Collection
Third picture: Pictorial Press Ltd

COLOUR SECTION
1. The Ronald Grant Archive
2. The Ronald Grant Archive
3. Pictorial Press Ltd
4. The Ronald Grant Archive
5. The Ronald Grant Archive
6. The Kobal Collection
7. The Ronald Grant Archive
8. The Kobal Collection
9. Pictorial Press Ltd
10. The Kobal Collection
11. The Kobal Collection
12. The Kobal Collection
13. The Kobal Collection
14. The Kobal Collection
15. The Kobal Collection